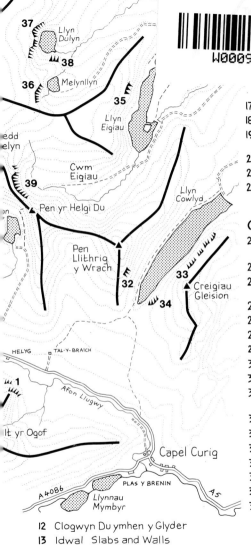

W0009869

17 Castell y Geifr
18 Drws Cwm Clyd
19 Pinnacle Crag of Cwm Cywion
20 Craig Blaen y Nant
21 Carnedd y Filiast
22 Craig Cwrwgl (Pillar of Elidir)

CARNEDDAU

23 Ysgolion Duon (The Black Ladders)
24 Llech Du
25 Craig y Cwmglas Bach
26 Craig Dafydd
27 Craig Braich Ty Du
28 Craig Lloer
29 Craig Ddaear
30 Carreg Mianog
31 Craig yr Ogof
32 Pen Llithrig y Wrach
33 Creigiau Gleision
34 Craig Llethr Gwyn
35 Craig Eigiau
36 Craig Fawr
37 Craig y Dulyn
38 Castell y Dulyn
39 Craig Yr Ysfa

12 Clogwyn Du ymhen y Glyder
13 Idwal Slabs and Walls
14 Glyder Fawr
15 Clogwyn y Geifr
16 Twll Du (The Devil's Kitchen)

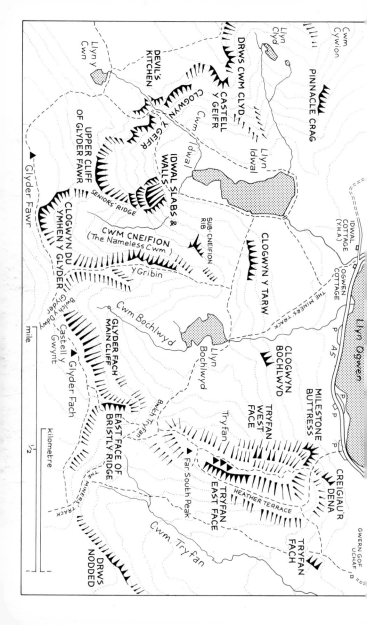

Lisa White in the Devil's Kitchen. Photo: Gordon Stainforth

Gareth Fletcher and Lisa White on *Cneifion Arête* (Mod), Cwm Cneifion.
Photo: Gordon Stainforth

Climbers' Club Guides
Edited by Ian Smith and Geoff Milburn

Ogwen and Carneddau

by Iwan Arfon Jones

with the guidebook team of Simon Cardy, Geoff Milburn, Andy Newton, Chris Parkin and Mike Raine

after Zdzislaw Leppert and Les Holliwell

Endpaper maps by Don Sargeant

Cover photographs by Ray Wood and Iwan Arfon Jones

Published by The Climbers' Club

Climbing in the Ogwen District First Edition 1910
by J M Archer Thomson, re-published in 1921 with an Appendix
by H E L Porter

Cwm Idwal First Edition 1936
Revised 1940 and Reprinted 1946, 1949, 1955
by J M Edwards

Glyder Fach First Edition 1937
by C F Kirkus

Tryfan First Edition 1937
Reprinted 1939, 1946, 1949
by J M Edwards and C W F Noyce

Craig yr Ysfa First Edition 1943
by M E Kretschmer and A D M Cox

Carneddau First Edition 1950
Revised 1966
by A J J Moulam

Tryfan and Glyder Fach First Edition 1956
Reprinted 1956, 1964, 1966 and 1973
by A J J Moulam

Cwm Idwal Second Edition 1958
Revised and Reprinted 1964 and 1967
by A J J Moulam

Cwm Idwal Third Edition 1974
by Ken Wilson and Zdzislaw Leppert

Carneddau Third Edition 1975
by Les Holliwell

Ogwen Second Edition 1982
by Zdzislaw Leppert

Ogwen and Carneddau First Edition 1993
by Iwan Arfon Jones et al

Front Cover: Lewis Smith on the first pitch of *Superdirect* (HVS), Milestone Buttress. Photo: Ray Wood

Rear Cover: *Aura* (E2), a modern classic on Craig yr Ysfa.
Photo: Iwan Arfon Jones

Jones, Iwan Arfon et al

Ogwen and Carneddau

(Climbers' Club Guides)

British Library Cataloguing in Publication Data

A catalogue record for this book is available from the British Library.

796.522

ISBN 0-901-601-52-7

Output by Pickards Typesetting & Design, Sheffield

Printed by Hi-Tec Print, Dinnington, South Yorkshire

Distributed by Cordee, 3a De Montfort Street, Leicester, LE1 7HD

Contents

Ogwen

List of Photodiagrams

Guidebook Disclaimer

This guidebook attempts to provide a definitive record of all existing climbs and is compiled from information from a variety of sources. The inclusion of any route does not imply that it remains in the condition described. Climbs can change unpredictably: rock can deteriorate and the existence and condition of *in situ* protection can alter. All climbers must rely on their own ability and experience to gauge the difficulty and seriousness of any climb. Climbing is an inherently dangerous activity.

Neither The Climbers' Club nor the authors and editors of this guidebook accept any liability whatsoever for any injury or damage caused to climbers, third parties, or property, arising from the use of it. Whilst the content of the guide is believed to be accurate, no responsibility is accepted for any error, omission, or mis-statement. Users must rely on their own judgement and are recommended to insure against injury to person and property and third party risks.

The inclusion in this guidebook of a crag or routes upon it does not mean that any member of the public has a right of access to the crag or the right to climb.

Before climbing on any crag in this guide please read the appropriate access and conservation notes.

Climbing Style

The following policy statement on climbing style was agreed in principle at The Climbers' Club Annual General Meeting on 25th February 1990:

The Climbers' Club supports the tradition of using natural protection and is opposed to actions which are against the best interests of climbers and users of crags. This applies particularly to irreversible acts which could affect the crags and their environs.

Such acts could include: the placing of bolts on mountain and natural crags; retrospective placing of bolts; chiselling, hammering, or altering the rock appearance or structure; excessive removal of vegetation and interference with trees, flowers, and fauna.

The Climbers' Club policy is that guidebooks are written to reflect the best style matched to the ethos and traditions of British Climbing.

Acknowledgements

Unlike many previous Climbers' Club guidebooks, which were the work of individuals, this book has been a team effort. First in a long list are the authors of the guidebooks that have gone before, particularly Tom Leppert; their work remains in many parts of this volume. The principal worker updating and modernising has been Iwan Arfon Jones, who has completed an excellent job, ably assisted by Mike Raine, Andy Newton, Chris Parkin and Simon Cardy. Simon has also undertaken the particularly onerous task of collecting together, and preparing for publication, the photodiagrams. For providing the photos that Simon didn't take thanks to Iwan, Malcolm Griffiths, Steve Ashton, Ray Wood and Ken Wilson. The photographers who have supplied the action shots are credited in the appropriate places, but Ray Wood should be singled out for providing an excellent set of pictures for consideration. Barbara Jones kindly supplied the access and conservation notes, which are particularly important in this sensitive area.

A great debt of gratitude is owed to Geoff Milburn, who as well as writing the Historical, compiling the first ascents list, and beginning the editing process on this volume, completed his 10 year stint as CC North Wales Editor. During that time he saw to fruition six guidebooks of excellent quality, notable for the well-researched and entertainingly detailed first ascents lists and the successful introduction of colour illustrations.

This guidebook is published in a new form; it is split into two volumes, to make the carrying easier on multi-pitch routes, but supplied within a single cover. The CC has already published one guidebook in this format, Avon and Cheddar, but much of the initial discussion and planning for this concept was done by the Ogwen and Carneddau guidebook team.

The team also wishes to thank all the following for their various and important contributions: Chris Ayrs, John Cleare, Noel Craine, John Darling, M Davies, Terry Gifford, Chris Gilbert, J Gregson, Chris

Jackson, Dai Lampard, Rhona Lampard, Jill Lawrence, Alan Leary, Tom Leppert, Bob Lewis, Steve Long, Paul Middleton, Andy Orton, Chris Pearson, Dubbo Smith, Gordon Stainforth, Ed Stone, Mike Turner, George White, Martin Whitaker, Bob Wightman and Dave Wrennall. Apologies to anyone whom we have inadvertently missed out.

Finally, a personal note of thanks must go to: Dave Farrant, who is my guide through the minefield of word processing and computer typesetting; John Willson, my fellow CC Editor; and Bob Moulton, CC Business Manager and voice of experience.

Ian Smith

Conservation Notes

The area included within this guidebook covers some of the most remote and beautiful mountains and cwms in Wales. The larger part is within the internationally important Eryri: Mountains of Snowdonia Site of Special Scientific Interest (SSSI), designated so for its geological history and features, once studied by Darwin and for its varied montane vegetation, in which the distribution of the arctic-alpine flora is related closely to the variation in rock types.

The extensive high plateau of the Carneddau has been dissected by a number of deep cwms, some of which provide superb high standard rock-climbing, for example on Llech Ddu, while others such as Ysgolion Duon come into condition when there is a hard winter. These north facing cwms and cliffs hold an attraction, not only for the winter climber, but also for the arctic-alpine vegetation which thrives on the shaded, damp and often loose texture of the rocks found here. Such a description is not attractive to the rock climber and herein lies a distinction which has been the saving grace for many plant communities in the mountains of Eryri. Most climbing takes place on the harder volcanic lavas which tend to be rather acidic, supporting grasses and heathers. In contrast, the softer ashes and pumice rocks are richer in nutrients and support plants which would have been common in early post-glacial times, but which are now restricted to these upland 'retreats' due to climatic change and disturbance by grazing and by human activities. These arctic-alpine plants such as purple saxifrage and moss campion are close to their southernmost limit in Britain today and although most are now beyond the reach of grazing animals, many are still vulnerable to the human touch.

There is a wealth of interest contained in the area encompassed within this guide, there for anyone to see with a mind open to more than just pure rock-climbing. Most cliffs require some effort to reach and on the walk in, the complex geology (the saucer shape of the rocks in the back of Cwm Idwal, by Twll Du for example), together with the varied bird and plant life throughout can distract the mind from the endless walk or the fear of what is to come! Even on the routes, the changing vista and the occasional interesting plant can add to the experience. More than in many other areas however, a plea must be made regarding the 'cleaning' of routes. The cliffs in this guidebook have by no means been fully explored and it is likely that its publication will stimulate a wave of new route activity. Such activity usually entails a degree of removal of vegetation but for many cliffs in this area, any cleaning could be disastrous, as a number of plants growing here are extremely rare and their numbers could be severely reduced by ill-considered action. These plants are protected by law, and offences are prosecuted under the 1981 Wildlife and Countryside Act, but we want to protect the plants and prevent damage or disturbance rather than chase their memory.

Similarly, there are a number of uncommon bird species in Snowdonia, ranging from the peregrine falcon through to the chough, merlin and ring ouzel. All these species can be found nesting or feeding within the mountain and crag environment used by climbers and can be disturbed, just as mountain vegetation can be, by inadvertent actions. Disturbance to nesting birds tends to be more obvious and perhaps more easily avoidable than that to plants, but the same protection applies, with penalties enforceable under law when an offence has been committed.

For the above reasons the Countryside Council for Wales would ask that anyone intending to explore a new cliff and put up new routes in sensitive areas should approach CCW first so that the cliff in question can be discussed and advice given on the likelihood of any rare plants, or birds, being damage or disturbed there. There is no intention to try to steal another person's routes, but the aim is to protect the scientific interest in the area. There is a wealth of interest for both climber and naturalist in the Carneddau and Ogwen; let us work together to keep it that way.

For information on the conservation interest of areas within this guide the CCW Warden, Mr Hywel Roberts can be contacted through the CCW regional office on 0248 372333.

Barbara Jones

Historical

In ancient times a Welsh prophet ventured to predict that a path would one day be created through the wilds of the Nant Ffrancon pass. He was promptly accounted as a madman, yet by the 18th Century a route did exist. The bridle-path however was described as one of the worst of its kind in Wales. Halliwell's 1860 account sets the scene nicely:

'At Tyn y Maes, a mile and a half further on, formerly a station on the old Holyhead road, the splendid pass of Nant Ffrancon commences; a pass which is always grand and striking, but seen, as we have seen it, with a full moon passing through changing clouds, casting its shadows on them as they rolled in heavy and constantly changing masses between the mountains, there is an impression of grandeur far beyond that made by any other scene I have yet witnessed in this country. The pass itself, about three miles long, is situated between two solemn mountain ranges, the river Ogwen flowing at the bottom, amidst dark fields of peat'.

Early travellers going down the Ogwen valley to Bethesda could hardly fail to notice Tryfan and inevitably they must have been attracted to its shapely summit. There were however deterrents such as the giant Rhitta who, according to local legend, was the sole inhabitant of Carnedd Llewelyn. Supposedly Rhitta was clothed in a garment made from the beards of the enemies that he had slain. Despite the threat of Rhitta a naturalist called Johnson reached the summit of Carnedd Llewelyn as early as 1639, but his guide could not be persuaded to take him 'to the steep parts where the rare plants only grow'. The rustic genuinely feared an attack from eagles as it was believed that they started from their nests after their prey with such force that it was unsafe to venture to the highest crags.

An anonymous 'tourist' made a guided ascent of Carnedd Llewelyn in 1837 despite poor weather conditions on the mountain:

'On our ascent we encountered some difficulty in consequence of the violence of the gale which swept over this towering elevation. The cold was intense; I should suppose it to be five or six degrees below the freezing point, and this while the sun was shining at noon day, and the temperature in the valley was sixty-two degrees of Fahrenheit. The snow lay very deep in some situations. We walked over a ravine which my guide informed me was at least forty feet in depth. In this, and similar places, he said that it would not disappear until the end of August'.

Members of a first generation of mountain lovers tentatively worked their way up the prominent ridges carrying eight-foot Alpenstocks to aid their progress. It needed men of vision to explore the Glyderau but so far the aim was to avoid the crags rather than to seek them out.

To make the transition from walking to true rock-climbing perhaps it was not a mountaineer but a fisherman who first set foot on Ogwen rock. John Henry Cliffe had already ascended some of the local mountains when, in 1843, he entered Twll Du (the Black Pit) or Devil's Kitchen, 'tempted to do so by a spirit of adventure'. The depths of the Kitchen did not however inspire him to complete the ascent.

After the formation of the Alpine Club in 1857 John Tyndall and other eminent Alpinists began to regard the Snowdonia mountains with respect. John Stogden, a remarkable pioneer, not only explored Swanage and Beachy Head but also made a winter ascent of Glyder Fach via the Devil's Kitchen track – and this he treated as an Alpine ascent. Haskett Smith recorded:

'When in February 1873 Glyder Fawr was crossed from Ogwen by way of Twll Du, with John Roberts as a guide, it was recorded in the Alpine Journal as something of a feat and something of an eccentricity'.

The winters at that time gave excellent snow and ice and the Alpine Club members soon realised the potential of the Welsh hills. Under good snow and ice conditions 13 members of an Alpine Club party ascended Carnedd Dafydd from Bethesda via Central Gully of Ysgolion Duon. They then descended to the head of Llyn Ogwen, went up Tryfan and continued over the shoulder of the Glyders to return to Capel Curig.

The birth of true rock-climbing in Ogwen is uncertain but it has been stated that Edward and John Hopkinson made a descent of part of the East Face of Tryfan prior to 1882. The gully epoch in Wales however was ushered in in 1887 when Roderick Williams, a Liverpool solicitor, completed *South Gully* on Tryfan. A year later, with his brother Tom, he ascended *North Gully* watched by a 12-year old boy, Geoffrey Winthrop Young.

'On the gallant top of Tryfan we saw two men emerge from the cliffs, roped together, the first sight of the rope! I believe this was in truth the occasion of the first ascent of the North Gully of Tryfan, and the beginning of modern rock-climbing in Wales'.

In 1894 a schoolmaster from Bangor, J M Archer Thomson, made the first climb on the Glyderau, the *Central Gully* of Glyder Fawr, and this like many other climbs to follow was to be of a standard of severity which at that time was unsurpassed in Wales. At one point the rope had to be threaded through a hole in the roof of a cave in order to overcome the hard moves.

'...it was found necessary to adopt a compromise between the wisdom of the serpent and the aimlessness of the crab, advancing by lateral jerks in a semi-recumbent attitude'. Thomson also explored Braich Ty Du and produced its first climb, *Right Gully*.

A year later other Severes led by Thomson were the *Gully of Clogwyn Du* and 'reputedly' the *Grey Rib* of Glyder Fawr. It was the Devil's Kitchen however which inspired the Alpinists and early in 1895 Thomson and H Hughes made the first winter ascent after an epic battle.

'After having surreptitiously appropriated the hatchet from Mrs Jones's coal-cellar they started at 10 a.m. for the Kitchen passing *en route* across Llyn Idwal, which was frozen to a depth of 7 or 8 inches. The chasm was filled up with snow and they were able to walk without difficulty up to near the capstone of the great pitch. Here ensued some remarkable gymnastics both on the part of the climbers and the hatchet. At one point the head of the hatchet flew off and had to be retrieved prior to being tied on again with string.
The rate of progress up the icy upper section was about five feet an hour and they finally reached the top at 7.15 p.m.'

Later when the snow had melted O G Jones attempted to solo the Kitchen but finally retreated owing to the dangerous condition of the finish. Another attempt, spearheaded by Oscar Eckenstein, and with the Abraham brothers in support, also failed in 1897 and it was left to W R Reade and W P McCulloch to make the first true ascent. When George Abraham later made an ascent he wrote:

'I cannot think that the ascent of Twll Du will ever become a popular climb. Its damp recesses would no doubt appeal to those famous and enthusiastic Yorkshiremen, who appear to revel in the wet and dismal depths of the very bowels of the earth'.

The second ascent was made in 1899 by O G Jones, J W Puttrell, George Abraham and F W Hill.

Jones and the Abrahams made a unique find with *Hanging Garden Gully* as they explored farther along the cliff, causing Abraham to write:

'We had some sensational back-and-knee practice, with the beautiful soft green carpet of the Garden about 100 feet directly below. My companion jokingly remarked that it might fulfil the duties of a gymnasium net, should we decide to make a hurried descent to gather more specimens'.

During the ascent they noticed a prominent crack over to the left and on the last day of the holiday Jones and George Abraham ascended one of the 'best' gullies in the area when they negotiated the black hole of the *Devil's Staircase*.

The Gully Epoch was to yield many intimidating dark clefts and perhaps the most hidden and remote was the *Great Gully* of Craig yr Ysfa. It was eventually subdued by a party led by Thomson in 1900. The 'Door Jamb' pitch was particularly notorious and it was quite common for human pyramids to be formed to overcome it. Other climbers waited for banks of snow in winter but even then on occasions had to resort to the pyramid technique. The route was to become one of the three great Welsh gullies. Thomson's description of the route's technicalities was uniquely provocative and as classic as the gully itself. A much more committing proposition however was to be the inescapable *Western Gully* of Ysgolion Duon which P H Cooke, Brushfield and Owen were to conquer a year later.

After the death of Jones, in the Alps, little of note was produced apart from *Gashed Crag* on Tryfan, by Buckle and Barlow, who were to explore the Ogwen area together for several years. In 1905 however George and Ashley Abraham not only succeeded on *Amphitheatre Buttress* and *Avalanche Gully* on Craig yr Ysfa, as well as the Severe *Hawk's Nest Buttress*, Glyder Fach, but also completed what was thought to be the hardest route in Wales. It was a real *tour de force* requiring 'spasmodic caterpillar-like movements' and during the two hour ascent much of the time was spent in devising theories as to how the problem should be approached. Before Jones had ascended Kern Knotts Crack (Gable) a friend had volunteered the immortal statement; "If you climb that place I will never speak to you again." *Monolith Crack* was said to be even harder and the description was added to the written record with some diffidence.

An even harder route was to follow in 1907 when Ward and Gibson found the fine mountaineering *Direct Route* on Glyder Fach. During the day they returned to the foot of *Gibson's Chimney* to lead a VS 4c pitch – the hardest of its day in Wales.

At this stage of development Archer Thomson completed his superb volume 'Climbing in the Ogwen District' (including the Carneddau) which charted all the known climbs, which had personally been checked by Thomson. When the guide appeared in 1910 it was considered by the Climbers' Club officers that the epoch of exploration had then closed.

George Mallory (of Everest fame) visited Craig yr Ysfa with Geoffrey Winthrop Young in 1909 to climb two minor routes then he returned alone for another line in 1910 despite the fact that after the odd nice pitch he was 'marooned' in a mass of vegetation.

Over a period of several years the names of Barlow, Steeple, Buckle and Doughty figured prominently and Barlow was responsible for the classical Milestone Buttress lines of the *Direct Route* and *Superdirect* (VS 4c – later top pitch HVS) and then was in the party which followed Steeple up *Grooved Arête* in 1911. Barlow and Steeple were to climb together for some years starting with the trivial *West End Buttress* on Ysgolion Duon in 1911. That same year Siegfried Herford and John Laycock, two climbers better known for their feats elsewhere, added new routes to Tryfan and in 1912 explored the Gribin to produce routes, the best of which was *Herford's Crack*.

A mystery of Tryfan was Harold Porter's ascent of *Cheek*, thought to have been accomplished while Porter was wandering up the crag alone. At the time it was the hardest route on the mountain and for some time no one responsible for guidebooks knew exactly where he had been.

During the Great War three routes appeared on the Idwal Slabs and the initial breach was *Hope* by Mrs Daniell. Her second, Ivor Richards who was later to marry Dorothy Pilley, then went on to follow David Pye up *Faith* and *Charity*. C F Holland referred to this development as the finest genuine slab climbing in Great Britain. The Slabs have attracted climbers ever since and their charm was well portrayed by Holland when he wrote: '...the great sweep of the Idwal Slabs has a rare quality of spacious breadth and simplicity, so that we gain a sense of freedom that has a peculiarly tonic effect upon the mind'.

High above the Slabs a lone holly tree had been spotted by Ivor Richards and he was determined to reach it if humanly possible. The assault was commenced with an ice-axe at the ready and with Holland positioned to give a shoulder if necessary. 'It was not until evening that a straightforward start to the climb was found, for the original take-off had been performed by means of a complicated and risky ladder, improvised with an ice-axe held aloft at arm's length by the second, whose position was so unsafe that he had to be secured with a rope flung over a projection luckily available overhead'.

Eventually the holly tree was reached but the chimney above proved stubborn and Holland, leading it in nailed boots, finally found a solution up the wall on the left of the ledge. The *Original Route* of Holly Tree Wall was to become a classic route in the years to come, and the only other line of great character from that era was *Tennis Shoe* which was accomplished by the Everest climber Noel Odell in 1918.

Cwm Llafar was rather off the beaten track (as it still is today) and no climbers had faced up to the forbidding challenge of Llech Ddu whose dark sombre cliffs all too easily intimidated the faint-hearted. In April 1917 Steeple and Barlow started at the centre of the cliff and attacked the 'steep wall of quivering vegetation'. After conquering the lower section they still had to find an escape up *Askant Chimney* in order to breach the impressive headwall of the cliff. Few climbers are likely to follow in their steps! Undeterred by their experience they returned two months later for *Corridor Gully*, *The Pillar Traverse*, and *Y Chimney*. The latter route was at that time quite technical and it was certainly a very serious proposition. Over the next four years they were to return to the cliff to find other lines of weakness.

In 1922 Richards and Pilley went up to Holly Tree Wall for a new route named *Other Kingdom*. At the foot of the cliff they discovered a piton protruding from a cranny in the rock. During the ascent the 'Finger of Fate' was hammered in to the face using a stone specifically carried up for the purpose, despite the fact that security was not really needed from the metal appendage.

During the early 1920s Welsh climbing failed to surpass the standard of the hardest Lakeland routes but things were soon to change. One factor that was to affect the climbing fraternity was the purchase of Helyg which George Borrow had referred to as a 'wretched hovel'. This event took place mainly due to the enthusiasm of Herbert Carr on behalf of the Climbers' Club. Another factor was the reissue, in 1921, of the Ogwen guidebook with an appendix of new climbs by H E L Porter (his initials were particularly apt for a climber), but a greater stimulus outside Ogwen was Carr's 1926 guidebook to the Snowdon area. Another base which appeared in the Ogwen valley was the Rucksack Club's cottage Tal y Braich Uchaf. It was however the Cambridge generation of Everest climbers and polar explorers which dominated the Ogwen scene: names such as Geoffrey Winthrop Young, Wyn Harris, Gino Watkins, Stewart Palmer, Peter Lloyd, Laurence Wager, Ivan Waller and Jack Longland. This generation used fast cars to get them to the hills as quickly as possible and in the spirit of the '20s Ivan Waller led the spectacularly steep *Belle Vue Bastion* on Tryfan's Terrace Wall – to the strains of music from a portable gramophone on the terrace below.

Climbing solo, as he had no companions, the 17 year old Colin Kirkus from Liverpool escaped two falls in the B Gully of Craig yr Ysfa and, after tackling Idwal's Holly Tree Wall, just managed to escape by first lassoing a bollard, with the rope that he carried, then swarming up the rope. In the summer of 1928 he pioneered his first two Welsh new climbs. One in the Moelwyns was done in the company of his brother Guy, while the other was done solo – but it nearly cost him his life. On Craig Lloer Kirkus started up an airy crest then tackled a difficult crack where he had to abandon his rucksack which contained his camera. Higher up the crag he approached an innocent-looking bulge but then got into difficulties when he made a grab for a hold. 'I was hanging from my hands alone. There were no holds above and I could not descend. My arms were getting tired. I looked down and saw a drop of nearly 200 feet below me. My arms were aching now and I felt that I couldn't hold on much longer. I just hung there and waited for the end. Then I got into a panic and made a sudden convulsive spring round the corner on the left, where my hands mercifully landed on a hold'. And so a life, and the whole history of climbing, was affected by a single thread of fate.

1929 was to be an especially good year as far as the weather was concerned and consequently some notable new routes appeared. Ted Hicks showed great promise as a leader, climbing 'in the Oxford bell-bottoms (fashionable at the time) flapping loose round his ankles'. First Hicks took a line past Richards' piton to produce *Piton Route* then he breached the East Wall with *Ash Tree Wall* and the harder *Heather Wall* which required stern use of the Helyg poker while gardening, as well as a timely change from boots to rubbers for the final lead. Two other bold routes were *Rowan Tree Slabs* and finally the *Girdle Traverse of Holly Tree Wall*.

It was Hicks who was to take in hand the young teenager Colin Kirkus, 'a rather queer-looking lad', who was to change the face of Welsh climbing. Six days after his nineteenth birthday Kirkus was taken up to Glyder Fach by a Cambridge party. There he astounded them all by offering to lead an extremely steep groove line. He was encouraged to climb the route with the safety of a rope from above but then promptly led the line with only Hicks able to follow him on what was to be *Lot's Groove*, which has been described as the first of the rubber climbs. The day after, he led what is now a 5a pitch, *Central Route* on Tryfan, and this time no one could follow him. Although on a good day Hicks was said to be as fine a technician on hard pitches as any other climber of his time, Kirkus had an extra inner drive and a keen eye for a new line. Later in 1929, after *Central Rib* on the Slabs, Kirkus succeeded, after Hicks had failed, on *Rake End Chimney*. The rock was wet and greasy and having removed his boots Kirkus attacked the overhang despite the fact that his chance of finding an exit was slim indeed. Nevertheless he managed to do what his companions thought of as impossible. The anchor man on the rope that day was Alan 'A B' Hargreaves, who not only accompanied Hicks and Kirkus on some of their finest climbs but also led many of the second ascents of the hardest routes of that era.

Occasionally a route is completed without fuss or acclaim and it is only years later when the true story emerges. One such route was *Javelin Blade* completed by Jack Longland at Easter in 1930. During the ascent Longland got off-route and the new climb was merely written up as a slightly harder variation on the Severe parent route; today the Blade is graded as E1 5b and as such it was retrospectively found to have been the hardest route in Wales for many years.

Since the probings of Steeple and Barlow things had remained very quiet in the Carneddau until the arrival of Kirkus. His first offering on Craig yr Ysfa was *Amphitheatre Rib* in 1931. Kirkus was climbing superbly in the aftermath of his brilliant breakthrough on the *Great Slab* of Clogwyn Du'r Arddu in 1930 and, after disposing of *Lot's Wife* the next day, he went on to tackle the *Pinnacle Wall* of Craig yr Ysfa. Not only was the wall unclimbed but it was outrageously steep with tremendous exposure owing to its position high above the lower wall. Pinnacle Wall was not technically hard but as a solo first ascent it lays claim to being Kirkus's finest hour, as anyone who has led the pitch may readily admit as they pull up the top moves. The *Direct Start* to Pinnacle Wall, which was completed a year later with Hargreaves, had 'no real point but difficulty'. Kirkus also tried to straighten out Pinnacle Wall even more but was ejected by the pitch. At this stage he also set his sights on Llech Ddu but was repulsed by fierce overhangs and excessive vegetation. He did however leave a final legacy on Craig yr Ysfa; *The Crack* quickly earned a reputation for being a hard proposition.

Although the Oxbridge influence had provided the main driving force for some years all the hardest attacks were spearheaded by the Liverpool contingent. Not only was Liverpool well-situated for forays into Wales but the conveniently positioned Helsby Rocks allowed a good training diet. Kirkus was not the only climber who was to thrive on the sandstone prior to greater deeds on the Welsh crags. His contemporary, Menlove Edwards, was also destined for great things and based at Helyg, Edwards spread out to explore the cliffs which had intimidated not only his predecessors but also his peers. Throughout the '30s Edwards made his mark in many ways starting with his exploration of the sepulchrally dank recesses of the Devil's Kitchen cliffs. During his dark moods Edwards would attack new sections of rock and power his way up the dripping overhangs casting aside the lethally loose outer skin of flaky rock and luxuriant vegetation. Many of his seconds must have approached routes with fear and trepidation only to experience further heart-stopping moments during the first ascents of routes which were undoubtedly far harder before subsequent teams got down to more solid rock. Edwards 'extended the diabolical domain with Rocks Buttresses, Pastures, Dumps and Dives'. Surprisingly Edwards did not stray north of the A5 for new routes apart from *Anvil Cracks* on Creigiau Gleision. Outside the Devil's domain he did however produce some fine Ogwen lines with *Sub-Cneifion Rib* (Cwm Cneifion) the *East Wall Girdle* (Idwal), *Soapgut* (Milestone Buttress), and the delectably delicate *Grey Slab* of Glyder Fawr.

Fifty six years after the ascent of Grey Slab evidence came to light that it had not after all been the first ascent as a month earlier Arthur Bullough of the Rucksack Club had climbed the same line which he called *Lost Boot Climb*, the boots had in fact been taken off for the crux and slung round the leader's neck, but when the laces snapped they fell to the ground from on high.

In the pre-war period a strong party of German climbers visited Britain and being unimpressed by the routes that they had been shown were eventually pointed at a blank piece of Tryfan rock. John Jenkins egged them on to try a new line but unfortunately *Munich Climb* was only done with the aid of three imported pitons and the gauntlet was thrown down to the British who saw this action as a declaration of war. A week later, when Jenkins showed the route to Menlove Edwards, a bronze karabiner and a piton could plainly be seen, so a vow was taken to remove the offending objects. Within two weeks Edwards had freed the route and Dick Barry removed one of the pitons with the well-travelled Helyg poker. Honour was finally satisfied.

The extensive exploration of the early 1930s was constantly monitored with the intention of producing a new series of guidebooks and the lion's share of this work was undertaken by Edwards whose prolific writing seemed to draw him away from the great problems which beset his life. His first guidebook was to be to the Cwm Idwal group in 1936 and this was followed in 1937 by the Tryfan guidebook for which Edwards had enlisted the help of the talented climber Wilf Noyce (later this pair also wrote the 1939 Lliwedd guidebook). The remaining third of the Ogwen area was included in the Glyder Fach guidebook of 1937, written by Kirkus, which was well-received by all climbers. Edwards had commented about the 1937 Scafell guide that 'You can read it, the dry print, but only with a headache'. Without wishing to adopt a single line approach to routes Edwards's hope was that 'the climber may get a good idea of things before ever seeing the cliff'. It was the Kirkus style however which won most acclaim as it was 'a straightforward and very clear piece of work, economical of words without being dry, and essentially easy to use'.

Sometimes a new guidebook will start another wave of exploration but in the late 1930s attention was drawn to the Carneddau cliffs as work had started on a new guidebook, so for several years little of note was done in the Ogwen valley.

The main Carneddau explorers were: Hodgkin, Cox, Palmer, Buzzard, Kretschmer and Noyce. It was David Cox however who stole the lead in 1938 with his solos of *Gomorrah* and *Spiral Route* on Craig yr Ysfa. He also led *The Grimmet*, an exposed route which some years later was ascended by C C members wearing party hats on each New Year's Day. Seventeen new routes were done in 1937 and 1938, then in 1939 and 1945 that number was doubled. A guide to Craig yr Ysfa was eventually completed by Cox and Kretschmer in 1943.

During the war years only two Ogwen routes really stand out: *Hawk's Nest Arête* on Glyder Fach, by Nock and Harrison, was a fine line, while *Manx Wall* on Clogwyn Du was completed by A J Lowe with a strong party.

Nully Kretschmer had summed up the pre-war attitude towards equipment when he wrote: 'The hard, sharp Tricouni nail succeeded the blunt clinkernail, then the fashion was reversed. From time to time the urge for self-expression produces fantastic patterns of nails. As in the Lakes the rubber shoe has come into its own, in spite of the boot expert who protests that everything will go in nails. The expert and the hardy sometimes use the stockinged foot on difficult passages and the exceptionally hardy climb bare-footed... The use of pitons and other artificial aids is rare in Wales and likely to remain so.' Things were about to change.

Those who streamed back to Britain after the war were hardened by battle and training in the Forces and many people who had endured several years of accute stress and heartache were soon to seek peace in the hills. Not only did climbers have the right mental attitude towards leading the hardest routes but wartime advances in equipment made available to the climbers such improvements as; ex-W.D. karabiners, Vibram-soled boots, nylon rope and refined belaying methods.

Of the characters hardened by army training Chris Preston stood out above the rest. He had been one of the party which clipped an hour off the record for the Welsh 3,000-footers, and after a day's climbing had raced up Snowdon in 48 minutes. His route *Advocate's Wall* on the Devil's Kitchen was merely a prelude to a major breakthrough. On October 7th 1945 Preston led the first route on Suicide Wall (*Suicide Wall Route 1*). By modern standards it is graded E2 5c, and one must remember that it was done wearing gym shoes – there were no runners – and it was utterly serious and committing from the moment that he made his big push. Not surprisingly there were only two repeats during the next 14 years, and the route remained for some years as the hardest route in the country. By comparison John Lawton's 1948 route *Suicide Groove* was far more amenable, but nevertheless it was an intimidating line and compared well with other hard routes of the day.

One pre-war push had been when Paul Work and I Ap G Hughes attacked the front of Llech Ddu but sadly after completing three very hard pitches they were forced to retreat. It was left to George Dwyer and Dickie Morsley to complete the *Central Route* of Llech Ddu in 1946. It was an inspired foretaste of what was to come in the future.

At Christmas 1945 the names of Peter Harding and Tony Moulam appeared on the new route list after they completed *Staircase* on Pen Llithrig y Wrach. It was a modest beginning from two climbers who were to go on to greater things.

From 1949 to 1956 things went very quiet in Ogwen although it did still act as a base for the opening up of the Carneddau where Tony Moulam was vigorously leading the exploration while working on a new guidebook. Moulam dominated all the exploration of the late '40s and '50s and although many of his routes were to fill gaps some such as *Widdershins* on Braich Ty Du and *Pieces of Eight* on Craig yr Ysfa were of better quality. His badly needed Carneddau guidebook was finished in 1951 (and was later revised in 1966), but before it appeared Moulam at last produced a brilliant route which was to capture people's imagination. His *Mur y Niwl* (Wall of the Mists) was a masterly piece of route finding up an improbable-looking wall. Even 30 years later people were to arrive at its foot and look out to the arête in disbelief, "It can't really go out there, can it?" Silence. A moment of realisation then in awed tones, "It does." *Mur y Niwl* gives an intricate line with immaculate climbing on the edge of a lot of fresh air. Few other routes of the 1950s deserve mention except perhaps for *Humour* on Lech Ddu in 1953.

If the Ogwen cliffs were brooding it was most apt as in June 1957 Edwards, in the middle of a personal conflict which raged inside him, returned to his old haunts for one last new climb. His aim was to follow the line of the waterfall in the heart of the Devil's Kitchen. 'He squirmed into the vertical crack down which the stream flows, and fought his way up it, puffing and gasping for breath. I shouted up to him to say I didn't want to do it, but the only reply I got was a bald head and a red face, glowering from the black dripping rock, looking like the very devil'.

Just over six months later Edwards took his own life, a tragic end for a tortured soul who had given so much of himself to the climbing world. Ogwen was still for a year until Ron James claimed two HVS routes of some note, *Devil's Nordwand* in the heart of the Edwards' domain and *Grey Arête* on immaculate rock overshadowing the slab which Edwards had visited more than a quarter of a century earlier.

One oddity was *Dover Road*, an A2 route, up overhangs on the left wing of the Amphitheatre of Craig yr Ysfa. Completed in 1955 the route would have been more at home in the Alps, which Bourdillon and Ward were aiming to visit, but the route remains unusual in that it was one of the few aid climbs to be completed on a mountain cliff in Wales. Another route which was controversial was *Agrippa*, completed in 1959 by the American climber John Wharton. Too many unnecessary pegs were used but in its later free form it provided a fine route.

In the early '60s all the action was elsewhere and Ogwen was left to beginners and those who were content to plod their way up well-charted paths albeit on vertical rock. One flash of inspiration was provided by Pete Crew and Bas Ingle in 1963 when they added the superb line of *Suicide Wall Route 2*. Another one-off was the *Devil's Bastion* by Herley and Blythe in 1965.

The Carneddau crags were about to be transformed by a generation of climbers who were prepared to tackle the most intimidating cliff faces, whatever the state of the rock. The major problem on Llech Ddu was to be gardening on a gigantic scale and Mo Anthoine and Ian Campbell took five days to remove several tons of vegetation from *The Groove*. It was well worth the effort however as the finished route was to be a sustained Mild Extreme of great quality.

The next climber to launch an attack was John Clements, backed first by Alan Bell and then Dave Potts. *Griseofulvin* (1964) and *Plumbagin* (1965) on Craig yr Ysfa were only HVS at the time, whereas the routes on Llech Ddu were slightly harder. The 1965 routes were; *Elliw* (E1), *Endor* (E2) and *The Great Corner* (E2). The latter gave yet another mega-trundling session as originally there was a huge ramp leading up towards the great roof – now the ramp has gone! The death of Clements in Glencoe brought an end to his Welsh ambitions and others were soon to step in for the many lines that were still waiting.

1966 saw the fine *Girdle Traverse of the Lower Amphitheatre Wall* of Craig yr Ysfa by Ron James but the main action was to be on Llech Ddu. Early in the year *Commuter's Crack* was climbed by Hatton, Jones and Moulam. The scene was then set for the arrival of the Holliwell brothers, Les and Lawrie. There was no doubt when the two Londoners were present on a crag as their constant banter was non-stop, but they had quickly adapted to hard Welsh climbing and had lots of ability, Lawrie in particular being forceful on technical problems and overhanging rock. They opened their account with the aptly named *Venom* (E3) which needed a point of aid owing to the looseness of the rock and the need to trundle some big blocks while leading. A week later *Iota* was added to the left wing.

During 1967 the Holliwells added only one route, *Scarface*, but it was an epic ascent both for the brothers as well as for other climbers present on the cliff as missiles rained down in profusion. 1968 was a busy year with *Zenith* (E1), *Blitzkrieg* (E1), *Skid Row* (VS) one of the last chimneys to be found, *Herostratus* (E3), *Cupid's Inspiration* (E2) and *Gytrack* (E1).

As the word spread about new route potential in the Carneddau several teams stepped in in the wake of the Holliwells. A party comprising Crew, Lowe, Alcock and Joe Brown went prospecting on Ysgolion Duon and bagged a long mountaineering route called *Flanders*. Trevor Jones then found the fine direct line of *Pinnaclissima* on Pinnacle Wall although the route was only led with two aid points. The big route of 1969 was to be *The Great Arête* of Llech Ddu and not surprisingly the route took several days to complete. Ed Ward Drummond and Ben Campbell-Kelly who completed the route used some aid but it was a fine achievement. The route was later to be freed by Pete Livesey in 1975. At the turn of the decade Les Holliwell filled in several obvious gaps for the guidebook while in 1971 Lawrie Holliwell, with Barry Whybrow, forced *The Fourth Dimension* a hard and challenging girdle across Llech Ddu. Just before the Carneddau guidebook went to press Rab Carrington, with Alan Rouse and Brian Hall, produced the superb pitch of *Aura* on the Lower Amphitheatre Wall.

In Ogwen between 1965 and 1971, apart from *Homicide Wall* by Peers and Whittle (a line which it is rumoured that Ted Hicks nearly succeeded on many years ago), all the quality routes were to be snatched by Martin Boysen and Dave Alcock. *Hebenwi* in 1969 was to be *the* route of Clogwyn Du giving exposed climbing in an intimidating position. It was on Suicide Wall however that the plum lines lay waiting, and in 1971

Boysen and Alcock added three routes in two days. *Capital Punishment* (E4 6a) was a real gripper which only capitulated with the aid of a piton. *Suspended Sentence* (E3) also needed a point of aid at the time. The last of the trio, *The Garotte* (E4 6a) was a forceful girdle of the Suicide Wall area and again minimal aid was needed to complete the route. It was not to be the final route on Suicide Wall as in 1977 Bill Wayman and Tim Jepson added a hard line, *Penal Servitude* (E4 6a). Then in 1979 the Yorkshire hit teams targetted in on the wall. Ron Fawcett struck first with *Mur y Meirwon* (Wall of the Dead) then shortly afterwards Pete Livesey made an even more serious foray with *Zero* (E6 6a).

Serious confrontation arose shortly after Martin Boysen used the oak tree below the Central Block of the Milestone Buttress to start a crack line, but in casual fashion he failed to write up the new route. Two young climbers later appeared on the scene and not realising the ecological significance cut down the oak. As they were unable to climb the line John Redhead was enlisted to complete the ascent of *The Wrinkled Retainer* (E4 6c). Boysen's original route was then given the name of Desecration Crack and in the midst of a host of accusations Redhead was wrongly charged with having wilfully removed the tree. In an open letter to the climbing world the two young climbers then admitted their thoughtless and irresponsible action, but the act was done and could not be rectified. John Redhead, who was to concentrate more in other areas, raised climbing standards considerably on Clogwyn y Tarw in 1979 with the bold lead of *Insidious Slit* (E4), while Ron Fawcett soloed *The Derelict*, an E3 pitch. That year saw the first appearance of Gary Gibson with *Wavelength Touch* on Holly Tree Wall, while his friend Derek Beetlestone found fierce climbing on the vague crack of *Demetreus* on the West Wall.

With the start of a new decade climbers started looking for some obvious gaps to fill and a typical product was Pat Littlejohn's *Night Moves* up the left wall of the Devil's Kitchen. Another oddity was the horrific roof of *Cobalt Dream* a 6b pitch on Drws Nodded on which Chris Shorter was eventually successful. Craig yr Ysfa was the crag which caught the attention of several top climbers and Martin Crook started things off with *Excalibur* on the Pinnacle Wall, while Paul Trower and Gordon Tinning broke out on to the Lower Amphitheatre Wall with *Solid Air*. It was Gibson however who stole the plums with *Turn the Centuries Turn* and the fine pitch of *Amadeus* leading up to the Mur y Niwl perch-stance. Llech Du being an unfashionable crag only saw brief action from Mick Fowler. He had previously freed Herostratus in 1978 and then returned to free Endor in 1981.

1982 was reasonably quiet with Yates and Boysen adding several routes, such as the excellent *Living Fossil*, to Craig Cwrwgl. Another noteworthy addition, after a two-year gap, was when Littlejohn returned to the other side of the Devil's Kitchen for *Hell's Gate*. A new team arrived on the scene in 1982 when Steve Boydon and Simon Cardy started their Ogwen campaign. Their excellent and atmospheric route, *Stratosphere*, on Clogwyn Du, was climbed on sight in swirling mist.

In 1983 John Harwood and Andy Sharp surprisingly found the fine line of *Crazy Horse* on the left wall of Soapgut, while on the East Face of Tryfan Hugh Banner proved that it was still possible to find easier-graded new routes. These included *Central Chimney*, *The Temple* and *The Flange*. The main action of that year however was to be up on Craig yr Ysfa where some big lines were still waiting. Martin Crook and Andy Newton prospected on Pinnacle Wall for a new girdle which became *Sea of Dreams*, while Boysen and Rab Carrington worked out *El Nino* and *Drought* opposite Mur y Niwl. Yet again Gibson stole the show with a big route, *The Haunted*, an E5 wall (with an unfortunate drilled peg) to the right of Pinnacle Wall.

Sharp and Harwood updated Gallt yr Ogof on an August day in 1984 when they launched an assault on the overhangs to the right of Sodom. *Red Cloud* was a reasonable E2 but the E5 line of *Warhorse* was a much harder proposition altogether. Boydon and Cardy were also active with two E3s, *Optical Illusion* on Drws Nodded and *Appendicitis* on Clogwyn y Geifr. By 1984 climbers were also adding small sharp pitches in their own right, some as short as 50 feet. Nick Dixon scoured Idwal for pitches such as *Thinking of the Girl* and *Breadline*, but two routes were in another league. *One More Calorie* on Holly Tree Wall was given E6 6b as Dixon was in doubt as to whether or not the route deserved to be given an E7 rating. His other line, *Teenage Menopause* to the left of Demetreus, on the West Wall rated a staggering E7 6b.

After a rather quiet year in 1985 Ian Carr opened his account a year later with *The Hangman's Return* an E4 up to the right of Homicide Wall. One obscure gem of 1986 was Jon de Montjoye's *Afterburner* on Gallt yr Ogof, a very good route which several teams later failed to find. After a pause, Boydon and Cardy returned in 1987 for several hard routes. On May 10th they climbed two routes on Clogwyn y Geifr. *Hell's Teeth*, to the left of Gehenna, was a fine hors d'oeuvre before the main course when they made an assault on the old aid route *The Devil Rides Out*. The free version was a spectacular and strenuous E5 which had been tried by at least one top team. A few days later they visited the Pinnacle Crag of Cwm Cywion and brought it up to date with an E4, *Poultry in Motion*. Perhaps their biggest surprise was a route snatched from under everybody's noses. *Game, Set and Match*, E6 6b, is a hard but well-protected pitch beside Tennis Shoe on the Slabs.

During 1987 George Smith, who later was to receive criticism for the use of unsightly pegs, produced two good routes, *Tree of Man* on the Milestone and *Bubbly* on Clogwyn y Tarw. Then in 1988, following the trend for short but highly difficult pitches, there was a concerted effort on Clogwyn y Tarw and local guide Chris Parkin led *Blue Smartie, Stonehenge* and the bold arête of *Travelling People*. Another team concentrating on the bouldering out of short but vicious pitches was that of George Smith and Ed Stone. The latter accounted for *Couteau* E6 6b while Smith was successful with *Rocking Chair Ridge* E6 6b, and *Le Fin* E7 6b. Glyder Fach also received a hard pitch from Noel Craine, *Kaya* E7 6b. It was to the left of Direct Route and this excellent line was soon to receive a direct finish by Johnny Dawes.

One curious story is that of Craig yr Ogof a crag which had been dismissed by Tony Moulam many years previously. It was also a crag whose name kept changing just to add to the general confusion. Rumour has it that Tom Leppert only released low key information in order to keep the crag for himself. Certainly he has found some superb routes the best of which was *Broadsword* in 1988.

In 1989 the lure of a big mountain route with lots of aid points remaining was too much for some climbers to resist. *The Fourth Dimension* on Llech Ddu was an obvious target which fell prey to Crispin Waddy and Dai Lampard's impressive efforts for a free ascent. A lack of traffic and far from solid rock made its cleaning-up an even more impressive achievement, but Waddy and Lampard had no truck with looseness however and eventually freed the route. That year also saw *Hyndsight* on Glyder Fach, which was perhaps the best of Chris Parkin's routes. During 1990 the secret of Craig yr Ogof was out of the bag and Tom Leppert and Paul Jenkinson, and then Iwan Jones, stepped in for lines such as the fine *Morgan La Faye*.

Coming up to date it is fitting that the history to this much loved area should end with discoveries on the higher crags. In May 1991 Dai Lampard found the superb *Mother of Mercy*, to the right of Amadeus on Craig yr Ysfa. In the spring of 1992 Simon Cardy opened up a secluded new cliff, Craig Ddaear, up in Cwm Lloer, with several routes, the best being *Sweating Peat*, and George Smith climbed the excellent *Glyder Crack*, a modern route with a traditional name, up on Glyder Fach.

To sum up perhaps C F Holland's 1924 words are apt in order to assess how little Ogwen has changed over the last 100 years:

'Ogwen has now a strong claim to rank among the very best of climbing centres, whether its attractions are assessed from the point of view of moderate climbers or from that of the rubber men, while for wealth of climbing within easy reach it is unequalled. It also possesses a great weight of climbing tradition, an apostolic succession to the mighty men of old'.

Certainly Ogwen and Carneddau has a special place in the heart of climbers whether they opt for the easy Slabs, the gloomy depths of the Devil's Kitchen, the exposure of Suicide Wall or the distant seclusion of Craig yr Ysfa. There will always be the wild stormy days on the high ridges and a warm fire waiting at Helyg or Ogwen Cottage. Winter in its season will coat the high cwms and in the sparkling silence groups will seek a peace of mind on Tryfan and the Glyderau far from the pressures of the bustling weekday city life. In the heart of the vastness the dark waters of Idwal will be rippled by a bustling breeze and far above a lone raven will head off purposefully in its quest.

Ogwen

Introduction

The cliffs of the Glyderau have been inextricably linked to the history and development of rock-climbing ever since its infancy as a sport in the late Nineteenth Century. Each generation has left a legacy of fine routes in the area. It is this thread of continuity, unmatched in North Wales, that makes Ogwen so appealing. This perception also gives the routes a unique atmosphere; almost as if one were exploring the evolution of climbing.

The majority of the crags are to be found on the flanks of the Glyderau; a dog-leg range of mountains forming the southern and western confines of the Ogwen valley. This hump-backed ridge extends from Y Foel Goch 678 582 westwards to Glyder Fach 656 583 and Glyder Fawr 643 579; then north westwards past Y Garn 631 595 to Carnedd y Filiast 621 627 and Elidir Fawr 612 613. Tryfan 664 594 is the exception, forming a spur jutting out at right-angles to the range. The approaches to the crags are given in the text, each one in its respective preamble; almost all are straightforward.

There is much of interest for all types of climbers, whatever their inclination. Even the less frequented faces are of worth; if only to provide an illusion of seclusion in such a popular area. There is a tremendous variety in the nature of the rock and the character of the climbing. Indeed, the choice extends from easy angled slabs, boulder choked gullies, smooth steep walls through to towering buttresses. Most of the rock is good; however, it should never be treated with disregard. This is particularly true in those areas where the rock has been burnished by the passage of countless pairs of hands and feet. Many of the routes retain a distinct mountaineering flavour; and are often used as a training ground for the higher ranges. Moreover, with some forethought, a number of routes may be strung together to form the basis of a long outing.

Some of the more modern and highly technical routes, as well as a few of the older but less attractive offerings, have had very few repeats. These should be treated with circumspection, as they may be very lichenous, vegetated or loose; or, perhaps all three!

The standard adjectival grading system is employed. It assumes that climbers can afford and use a modern rack of gear, are wearing rock-boots and have the aptitude to use their equipment. The grades are as follows: Moderate, Difficult, Very Difficult, Severe, Hard Severe, Very Severe, Hard Very Severe and Extremely Severe.

The Extremely Severe grade is an open-ended system of increasing difficulty, represented by the symbols E1, E2, E3, E4, E5, E6 and currently E7. These, like the other adjectival grades, represent the overall impression of difficulty, taking into account the technical difficulty, strenuousness, seriousness and position of the route.

Numerical pitch grades are included in the text, and should be familiar to most climbers; they are 3a, 3b, 3c, 4a, 4b, 4c, 5a, 5b, 5c, 6a, 6b, 6c and 7a. The few points of aid are also mentioned, according to the number deployed. There are no real artificial routes of note. Pitch lengths are given in feet, reflecting the traditional style of the area; a rough conversion into metres can be achieved on subdividing by three.

The grades given are a consensus of opinion from a large number of local activists. However, anomalies may occur, particularly on the more recent routes, those recently rediscovered and the ones which are merely obscure. The high amount of polish on some of the easier routes has altered their grades; this problem is exacerbated during periods of rain. Poor weather will also increase the difficulty of all the other routes, particularly those which tend to be lichenous or vegetated.

The familiar star system has been used to indicate the quality of the routes, irrespective of grade. A route must be excellent in all respects to qualify for three stars, and even a one star route must be out of the ordinary. Absence of stars does not mean that a route is unsatisfactory, as poor climbs are specifically described as so in the text.

If pegs are mentioned in the text, either as waymarks or as belays, it should not be taken as a guarantee of their worth or presence. Many pegs have been in place for years, therefore, their condition must be a case for distrust, with the emphasis on the rust! Pegs regularly disappear and searching for a missing peg can confuse. It *must* be remembered that the ground has little sympathy for the climber who fails to back up pegs with modern protection devices.

Although there are a few rusty 'biscuit-tin' bolt hangers in Tin-Can Alley above Ogwen Cottage, relics of the Dolomitic age of excesses, bolts of any form are not warranted on any of the cliffs in this guidebook. Visiting parties should note that the appearance of a bolt will lead to two actions; the rapid removal of the bolt and the vigorous discouragement of further shameless deeds by the perpetrators.

It was strongly intended that the Crafnant crags would be included in this volume. However, negotiations with the Mynydd Climbing Club failed to produce an agreement. The MCC intend to produce their own guide to these excellent crags at some undetermined time in the future.

Gallt Yr Ogof

(Slope of the Cave)

OS Ref. 693 595

The long ridge from the Glyderau extends a lofty spur into the Ogwen Valley between Capel Curig and Tryfan. It ends in a cliff which appears quite sheer in outline. Gallt yr Ogof is not superficially attractive, being north-facing, dark, and heathery. Yet these first glances are deceptive and give no inkling of the variety of routes here. The rock is generally clean, has plenty of holds and is of such a rough texture that the occasional smooth intrusion comes as a shock.

There is much heather, though it seldom interrupts the climbing, and it adds an old-fashioned feel to the place. The cliff is only a short walk from the road. There is a footpath west of the Helyg hut, or an approach over a small bridge from the campsite and parking area at Gwern y Gof Isaf 685 601 can be made along a rough track.

Gallt yr Ogof turns out to be quite complex. The main area comprises two cliffs, one set above the other. The Lower Cliff is by far the biggest expanse of rock; slanting over this is the steep Upper Cliff, with the tall dark cave that gives the cliff its name. To the left the cliff exposes a fine wing with a number of jutting overhangs. This is Dolphin Buttress, round the back of which (and facing east) is the little Skyline Buttress, rising above the smooth band of red slabs that provides the first two climbs. Beyond, only the summit rocks of Nant y Gors remain, the haunt of peregrine and buzzard.

Red Slab (150 feet, Severe) is not as hopeless as it first appears, and is marvellously rough. The best line trends up leftwards to the heather ledge beneath the grey cornice.

Netts   300 feet   Difficult   (1955)
A pleasant route on the right-hand area of slab and just up from a smooth grey slab. A heathery ramp slants up cutting a square break through the bulge at 40 feet.
1 90 feet. Climb up the slab just on the left and step over the bulge to a ledge on the right. Spike belay.
2 90 feet. Go straight up to a smooth slab beneath a short overhanging wall. From the middle of this, ascend delicately leftwards to heather. Walk 50 feet to the left.
3 20 feet. The slab on the right of the white groove.
4 100 feet. Go straight up again, staying on the edge, then finish over a steep little nose on the left.

Skyline Buttress

This is the most easterly buttress, quite high up and not immediately obvious. The left flank is steep and provides the climbing, although the **Original Route** (300 feet, Moderate, 1939) takes its crest in two easy stages.

Capstone Climb   120 feet   Very Difficult   (1940)
An interesting and steep little climb on good holds. Start over to the left, in the shade of an oak and a birch.
1 30 feet. Take the steep left edge to a heather ledge.
2 50 feet. Climb the next steep wall, swing up on to some large flakes then go through the trees and belay on the edge.
3 40 feet. Ascend the edge again. Scrambling remains.

The Rocking Stone Climb   100 feet   Very Difficult   (1939)
A rather scrappy route with little distinction. Start by the Luncheon Stone, 40 feet left of a low stone wall.
1 50 feet. Take the easy slab up to the left then go back right to a heather terrace.
2 50 feet. Climb the heathery recess to where it steepens at the hanging blocks. Work out left over these. Open scrambling leads to the top.

The next route ascends the left-hand of three prominent buttresses above Skyline Buttress.

★★Afterburner   70 feet   E5   (1986)
Takes the obvious central crack on the steep face of the buttress. Start

Zdzislaw 'Tom' Leppert, author and co-author of the two previous guidebooks to Ogwen. Photo: Howard Williams

Tom Leppert on the first ascent of *Ghostrider* (E3), Drws Nodded.
Photo: James Yeardsley

On the Central Buttress of Tryfan. Photo: Abraham Bros. Courtesy of Fell and Rock Climbing Club and Abbot Hall Art Gallery and Museum

The North Buttress of Tryfan; the traverse to Belle Vue Terrace. Photo: Abraham Bros.
Courtesy of Fell and Rock Climbing Club and Abbot Hall Art Gallery and Museum

at a peg belay below the crack.
1 70 feet. 6a. Ascend the crack, passing a peg at half height, the crux is just above, to a final steep wall.

Hebog Buttress

On the lower cliffs left of Dolphin Buttress a slate topped stone wall rises up to the foot of a small buttress. The continuation wall attains the foot of a larger and compact area of cliff, where the next routes will be found.

★**Shorter Oak** 60 feet E1   (1990)
Start at a bilberry ledge under a short groove.
1 60 feet. 5b. Ascend the wall just right of a short groove to a thread. Move left on to the slab then continue up the slab to a rounded finish.

The Littlest Rebel 50 feet E5   (1990)
Takes the wall to the right of Shorter Oak.
1 50 feet. 6a. Climb the wall past a crucial placement (Rock 1) to good holds. The upper section is easier and again rounded.

Dolphin Buttress

This is just left of the main cliff and has a graceful crest with a steep right face. The lower end quickly breaks loose from the deep heather and rises as a smooth slabby wall broken only by overhangs. Much farther up an obvious clear-cut crack is taken by Crack and Wall.

The Overhangs 240 feet Very Severe   (1944)
Develops into a surprisingly good and open route. The buttress presents three square overhangs at its lower end. The route goes up left of these to a clean upper rib. Start beneath overhanging rock by a smooth slab.
1 60 feet. 4a. Start up a heather-choked groove; there is a holly above. Traverse left beneath the overhang and climb a cracked bulge to a heather ledge. Belays are higher up.
2 40 feet. Climb the sloping steps and belay at the large flake under the third overhang.
3 40 feet. Hand-traverse left beneath this overhang and go up an easy groove to a spike belay.
4 100 feet. 4a. The main rib, on the right, is followed in its entirety. Always bold and quite delicate

Gallt Yr Ogof

Photo: Simon Cardy

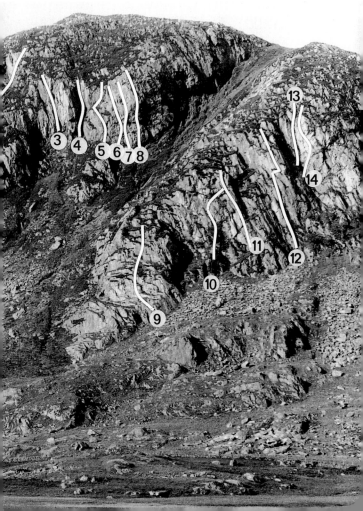

Variation
3a 110 feet. Traverse right from the third overhang and take difficult slanting cracks onto the smooth scoop of slab. Climb the open groove above to the top.

Crack and Wall   130 feet   Very Difficult   (1944)
A short climb consisting of a selection of problems. Start below the obvious wide crack.
1 40 feet. The crack, which needs to be started with conviction.
2 30 feet. Traverse left and take a shallow groove to a small stance beneath the inverted 'organ pipes'.
3 60 feet. Boldly climb straight over the overhang to the groove above, which is taken to the top.

A poor route, **Airy Corner** (120 feet, Difficult), takes the parallel earthy cracks and slabby corner to the easy ground on the right.

The Upper Cliff

Situated above the lower section, the routes on the Upper Cliff enjoy a flatteringly open aspect. The whole cliff is quite steep, but suffers badly from drainage.

The tall dark cave is the most immediate feature, separated from a V-chimney by a startling nose dubbed Jonah's Whale. Jonah's Buttress is just right of all this. The cliff has a long western face that runs steeply uphill. The lowest end shows several sharp overhangs, around which The Mulberry Bush picks a line. The height gradually reduces but the routes remain good. Table Climb is on the shelving grey rock that runs into a unique area of ledges, and Slab Route is above the big square overhang farther up. **Old Route** (350 feet, Moderate, 1910) takes the long gentle ridge that defines the left edge of the cliff. A good scramble, where a rope seems hardly necessary.

★**Black Maria**   180 feet   E1   (1965)
The deep V-chimney left of the tall cave. It is often damp, and is then an absorbing and slippery exercise. Start by scrambling up to its foot.
1 120 feet. 5b. Climb the chimney past a suspect flake. When the crack closes get onto the right arête for a few feet, before returning to the chimney.
2 60 feet. 4b. The leftward-slanting crack leads to the top.

Maria   160 feet   Hard Very Severe   (1959)
The obvious tall cave holds a strong element of fascination to those willing to explore its chilling depths. Start within the dark, wet interior.
1 40 feet. 4b. Climb slabby rocks to a stance on the left beneath the

huge overhang.
2 50 feet. 5a. From a little lower climb the right-hand wall, on widely-spaced holds, to a ledge. Traverse back into the corner and go up to an earthy stance and thread belay.
3 70 feet. 4c. Tackle the greasy crack, facing right.

Jonah's Buttress   140 feet   Very Difficult   (1933)
The rounded buttress right of the cave is steep in parts, though thankfully these are only short and there is a grassy bay high up. Start where some sloping rocks point up into a recess.
1 70 feet. Climb up into the recess, traverse right over some square blocks, then take a crack up to the grass ledges.
2 70 feet. Traverse up to the right round a rib, where a slabby break leads to the top. Or, take the little rib on the left of the bay, overlooking Jonah's Whale.

Sodom   210 feet   Very Severe   (1969)
This is on the left edge of the zone of overhangs at the turn in the cliff, right of Jonah's Buttress. Start beneath the lowest overhang.
1 50 feet. 4b. Climb to the overhang and move up right to reach a small stance with a spike belay.
2 60 feet. 4c. Traverse left and go up a shallow groove to a square overhang. Pass this on either side to a stance.
3 100 feet. 4a. Traverse right and climb an obvious groove, stepping out right at the top.

★**Red Cloud**   195 feet   E2   (1984)
A direct line through the overhangs right of Sodom. Start 25 feet right of Sodom at a shallow groove beneath the left end of the overhangs.
1 50 feet. 5b. Ascend the groove to the belay spikes on Sodom.
2 75 feet. 5b. Move up to the overhang and climb through it via a crack-line. Continue up a rough wall to a good ledge and belay
3 70 feet. 5b. Climb the wall rightwards to the arête and continue up this to the top.

★**Warhorse**   155 feet   E5   (1984)
The impressive line through the overhangs right of Sodom via an obvious overhanging crack. Start beneath the crack at a shallow undercut groove, about 30 foot right of Red Cloud.
1 70 feet. 6b. Enter the groove over an overhang and climb it with difficulty. Traverse right as for The Mulberry Bush to the cave belay.
2 85 feet. 6a. Traverse back left to the overhanging crack and climb it and easy ground above to the top.

The Mulberry Bush   280 feet   Hard Very Severe   (1969)
A good route that tactfully takes a rightward-rising line under the three main overhangs.
1 50 feet. 4a. As for Sodom.
2 70 feet. 4c. Traverse right beneath the overhang and continue the traverse with a delicate move to a small ledge at the last overhang. Get round this to reach a stance.
3 60 feet. 5a. Move out right, pull over the overhang and continue the traverse, with a delicate move to a small ledge at the last overhang. Get round this to a stance.
4 100 feet. 4b. Traverse right to the arête, climb directly to a shallow scoop, then easily to the top.

Table Climb   160 feet   Severe   (1937)
The cliff now relents to sloping grey shelves and black scarp walls. There is a nice open route here. Start beneath the Table, the largest of the shelves.
1 55 feet. Climb onto the Table. Go a little way up the obvious crack before moving round the low rib on the right to reach a stance below a dark wall.
2 35 feet. Continue on the rib to an overhung ledge, follow this rightwards to where big holds lead to a large belay.
3 70 feet. Climb the groove to the left, then a rounded slab, difficulties soon ease.

Route II   130 feet   Very Difficult   (1949)
This route, and the next, merge in an area which can only be described as the 'Ledges'. Start at a groove, 50 feet up from Table Climb.
1 55 feet. Ascend the groove, leaving its left edge to the ledge area. Belay by an ash tree.
2 25 feet. Go rightwards along the upper ledge.
3 50 feet. From the right-hand side, climb a wide shallow groove and minor ledges, going left.

Route I   130 feet   Very Difficult   (1949)
A scenic, circuitous route. Start at a broad gangway sloping up to the left, 50 feet right of Route II.
1 30 feet. Climb easily in the corner to the top of the gangway.
2 50 feet. Move down to the ledge and cross to a crevassed ledge, on incut holds. Pass an ash tree to the corner of the black wall, then go up to the next ledge.
3 50 feet. As for pitch 3 of Route II.

Slab Route   100 feet   Very Difficult   (1937)
A short climb in a good position above the sharpest overhang at the upper end of the cliff. Start where a dark open crack splits the lower wall.
1 80 feet. Climb the crack and awkwardly reach a small ledge on the right. Traverse right onto the slab, then follow the obvious line left of the overhang.
2 20 feet. Climb the gully on the left.

Dandelion Wall   120 feet   Very Difficult   (1949)
The first break in the overhang right of Slab Route. Start at a vertical crack.
1 50 feet. Climb the crack then go diagonally left to belay below the overhang.
2 70 feet. Traverse on small ledges to the right. One can now go left again to easy ground, but the more natural line is the crack and steep groove on the right.

Fence Climb   100 feet   Very Difficult   (1937)
A short route up to the fence at the end of the cliff. Start 30 feet right of Dandelion Wall.
1 100 feet. A sort of pillar leans against the face forming a series of cracks running to the top. Climb these.

The Lower Cliff

The lower cliff consists of slabby buttresses flanked by steep gaunt walls. It has the biggest selection of routes and they are varied in character. A good place for the afternoon or a short day. The left-hand side is low, steep and compact. Chalkren Stairs finds a way up out of the trees. To the right a small, overgrown, slabby area is overlooked by a steep arête with a projecting roof. Green Gully, the huge open bay in the middle of the cliff, is certainly lush. Its splendid right wall hangs like a bewitching yellow veil. From the lowest part of the cliff a rocky spur leads up to Bee's Buttress and the largest slabby face. It is somewhat spoilt by the bands of heather, yet the climbing is often open and rewarding.

Three Pitch Buttress (150 feet, Difficult), on the left of the Lower Cliff, is pleasing enough: the slab at its foot is followed by a little wall and then a steep groove.

Mad Jack McMad   70 feet   E2   (1991)
This route climbs the thumb-shaped west facing wall between Three Pitch Buttress and One Pitch Gully. Start below the centre of the wall.
1 70 feet. 5c. Gain the obvious right trending crack past two old aid pegs, crux, to finish up the arête.

To the right is **One Pitch Gully**, an easy step providing a short cut to the Upper Cliff.

Chalkren Stairs   150 feet   Very Severe   (1936)
An interesting and unusual climb in a rather sombre situation. Start right of One Pitch Gully, where the rock is steep and green, and find a way through the tree-covered lower slopes.
1 50 feet. 4b. Get into a steep V-shaped scoop from the left, then climb up through the funnel above. Go up the slab to belay on a small rock ledge on the left.
2 30 feet. 4c. There is a long overhang above and a ledge on the right perched beneath it. Make an awkward little traverse to reach this ledge, the Sing-Song Ledge.
3 20 feet. 4a. Descend a little then go up steeply to the next step on the edge of the buttress.
4 50 feet. 4a. Climb the ragged crack farther to the right.

Variation
3a 80 feet. 5a. Gain the steep crack above the left-hand end of the ledge, then move left to an exposed position by a doubtful spike. Finish directly.

★**Mosquito Slab**   230 feet   Very Severe   (1968)
Follows the rising slabs to the left of Old Man Buttress. It has a surprisingly elegant third pitch. Start at the open corner at the foot of the buttress.
1 50 feet. Climb the corner, exit left then go easily to a tree on the right.
2 60 feet. 4a. Take the slab on the left to where it bulges then go up right to the large grass ledge.
3 70 feet. 4c. Move delicately out onto the clean sweep of slab and climb the crack in the overhang above.
4 50 feet. 4a. The ragged crack of Chalkren Stairs.

Old Man Buttress   230 feet   Very Difficult   (1934)
A vegetated struggle up the front of the buttress between One Pitch Gully and Green Gully. Start at the lowest part of the buttress. Wander up easy ledges then take a ramp, with an awkward finish, which leads into the wide trough above.

Easy Pinnacle Route   160 feet   Moderate   (1934)
An entertaining scramble in the forbidding area just right of Old Man Buttress. Climb the corner beneath the hanging right wall to where a long pinnacle strut forms a wide crack, making an easy passage into the trough above.

The Curate's Egg 210 feet Hard Very Severe   (1968)
Quite good, open climbing. To the left of Green Gully is a clean arête
with a sharp roof. The route goes up into the shallow corner just to the
right of this. Start above the first bit of Green Gully, at the arête.
1 70 feet. 5a. Climb up into a steep little corner, move round the
arête above a small tree into a groove and go up to grass ledges.
2 140 feet. 4c. Move left onto the nose then climb straight up the
edge to a crack. This leads into the long corner, which is followed to
the top.

Green Gully (300 feet, Moderate) is a wide green slope shadowed
by an impending right wall. A reserve for the hardy expert in
vegetation techniques, as considerable depths of rushes and grass
will surely be encountered.

★**Samson** 140 feet E2   (1972)
The big corner rising out of Green Gully in a dominant position makes
a great climb. Start with much wading and one awkward rock step,
in the preliminaries of the gully.
1 140 feet. 5b. The corner direct; any tendency to rush will be
quickly quashed by the obvious need to eke out energies. The slanting
crack near the top forms an alternative finish.

★**Roseda Wall** 180 feet Hard Very Severe   (1968)
A magnificent, exposed route on the big yellow wall overhanging
Green Gully. It is packed with interest and quality. Start high up
Green Gully, at the corner of Samson.
1 70 feet. 4c. Traverse onto the right wall and climb steeply past a
large spike. Move right and mantelshelf onto a shattered ledge. Good
thread belay farther right.
2 70 feet. 5a. Cross the wall beneath the overhang to a crack and
gain a cosy niche. Climb the steep exit crack to an airy perch.
3 40 feet. 4c. Go left into a verdant alcove and climb the
overhanging groove on good holds; a fine finish.

★**Bee's Buttress** 200 feet Hard Severe   (1933)
A good route on the nose of the buttress at the very edge of the steep
scarp wall. Extraordinarily exposed. Start by going up heather and
rock at the toe of the buttress.
1 70 feet. 4b. Climb a short crack on the left edge, get out onto a
slab on the right and take the crack above.
2 60 feet. 4a. Ascend the exposed gangway on the left, then a crack
on the right to beneath the final overhangs.
3 70 feet. Traverse right, then make for an easy break back left
above the overhangs.

Gnat's Gnose   195 feet   Severe   (1937)
Quite a good climb, on the slabby area right of Bee's Buttress. The
rock is good and the heather soon subsides. Start right of Bee's
Buttress, by a fallen tree.
1 50 feet. Go straight up to a wide, shallow chimney.
2 65 feet. Climb the chimney, stepping out right, take the slab on the
left, and go round a corner to another slab. Climb this slab, which is
quite difficult, and belay on a quartz ledge along to the right.
3 80 feet. Climb straight up steeply, then go a little way left to a
recess. Take the rib on the left and traverse to the right beneath an
overhang, going over this at its end. The rest is a scramble.

Steep Wall   220 feet   Very Difficult   (1935)
A series of excellent pitches on steep rock walls are linked to make a
good climb of interest and exposure. The heather bands do not
interrupt the actual climbing. Start at a long slab coming out of Black
Gully, between where its left edge becomes undercut at a tiny overlap.
1 50 feet. Go easily up the slab and belay at a pinnacle on the
heather terrace.
2 60 feet. Climb the slabby wall just left of the pinnacle, then cross
the steep little wall trending to the right above it. Take a shallow
groove to a ledge.
3 50 feet. Take the rounded rib behind the belay, then go over to the
right and climb to the top of a steep rib.
4 60 feet. On the right is a steep wall with an overhang across its
top. Step up on the left and follow a line of holds that lead rightwards
beneath it, then go up a rib to the top.

H & J Variations   50 feet   Difficult
Two good little pitches.
1a 30 feet. Climb the steep slab on good holds, near the entrance to
Black Gully.
2a 30 feet. Take the groove against the overhangs on the right then
scramble up to the last pitch.

The Chant is a wandering girdle traverse of the Lower Cliff. The
original way (Very Severe) includes the crux pitch of Chalkren Stairs,
though another line avoids this difficulty by coming down low and
continuing via Old Man Buttress. This is almost cheating but levels the
standard out at Very Difficult. Elsewhere the climber is fairly free to
choose his way.

To the right of the wide wet chimney of Black Gully, twin buttresses
snuggle close together. They are very uninspiring, ugly sisters yet they
have been climbed in several places. **Hop Wall** (160 feet, Very Difficult)

is on the left buttress; **Stack Wall** (130 feet, Severe, 1936) is on the right.

Farther right, patches of rock come down a little lower and face Tryfan. These are good and rough, and can be linked to give **West Ridge** (150 feet, Difficult). Start up the chimney left of the gully then follow the right edge of the rib. A line up the steep wall beyond, not obvious, is Severe and makes a good finish.

Nant Yr Ogof and **Cwm Tryfan**

(Valley of the Cave)

Between Gallt yr Ogof and Tryfan are two quite individual cwms separated by a low narrow spur called Braich y Ddeugwm.

The left-hand cwm, Nant yr Ogof, is pleasantly open and grassy. A line of outcrops and craglets extends into the cwm from Gallt yr Ogof, and nestling in its back is a small crag. A steady walk leads up the cwm from Gwern y Gof Isaf 685 602.

Cwm Tryfan is a very different place. The East Face towers over one side, the steep scree-covered slopes of a high curving ridge shut off the head; on the left, rock bands rise tier upon tier culminating in Drws Nodded, which stands like an eerie cenotaph. Cwm Tryfan can be reached from Gwern y Gof Uchaf 673,603, whence, from behind the farmhouse, a footpath leads past Little Tryfan. The crest of this remarkable promontory of slab is very easy and relieves the monotony of a sharp rise into the Cwm.

Craig Nant Yr Ogof

OS Ref. 677 585

This is the little crag at the head of Nant yr Ogof. It is highest on the left, where it is buttressed by a flat pillar; there is a steep, straight crack in the centre and farther right, beyond a projecting nose, is Youth Crack.

Yeoman Service 150 feet Severe   (1954)
The top pitch is good but the lower pitches are rather messy. Start at the foot of the pillar beneath a low roof.
1 40 feet. Go up grass until under the roof, or climb there by a little groove in the wall down to the left. Take the break on the right to another grass ledge.
2 45 feet. Climb the crack then the groove to the top of the pillar.
3 65 feet. The wall above is good, and steep. Reach a line of holds and follow them across to a niche, then go right again to a groove and the top.

Breach of Promise 140 feet Very Severe   (1979)
A good climb and the cleanest line here. It is the straight crack out of the alcove in the centre of the cliff. Start directly beneath the crack.
1 40 feet. 4a. Climb up through a little open chimney then cross a slab to the alcove on the right.
2 100 feet. 4c. From the back of the alcove climb the very pleasing crack to the top.

Youth Crack 100 feet Difficult   (1931)
This is the break that eventually becomes a crack. Start by scrambling up to the right over the lower boulders.
1 100 feet. Climb over a jammed block into the break and then, higher up, the clean rough crack to finish.

Drws Nodded

(Door of Shelter)

OS Ref. 672 586

A steep, compact cliff, which has two distinct sections. The left half is clean and dignified, and crowned by a long stately overhang. The right half is very scruffy by comparison.

The Left Half

To the left of the overhang is a square corner with Plain Crack in its left wall. The roof is a major challenge and it is now done without aid. There is a clean right-hand arête before the vegetated gully corner.

Analyst's Flue   90 feet   Difficult   (1948)
A chimney in the short face round to the left of Plain Crack. Start below the chimney.
1 50 feet. Climb up to the grass strip beneath the chimney.
2 40 feet. Finish up the chimney.

Plain Crack   120 feet   Severe   (1936)
A good crack, which lives up to its name. Start at the foot of the grassy corner, left of the overhang.
1 100 feet. Climb the wall out of the corner to gain the crack. The crack is quite steep and open with an awkward bulge before it eases.

Optical Illusion   120 feet   E3 (1 pt. aid)   (1984)
Ascends the steep narrow wall right of Plain Crack. Start at the foot of the big grassy corner as for Plain Crack.
1 120 feet. 6a. Climb the corner for a few feet then venture rightwards to the middle of the wall. Climb directly past two pegs, the second peg being used to maintain upward progress, crux. Easier but bolder climbing leads straight up for 50 feet until forced to escape out rightwards to where the difficulties abate.

★★Ghostrider   140 feet   E3   (1984)
A steep arête rises to support the left-hand side of the main overhang. Start at a corner cut into the arête.
1 140 feet. 6a. Ascend the corner until one is forced out right to a giant thread under an overlap. Surmount the overlap and keep close to the edge of the arête until it is possible to make a hard mantel high

on the right. Use some fangs of rock to regain the arête and continue up the crack above.

★**Cobalt Dream** 140 feet E4   (1981)
The sensational main overhang goes free. Start below the crack in the right wall.
1 40 feet. 4b. Ascend blocks to a small balcony.
2 100 feet. 6b. Take the thin crack to the roof. The crack runs horizontally out across the roof for 15 feet, where it widens to a suffocating nightmare. A specialist's pitch. Large Friends will be found to be useful.

★**Evening Flight** 140 feet E1   (1973)
A steep climb that waives an easy escape. Start at a steep groove in the right arête.
1 90 feet. 5a. Climb the groove. It has a good crack but it is still awkward to reach the ledge on the right.
2 50 feet. 5b. Go leftwards onto the front then, with a lurch, grasp the fang above the overhang and pull into an easier groove.

The gully corner and **Unbar Route** (100 feet, Difficult, 1936), on the left, are examples of an audacious type of climbing that has long been unfashionable. They are best when the fruits are ripe.

The Right Half
Here the rock is not so reliable and is very mossy. There are several cracks and corners but they make a poor impression.

Garden Path 110 feet Hard Severe   (1942)
An open crack, made more interesting by a direct finish. Start at the straight crack, 30 feet right of the gully.
1 70 feet. 4a. Climb the crack (a rock finger points up into it), passing a small overhang, to a grassy stance.
2 40 feet. 4a. Desert the crack by a delicate traverse to the ledges on the right. Or, harder, follow the crack through the overhang.

Barbed Corner 90 feet Severe   (1936)
More constricted and just as mossy as the previous climb. Start at the corner, which is only obvious from the right.
1 90 feet. The ground is loose for a few feet before you arrive in the corner. Climb past the sharp overhang and continue more easily to the top.

Tryfan Fach

(Little Tryfan)

OS Ref. 672 601

This well-known feature of the valley, a miniature in outline of the parent peak, is situated at the base of Cwm Tryfan and only a short walk beyond Gwern y Gof Uchaf, from where it appears as a rock spur emerging from the hillside. Its left face is only short, but the other, on the west, is a remarkable expanse of slab. It is a great place for beginners to learn the ropes, and handy enough for amusement on a wet day.

The uppermost area must be condemned, as it is broken by too many heather terraces. The lower slabs, however, are smooth and clean for 200 feet, and at an angle that just suggests more difficulty than really exists, for there is an abundance of sharp and incut holds. The slab can be climbed almost anywhere, though some care should be taken as the stances are small and few; it seems best to stick to the natural lines. The repetitive moves need not bore, and can add momentum to an ascent.

Little Tryfan Arête 240 feet Difficult
A pleasant introduction to the cliff it is low in its grade and can be made even easier, by missing out a couple of sections. Start at a pile of boulders beneath the well worn arête, at the leftmost edge of the slabs.
1 80 feet. A number of variants lead to a large ledge and good belays.
2 80 feet. Keep to the very edge of the arête as much as possible to heighten the sense of exposure.
3 80 feet. The climbing and the angle both ease off considerably towards the top

Crack 1 240 feet Difficult
An obvious line which only just manages to attain the grade due to the polished nature of the rock. However, it does provide a diverting exercise for the beginner. Start at the base of a wide crack, just to the right of the arête.
1 80 feet. Follow the wide crack to a stance at some rounded flakes.
2 80 feet. Keeping to the right of the arête, continue up the crack.
3 80 feet. Trend up rightwards to finish.

Crack 2 200 feet Difficult
Another popular route. Start directly below a large triangular niche

30 feet above the base of the slabs.
1 120 feet. Climb up to the niche, then from its left-hand end continue up a crack to join the route above.
2 80 feet. Easily rightwards as for the previous route.

Crack 3   200 feet   Difficult
Slightly harder than the three climbs above. Start below and to the right of the large triangular niche.
1 80 feet. Climb directly to a thin crack, going straight up the slab. Follow the crack to a shallow rectangular recess at the point where the cracks fork off to become two lines.
2 120 feet. Follow the right-hand crack, with continuous interest, to the top. Obviously, the left-hand branch can be tackled, instead.

Slab 1   190 feet   Very Difficult
A pleasant route. Start 10 feet to the right, directly beneath the left side of a white bulge (or boil?) at about 60 feet.
1 80 feet. Ascend the slab via thin cracks, move up leftwards through the left-hand side of the pale bulge to reach the shallow square recess of Crack 3.
2 110 feet. Reject both of the branches of the forked crack and climb directly up the tongue of slab betwixt the cracks. Move right to the belay.

Slab 2   190 feet   Severe
A delectable little climb. Start below the right-hand side of the white bulge at 60 feet.
1 80 feet. Climb up to the right-hand side of the pale boil, go over, on good holds, to reach tiny footledges, the stance.
2 110 feet. Continue directly, via a series of shallow slanting cracks, to belay on a large ledge.

Crack 4   190 feet   Difficult
Another delightful offering. Start at the foot of a ragged crack, between the boil and the next large triangular niche.
1 90 feet. Follow the crack past a large perched flake to good belays.
2 100 feet. Follow the crack, in much the same vein, to the top.

On the right is a second and even larger triangular niche, which eventually tapers off into a wide crack.

Chimney Crack   160 feet   Difficult
Easier if dry, the route still contains a number of soil ledges. Start in the niche, about 20 feet above the base of the slabs.

1 160 feet. Ascend the glaringly obvious line, which can be split almost anywhere if your ropes don't reach in one run-out.

To the right is a large rectangular slab of perfect grey rock.

Left-Hand Slab Route   190 feet   Difficult
Well-protected and pleasing climbing. Start below and right of the large niche.
1 90 feet. Follow the left-hand side of the slab, to belay at the base of a curving crack.
2 100 feet. Either follow the crack, or, continue up the slab just to its left on delicious incuts.

Central Slab Route   200 feet   Very Difficult
A surprisingly fine climb. Start below the centre of the slab, yes, you really do!
1 95 feet. Climb in a straight line, a real directissima, then crabwalk leftwards to belay at the base of the curving crack.
2 105 feet. Move back right, to continue in as straight a line on the upper section of the slab.

Right Rib   130 feet   Severe
Some delightful moves, but with less protection on its crux than is usual on these slabs. Start at the right-hand end, before the descent gully. Start below a crack, with perched flakes above.
1 130 feet. Ascend up to and past the flakes to a sloping ledge, follow the smooth looking rib above to belay just behind a large boulder in the descent gully.

The gully to the right is very polished, and care should be taken in descent. To the right is another slab with some vegetated and lichenous areas; however, these do not impinge on the climbing.

Left Edge Route   170 feet   Very Difficult
Very artificial but with some good climbing, protection is quite sparse; placing gear in Stepped Crack to the right brings the grade down to Difficult. Start at the very left edge of this area of slabs.
1 110 feet. Climb the rib, keeping to its edge, to belay at a crack above.
2 60 feet. Easily to the top.

Stepped Crack   170 feet   Difficult
Start just to the right of the previous route, at the base of a crack.
1 110 feet. Follow the obvious crack, which leads up slightly

leftwards to a crack belay.
2 60 feet. Wander up to the top.

Mossy Slab 200 feet Severe
A lovely little route, hardly affected by the presence of the moss, in dry weather. Start at the foot of a sequence of thin cracks which lead up to a heather patch at 80 feet.
1 80 feet. The cracks are followed directly, but never too hard, until one can reach up and pull over and on to the heather.
2 120 feet. Go over a slight overlap and climb easily to the top.

Overlap Slab 200 feet Severe
The route only just manages to reach this grade. Start 10 feet right of the previous climb.
1 80 feet. Climb directly to reach the narrow overlap to the right of the stance of the previous route.
2 120 feet. Continue over the ripple and ramble on up to the top.

A traverse can be made on the slab starting from the ledge on the left edge; the first part takes the two horizontal cracks about 100 feet up. Around the foot of the slab, on the east face, are a couple of harder problems; a short steep groove and some thin cracks provide entertainment. The ridge which forms the crest of the slab is really only an airy walk after the initial steps.

The East Face of Bristly Ridge

OS Ref. 662 587

From the head of Cwm Tryfan the haunting towers and pinnacles of Bristly Ridge dominate the scene. The eastern flank is supported by a series of flying buttresses, each topped by a fine tower forming part of the backbone of the ridge. Like Tryfan, the face catches the morning sun, and the climbs too are much alike, though these benefit from their additional steepness, and the more remote setting is strongly felt. A fragment of the face curves round above the initial screes of Bristly Ridge. This is a good place for a spot of exercise after lunch at the Bwlch on an otherwise lazy day.

Giant's Steps Buttress 185 feet Very Difficult   (1944)
A pleasing and easily recognised route on the first buttress beyond

the scree when approaching from Bwlch Tryfan. Start on a terrace running off right from Big Boulder Gully.

1 35 feet. Go up broken rocks to a ledge with myriad belays.
2 50 feet. The weakness up to the left leads to a flat platform. Then walk over to the next step.
3 60 feet. Step up by a spike onto the tower on the right and climb a leftwards-leaning groove. Belay on the right.
4 40 feet. Take the left-hand groove on flaky holds.

The face temporarily falls back into a stony amphitheatre. The chimney on the right is filled with chockstones; **The Stovepipe** (50 feet, Difficult). **Dissected Buttress** (150 feet, Severe) stands in the centre with **Big Boulder Gully** (100 feet, Difficult) on its left. The main branch of this is obvious.

Two Tower Buttress   370 feet   Very Difficult   (1944)
Just beyond a sort of broken gully a clean tower, The Chateau, cuts the skyline and promises a good finish. Start on the easy-angled rib below the tower.
1 90 feet. Climb the rib to a ledge, cross the gangway and take a steep crack to a grass ledge overlooking the gully.
2 20 feet. To the top of the first tower.
3 120 feet. Pleasantly ascend the serrated ridge to a shark's fin formation.
4 20 feet. Climb the steep wall in the centre of the next tower.
5 80 feet. Follow the steep pinnacled ridge.
6 40 feet. Take the two-tier chimney on the left side of The Chateau to arrive on the ridge.

Variation
The Chateau   100 feet   Severe   (1944)
A harder finish to the summit tower, though the ridge just right of the gully may be taken to lend it independence.
4a 100 feet. Follow the grass round to the right-hand side of the tower, where a rather loose chimney leads to the top. Central Gully is a scree-chute started by a mossy glacis. It makes a good way back to the foot of the face.

★**Great Tower Buttress**   470 feet   Severe   (1944)
The Great Tower dominates Bristly Ridge and is the most honest mountaineering challenge of the face. Start in a small bay left of Central Gully.
1 140 feet. Climb a flake from its left, then a little chimney and some scrambling lead up to a big square block.
2 60 feet. The steep crack in front of the block is tough, then climb

the wall right of a chimney to a niche.
3 120 feet. Pleasant ambling over pinnacles leads to a smooth little slab which slants up to the left.
4 70 feet. Climb the steep groove above. After passing a bulge, cross to the right to finish on the edge.
5 80 feet. The Great Tower. A crack splitting its face is the only weakness and makes a splendid finish.

Brown Gully (300 feet, Difficult) now slants up to the left and separates the next buttress. It is not too unpleasant. Start at a chimney on the left of the mossy wall guarding its foot and follow chimneys and then the left-hand branch of the gully.

Skyline Buttress   290 feet   Severe   (1936)
This roughly follows the outline of the face as seen from Bwlch Tryfan. Interest and position steadily improve. Start at a shallow gully 20 feet left of Brown Gully.
1 45 feet. Take a chimney on the left to a grass landing.
2 90 feet. The nose on the right, then go easily to a tower.
3 55 feet. Climb a crack and move up a scoop in the right wall. Delicately traverse the front face to a crack on the left.
4 80 feet. Go up a slab well-supplied with holds then take the steep wall on the left to a knife-edge ridge.
5 20 feet. A final awkward wall leads to Bristly Ridge.

Variation
3a 80 feet. The crack in the tower is climbed direct until a nasty bulge gives a passage into the chimney above.

Tryfan

(Three Peaked)
OS Ref. 664 594

The East Face

The jagged outline of Tryfan makes a sudden and dramatic appearance as you travel along the road from Capel Curig. A magnificent rock peak, it contrasts sharply with the surrounding mountains. The scrambler will immediately eye the North Ridge, whilst the climber will feel drawn to the towering buttresses that compose its remarkable East Face. Here the vertical strata burst up, leaving sharp-edged subsidiary ridges that give the face its splendid mountaineering routes. They all offer the special joy of finishing a climb on a summit.

The climbing is old-style stuff, never too serious, with a good hold or a ledge usually to hand, leaving the senses free to revel in the delights of the situation. It is a glorious place on a sunny day when the rocks have been gently warmed. The East Face can hardly ever be said to be out of condition; the clean rock is quite climbable when wet and it is sheltered from the stormy westerlies. Even in the occasional deep snows of winter, the main routes can be done; they then provide the sort of challenge that makes for a memorable day.

Llwybr Llechan Goch (Path of the Red Slabs) or the Heather Terrace can be clearly seen cutting across the face below the three main buttresses. Nearly all the routes start from this. The Terrace can be reached by taking a track from the road onto the North Ridge then following other paths round to the left to its lower end. There is also a good path from behind Gwern y Gof Uchaf farm. It leads past Little Tryfan, then labours up a steep chute to reach the Terrace.

The climbs are described from right to left, in the manner in which they are approached when walking along the Heather Terrace from the north.

The initial slopes above the northern end of Heather Terrace are only occasionally broken by rocks of any significance. No Gully is barely a furrow, heather-filled, running up towards the not-too-distant North Ridge. Scattered about are No Gully Outcrops, where an oblique chimney and a groove are probably the best of the little pitches.

Bastow Buttress   200 feet   Difficult
This is the twin buttress, the first of the steep rock to come down to
Heather Terrace, standing just right of Bastow Gully. The right-hand
buttress, with the sharp little overhang, is the most interesting; it is
distinguished by a quartz-marked ledge and a leaning pillar forming
a cave. Either buttress leads to scrambling and Bastow Mines on the
right. There is a tall split-off flake at the foot of the central groove,
which provides a route of about 100 feet.

Bastow Gully is the first real gully and is a deep one. Its bed is a uniform
easy slope and strewn with boulders.

Nor' Nor' Buttress   570 feet   Difficult
A route with some delicate pitches between leisurely scrambles. Too
often it is hurried past for the higher routes. Start at a narrow
gangway slanting up the right side of the tall grey buttress 60 feet left
of Bastow Gully.
1 90 feet. Take a groove and crack to the gangway, which is
followed to a big ledge. Harder than it looks.
2 100 feet. Climb a crack then follow the ridge easily.
3 100 feet. Take a steep little rib overhanging Nor' Nor' Gully and a
second sharp rib on the right to easy ground.
4 50 feet. After a further step the route steepens again.
5 40 feet. Ascend a smooth, steep slab on the right edge, where it
feels most exposed.
6 100 feet. Scramble up towards Nor' Nor' Gully and the final rocks
below the North Ridge.
7 90 feet. Climb the cracks left of the gully to finish.

Variations
Enigma Variation   80 feet   Very Severe   (1949)
1a 80 feet. 4b. There is a prominent overhang in the centre of the
buttress. Climb the left-hand groove to the overhang and move right to
a small ledge. Now climb easily on the front.

Opus One   100 feet   Very Difficult
1b 100 feet. Take easy rocks to a steep groove just right of Nor'
Nor' Gully. Climb the groove and a slab then the right-hand of two
cracks to the big ledge.

Nor' Nor' Gully (1891) is a steep-sided corridor with three short easy
pitches, the first being 'The Tombstone', jammed across the gully a little
way up. Higher it becomes a wide open slope running up to the North
Tower. However, its true continuation is straight up and narrow.

Between Nor' Nor' Gully and Green Gully the face is broken by a grassy slope. The upper rocks are the northernmost extension of Terrace Wall. The lower rock band achieves some height and boldness towards Green Gully; and perched above the right end, overlooking Nor' Nor' Gully, is the small Yew Buttress.

Mea Route   130 feet   Very Difficult   (1954)
The stepped right wing of Yew Buttress. Start to the right of the thick grass pasture enclosed by the two wings of the buttress.
1 55 feet. Go up a crack in the slab onto the crest. Climb a little wall and the next step by a crack, to a ledge.
2 40 feet. Climb the slab close to its right edge.
3 35 feet. Step onto the front of the buttress, from lower down, and climb in a fine position to the top.

Yew Buttress   120 feet   Hard Severe   (1936)
A deceptively difficult route that attempts the centre of the buttress but is forced off to the right. Start at the back of the pastures.
1 40 feet. 4a. Climb a series of ledges in the open corner, stepping up right and then left to the highest one.
2 80 feet. 4a. The wall ahead is steep and smooth, but there is a groove on the right, which can be reached by boldly swinging from the cracks above. Climb straight up the groove, or its left edge, and finish on slabs.

Snowstorm   500 feet   Very Severe   (1957)
The grand beginnings vanish in the dank confines of Green Gully, from which it makes a thankful escape. Start on Heather Terrace, just right of Green Gully where a big corner is topped by a square overhang.
1 60 feet. 4c. Climb the crack to the overhang, then traverse rightwards to the arête. Now scramble up the grassy slopes close to Green Gully, for about 200 feet.
2 40 feet. Go up a rib right of the Gully to a spike.
3 75 feet. 4b. Step from the spike and climb a steep little groove and rib into the deep cleft of Green Gully.
4 50 feet. 4a. Traverse across the steep left wall and climb directly to a stance below an overhanging crack.
5 75 feet. 4c. Climb the crack to a platform, then the left wall, finishing up a steep groove on the right.

Green Gully Buttress   130 feet   Difficult
A pleasant little climb and a good approach to Yew Buttress or the interesting part of the Gully. Start at the first groove right of Green Gully.

East Face of Tryfan

1. South Rib	Mod	5. Munich Climb	VS
2. Arête Climb	D	6. South Gully Rib	D
3. Apex Route &		7. Central By Pass	VD
South Chimney	M/D	8. Overlapping Rib Route	D
4. Gashed Crag	VD	9. Pinnacle Rib Route	D

Photo: Ken Wilson

1 70 feet. There is a tiny chimney in the corner. Climb this and the groove to its end.
2 60 feet. Take the rock ridge on the right to the slopes, then wander over to Yew Buttress on the right. The crest of its left wing is a good continuation at a similar standard.

Green Gully (450 feet, Difficult, 1913) appears at Heather Terrace as an open runnel full of grass and showing a few slabs of rock. higher up, though, it becomes a deep cleft providing short, confined pitches of traditional form. Scramble up to where it meets the upper wall or, better, climb Green Gully Buttress. Get into the cleft from a crack on the right and climb a 30-foot chimney. This is followed by three similar short chimneys, all good sport, before coming out over jammed boulders.

North Buttress

This extends from Green Gully to North Gully. It is the most concentrated climbing area on the mountain because it includes Terrace Wall, the steep high wall that forms an imposing barrier across the upper part of the buttress. The Grooved Arête is obvious in the right flank of the Terrace Wall. The North Tower stands apart, round on the North Ridge.

★★★**Grooved Arête**   560 feet   Very Difficult   (1911)
The most inspiring and well-known route on Tryfan. The climbing is neat and always open. It steadily increases in difficulty until one is quite committed, and high on the mountain. Start at the short rib 20 feet left of Green Gully.
1 40 feet. Go up the corner behind the split-off flake.
2 50 feet. Climb the front of the rib, then go up to a tall spike.
3 100 feet. Climb the narrow grooves in the rib on the left, delightfully delicate and best done without interruption.
4 60 feet. Climb the next step and easy ground to a belay. This is followed by a walk of 100 feet rightwards to the long thin rib which drops down from the right-hand end of the rock barrier above.
5 90 feet. Follow the rib, firstly on its right, then on the left to reach a block belay.
6 120 feet. Start on the arête, moving left into the main groove as it steepens. Work up to the left across a minor groove and a little rib. The position just left begins to take on an air of seriousness as one gratefully arrives at the Haven.
7 60 feet. The Knight's Slab. Climb the steep crack from the left end of the Haven. A quick glance will confirm that this is to be the crux. Cross the slab by a sequence of Knight's Moves (the holds are small) and step round the upper right-hand edge to a corner niche.
8 60 feet. Climb the dark corner to a large platform.

9 100 feet. Either wander off to the North Tower or continue on black rock with big rough holds. Climb this directly to finish.

Variations
Super-Direct Route 80 feet Very Severe
Takes the arête more or less in its entirety. It is very exposed. Start at the ledge in the main groove, 30 feet below the Haven.
6a 80 feet. 4c. Traverse out onto the wafer edge of the rib. Climb a little way up it then cross the slab round on the right to an overhanging corner. Come back on the rib to the corner niche.

Direct Route from the Haven 50 feet Severe
6b 50 feet. There is a steep continuation of the main groove on the right, near the edge, but it falls short of the Haven. Climb the awkward, overlapped slab to reach the groove. It leads directly to the corner niche.
7a 60 feet. From the corner niche one can climb the steep and exposed right wall of the arête.

Quarter Gully Ribs Left of Grooved Arête, two ribs stand on either side of the grassy groove of Quarter Gully. The right-hand rib is only 80 feet but is split by a fine steep corner. The other is more continuous and useful. It leads up to Terrace Wall and has some interesting climbing at about Difficult standard.

North Buttress 640 feet Moderate   (1899)
Pleasant straightforward climbing, the easiest way up the face. It is a little vague in the middle but revives with an airy traverse along the top of Terrace Wall. There are several V-grooves right of North Gully. The first is very deep, the second is the usual start.
1 80 feet. Go up the groove, then climb a rib and through an overlap by a little V-slot.
2 120 feet. Step onto the steep rib on the left and follow it to a large grassy bay littered with boulders.
3 100 feet. Climb the slabby band to Terrace Wall.
4 150 feet. Scramble up broken rocks along the foot of Terrace Wall to a ledge coming in from North Gully.
5 90 feet. The Traverse. Climb up a scooped slab and traverse right behind a perched flake, after which a little groove leads to Belle Vue Terrace.
6 100 feet. The easy corner at the back of the Terrace. Follow a little neck to the North Summit, where a continuation chimney can be found in the North Tower.

Variation
1a 100 feet. The deep V-groove and the rib on the left may be taken to start. This is a little harder.

Terrace Wall

The pride of the East Face; a cheerful sunny spot, which gives a refreshing opportunity to indulge in some gymnastic climbing. The wall is barely 200 feet high, but it has such an airy aspect, near the summit of North Buttress, that there really are days when you can be climbing above the clouds.

Most of the routes are left of the Bastion Edge, on the slabby front of the Wall. Its portentous nose points out over the Cwm and hides the mysterious back wall.

The front is divided by two shallow vertical corners; the left one runs up the height of the wall. This is Long Chimney, with the six foot Finger Stone standing at its foot. A narrow overhang extends from Long Chimney almost to the Bastion Edge, and over this Bollard Slab slants up towards Belle Vue Terrace. Left of Long Chimney, above the remains of the overhang, are two little platforms known as the First and Second Ledges; higher up is the obvious perched flake on The Traverse of North Buttress Route. The simplest way of returning to the foot of the Wall is to descend the upper section of North Gully and traverse back in.

★★**Belle Vue Bastion**   160 feet   Very Severe   (1927)
The Bastion Edge is an imposing prospect. It is certainly the best route on Terrace Wall, and was recognised as such even in the early days before its ascent. Start at the right-hand end of the front of the wall.
1 90 feet. 4c. Go up the easy rocks and round the right edge, where a subsidiary slab leads to a small ledge. Get onto a higher ledge and make an awkward step up to the scooped slab. Follow the curving groove moving left onto the rib to reach the Grove of Bollards. Or, make a difficult step left to the rib once the slab is gained.
2 70 feet. 4a. Traverse out right onto an exposed little bracket on the nose. Climb straight up the edge and gain a difficult mantelshelf on the front. Continue up to Belle Vue Terrace.

Central Route   80 feet   Very Severe   (1929)
The obvious corner between the Finger Stone and the right edge. A steep pitch providing an exciting moment or two. Start beneath the hanging corner.
1 80 feet. 5a. Go up the initial steep rock and climb straight up the corner. It is vicious, but reliable, as it comes through the overhang. Belay on Bollard Slab.

★**Scars Climb** 145 feet Very Severe   (1936)
A route with some steep climbing on the improbable rock between the
features of Long Chimney and Central Route.
1 35 feet. As for Cheek but belay at a small ledge just beneath the
V-shaped alcove.
2 60 feet. 4c. Go up to the alcove then sidle out right to take the
overlap on side holds. Move right again and climb the rib, which is
the left ledge of the groove of Central Route, to the Grove of Bollards.
3 50 feet. 4a. Go easily up Bollard Slab to a shallow corner where a
flake crack comes down the final wall from a ledge up on the right.
The crack is quite easy once it is reached, then again go round to the
right from the ledge to finish.

Variation
Spider Wall 60 feet Very Severe
2a 60 feet. 5a. Traverse right along the quartz ledge beneath the
line of the overhang, cross Central Route, then move up the steep slab
and rib to Bollard Slab.

Cheek 165 feet Severe   (1912)
A meandering route, which crosses Long Chimney beneath the main
overhang before gaining any distinction. Start at easy rocks 30 feet
right of the Finger Stone.
1 50 feet. The rocks curve up and left making an easy gangway
beneath the overhang. Follow the gangway and belay at its end.
2 45 feet. Cross the break of Long Chimney on a smooth slab and
make for a groove just past the little rib to the left. Continue to the
Second Ledge with no further difficulty.
3 70 feet. From the left go easily on slabs to a thin diagonal overlap.
Move steeply to the right over this then ascend a further slab to the
perched flake on The Traverse.

Beeline 90 feet Very Severe   (1946)
A direct and bold way to Bollard Slab. Start at a shallow groove just
right of the Finger Stone.
1 30 feet. Climb the groove and its right-hand rib to belay as for
Cheek, beneath the overhangs.
2 60 feet. 4c. Pull straight over the overhang, using a big hold, and
move up to Bollard Slab. The last pitch of Scars seems the most
appropriate finish.

Long Chimney 210 feet Hard Severe   (1927)
A good climb, surprisingly smooth and open, and not bearing any
resemblance to its name. It is actually the continuous shallow corner
running up the middle of the face. Start at the Finger Stone.

1 80 feet. 4b. Climb straight up the overlapping leaves following the main groove through the bulge, then more easily up to the Second Ledge.
2 60 feet. 4a. Ascend on small holds, up the little open corner above. Belay at the perched flake on The Traverse.
3 70 feet. From above the flake follow the continuation crack and finish up a short wall.

Variation
The Right-Hand Branch   120 feet   Severe   (1936)
2a 80 feet. 4a. From the Second Ledge take the large right-hand corner, quite smooth at first, up to Belle Vue Terrace.
3a 40 feet. Finish easily up the continuation chimney.

Linear Climb   135 feet   Severe   (1938)
Quite a steep and direct route to the perched flake on The Traverse of North Buttress Route. Start just left of the Finger Stone.
1 75 feet. Take the groove left of Long Chimney to the overhang and a smaller groove on the left to reach the First Ledge. Continue easily to the Second Ledge.
2 60 feet. Climb straight up the open wall to the perched flake.

★Terrace Wall Variant   160 feet   Very Difficult   (1899)
An interesting climb finding an easy winding route up through the steep wall. Start left of the Finger Stone, midway between it and where Terrace Wall peters out to slabs.
1 80 feet. Start up the open corner which is tilted to the left. Leave this, more steeply, by a slanting crack that leads rightwards to the First Ledge. Climb the groove to belay at the Second Ledge.
2 40 feet. Go to the right, step across the corner of the right-hand branch of Long Chimney, and climb a steep bit to Bollard Slab.
3 40 feet. From the top of Bollard Slab, move left over Long Chimney again and go up a slab to Belle Vue Terrace.

The Girdle Traverse   320 feet   Very Severe   (1936)
A route with more of an expedition quality than is normally expected of Terrace Wall. By far the hardest section is the descent of the Bastion, from which it continues on the back wall to finish on a fine rib. This is worthwhile in itself. Start on the left-hand side of Terrace Wall.
1 60 feet. Join Terrace Wall Variant and follow it to the First Ledge.
2 50 feet. 4a. Go down slightly crossing Long Chimney then traverse the steep face to Bollard Slab.
3 50 feet. 4c. Descend the crux of Belle Vue Bastion to the subsidiary slab.

4 40 feet. 4a. Step into a mossy groove and go up to a ledge close to the edge of the rib on the right.
5 120 feet. 4b. Climb the rib (there is an open crack in its side) then on its edge again to finish.

The Back Wall

A short scramble round to the right of the Bastion Edge gains an area of rock set back to form a bay, the routes are described as they are approached.

The Temple   150 feet   Hard Very Severe   (1983)
Although the upper pitch looks rather improbable it is easier than Central Chimney. Start just to the right of the Bastion at a groove.
1 60 feet. Ascend the groove without particular event to a stance.
2 90 feet. 5a. The second pitch of Central Chimney lies a few feet to the right but this climb takes the unpromising looking steep slab ahead. This turns out to be much more reasonable than it appears, finishing at the top of the Bastion.

Central Chimney   150 feet   Hard Very Severe   (1983)
Start at the base of a groove line which leads directly to a short overhanging V-chimney at the top.
1 60 feet. 5a. Gain the groove easily, it then steepens and becomes quite awkward before exiting to a ledge.
2 90 feet. 5a. Continue up the groove more easily to the foot of the final V-chimney which provides a sharp finish.

The Flange   170 feet   Hard Very Severe   (1983)
To the right of Central Chimney there is a sweep of curious overlapping flanged slabs. Start at the base of these.
1 90 feet. 5a.Climb the slabs to the corner; fine views of the Knight's Slab which is directly below. Exit to a grass ledge, which can also be reached from Grooved Arête on the right.
2 80 feet. 5a.The arête above is taken to the top.

The North Tower

This is the North Summit of the mountain and is connected to the North Buttress by a little neck of ridge. It has a narrow east face, which provides the continuation chimney of North Buttress and two problem cracks on the left. There is a longer, steep north face. This extends across the North Ridge, where from the right we find:

Eighty-Foot Route   80 feet   Difficult
The best climb here, on the steep little buttress on the right. Climb

straight up the grooves and cracks on the left edge, avoiding the easier ground on the right.

The Bridged Cleft faces down from the higher rocks of the ridge. One can strike up anywhere and finish through it.

Spillikin Wall   80 feet   Moderate
Goes up the break close to the left edge of this face and tends to avoid all the difficulties.

Pinnacle Route   80 feet   Difficult
Just around the corner, on the east face, there is a tall leaning pinnacle. Climb the amusing chimney in the back of this and take the obvious weakness onto the north face.

North Gully   295 feet   Difficult   (1888)
This is the best of Tryfan's rather disappointing gullies. There are several good pitches in the lower half; they tackle the great wedged boulders, which are formidable obstacles. The rest is a scramble. Something to do during bad weather. Start below Heather Terrace.
1 30 feet. Go up the gully bed and through a gap in the cave roof onto the Heather Terrace.
2 45 feet. The gully steepens to a staircase pitch.
3 40 feet. A larger cave lies above, with a large gap in its roof. Then scramble up the scree and boulders for 150 feet.
4 30 feet. The final pitch is again a steep boulder. One can pass it on the side walls, but the purest way is direct.

The upper part of the gully is an open funnel, where a narrow passage on the left passes under an elegant arch to finish on the ridge. However, one may climb the **North Peak Wall** (100 feet, Severe), straight ahead; start up the central groove, then climb the left-hand groove to a small cave and bear right to the top.
There are further possibilities for routes in this area, some have been climbed, and some have been claimed; they are left for the enthusiast to discover.

Central Buttress

This is the vast bulwark beneath the main summit of Tryfan. It is topped by the summit blocks of Adam and Eve. Its dark upper section overhangs North Gully, and a great beak juts out in the form of a battleship bow to hint of serious routes, but this is not supported lower down. Farther along it is much more inviting. Two grand ridges, astride a grassy bay, rise pleasantly to converge at the fine, pointed Pinnacle. Behind this is

The top pitch of *North Gully*, Tryfan. Photo: Abraham Bros. Courtesy of Fell and Rock Climbing Club and Abbot Hall Art Gallery and Museum

On the Milestone Buttress, Tryfan. Photo: Abraham Bros. Courtesy of Fell and Rock
Climbing Club and Abbot Hall Art Gallery and Museum

the Yellow Slab, which extends leftwards as a smooth band below the Final Wall.

North Side Route   220 feet   Hard Severe   (1936)
A route for the more dogged devotee of Tryfan climbing. Solid, but not as clean or well-positioned as the Terrace Wall climbs. It takes the left wall of the upper part of North Gully and then the rib right of the great battleship bow. Start just above the junction of Little and North Gullies; a bit difficult to find.
1 60 feet. Up to the right is a perched block. Scramble up grass and rocks until beneath this, then traverse to a triangular grass ledge in a little nook on the left.
2 70 feet. 4a. Climb a crack in the smooth slab, cross round a rib and go easily up to a ledge in a recess.
3 30 feet. 4a. Climb a steeper, but much shorter, slab of wafery rock at a weakness.
4 60 feet. 4b. Climb the side wall of the rib on the left to a small ledge. Move delicately round into a fine position on its front. Follow the bubbly edge to the top.

Northern Rib   425 feet   Difficult   (1948)
The stepped rib set apart by the converging North and Little Gullies gives some interesting climbing. Start at a flat-topped boulder between the gullies.
1 35 feet. Start up a crack, by a small detached flake, step left into a groove and climb to a large grass terrace.
2 60 feet. The prominent easy chimney in the next tier leads to a clean slab. Thread belay at the top.
3 60 feet. Climb up the wall then the left edge of the rib overlooking Little Gully.
4 85 feet. Cross a small col, where Little Gully comes over to join North Gully, and climb the pleasant rib ahead.
5 60 feet. Climb a grass rake and the chimney on the right.
6 70 feet. Go straight up the nose and a delicate rib.
7 55 feet. Continue in the same line, on a wall and easy groove, to a ledge. Ahead is the final imposing section, where Crevassed Rib and North Side Route finish. These are very much harder; the only easy way is to traverse into North Gully.

Little Gully is shallow and runs up to the right to join North Gully. It is not easily identified from Heather Terrace, but is worth noting because it is a safe descent, which dodges the hard section of North Gully.

Crevassed Rib   540 feet   Severe   (1931)
Quite a good route taking the series of buttresses that lead up to the

prominent battleship bow. One must not be thwarted early on and, though the difficult bits are well-separated, the dramatic finish makes up for all. Immediately left of Little Gully is a leaning wall, across which there is a small overlap. Start from the foot of this wall, near its right end, between two blocks, one fallen and one standing.

1 60 feet. Climb the groove and go through the overlap, which is not easy, then a crack on the left leads to a ledge.

2 150 feet. Climbing and scrambling until the general ridge becomes more defined.

3 70 feet. Things now improve. Climb a steep wall by a thin crack, and then an open groove.

4 120 feet. Continue up grooves in the line of the rib, then go on up to the final section, where there are two curving ribs. The battleship bow now hoves into view.

5 80 feet. Climb directly up the edge of the left-hand rib to a ledge beneath the bow.

6 60 feet. Ignore the easy groove on the right. Go up to the bow, make a neat little traverse below it to join a curving chimney round on the left. Or, from lower down, walk left and climb the complete crack and chimney to finish.

★★ Pinnacle Rib Route (Second Pinnacle Rib)   535 feet   Difficult
(1894)

This is the original route to the Pinnacle. The climbing is better and more continuous than on the sister route, though lacking some of its charm. Start at the first groove on the right-hand side of the grassy bay between the two main ribs.

1 80 feet. Go up the groove, which is tucked behind a little rib.

2 100 feet. Climb the thin rib ahead; at one point a steep nose is cut by a tiny V-groove.

3 150 feet. Continue on the ridge over a series of steps to a ledge by the Pinnacle. Overlapping Rib Route is just to the left.

4 50 feet. Climb the blunt arête; the sharp continuation edge is the proper way but it is good Severe, so traverse left to a ledge above the Yellow Slab. The routes now merge.

5 75 feet. Continue quite steeply, where the strangely contorted leaf-like rock forms a curving groove.

6 80 feet. Go up the easy slopes below the Final Wall, where one can find a pitch, or walk to the summit.

★ Overlapping Rib Route (First Pinnacle Rib)   540 feet   Difficult
(1914)

This delightfully simple mountain ridge makes a good introduction to climbing on Tryfan. One can relax in its gentle atmosphere, with only the Yellow Slab to demand a moment's concentration. Start about

halfway along the wide base of the rib, which stretches from the grassy bay into South Gully.
1 20 feet. Climb the slab that slants up to the right beneath a steepness. Step left to a sloping platform.
2 120 feet. The steep crack ahead leads onto the ridge, which now becomes more defined and gives some pleasant climbing.
3 100 feet. Broken steps on the ridge lead to the Pinnacle.
4 45 feet. 4b. The Yellow Slab is the smooth barrier behind the Pinnacle. Climb the edge of the slab and step right to reach a groove in its face. Neat footwork is needed, though there are often others stranded here, eager to extend advice. This can be avoided on the right.
5 75 feet. Climb the curving groove, as for Pinnacle Rib Route.
6 80 feet. Continue easily up to the broad slopes below the Final Wall. One can walk round this to the summit of the mountain.

Variations
1a 120 feet. Any of the initial grooves may be taken.
4a 45 feet. Climb the wall and bulge just right of the Yellow Slab, or yet again the steep slab left of the Yellow Slab.

Central By-Pass   470 feet   Very Difficult   (1945)
Although essentially this route is a series of variations on Overlapping Rib Route, it is worthwhile just for its finish on the sweeping band of slab left of the Pinnacle. This is quite remote in atmosphere. Start as for Overlapping Rib Route, the route with which it shares its stances.
1 120 feet. Pitch 1 of Overlapping Rib Route, or any of the long grooves, may be taken to the large sloping platform.
2 90 feet. From round on the left, climb a thin crack in the edge of a lozenge-shaped slab and swing up to a ledge. Pass a flake, and belay at a toppled pinnacle.
3 80 feet. Step from its top and regain the rib. Go down to the left and take a slanting crack to a recess beneath a rock cannon. Go easily up to the Pinnacle.
4 40 feet. Climb a straight crack and grassy groove near the left edge of the Yellow Slab to a block on the left
5 40 feet. Work up the steep slab, trending leftwards to a ledge below an overlap in the middle of this area.
6 100 feet. Climb up to the overlap and follow a good crack beneath it to the right. Go right again and up a groove, passing a second overlap, to the Final Wall.

Stoat's Groove   160 feet   Very Difficult   (1945)
Quite a nice little climb, though a trifle lush in parts. Start in the right-hand corner of South Gully Rib.

1 40 feet. Climb the right-hand groove to a grass ledge.
2 70 feet. Take the delicate slab and the steepening groove to the long narrow ledge below the slabby band.
3 50 feet. There is another groove near the left end of this. It leads to the Final Wall.

South Gully Rib   150 feet   Difficult
The steep little rib in the centre of South Gully makes a pretty climb of three pitches. It can be approached directly from the gully or from Overlapping Rib.

The Final Wall

This is the steep wall below the summit blocks of Adam and Eve. It is an interesting little place, which gives one more good pitch before reaching the summit.

Thomson's Chimney   60 feet   Hard Severe
The shallow corner chimney makes a testing problem. Start at its foot near the right-hand side of the wall.
1 60 feet. 4b. Climb up onto the ledge on the left. Move across into the chimney and climb to the top.

The Wall   90 feet   Hard Severe
This is a steep and excellent finish. Start by a split-off flake 30 feet left of Thomson's Chimney.
1 90 feet. 4a. Climb straight up the wall to a narrow ledge. Step right and continue directly to the top.

Variation
Ghost Chimney   100 feet   Very Difficult
1 100 feet. Go up to the narrow ledge but follow it leftwards to climb the chimney round the edge.

South Buttress

The soaring ridge of Gashed Crag dominates the buttress, dwarfing a large expanse of rock to its left. This area may not be as appealing as the rest of Tryfan, but it does have a lot to offer those who wish just to climb in peaceful surroundings. They will find the rock architecture fascinating.

South Gully   Moderate   (1887)
A broad and easy gully that gives the South Buttress a steep flanking wall. There is much latitude in the choice of route and it provides an

easy way down. It is not the easiest way up the mountain, but makes no pretence to have any pitch longer than 30 feet.

★★**Munich Climb**   230 feet   Very Severe   (1936)
An excellent climb that is most fully enjoyed if approached with confidence. It is varied in character and begins by tackling the long rib in the upper part of the left wall of South Gully. Start by going up to the large grass ledge in a recess left of the rib.
1 40 feet. 4b. Step down and take the groove close to the right edge of the rib.
2 30 feet. 4c. Climb the steep, narrow slab ahead. The finish, on the very outside edge, is hard and exposed. Stance and belay amongst the blocks beside a sharp nose.
3 60 feet. 4a. From the right boldly step up and onto the nose, then traverse left to reach Teufel's Crack. Climb this fine juggy crack to an easy rake.
4 70 feet. 4a. From behind the big block a little way along the rake, climb an ill-defined groove and belay at the horizontal break.
5 30 feet. 4a. Climb the black wall trending rightwards. This just leaves the final chimney on Gashed Crag to the South Summit.

Variations
There are a selection of initial grooves and even a dripping corner direct to Teufel's Crack. All are much inferior.

South Gully Wall   220 feet   Very Severe
A steep and exciting climb keeping to the wall above the void of South Gully. Stances are shared with Munich Climb.
1 40 feet. 4b. Pitch 1 of Munich Climb.
2 40 feet. 4c. From a ledge on the right move onto the wall, and follow a shallow groove to the stance amongst the blocks.
3 50 feet. 4c. Climb the very steep crack above the right end of the ledge and belay on the easy rake.
4 60 feet. 4b. Take the long crack, 15 feet right of the big block, to the horizontal break.
5 30 feet. 4b. The overhanging right edge of the wall, to the final chimney of Gashed Crag.

★★**Gashed Crag**   550 feet   Very Difficult   (1902)
A great climb of strong mountaineering character. The most continuous ridge on Tryfan's East Face and easily identified by the Gash, a deep V-notch in the huge buttress towering out of South Gully. Start beyond South Gully, where the path rises sharply to a steep little buttress with overhangs.
1 40 feet. Climb a small groove at the right edge to the overlap. Step

onto the rib then go up to the right.
2 80 feet. Cross the corner and climb an awkward crack to a ledge on the left then take a narrow groove that cuts the crest of the rib. Walk over to the main ridge, where a series of ribs leads up to the Gash. Belay at a spike.
3 50 feet. Climb up to the Gash, following the thin ribs.
4 60 feet. The roof of the Gash halts progress on the ridge but out of sight, round to the right, is a chimney. This is so smooth and tight that it can easily become a very personal struggle.
5 250 feet. Step right and up until a difficult move left regains the crest of the ridge. This is followed energetically to the foot of the Summit Wall. Belay at intervals.
6 70 feet. Go over to the right, take a deep groove and then an awkward narrow chimney to the South Summit.

Variation
Left Wall Way   120 feet   Severe
A hard variation, but useful if the chimney becomes blocked.
4a 40 feet. From the Gash move out left onto a small recessed slab beyond the overhang, go up to the top of this, then climb to a ledge on the left.
5a 80 feet. Climb up to the right, then more easily past a deep cave, and rejoin the main ridge on the right.

★**Bubbly Wall**   80 feet   Hard Severe   (1936)
A steep exhilarating piece of climbing on the Summit Wall. Over to the left of the final chimney on Gashed Crag is a sharp nose with twin chimneys on either side. Start on the break on the front of the wall.
1 50 feet. Go up the scooped rocks and make for the overhanging chimney just left of the nose.
2 30 feet. 3b. From immediately below the nose make a difficult step out onto the edge of the left wall and climb it.

South Chimney   420 feet   Moderate
This starts as a chimney, becomes a crack, then degenerates into a grassy trough. It begins 150 feet above Heather Terrace and runs up the buttress left of Gashed Crag.

Apex Route   210 feet   Difficult
Takes the secondary rib between Gashed Crag and Arête Climb. An interesting alternative if Gashed Crag is crowded. Start on the left edge of the steep little buttress that Gashed Crag starts up.
1 70 feet. Climb steeply, keeping on the edge overlooking a thin inset slab, then take the crack in the crest.

2 140 feet. Climb straight up the rib to a grassy bay then get onto the slab on the left and join Arête Climb.

★**Arête Climb** 470 feet Difficult (1894)
It is a pity that this ridge is not as distinct as the others. It provides good climbing in an interesting area but lacks the usual openness of climbing on Tryfan. Start some 40 yards left of South Gully, where a low relief rib leads up to the Block Tower.
1 80 feet. Climb the clean thin crack in the front of the long rib to a small ledge.
2 70 feet. Continue on the rib.
3 80 feet. There is now a smooth slabby wall. Start up a crack in its centre then move to the sharp right edge.
4 35 feet. The Block Tower is taken close to the left edge; a good pitch. It is Very Difficult but can be avoided on either side.
5 110 feet. Clamber over large blocks and up a broad rib with plenty of good holds. A steep little wall and a difficult crack leads to a large terrace.
6 50 feet. Follow the left-hand of the two pointed ribs that flank the recess above the terrace.
7 45 feet. Ahead is the summit wall with ominous bands of overlaps and quartz, and a sharp nose over on the right. Go straight up until beneath the overlap, about 30 feet left of the nose, then climb the steep slab on the left.

South Rib 530 feet Moderate (1912)
A vague ridge runs up the buttress to the left of the large grassy slope. It gives several good pitches, which are rather well-spaced but good for beginners. Start 20 yards along the upper branch of Heather Terrace.
1 100 feet. Climb the broken rib, which is to the left of a pillar, then walk across to the main rib on the right.
2 180 feet. The rib gives some easy climbing. Cross a gap then climb a second rise, which is difficult to start.
3 100 feet. Scramble to the next lot of rocks on the right.
4 120 feet. Climb a slabby wall to a steep pillar, which is taken direct. Beyond this cross two crevasses and go to the horizontal ledge below the Summit Wall.
5 30 feet. Take the steep groove on the left to finish.

Dud Ridge is the rambling, stepped ridge of disjointed rocks just right of the grassy dip in the South Ridge.

Far South Peak

This stands in isolation on the South Ridge close to Bwlch Tryfan, from where it is best approached. There are a couple of good small climbs set about the rock finger of the Index that points defiantly over Cwm Tryfan.

Index Climb   200 feet   Moderate   (1911)
This is an easy route that takes the steep little walls, broken by big ledges, on the rough rib right of the Index.

Progressive Cracks   110 feet   Very Difficult   (1922)
A good little climb, steep and on good holds. To the left of the Index is a steep slab, below which is an even steeper wall capped by a flat roof. Start here.
1 20 feet. Climb either crack to the broad ledge running from the Index. The left one has more interest at the roof.
2 40 feet. Take a crack across the smooth slab into a deep groove. Climb this and out left to ledges.
3 50 feet. Go up to the final tier and climb a thin crack just left of the bulge. The hardest pitch.

Variation
Beside the Index   100 feet   Very Difficult
Start on the broad ledge just left of the Index itself.
2a 100 feet. The slab can be climbed by slanting up to a stance in the groove on its right. Move back left and climb the steep rib and a further step to the top.

North Rib   245 feet   Difficult (final move Severe)   (1947)
Start at the same level as the Index rock, 60 feet to the right of it. There is a conspicuous deep cave gully on the left of the rib.
1 45 feet. A subsidiary slab leads to a large heather platform, then the rib proper starts with broken, slabby rock leading to a prominent bulge broken by a thin crack. Stance and belay on the right corner of the rib.
2 75 feet. The bulge can be climbed direct by the crack, but the original and more interesting way is to traverse left to a flake pinnacle and crack on the left corner. Ascend the crack and step over from the top of the pinnacle on to the main face and so up to a stance.
3 70 feet. A steep rib directly ahead is climbed on good holds to a very large ledge.
4 25 feet. Broken rock lies ahead. There are three alternatives:
a) There is a cave and overhang round the right corner. One can climb out of the cave by the right wall and round the overhang.
b) An easy gully on the left of the wall.

c) Across heather there is a smooth overhanging wall which might go with the aid of a thin crack up its face.

5 50 feet. Straight ahead now is another steep rib cleft by a crack. This can now be climbed, but a better route is to stride across the crack low down and on to the corner. To attain the small square mantelshelf on the corner is a good problem in balance.

Creigiau'r Dena   (Crag of the Thin River)

OS Ref. 667 602

These rocks lie to the left of the Milestone Buttress, and are even closer to the road. They are scattered over a wide area and form an overgrown rockery, where one can wander through a maze of loosely-linked pitches and problems that still retain much of their natural modesty.

The Giant Steps (200 feet, Moderate) is the most easterly climb. They are obvious with four risers. **Glandular** (100 feet, Difficult) takes the large west-facing quartz slab nearer the main crag. The better routes are arranged about the Great Flake, which appears as a smooth face in the centre of the area.

Left Ridge   225 feet   Very Difficult   (1952)
A good little route which defines the left-hand side of the main face. Start above the boulder of Anniversary Approach, by a large flake.
1 60 feet. Ascend a groove then go out rightwards to flaky holds. A scramble leads to a belay in the groove left of the Great Flake.
2 120 feet. Gain the rock rib on the left and follow it to a grass amphitheatre.
3 45 feet. Climb two short walls on the right of the amphitheatre.

Flake Cross   60 feet   Severe   (1952)
A rather pointless route crossing the Great Flake. Start at the base of the groove on the left-hand side of the flake.
1 60 feet. Move down right on the heather ledge, until a precarious traverse leads across to the crack. Move up and continue the traverse to the right-hand side of the flake to finish up the edge.

★**Great Flake Crack**   120 feet   Hard Severe   (1952)
A little gem, both strenuous and technically absorbing. A good jamming technique is a must, otherwise it may seem harder! Start at

the foot of the crack in the centre of the flake's main face.
1 55 feet. 4b. Layback, until it is possible to jam the crack; or, much more interesting, jam the whole way to the easier upper section. Belay at the crevice.
2 65 feet. Step across the chasm on to the wall beyond. Move up bearing rightwards to a field, zigzag up heather and rock to broken ground.

Anniversary Approach 260 feet Difficult   (1949)
A favoured route because it chooses an interesting way. Start at a small buttress just beneath the main face.
1 40 feet. From the right corner swing onto a slab, then go left beneath the overhang and up a harder groove.
2 50 feet. Easily ascend to a sporting flake leading to the terrace.
3 60 feet. Tackle the chimney behind the Great Flake.
4 110 feet. Step across the crevasse and climb the arête on the right, or the crack beyond it, to more broken ground.

The left side of the next section of crag gives **Wall Direct** (150 feet, Very Difficult, 1953), a climb on small sound holds.

Easter Ridge 270 feet Very Difficult   (1952)
The best of these routes and quite exposed in parts. Start at the foot of the right-hand buttress.
1 40 feet. A short sharp chimney and a traverse to a ledge.
2 60 feet. Climb the slab, moving up the arête to the terrace.
3 50 feet. Go up the centre of the wall and a subsequent corner.
4 50 feet. Approach the overlap by a steep step and a little slab. The crack over the overlap is easier than it looks.
5 70 feet. Go over an easy-angled slab and up a shallow corner on the right. Traverse out beneath the overhangs to escape to easy ground, or go straight up the crack from the slab. **The Anniversary Girdle** (400 feet, Very Difficult) may be regarded as a devious way to the Left Ridge, but it does combine the good sections of the crag. Follow Easter Ridge for three pitches then descend a hole on the left to reach the foot of the chimney of Anniversary Approach. Climb the chimney and cross the top of the Flake to gain the Ridge.

One can now scramble up to a further broken section of crag, above the path between the North Ridge and the top of Milestone Buttress.

Anniversary Route 390 feet Difficult   (1948)
A route for beginners, being broken and escapable. Start at the base of a little gully with a narrow diagonal slab just to its left. Each pitch may be split further.

1 120 feet. Ascend the slab, becoming progressively easier, to belay at a heather platform beneath a pinnacle.
2 100 feet. Either the quartz slab direct, or via the pinnacle and a stride. Broken ground leads to a belay beneath a short wall.
3 110 feet. Step in to the shallow groove on the wall above, from the left. Climb the groove then a flake crack to a heather ledge. Avoid the easy rock above by climbing two steps.
4 60 feet. The steep wall above, either by the wall or the crack leads to a final rough wall.

Variation
Twin Variant Takes the step-like area of rock to the left of the pitch 2 finishing up a final tremendous block

The Milestone Buttress OS Ref. 663 601

The North Ridge of Tryfan makes a long and spectacular descent into Ogwen Valley. On the west side, tucked away under its foot as it splays out to meet the valley floor, is a final buttress. It was named because of its position above the tenth milestone on the road from Bangor, but this has long since disappeared.

Being just a few minutes up from the road, and a cliff where many young people get their first taste of the sport, the Milestone is a very busy buttress. Yet from its comfortable ledges there are always moments when one can gaze across Llyn Ogwen and reflect on more peaceful times.

The Buttress has a pronounced central ridge and a slabby front that faces more to the west. This gets the afternoon sunshine and is very popular, even when it rains. To the left, the buttress extends a long, sinister wing, known as the Back of the Milestone.

The rock is excellent, entirely solid, but there is a marked difference between the eccentrically juggy front and the steep, slippery walls of the back, which call for a neater style. The vertical splits are all frustratingly smooth.

The Back of The Milestone

This is rather complex, and consists of two walls separated by the rambling spur of the Easy Section. Its shadowy secrets seem hidden by the greenery, which gives the place an atmosphere missing from the front.

The First Wall is to the left of the long sweeping corner of Soapgut. The Second Wall, which is concealed behind the Easy Section, is where we find the initial routes and End Gut. This is an open gully high up on the left, and is the only recommended, but awkward, descent from this side.

Hangman Gut 70 feet Severe   (1936)
In the left end of the Second Wall is a vegetated recess of distinctly unhealthy appearance. Start at its cut-away foot.
1 70 feet. Get up into the groove, then climb to a ledge on the right wall and make a steep grassy finish.

Hangman's Wall 110 feet Very Severe   (1948)
Much more of a rock climb than the previous route. Start at the square corner just right of Hangman Gut.
1 50 feet. 4b. The greasy groove to a squat bollard.
2 60 feet. 4c. Climb the steep twin cracks above the bollard. Traverse left and finish up left of a corner.

Bishop's Gut 120 feet Very Severe   (1956)
A really good pitch that escapes the confines of this dreary area. Round to the left of the tall pinnacle is a sheer corner. Start about 10 yards left of this.
1 90 feet. 4c. Go up a groove and move right over a sloping ledge to a grass patch below the corner. Climb the corner.
2 30 feet. 4a. The easier crack in the next wall.

★Au Suivant 75 feet E3   (1986)
A nice open pitch taking the narrowing wall to the right of Bishop's Gut and left of a tall pinnacle. Start at a thin crack in the wall.
1 75 feet. 6a. Follow the thin crack up into the scoop. Continue up a shallow groove and twin cracks in the headwall to the top.

★En Passant 120 feet E1   (1982)
The steep crack between the corner and the pinnacle offers an opportunity. Start well below the crack.
1 90 feet. 5b. Move up through an awkward slot and climb the crack to the cold comfort of a finish lacking good holds.
2 30 feet. 4a. The crack behind a tilted column.

From below the tall pinnacle, the easy section seems less chaotic. Only the best lines have been described, to avoid confusion. Indeed, one can perambulate across the ledges and discover many other combinations and variations of pitches.

Cantilever Route   140 feet   Severe   (1916)
Not an easy route, though it is very entertaining. The Cantilever is a thin finger jutting out from a groove 50 feet right of the pinnacle and about level with its top. Start on the upper grass tongue that rises into this area.
1 40 feet. Go up a little cracked slab to a recess.
2 40 feet. Climb the split-off cleft of Wing Chimney.
3 30 feet. Ascend the easy groove and swing energetically over the Cantilever. Continue to a large grass terrace.
4 30 feet. Climb the slanting crack in the next wall.

Holly Route   150 feet   Moderate   (1916)
Little more than a scramble. Follow the upper of the two grass tongues into the broken area. Ahead a series of scooped slabs and two easy steps lead to Broad Ledge.

Postern Gate and Holly Crack   120 feet   Moderate   (1916)
Threads an easy way rightwards to the steeper area. Start at the two grass tongues.
1 30 feet. Go along either to the right and drop down into the Postern Gate, a passage between the detached slabs.
2 40 feet. Step out onto the right wall and climb up the grass ledges across to the V-ledge. Its right branch leads to a holly.
3 50 feet. Holly Crack. Reach the tree from the little corner on the right and climb the crack behind it. At the overhang a ledge on the right is only a step away. A groove then leads to easy ground. The Oblique Trench, on the right, avoids the main interest.

Variation
Gate Chimney   30 feet   Very Difficult
The slippery slot left of Canopy Route leads directly to Postern Gate. It proves to be an exhausting problem.

The climbs on the First Wall of this wing of the Milestone are quite short, but they do have an air of seriousness about them. Each has something interesting to recommend it.

Canopy Route   180 feet   Difficult   (1916)
A good route, with a short taste of real exposure. Start in the left-hand corner, where the obvious Canopy projects over a rectangular scoop of slab.
1 70 feet. The slab is enticingly easy, but soon one has to take the

steep groove on the right to get round the Canopy. Belay on the
ledge above it.
2 20 feet. Go up to a V-ledge; its left branch leads to a comfortable
stance in the Square Recess.
3 90 feet. Take the slab to the right, under a little wall, until a break
on the left and two easy steps lead to Broad Ledge.

Vae   170 feet   Hard Severe   (1959)
A good starting crack but the rest is optional. Start in the little corner
right of Canopy Route.
1 50 feet. 4b. Climb the crack, which becomes appreciably harder
the farther one progresses, to a stance above the Canopy.
2 50 feet. Climb the steep crack on the right, and wander up the
grassy bay to a cave farther to the right.
3 70 feet. 4a. Climb the overhang left of the cave and then a steep
crack with a rowan in it.

★**Boot Crack**   80 feet   Hard Very Severe   (1966)
This is the crack in the rounded arête right of the Canopy. A great
problem pitch in a fine position. Start at a large spike on the grassy
ledge below the arête.
1 80 feet. 5a. The crack is awkward to start, and the arête very
steep, but it soon bends to the left on to the face and matures to
satisfaction.

The Pals   80 feet   Hard Very Severe   (1991)
A pleasant enough pitch. Start just right of Boot Crack at the base of
a groove.
1 80 feet. 5a. Ascend the open groove to a vegetated ledge; then
climb the crack in the wall above to gain a juggy finish.

Rope Wall   200 feet   Severe (1 pt. aid)   (1934)
An amusing route, though this may depend on one's adaptability and
temperament. The antics demand care to avoid trouble. A long
horizontal ledge splits the wall into two tiers. Start by a shallow
groove running up to the centre of the ledge.
1 40 feet. Gain a little stepped ramp, left of the groove, and follow it
to the ledge. Belay on the right.
2 40 feet. An open crack and groove slants up rightwards to a small
stance on the edge, poor belays.
3 60 feet. The position appears to be inescapable, but on the right
above the steep corner is a ledge with a stout belay. Throw a rope
over this, then gamely swing into the corner and swarm up the rope.
Climb up and left through heather to gain a high tree belay in order

to protect the second.
4 60 feet. Climb up and right to finish up an awkward short corner.

Bowline   90 feet   Very Severe
An alternative way up Rope Wall, but not so much fun. Start as for
Rope Wall, at the shallow groove.
1 40 feet. 4b. Climb the groove to the long grass ledge.
2 50 feet. 4c. Go along the ledge to the right and climb the steep
corner.

★★**Crazy Horse**   180 feet   E3   (1983)
A continually interesting climb up the left wall of Soapgut. Start at the
huge flake left of the corner.
1 55 feet. 5c. Climb up behind the flake (don't push too hard) and
continue up the shallow corner to a ledge. Move right and belay in
the corner.
2 90 feet. 6a. Climb the thin crack in the wall left of 'The Narrows' to
a ledge. Move diagonally left to a rib and follow this to a grass ledge
and tree belay.
3 35 feet. 5a. The vertical jam crack behind the tree exiting left at the
top.

★★**Soapgut**   200 feet   Hard Severe   (1935)
This is the great curving corner which is the most natural line of the
Milestone Buttress. It is often as slippery as the name suggests, but an
ascent is always exciting and can be made more continuous by
joining Chimney Route. Start below the corner; a gigantic arrow-head
is a needless pointer.
1 60 feet. Climb the steep corner, the crack in which is most
endearing, and make a troublesome mantelshelf to the halfway ledge.
2 40 feet. 4a. The crux pitch. Make a rather insecure stride to a tiny
ledge out on the right wall, then work back left and climb through the
Narrows.
3 100 feet. Easy going now, up the remainder of the gut, though for
more interest the last pitch of Chimney Route can be taken. It can be
found around the rib on the right.

Variation
Squint Start   75 feet   Hard Severe
A harder and more varied way to the halfway ledge. Start on the
outer edge of the left wall, beyond the great flake, where a deep
groove curves up to a ledge by a propped flake.
1a 60 feet. 4a. Climb the groove and gangway to the ledge.
2a 15 feet. Go around the edge on the right and balance across to
the halfway ledge.

Soap Crack and Rib   190 feet   Hard Very Severe   (1962)
The sweeping rib of Soapgut is a worthy climb, with contrasting pitches. Start in the corner of Soapgut.
1 70 feet. 4c. Climb the crack in the right wall. It stays good until a tricky traverse is made to the right.
2 120 feet. 5a. Climb the long scant rib that rises in two sections to the top.

In about the middle of the buttress is a slabby bay, stacked with grass, over which the Central Block's bold proportions tower. This is the Central Break. A narrow ledge comes in from below Soapgut, though one can scramble here from Ordinary Route or use the next climb on the subsidiary wall.

Wall Climb   65 feet   Very Difficult   (1927)
A neat way to the Central Break. Start right of the stone wall. Take either of the two ways to the steep scoop, then go up to a ledge on the right. Follow this round to the Central Break.

Variation
Direct Finish   20 feet   Very Severe   (1932)
The wafer-edged crack that rises from the ledge is a vicious piece of jamming and laybacking.

The Central Block
The stands above the grassy Central Break, with the much abused tree making a comeback.

Chimney Route   70 feet   Hard Severe   (1913)
A short, fearsome climb in the corner high up and bounding the left side of the Central Block. Start by scrambling over the Central Break to a lonely rowan on the left edge.
1 20 feet. Take the easy corner to a sloping stance.
2 50 feet. 4a. Begin in the corner, then move to the crack in the right wall. This seems just as hopeless and smooth but it is the only escape from the chimney.

The Tree of Man   80 feet   E5   (1987)
Takes the crack round to the left of The Wrinkled Retainer. Start beneath a peg.
1 80 feet. 6b. Lasso the first peg and with its protection gain the wall directly above. Very sustained climbing, with small wires for protection, may eventually lead to the top. Slightly easier for those with above average stature.

Ivan Waller repeating his route *Belle Vue Bastion* (VS), East Face of Tryfan, 58 years after making the first ascent. Photo: Ian Smith

The top moves on *Pulpit Route* (Diff), The Milestone Buttress. Photo: Ray Wood

Climbers on the tricky Final Crack of *Direct Route* (Hard Severe), Glyder Fach. Photo: Ian Smith

Lot's Wife (VS), one of the classic Kirkus routes on Glyder Fach.
Photo: Jim Gregson

★The Wrinkled Retainer   90 feet   E4   (1979)
The long slanting gash in the face of the Central Block is a fierce and
compelling line. Start from the desecrated tree that once lent the line a
more reasonable start.
1 90 feet. 6c. Climb desperately to gain a ledge, then continue more
easily up the steep groove above. A more amenable approach, to the
upper reaches is afforded by starting up Crosscut. (E4 6a)

Crosscut   130 feet   E2   (1979)
An unsuspected and delightful route that cleverly crosses the Central
Block low down, to ascend the left side face. Start at the foot of the
Central Block.
1 90 feet. 5b. Go up the easy corner on the right and take the offset
ledge leftwards into the niche of The Wrinkled Retainer. Continue
precariously leftwards round the left edge and on to the side face to a
thin crack then climb diagonally up to a small stance.
2 40 feet. 4b. A straightforward crack leads to the top.

Rope Crack   40 feet   Severe
The corner that leads directly to the Corner Chimney platform. Start as
for Crosscut.
1 40 feet. Climb the corner crack; the upper half is a slimy and
strenuous layback.

The Front of The Milestone
The buttress presents a distinct central ridge with a clearly defined left
edge. Its upper section is characterised by a pair of parallel leaning
chimney cracks. The rest is built of flanking slabs, of an easy angle,
coming to an end at Little Gully on the right. The gully gives the easiest
descent, though, with care, the upper end of the slabs can be descended
diagonally towards the foot. All the routes are clean, but well-polished.

The subsidiary wall of the buttress is very low at its right end, but a
chimney or a groove provide some optional sport on approach.

Ordinary Route   230 feet   Difficult   (1899)
The original route of the buttress weaves an easy way up the central
ridge, with surprisingly little exposure. The attraction is its hearty
old-fashioned pitches. Start just left of the foot of the central ridge.
1 100 feet. The easy staircase on the left leads to a long scoop, just
left of the ridge, which then curves up to the large ledge at the top of
the first section.
2 40 feet. Step from the pinnacle and fight the widening left-hand
crack to reach a comfortable nook.
3 50 feet. Take the crack cutting leftwards across the ridge, 'over the

Milestone Buttress

1. Superdirect   HVS
2. Direct Route   VD
3. Slab Start
4. Rowan Route   D
5. Pulpit Route   D

5

garden wall', and step into a corner round the back. Ascend a crack, which soon grows into a chimney and then becomes a deep cave.
4 20 feet. The easy slab beyond the boulder.
5 20 feet. Corner Chimney is on the left, but ours is the simpler chimney in the back wall.

★★**Superdirect**   250 feet   Hard Very Severe   (1910/1941)
The crest of the central ridge makes a very good climb, providing all the easy options are waived. Start at the steep toe of the central ridge.
1 100 feet. 4c. Above is an inverted V-scoop. Climb up to this by a bastard layback. The rock shines from many years of attention. Follow the straight crack in the rounded crest to the large ledge.
2 90 feet. 4c. A small overhung slab leads onto the edge; a bold reach is needed to overcome a steep nose and the final sharp arête.
3 20 feet. 4a. The amusing little rib on the left.
4 40 feet. 5a. A serious finale on the Central Block. Follow a line of flakes to the left across the Block to a recess in the front, then make a very solitary finish up an open crack.

★★★**Direct Route**   250 feet   Very Difficult   (1910)
This is certainly the most popular climb in the valley and the classic of the Milestone. Continuously interesting, never too easy it is even harder in poor conditions but always satisfying. Start at the slab set in the right side of the central ridge.
1 100 feet. Trend leftwards to a scoop in the slab, and swing up into the groove behind the overlapping border of the slab. From the top of the groove step back onto the slab and climb to its apex. An awkward exit through a crevasse then leads to the large ledge.
2 40 feet. From behind the pinnacle climb the smooth left-hand corner to gain a comfortable nook.
3 50 feet. Continue up the steepening crack until a jutting block halts progress. Semi-hand-traverse out leftwards below the block, move delicately round its edge, and seek security in the cave behind it. Thread belays low down. Scramble up a few feet to reach the large scree covered ledge. Belay by the steep left hand corner.
4 30 feet. The Corner Chimney. It is a struggle to gain a chockstone and then to leave it. Escape up the left wall, though there is an upper, more constricted, storey for the insatiable.
5 30 feet. Finish pleasantly on the slabby wall beyond.

Variations
1a 100 feet. The apex can be reached from anywhere on the slab. The ways are obvious and well worn.
2a 90 feet. The right-hand crack can be followed to the head of Rowan Gully. The left exit leads to Corner Chimney.

Rowan Gully has little contemporary merit. It is the shallow depression that separates the central ridge from the flanking slabs.

★★**Rowan Route**   290 feet   Difficult   (1910)
An excellent climb for the beginner, being varied and having good ledges and belays throughout. Start at the long rib with a flanking slab to the right of Rowan Gully. The twin pinnacles of the Bivalve are prominent above.
1 70 feet. Climb up the rib, staying on the very edge, to the terrace of bollards and spikes.
2 50 feet. Take the open groove up to the ledge on the right, passing the Bivalve, then a rib to the next ledge.
3 50 feet. Above is a small shallow chimney; approach this from the slabs on the right and climb up it.
4 120 feet. Scramble up over easy slabs, and finish up the little wall at the top or the chimney over to the right.

★**Pulpit Route**   230 feet   Difficult   (1911)
Another good climb for the novice, mainly on easy slabs, though there is the amusing Ivy Chimney finish. Start between Rowan Route and Little Gully, at a slabby rib leading up to the remarkable triple-decker Pulpit.
1 90 feet. Climb the juggy slabs on the rib, then the narrow slab on the right to the top of the Pulpit.
2 70 feet. The way ahead is steep and smooth. Take the slab on the left and climb through a square trough in a low wall to ledges. Belay here, then walk over to the deep cleft in the wall overlooking Little Gully.
3 50 feet. The Ivy Chimney. Go up into the chimney and make an exciting exit through a hole on the right or pull straight over on good holds.
4 20 feet. Climb the steep little wall above, taking care with the loose rock on the right.

Little Gully Wall   70 feet   Hard Severe   (1934)
A good steep climb, on rough rock of interesting structure. Start in Little Gully, where it narrows.
1 70 feet. 4b. Climb the left wall trending right, with several long reaches between the pockets. Don't go over into Ivy Chimney, but move right for a few feet and climb to the very top of the wall, to pull over the apex. Sustained.

The Black Vegetable   75 feet   Hard Very Severe   (1983)
Often wet. Start at a crack in the wall opposite to Little Gully Wall.

1 75 feet. 5a. Some interesting moves up the crack provides sport only in the driest of summers.

The Sylvan Traverse 730 feet Moderate (1916)
A great outing that makes a grand tour of the principal sights of the buttress. Best done as a large jovial party, but with the pitches kept short for maximum entertainment. Some prior knowledge of the main features is useful; and a well-stocked picnic hamper essential. Lunch may be taken on a convenient ledge above Rope Wall, from where the ways are many and can be varied according to one's disposition. Start at the foot of Pulpit Route.
1 90 feet. Climb the slabs to the top of the Pulpit.
2 100 feet. To the cave on Ordinary Route. Cross the slabs on the left to the ledge just above the Bivalve. The head of Rowan Gully steepens here but one can climb a little wall to the through way into the cave.
3 80 feet. To Chimney Route. Slide down the crack at the far end and cross a grassy slab. Descend the corner made with the Central Block or a more immediate crack; both are rather smooth. If slippery, they can be roped down. Walk along the top of the Central Break and round a corner to Chimney Route.
4 60 feet. To the bollard on Rope Wall. Take the crevasse on the left, over the spike on the rib and descend the other side to Soapgut. Press on over another crack to the ledge.
5 120 feet. To the Square Recess on Canopy Route. Scramble on ledges above the steep wall to a short overhanging corner. Go down a bit then cross the wall, past Richards' wobbly spike, to join ledges that run down to a V-ledge. Climb up the far branch to the Square Recess.
6 130 feet. To the ledges above the tall pinnacle. Climb the little slab under the wall, to the right, then go back left across and along a leaf to below the jutting finger of the Cantilever. Carry on round the next steep corner, to High Tree Ledge, then up the easy rock stairs to some grass ledges. One can make a daring leap to the pinnacle from here. Ascend the slab to a more extensive grass tract.
7 150 feet. To the finish. Climb the crack in the back wall and follow a pathway of connecting ledges along an avenue of stone pillars to the head of End Gut.

The West Face of Tryfan   OS Ref. 663 597

At a casual glance only the tower of Notch Rocks, in its stately position on the North Ridge, makes any impression. A closer look reveals a line of flat buttresses standing over the scree-slopes. Most of the climbing will suit the ardent scrambler; the more adventurous will find their own way. The lower rock lies between two broad gullies which can be reached from the top of the Milestone by crossing the head of Little Gully, making it quite easy to escape from the suffocating numbers to a more tranquil mountain atmosphere.

Columbyne   500 feet   Difficult   (1953)
Difficult to locate, but quite interesting with a lot of hearty scrambling. Start beneath the three parallel cracks in the left wall of the low-relief buttress between the two watercourses.
1 90 feet. Take the right-hand crack, swing onto the front then climb a steep wall to easy slabs and a ledge.
2 120 feet. A short corner left of the crack leads to a crevasse. Climb behind the pinnacle on the right, then up a rib.
3 90 feet. The chimney above the mantelshelf gives access to slabs and a narrow heather terrace below the tower.
4 50 feet. Climb a slim corner crack to a turf stance.
5 80 feet. The traverse. Go round the right-hand corner, delicately cross the face and step awkwardly into the gully.
6 70 feet. The crack in the pinnacle and an arête to finish.

Pierrot   265 feet   Very Difficult   (1953)
A natural rising line that is almost inescapable. Far better than it appears at first sight. Start at a tower, actually in the bed of the right-hand gully.
1 80 feet. Climb two slabs and a crack in the tower. Step left from a blade-like flake onto the face. Scramble to belays.
2 70 feet. Ascend a rock staircase and a short awkward chimney on the left. Belay behind a huge tilted block.
3 65 feet. A shallow groove leads to the ledge on the traverse of Columbyne. Take a groove from its left edge.
4 50 feet. Straight up the wall until the angle eases.

The Wrinkled Slabs (300 feet, Moderate) are just round to the right. The lower slab is weathered in rough corrugations; the upper, which is removed to the left, is smoother. A rib simply stuck on the edges of both is a curious feature, and more interesting than the usual ways.

Castle Rocks (1907) are steeper; they overlook the Wrinkled Slabs and provide the natural continuation. Either of the chimneys takes one onto the ridge, which can be followed fancy-free.

The next three buttresses to the right offer much in the way of pleasant scrambling and the delights of discovery, and so remain uncharted, though the rightmost is quite continuous and does deserve a mention:

Cannon Ridge (400 feet Difficult). A good mountaineering climb can be made by way of this buttress up almost the whole of the West Face to the North Ridge. The Cannon is located at the top of the initial 150-foot curving rock spur.

A narrow, stony runnel now separates the mountainside from the broken outcrop of Brag Rocks. Two recesses cut deeply into the main face causing the corresponding buttresses to stand out in sharp relief. The main features, each of which gives a 300-foot route of Moderate standard, are described from left to right going up the scree-slope:

V Buttress, on the left, is of three tiers, which tend to deteriorate before 300 feet is achieved.

V Cleft has a narrow mouth that opens out into a wide amphitheatre. A 70-foot pitch in the right corner leads to a glacis.

V Arête. If the top edge of the right wall is followed an easy route can be had. The position has exposure.

Y Gully (1894) is narrower and more shallow than V Cleft. The right-hand branch is a trough, which proves quite interesting as long as you are prepared to immerse yourself entirely

Y Gully Edge. The idea is to keep on the edge, to appreciate the atmosphere.

Notch Rocks are high up; the sharp Notch in the skyline of the North Ridge can be clearly seen, directly above V Cleft. The whole group is composed of the best Tryfan rock. **Notch Buttress** (100 feet Moderate 1905) takes the cracks in the more northerly aspect, which is steeper than the arête. **Notch Arête** (300 feet Moderate) is on the right. A chimney behind a huge split-off pillar is unmistakable. The shape, altitude and easy poise of the ridge above make it most acceptable.

Clogwyn Bochlwyd   (Bochlwyd Buttress)

OS Ref. 657 597

This attractive little buttress is a landmark on the long haul up to Cwm Bochlwyd. It stands out well against the hillside by the stream that cascades from the Cwm. A smooth, steep grey face, ideally suited for a visit when on the way up to Glyder Fach, or better still on return, when one can relax in the evening sunlight.

The rock is good, and with so many holds that a number of variations on the described routes are possible. However; in damp conditions, the rock can become quite greasy.

Shadow Arête   200 feet   Difficult   (1956)
A pleasant climb with a fine top pitch. The arête is at the far left-hand end, beyond the very broken area. Start at its foot, by some slanting quartz ledges.
1 70 feet. Climb onto the ledges then take the thin crack on the left to easy ground. Belay over on the right.
2 40 feet. Walk round the boulder on the right then climb up to a belay in a Corner.
3 90 feet. Move out onto the edge of the slab and climb the steepening arête on good little holds to the top.

We now move back right to the main face.

★Wall Climb   150 feet   Hard Severe   (1929)
An exposed and fascinating route for such a small buttress. Start left of the chimney, beside two sloping gangways.
1 85 feet. 4a. Take the upper gangway leftwards. Step down, overcome an awkward mantelshelf in a steep position, then climb straight up to a stance by a wretched tree.
2 65 feet. 4a. Take the groove up to the right, then move out onto the face, where some delectable climbing leads to the top.

★★Bochlwyd Eliminate   120 feet   Hard Very Severe   (1962)
Takes the smooth grey face of the buttress. Start at a quartz slab below the gangway on Wall Climb.
1 120 feet. 5a. Easily up the slab and rib to the traverse on Wall Climb. Climb the small open groove ahead and swing along a hand traverse to a ledge on the right. Climb over a block and finish

Clogwyn Bochlwyd

1. Bochlwyd Eliminate	HVS	5. Two Pitch Route	S
2. Wall Climb	HS	6. Five Pitch Route	S
3. The Wrack	E2	7. Marble Slab	S
4. Chimney Climb	S	8. Arête and Slab	D
4a. Direct Start			
4b. Severe Start			

Photo: Simon Cardy

leftwards up the face. The pitch can be done more directly but this is not so much fun.

The Wrack   100 feet   E2   (1963)
The steep groove left of the chimney gives an impressive climb. Start at the toe of the buttress, just right of Wall Climb.
1 110 feet. 5b. Go diagonally rightwards over the stretch of slab guarding the foot of the buttress to reach the groove. Boldly climb this to a small ledge on the left. Re-enter the groove and finish out left of the overlap.

Rhwyn   110 feet   E4   (1988)
Takes the arête left of the chimney. Start just left of the tall slot of Chimney Route Direct at a short wall.
1 110 feet. 6a. Climb the wall, keeping to its right edge to gain a small slab. Enter the overhanging groove on the right, then climb the right-hand side of the groove to attain the rib above, which is followed to the top.

★Chimney Climb   110 feet   Severe   (1909)
This is the original route of the buttress. It provides ample entertainment in any conditions, and is low in its grade. The main chimney comes down into a tall slot, which forms the direct start, but it does have a dislocated twin 10 yards to the right. Start here.
1 40 feet. Bridge up the smooth-sided chimney or climb the face to a sloping ledge. Belay at its left end.
2 70 feet. Get into the main chimney, wriggle up and step onto a block. If this can be done without creating uneasiness, you simply reach up and pull into the upper parts. Otherwise you are left nervously pondering over the obstruction. The rest comes easily.

Direct Variations
1a 30 feet. A crack leads up rightwards from the tall slot. This is Severe. The main crack on its left is the ultimate in purity and is considered to be much harder.

Two Pitch Route   100 feet   Severe   (1935)
Quite a fine climb with a good exposed finish. Start at the foot of the right-hand chimney.
1 40 feet. Climb straight up the wall right of Chimney Climb to a shallow scoop. Leave this by its left edge and head on up to a ledge just right of a rock nose.
2 60 feet. Go up to the left, then traverse left round an undercut block, and finish on the steep rib which forms the right wall of the chimney.

Five Pitch Route 110 feet Severe   (1935)
A little broken, but a good climb of short sharp pitches. Start where a
detached slab rests against the buttress. Obviously, it is possible to
climb this route in one pitch!
1 20 feet. Climb easily to the top of the slab.
2 25 feet. Go up the crack to the obvious niche. The exit is awkward,
then a crack leads to a small stance.
3 15 feet. Go on up to the grass ledge on the right.
4 30 feet. Traverse 10 feet left, then make for a little rock recess on
the right. Its exit is quite difficult.
5 20 feet. Slabs now lead to the top.

One Pitch Route 100 feet Hard Severe
1 100 feet. 4a. A slight eliminate which follows a line of holds to the
left of the overlaps on Marble Slab. Protection can be arranged in the
routes on either side.

Marble Slab 60 feet Severe   (1935)
Only a little climb, but a pretty one. Its essence lies in technique. Start
at the bollard near the right end of the buttress.
1 60 feet. Climb the crack just left of the bollard to an overlap. Pull
over onto the slab, and ascend it to join Arête and Slab at the ledge
on the right.

Arête and Slab 110 feet Difficult   (1927)
A pleasant climb that skirts the right edge of the buttress. Start at the
arête on the extreme right-hand side.
1 60 feet. Climb the deep crack that splits the arête to a stance. Then
cross the ledge and belay on the left.
2 15 feet. The steep wall on good holds leads to a sloping ledge.
3 35 feet. A timorous step onto the slab on the left is followed by
some delightful climbing to the top.

Gargoyle Traverse 340 feet Very Difficult   (1926)
A traverse of character, on which the interest is well-maintained. Start
nearly 30 yards left of the main face and lower down, by a large
smooth slab.
1 60 feet. Scramble up to a rounded rib and take the indefinite
chimney on its right to a large block. A rock cannon protrudes on the
right.
2 40 feet. A heathery scramble across to a detached flake.
3 50 feet. The wall above and the corner to a grass platform.
Continue diagonally until one reaches the sad ash tree. The
'gargoyle' glowers down from the left.
4 30 feet. A delicate and exposed traverse leads to a small stance.

5 50 feet. Descend close to the edge of the chimney, only entering it at 20 feet to drop through the narrows. Bollard belay.
6 45 feet. Climb straight up to a detached flake, gingerly step from its top and traverse to a ledge at this level.
7 40 feet. An easy chimney on the right to the next ledge.
8 25 feet. Climb the steep nose above.

Many other entertaining routes could be devised on this friendly little crag. The most amusing must be a counter traverse to the last route.

Rising Damp   210 feet   Very Severe   (1977)
A right-to-left girdle of the crag. Start at the foot of the Arête and Slab.
1 60 feet. 4b. Climb diagonally leftwards over the bollard then below the overlap to a good stance just past the crack of Five Pitch Route.
2 30 feet. Continue horizontally to Chimney Climb.
3 90 feet. 4b. Move out left and descend the arête of the chimney, traverse the wall for 40 feet to a ledge below a block. Climb up leftwards to the tree.
4 30 feet. 4a. Move along a quartz ledge to finish up the edge.

Glyder Fach   (The Small Mound of Rocks)

OS Ref. 656 586

This was once a popular cliff which had drifted away from climbers' attentions, however, in the past few years interest has been rekindled. This cliff is a great place and must surely have the finest collection of medium-grade routes in the area, as well as some hard modern routes.

From beside Llyn Bochlwyd, after the steep approach to the Cwm, the cliff seems lost among the high surrounding ridges and the tumbled mass of the mountain's north face. Avoid the steep screes below the cliff by making use of the track to Bwlch Tryfan and cutting across the hillside. If you are lucky you may catch the sun slanting across the face, highlighting the tall grey pillars and edges, sending them soaring out of all proportion, and after first acquaintance with this clean, rough rock you will wonder why you have not been here before. The climbing is the solid, strenuous sort; being clean the rock is quick-drying, and by its very nature inspires confidence.

The East Buttress is tall and compact, and is bounded on the right by the wide and curving Main Gully. Main Gully converges with East Gully, which is on its right, and between the two lies the broad belt of the Alphabet Slabs. Gable Buttress rises to a massive point almost at the summit of the mountain. This huge unsightly area has three very good little buttresses, which should not be neglected. The West Gully serves to separate what remains, which is an indefinite easy-angled expanse known as the West Buttress.

East Buttress

This is the most striking of the buttresses and displays all the best features of Glyder Fach, tall walls of beautiful grey rock cut by steep cracks and clean corners.

Oblique Buttress and Gully are easily seen slanting up the left side of a complex of ribs and walls. This central area is quite bewildering on a first inspection, and through it Slab Route and Direct Route pick their reasonable but tortuous ways. The Luncheon Stone and the standing Capstan, 12 yards farther right, are both serviceable and useful landmarks at the base of this area. Arch Gully only becomes apparent high up. Towards the right-hand end the columns are pronounced. A massive block pillar adjoining the cliff gives the short but classic routes of Lot's Wife and Lot's Groove. The Chasm is a dark vertical cleft immediately right of the pillar; this is part way up Main Gully. The gully itself curves round the right-hand end of the buttress, and provides the easiest means of descent.

Square Chimney 105 feet Severe   (1912)
The obvious vertical cleft at the extreme left-hand end of the buttress is a climb of the very traditional type. Start by scrambling up to its foot.
1 15 feet. Climb the crack on the right to grass.
2 70 feet. Climb the chimney; it will only yield to a determined approach. Go up slabby ground to a spike belay.
3 20 feet. The left wall is preferable to the gully.

Square Chimney Buttress 180 feet Severe   (1931)
A climb with a strong mountaineering flavour and individual character. Quite short, but packed with interest. Start at a small corner down and right of Square Chimney.
1 35 feet. Climb the wall by cracks and go leftwards and up grass to a spike belay.
2 80 feet. Take the corner on the right, and follow a narrow crack until one can traverse right into a grassy chimney. Climb the chimney and belay at the chockstone.
3 40 feet. Delicately traverse the overhung slab on the left. Go up an

Glyder Fach

Photo: Steve Ashton

awkward scoop and the subsequent chimney.
4 25 feet. Left again taking a crack to finish.

Oblique Buttress Direct   220 feet   Very Severe   (1985)
A direct line on the original, rather wandering, route. Start just left of
this.
1 50 feet. 4a. Climb easy ribs to a good thread belay in the centre of
the buttress.
2 60 feet. 4b. From a grassy ledge above the belay, climb a groove
system and cross the overlap on good holds. Continue to meet the
original route at a good ledge.
3 60 feet. 4c. Climb the steep crack near the left edge and pull up
via holds on the edge. Step right and continue to a grass ledge
(possible belay). Traverse 15 feet right to a small stance overlooking
Oblique Gully.
4 50 feet. 4a. Jam the crack in the wall to exit near the summit of the
buttress.

★Oblique Buttress   195 feet   Severe   (1918)
This is the narrow, unbroken face slanting up the cliff. The rock is
good and the climb quite steep. Start at the initial slab beneath a
steep crack which curves over into Oblique Gully.
1 70 feet. The easy slab and rib lead up to a small grass ledge in a
steep cavity.
2 40 feet. Climb the very steep crack out of this, then over a pinnacle
and so into Oblique Gully.
3 35 feet. From the top of the pinnacle, step onto the front of the
buttress and go easily to a bunch of spikes.
4 50 feet. Traverse left and climb the clean rib, just beyond the
grassy groove, and finish by delicately gaining a mantelshelf on the
right. Some scrambling remains.

Oblique Gully   190 feet   Very Difficult   (1907)
Certainly the best of the long gullies on the cliff. The gully defines the
right-hand edge of Oblique Buttress. Start by scrambling up grass to
the foot of the obvious chimney.
1 70 feet. The chimney is quite difficult but submits to a classical style
of assault. Climb some broken slabs and belay in a small recess
where the back wall steepens.
2 70 feet. Step up to the right and then back left over a small
chockstone and continue easily, or take the slabs on the right which
are harder and more open. The next little steep step should be taken
on the right.
3 50 feet. Go easily up to and surmount the final chockstone, messy,
then make a rather awkward step out to grass.

Gryngolet 240 feet   Hard Very Severe   (1980)
Quite a good route on the buttress right of Oblique Gully. Start at the
crack in the right-hand branch of the gully.
1 60 feet. 5a. Start up the short crack, moving right onto a rib, then
go up to a grass ledge. A groove now leads to a foot traverse across
to the crack on Errant Route.
2 50 feet. 4a. The crack to the large bay.
3 80 feet. 4c. Climb the corner on the right, escaping, where it
steepens, to the left and up a crack in the centre of the face. Or climb
the corner direct.
4 50 feet. Finish easily on more broken ground.

Errant Route 300 feet   Severe   (1936)
A tortuous route, yet it does find two excellent pitches, one of which is
the obvious diagonal crack in the steep section of cliff to the right of
Oblique Gully. Start midway between Oblique Gully and the
Luncheon Stone.
1 70 feet. Make the best of the wet grassy area up to a stance beside
Arch Gully.
2 50 feet. Climb a nasty little overhanging crack, then a slab on the
left leads to a ledge by the diagonal crack.
3 50 feet. Climb the steep crack, with some good jamming and then
better holds, up to a large bay.
4 70 feet. From the right end of the bay go up the slab and take a
crack in the rib crest, then make a series of exciting swings up a line
of flakes overlooking Arch Gully. Belay at an airy stance at their top.
5 60 feet. Continue on the extreme right-hand edge, move right
across Arch Gully to finish on a pleasant slab.

Arch Gully 275 feet   Difficult   (1936)
Undistinguished at first, a loose collection of grooves, but the gully
develops and it has its charms. Quite hard when wet. Start 15 feet left
of the Luncheon Stone.
1 45 feet. Climb a small corner immediately left of the big
right-angled corner and follow a slanting crack leftwards.
2 40 feet. A grassy rake leads up into the gully.
3 45 feet. Take a groove up to the right then climb a slimy corner. To
the right, the Spiral Variant of Slab Route is tempting, but be diligent
and follow the gully.
4 50 feet. A grass-filled constriction lies ahead until the gully opens
out at the arch, which is just down to the right.
5 50 feet. Climb a corner and move up the gully, passing the tall
flakes on the left wall, to beneath the capstone.
6 45 feet. The exit seems blocked though a hard pull will bring one

over the capstone, but with a sharp increase of exposure. The
left-hand corner leads to a final rib.

★Slab Route 240 feet Very Difficult   (1907)
A very good climb, being steep and clean. Sadly it is interrupted and
has to find a final, though excellent, pitch on the other side of Arch
Gully. Start at the rib immediately left of the Capstan.
1 20 feet. Climb the rib to a ledge on the left.
2 75 feet. High above is the Slab; a narrow and exposed gangway
slants up to the left. Go up the break on the right then climb across
the Slab. Difficulties increase and balance becomes more awkward
as one progresses.
3 50 feet. Climb the rib on the right and continue on a slab, passing
the fallen flakes that span Arch Chimney.
4 45 feet. Cross Arch Gully and belay at the tall flakes on the left.
The damp, grassy bit is now done.
5 50 feet. Swarm up the flakes, escaping the gully, and step from the
last of these to an exposed little ledge on the front. Climb up and
across the wall finishing by a shallow scoop on the left.

Variation
The Spiral Variant 70 feet Difficult   (1917)
A reasonable diversion to avoid the difficult Slab Pitch. Start on the
ledge at the top of Pitch 1.
2a 70 feet. From the left end of the ledge make a long stride into a
corner chimney, and climb to some spikes. Now tackle the awkward
corner above to rejoin the route.

Arch Chimney 80 feet Hard Severe
A difficult problem pitch, but worthy of attention. Start at the top of
pitch 1 of Slab Route.
1 80 feet. 4b. Ascend the little slab in the break on the right, and
make a difficult entry into the bottomless chimney further up to the
right. Go easily up this, passing between the arches to a stance. We
are now in Arch Gully, the upper half being the natural continuation.

★★★Direct Route 265 feet Hard Severe   (1907)
This is the most popular route on the cliff. Normally climbed as
described, and as such it is far from direct. Yet it remains a grand
piece of mountaineering, on perfect rock which is sometimes very
steep and always demanding. The many variations add spice to a
subsequent visit. Start where a steep, flat rib drops to just behind the
Capstan.
1 40 feet. Start up easily to the left of the rib to reach a ledge and
arrowhead belay below a V-shaped recess.

Glyder Fach: Direct Route and Variations

Direct Route	HS	6. Hodgkin's Var.	S	
Gibson's Chimney	VS	7. Kaya	E6	
Winter Finish	VD	8. Brown's Corner	HVS	
Left-Hand Crack	VS	9. The Watchtower	E1	
Right-Hand Crack	HVS	10. Lot's Wife	VS	Photo: Ken Wilson

2 60 feet. 4a. Steeply now up the right edge of the recess on some superb holds, which continue as a rightwards traverse to security behind a great block leaning out of a deep bay.

3 20 feet. The smooth scoop out of the bay leads to a ledge on the left. Gibson's Chimney is above.

4 30 feet. 4a. The Rectangular Excursion. Traverse the narrow ledge across the front, continue on the Finger and Toe Traverse round the left-hand edge, and step to the fallen spike delicately spanning Arch Chimney.

5 60 feet. 4b. Go up the corner on the right to the Hand Traverse, a crack rising from left to right, and of some repute. It is disconcertingly smooth, but a wedged foot or even a knee will halt any tendency to swing alarmingly. The wide crack above is thankfully simple and brings the Excursion to an end on the Verandah.

6 25 feet. Walk to the right end of the Verandah and climb a slanting coffin-like chimney and crack to a small platform. A strenuous crack just to the left of this leads to the same place.

7 30 feet. 4c. Above is the Final Crack, set in a narrow vertical corner. This will prove to be the crux of this route; the thin crack in the left wall offers some assistance.

Variations
Brown's Corner   70 feet   Hard Very Severe
The big corner leading directly to the Verandah.
3a 70 feet. 5b. This is the right-hand corner of the deep bay. It becomes much easier once the niche in the right wall is reached.

Gibson's Chimney   50 feet   Very Severe
This is the very shallow square chimney that cuts straight up the face to the Verandah and is '... unquestionably the best route to take', but only for the strong-willed.
4a 50 feet. 4c. The chimney rises from the ledge above the deep bay. In the first part the holds are small, in the upper part notably absent.

Alternative finishes: there seems to be a selection to suit all tastes, starting at various places along the Verandah.

The Winter Finish   80 feet   Very Difficult
This is a corner round to the left, quite easy and often overlooked.
6a 80 feet. Return to the wide crack on the left then go round to the left along a broad flake into the corner. Climb past a collapsed flake and go up a crack on the right.

The Tombstone Crack 50 feet Hard Severe   (1985)
1 50 feet. 4b. Ascend the obvious crack in the wall right of the
Winter Finish, gained via the impending flake below.

The Final Flake is a projecting pillar on the upper wall, tilted slightly
forward with a fearsome crack on each side:

The Left-Hand Crack 50 feet Very Severe
6b 50 feet. 5a. This is the more straightforward but more intimidating
of the pair, and a good test of hand-jamming.

The Right-Hand Crack 50 feet Hard Very Severe
6c 50 feet. 5b. The crack can be reached directly from the Verandah
and involves some brutal jamming and laybacking.

Hodgkin's Variation 50 feet Severe
Provides a steep and elegant alternative to the Final Crack
6d 50 feet. Make a difficult start in the right hand corner of a square
recess in the back of the Verandah. From the ledge follow the corner
crack steeply until forced to layback.

★ **Glyder Crack** 80 feet E6   (1992)
The demise of yet another last major problem has resulted in a stiff
testpiece which takes the thin crack around the arête, and left of
Kaya.
1 80 feet. 6b. From the huge block of Direct Route climb easily into a
long pod (Friends at top). Move rightwards into the crack and make
very sequency moves, past two pegs, to the ledges above. Ascend
the short groove above to belay. A fine, sustained pitch.

★★ **Kaya** 60 feet E7   (1988)
A bold route which ascends the left arête of the great block pillar.
Start on the left-hand side of the arête, where a small RP protects the
initial moves.
1 60 feet. 6b. Gain the front face of the arête and climb up past two
pegs, hard, then move back left round the arête to climb its left side to
reach good holds. Another swing right, then moves up past a further
two pegs allows one (possible escape rightwards) to finish up the
superb headwall past two more pegs.

The Watchtower 120 feet E1   (1980)
A good steep climb on the face of the great block pillar, but a blind
eye must be turned on the digression to the Wife. Start by moving left
to the front of the pillar after Pitch 2 of Chasm Route.
1 120 feet. 5c. Climb the steep leftwards facing corner then make an

Glyder Fach: East Gully Area

1. Arch Gully	D	10. Delta	D
2. Slab Route	VD	11. Omega	S
3. Direct Route	HS	12. East Gully Arête	D
4. The Right-Hand Crack	HVS	13. Get Close	HVS
5. Lot's Wife	VS	14. Hyndsight	E4
6. Chasm Route	VD	15. Last Pretender	E2
7. Alpha	VS	16. Hawk's Nest Arête	VS
8. Beta	Mod	17. Hawk's Nest Buttress	S
9. Gamma	S	18. Back Door	VD

awkward traverse left to the foot of the shallow groove in the upper half of the face. Finish directly up this.

★**Lot's Wife** 120 feet Very Severe   (1931)
The crack on the right-hand side of the pillar face makes a nice climb. The only real difficulty is early on. Start at the groove formed by a tall thin rib left of the deep cleft of Chasm Route.
1 100 feet. 4c. Climb the groove using a fingery crack and get onto the rib on the left. Jam the crack on the left then move up right past a splinter and through a narrow slot to a recess.
2 20 feet. The slanting crack to the Verandah.

★★**Lot's Groove** 110 feet Hard Very Severe   (1929)
A harder and more sustained pitch than the previous route. The groove runs up the wall immediately left of the Chasm. Start at the end of Pitch 2 of Chasm Route.
1 90 feet. 5a. Climb the groove, mainly bridging moves of increasing delicacy, until beneath the overhang. The crack splitting this is only a problem for a few feet.
2 20 feet. 3b. The slanting crack on the right.

★★**Chasm Route** 280 feet Very Difficult   (1910)
An honest old-fashioned climb demanding a workmanlike approach. It definitely improves when the day is wild and windy. Up in the wide part of the Main Gully a deep rent appears to split off a portion of cliff. This is the Chasm. Start at the foot of the clean flat rib leading up to the Chasm.
1 70 feet. Climb the front of the rib and use a good jamming crack to gain the ledge on the left. Belay on the left.
2 20 feet. Go round to the right to the Chasm.
3 50 feet. Enter the Chasm, which is steep and smooth sided, and climb it. The crack on the right will be useful, as will long arms. Make an exit to the right from the upper part.
4 20 feet. Easily over blocks to a corner on the left.
5 25 feet. Climb the crack in the steep left wall until ample holds leads out to the left edge.
6 45 feet. Take the narrow gangway back into the gully bed. Pass under a fallen splinter and go up a corner to the chimney on the left.
7 50 feet. Above is the famous Vertical Vice. Get to it by squirming through the chimney. Climb the Vice, some vigorous efforts being needed to escape from its jaws, and finish up a corner crack.

Variations

Corkscrew Crack   50 feet   Severe
7a 50 feet. The crack in the left wall, just before the Vertical Vice, is climbed as its name implies.

Chasm Crack   40 feet   Very Severe
7b 40 feet. 4c. Lower down than Corkscrew Crack awkward twin cracks can be found in the right wall, which is the side wall of Chasm Rib.

★**Chasm Rib**   110 feet   Severe   (1931)
This is a slender rib that rises directly above the Chasm pitch and is best done in association with the initial pitches of Chasm Route. Confinement then leads to exposure. Start in Main Gully, above the Chasm.
1 20 feet. Go easily over blocks to a damp corner on the left (Pitch 4 of Chasm Route).
2 60 feet. Start up the crack in the left wall but break out right across the corner to a ledge on the front of the rib. Climb the steep series of cracks above to a stance.
3 30 feet. Ignore the chimney above, traverse right and take the second of two wide cracks in the edge of the rib.

Chasm Chimney   140 feet   Difficult   (1931)
A pleasant climb in the obvious block-filled chimney. Start in Main Gully, just right of Chasm Rib.
1 75 feet. From the block in the chimney go up on good holds and carefully climb the overhang into a bay.
2 65 feet. Mantelshelf up to the crack on the right then gain the rib on the left. Finish pleasantly up a scoop.

Girdle Traverse of East Buttress   375 feet   Severe   (1956)
Several traverses could be made but this one is both interesting and not too difficult. Start below Square Chimney, at the left-hand end of the cliff.
1 35 feet. Go easily up to the right and the spike on Square Chimney Buttress.
2 60 feet. Climb the corner on the right, cross ledges and follow grass to the edge of Oblique Buttress.
3 35 feet. Reverse the traverse of Oblique Buttress to the pinnacle and descend into Oblique Gully.
4 80 feet. Climb the gully and cross to a nick on the edge.
5 50 feet. From along the ledge climb to a crack, on rattling holds, and then down the flakes into Arch Gully.
6 35 feet. The Hand Traverse of Direct Route.

7 40 feet. Make an exposed traverse just below the Verandah to gain it near the right end.
8 40 feet. Go over the edge and down Pitch 5 of Chasm Route.

Main Gully now intervenes, separating the compact East Buttress from the more sprawling mass of scattered buttresses which make up the rest of the cliff. It provides the easiest means of descent. The walls of the gully are short but seamed with steep crack; **Lot's Child** (60 feet, Very Severe, 1948) takes the obvious groove, about midway up, in the right wall.

Main Gully Ridge (230 feet, Moderate, 1936) starts above the Alphabet Slabs and overlooks the gully. The crest is pleasant but rather too easy in ascent, though as a descent it is useful as all difficulties can be avoided.

The Alphabet Slabs

This wide band of slabs is smooth and delicate. The routes are short; they make a delightful contrast to the steep stuff round about, and are ideal for finishing off the day. One can climb almost anywhere on the slab and, over the ages, there have been many claims; however, there may not be enough letters in the alphabet to describe them all! Therefore, only the better routes are described. Alpha is on the edge; the obvious break slanting from right to left gives Beta, and Delta runs up the shallow depression in the slab farther right.

Alpha   100 feet   Very Severe   (1912)
A delicate climb that takes the extreme left-hand edge of the slabs. Quite testing near the top. Start on the left, just in from a small chimney.
1 100 feet. 4b. Climb straight up the slab to a little niche on the edge and then up to a quartz break. A hard move is made on the edge again before finishing more easily. This area of slab can be climbed in several ways further right.

Beta   90 feet   Moderate   (1912)
A simple little climb taking the slanting break that widens to a chimney in the centre of the slabs. It makes a useful approach to Main Gully Ridge. Start on the terrace, at the break.
1 90 feet. Climb the slab just left of the crack and go up to the chimney. Climb onto the slab left of this, cross back right to a ledge and follow slabs to the top.

★Gamma   150 feet   Severe   (1936)
An absorbing climb of some delicacy on the clean smooth slab right

of Beta. Start just to the right of Beta.
1 80 feet. Step up onto the slab and go right and then left up a shallow depression, possible belay. Traverse left and reach for a thin crack, then proceed up and right to a good belay.
2 70 feet. Go on up easier ground to a steeper wall, then finish up the awkward little wall.

Delta   140 feet   Difficult
A pleasant route following the line of least resistance. Start left of the grassy runnel that terminates the slabs.
1 70 feet. Go delicately up leftwards to reach a small ledge in the centre of the slab. Follow a crack just left of the vague hollow above. This is not easy to reach.
2 70 feet. Easy slabs are followed by ledges to the top.

Omega   110 feet   Severe   (1949)
Takes the corner in the steeper rock before East Gully. Start on a grass ledge in the middle of this area.
1 110 feet. Go diagonally left into the scooped corner and climb it to a quartz ledge. Continue in the corner, and then go up a wall to the terrace and a junction with East Gully Arête.

East Gully Arête   445 feet   Difficult
A climb in two parts; steep below the terrace, easy above. Quite suitable for beginners, with a good mountain atmosphere. Start just round to the left of the foot of East Gully.
1 50 feet. Climb straight up from a quartz block, and avoid a steep little wall by moving to the edge of the gully and then returning up left to a small ledge.
2 75 feet. Step right from a bollard and ascend the delicate slabs. A flake on the left leads to a bay. Climb an awkward groove to the terrace.
3 320 feet. The route now changes in character and becomes a simple breezy ridge, where most interest will be found close to the gully.

East Gully   80 feet   Severe   (1895)
Only a short gully problem, but a jolly good one. The gully is obvious, a deep black slot. Start at its foot.
1 60 feet. Climb the chimney or the slab, squirm upwards and take either of the cracks to a commodious platform.
2 20 feet. Climb into the dark cave below the capstone and gain a footing on the narrow ledge on the left wall. A final pull on a small chockstone only leaves the struggle to reach the upper part of the

gully. The rest is useless and best abandoned for a route on the next buttress.

Gable Buttress

This is the immense precipitous mountainside stretching between the East and West Gullies. Set in this vast conglomeration are three steep and distinct buttresses; on each will be found a route or two that will more than satisfy a diversion into this area.

The next two routes are found just above the 'terrace' where it crosses East Gully.

★★**Get Close**   85 feet   Hard Very Severe   (1989)
Start below the crackline in the left wall of the thin tower.
1 85 feet. 5a. Ascend the crack until a move rightwards into a groove in the right arête of the wall is possible, follow this to the top.

★★**Hyndsight**   85 feet   E4   (1989)
An superb pitch in a brilliant position on the front face of the tower. Start directly below a small spike at 60 feet.
1 85 feet. 6a. Climb steeply up the wall to gain the small spike on the arête. A move left allows protection to be placed in the groove of Get Close. Regain the front face and climb up delicately to a rounded finish

★**The Hollow Men**   90 feet   E1   (1985)
A good route up the square cut groove.
1 90 feet. 5b. Climb the left-hand side of the groove on good holds to a ledge at 40 feet. Continue up the groove, making some hard moves to reach a layback crack. Finish up this.

Hawk's Nest Buttress

This exciting little buttress can be reached easily from along the terrace above the Alphabet Slabs or from the right. It looks so small against the chaotic hillside, yet its sheer bold profile is attractive and gives a strong hint of the type of climbing to be expected.

Hawk Slab   90 feet   Very Difficult   (1936)
This is just left of the arête and is delicate in places. Start to the right of the wall of tottering blocks.
1 40 feet. Take the easy slab to a ledge.
2 50 feet. Go straight up then bear left over a block. Avoid the grassy bay by climbing the thin slab on the right to reach a large square bay.

★The Last Pretender   120 feet   E2   (1980)

A dirty corner leads to the impressive jamming crack in the left wall of Hawk's Nest Arête. Start below the corner, just left of the Arête.
1 30 feet. 5a. Climb the overhanging corner to the square bay.
2 70 feet. 5c. The crack is now obvious, steep and uncomfortably wide, and whichever way you face it seems to be wrong.
3 20 feet. Finish easily on the back wall.

★★★Hawk's Nest Arête   130 feet   Very Severe   (1940)

The buttress is distinguished by this clean steep edge. A superb climb and one of the best pitches on the cliff. Start directly beneath the arête.
1 90 feet. 4c. Climb easily at first to a perched flake, then continue, more steeply now, on the edge to a small ledge. Move right along this and go up an open little chimney to reach a flake, which leads back leftwards.
2 40 feet. Follow the crack to the top.

★Hawks's Nest Buttress   180 feet   Severe   (1905)

A route of character, taking a slanting line in the buttress. The climbing is strenuous in parts, delicate in others, and enjoys a very open aspect. Start directly beneath the sharp arête.
1 50 feet. Go easily up the lower edge of the arête then up the slab on the right to belay at a perched flake.
2 50 feet. Move across the rib on the right and follow a crack up to a niche beneath a jammed block. Reach for a mantelshelf on the right, and get onto it before stepping back left and going up into a deep recess.
3 30 feet. Climb easily to a sloping rock platform.
4 50 feet. To the right a curious tower of upright blocks is bridged at the top. Climb the chimney behind the tower and an easy slab to finish.

Variation
2a 60 feet. From the niche beneath the jammed block move leftwards to good holds, then climb straight up to pitch 4.

★Needle's Eye Climb   190 feet   Very Difficult   (1925)

Another good climb, with a novel problem of its own in a similar, though not so open, situation as the last route. A terrace drops below the buttress to where a small capstan stands at the foot of a narrowing chimney. Start here.
1 60 feet. Begin on the clean slab and trend left to a mantelshelf to gain the top part of the chimney.
2 50 feet. Go easily up to a nook on the right then right again up a rib.

3 55 feet. A rock ledge leads out left to a vertical slot behind a thin pinnacle. This is the Needle's Eye, and is quite delicate to reach; then one must persist with the smooth crack until it becomes wide enough to pass through into the cave behind. Climb straight up, step off the top of the pinnacle and go on to a corner on the left.
4 25 feet. Finish up either the awkward crack in the left-hand corner or by the bridged chimney behind the tower.

Shark Pinnacle (25 feet, Moderate) is the remarkably life-like feature clearly visible above the buttress when approaching.

Groove Route (200 feet, Moderate, 1898) follows the grassy runnel between this buttress and Little Buttress. It is dirty and worth avoiding.

Little Buttress
This steep block of buttress is situated a bit lower down and right of Hawk's Nest Buttress.

Back Door   100 feet   Very Difficult   (1949)
A short strenuous chimney in the back of the buttress.
1 50 feet. The chimney is obvious; climb it, and the difficult crack, into the bowels of the buttress.
2 50 feet. Continue up cracks to the top.

Wristy Business   55 feet   E2   (1989)
Just to the right of Back Door is a wide jamming crack.
1 55 feet. 5c. Swarm up the crack, then span right out across the steep wall to gain a thin crack which gradually opens out. Finish up grooves.

Little Buttress   190 feet   Severe   (1936)
An energetic climb up the crack in the front face. Start directly below the face.
1 60 feet. Go easily to a block, then up a crack to a ledge where the buttress steepens.
2 60 feet. Using a pinnacle step left to the crack. Climb this and the strenuous chimney above. Belay a little higher on the left.
3 70 feet. Move round to the left and follow the crack, finishing on the front of the bulge on the right.

Dolmen Buttress
This pleasant little buttress is perched high up to the right overlooking West Gully. It possesses two fine wings, between which is the sloping grassy Courtyard, and is topped by a great pyramid-shaped block. The

buttress can be easily reached after completing a route on Hawk's Nest Buttress by wandering along a narrow terrace, or from below by climbing **Lower Dolmen Rib** (150 feet, Difficult, 1955).

★★**Route II**   150 feet   Difficult   (1914)
An excellent climb, steep and positive, up the crest of the left wing of the buttress. Start just round to the left of the toe of this wing at a shallow depression.
1 50 feet. Step up steeply to a little niche and climb straight up to the steep groove on big holds. Move right onto the exposed crest and climb this to a small stance.
2 40 feet. Take the edge again, move left across a slab and back up to a small corner, which leads to a large sloping platform. Walk over to the chimney behind the pyramid-shaped tower.
3 60 feet. Go up into the chimney and climb out of its depths passing between the huge jammed chockstones.

Druid Route   130 feet   Severe   (1949)
This route is on the steep face of the right wing. Start between the grassy depression at the back of the Courtyard and the mossy groove of Route 1, at another steep but clean groove.
1 40 feet. Two steep grooves merge. Start up the scooped left-hand one and exit left from the higher one.
2 40 feet. Climb the left-hand corner of the recess. A steep crack then leads to a ledge.
3 50 feet. Take the crack behind, then go easily over blocks and climb the right edge to the top.

Route 1   140 feet   Difficult   (1912)
A pleasant and varied route. Start on the Courtyard, at a mossy groove in the middle of the right wing of the buttress.
1 40 feet. Climb into the niche, bridge up the steep groove and step out right to a ledge.
2 20 feet. Go over blocks and round the corner on the right to a chimney in the back of a recess.
3 30 feet. Climb the chimney.
4 50 feet. Take the easy crack up leftwards and a slab on the right to finish.

West Buttress

West Gully (1894) is the furthest right of the big gullies. It is scree-filled, but the diligent will find some climbing when approaching the next route.

Sidewalk   120 feet   Very Difficult   (1950)
Start in West Gully, where the right wall attains reasonable

The Corner Chimney pitch on *Direct Route* (Diff), Milestone Buttress.
Photo: Abraham Bros. Courtesy of Fell and Rock Climbing Club and Abbot Hall Art
Gallery and Museum

Sean Williams on *Direct Route* (Diff), Milestone Buttress. Photo: John Cleare

John Redhead climbing *The Wrinkled Retainer* (E4), Milestone Buttress.
Photo: Andy Newton

Direct Route (Hard Severe), Glyder Fach. Photo: Eric Byrom Collection

proportions 200 feet above Dolmen Buttress.

1 50 feet. Follow the flaky holds to a square ledge on the right, then climb a shallow groove to a grass niche.

2 70 feet. Get onto the little slab below the overhang, and go rightwards to finish up a steep cracked rib. The rest of the West Buttress is an expanse of broken hillside with no definite climbing, though it provides some scrambling on splendid rock for the lone wanderer. **Intermittent Gully** (300 feet, Moderate, 1898) commences with three short chimneys but deteriorates to a vague depression. Much farther right, **Hyperbolic Slab** (100 feet, Moderate) is of little interest.

Castell Y Gwynt   (Castle of the Wind)

OS Ref. 655 582

A mass of tall spikes and blocks rise in splendid confusion to form a little summit on the main ridge between the two Glyderau. Innumerable cracks and chimneys will quickly sap the strength of those who care to linger. The north face overlooks Cwm Bochlwyd and is high enough to give several routes.

The North Buttress comes down to the left of a large slab. **Hard Frost** (300 feet, Difficult) takes the weakness up the right edge of the buttress before tailing off into broken ground.

Crab Slab   150 feet   Very Difficult   (1949)
The large slab makes a corner with a rib on its right. Start above the scree gully running up to the slab.

1 70 feet. Climb diagonally up for 20 feet to a grassy crack. Continue to a stance on the left skyline.

2 60 feet. Go up the left edge of the slab.

3 20 feet. A narrow slab on the right leads to the top.

Frost's Climb   180 feet   Difficult   (1934)
A surprisingly good climb on the crest of the slabby rib at the extreme westward end of the face.

1 70 feet. Go up the rib, past a block, to a small stance.

2 90 feet. Climb the nose, then go up the slab neatly by its left edge to arrive on a shoulder.

3 20 feet. Finish pleasantly, still on the edge.

To the west the Gribin Ridge now encloses Cwm Bochlwyd. It shows a small face, which breaks up very quickly as it falls towards the llyn. This very shabby piece of hillside has known glamorous times. In January 1909 a staunch team comprising G H L Mallory, R L G Irving, D Murray and H E G Tyndale chose to climb the two-storey chimney on the left-hand end of the face (100 feet, Very Difficult). Much of this is too rotten to contemplate. Then, much later, C F Kirkus and R C Frost came searching for the original climb, but produced **False Route** (160 feet, Severe). This is on the steeper rock in the centre, though there are so many ledges that one is never bothered by commitment to any line.

Clogwyn Y Tarw
or **The Gribin Facet**

(Crag of the Bull)

OS Ref. 650 596

The rocky arm of the Gribin Ridge stretches down to end abruptly with Clogwyn y Tarw. This long, low cliff is only a short distance above, and parallel to, the well-trodden track from Ogwen Cottage to Llyn Idwal.

The cliff primarily consists of four buttresses; the central pair, East Buttress and Central Buttress, being the most distinguished. The routes here will satisfy most climbers, from the beginner to the expert.

The rock is bold and clean; there is nothing contrived about any of the routes. The deep cracks and corners give shelter from the worst of the storm if one is forced to do something in a period of foul weather to maintain sanity, and all have the distinctive Ogwen flavour.

The Far East Buttress

The rambling left-hand buttress is split into steep tiers by several large grassy terraces. These interrupt the climbing but do keep the exposure to a minimum. A large ash tree at the base of the cliff is a useful landmark.

Home Climb   260 feet   Very Difficult   (1922)

An entertaining selection of pitches that will delight the beginner, as there is very little exposure. Start at the big tree below a V-recess.

1 45 feet. Gain the recess, with some help from the tree or by coming in from the right, and take the slab on the left to a crevasse stance.

2 45 feet. The central of the three slanting grooves above is the usual way. The right-hand one is harder.

3 20 feet. A square groove makes a steep little problem.

4 80 feet. Walk over to the right, where a tight chimney must be overcome to reach a large grass terrace.

5 70 feet. A stiff little crack in the boulder on the left leads to a finish on a long slabby rib.

Variation

5a 60 feet. A series of chimneys farther left is less direct but more traditional.

Draw 50 feet   Hard Very Severe   (1963)

The wide crack behind a withered tree. Start 20 feet right of the large ash tree.

1 50 feet. 5a. The crack is ill-defined at first; an alternative start to Home Climb veers off to the left. Where it steepens it is very awkward, but this is quite short, and soon Home Climb can be joined.

Late Night Final 245 feet   Severe   (1947)

Makes the best of this part of the cliff, and has quite a difficult start. Start about 50 feet right of the large tree, where a steep left-facing groove comes down to a heather ledge.

1 65 feet. Get onto the narrow ledge and climb the groove, which rises to a crack. Pull out right at the top. An easy groove leads up left to a thread belay.

2 75 feet. Take the ramp on the right; it breaks through the overhangs to gain an area of grassy steps.

3 45 feet. Avoid the messy corner by climbing a groove on the left, past some shattered flakes, and a deep crack farther left to the grassy terrace.

4 25 feet. Over to the right a scarred, cracked boulder leads to a quartz glacis and a crevasse belay.

5 35 feet. Climb the wall above on small holds and enter a shallow groove, with an easy mantelshelf to finish.

Away Variations

2a 75 feet. Cross onto the open slab on the left and go up this to the left-hand end of the grassy steps.

3a 40 feet. 4b. The steep crack about 30 feet left of the messy corner may be taken, but it is Very Severe.

East Buttress

This is the most impressive buttress of Clogwyn y Tarw; it presents a sharp contrast of a steep wall and an easy-angled slab.

Clogwyn Y Tarw

1. Yob Route   VS   5. Slab Recess Route   Mod
2. Llyn   HS   6. Rocking Chair   VS
3. Slab Climb   D   7. Couteau   E6
4. Recess Monkey   E4   8. Le Fin   E7

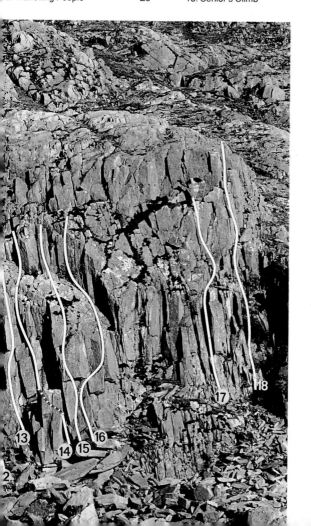

The intriguing dark wall is crossed by Thrasher, and Synapse takes the obvious slabby groove below the overlaps of the nose. All this is flanked by a huge inset slab, which gives an entirely different aspect to the buttress. It runs to the full height of the cliff and provides the trade routes, which are ideal for the novice. On the front of the wall, below the slab, a square corner part way up is the feature of Yob Route and the curving crack of Llyn is most obvious.

The broken area farther right is the quickest descent from all the routes on this and the Central Buttress.

Thrasher   100 feet   Hard Very Severe   (1970)
Not a very satisfying route, being rather dirty. Start at the top of the broken bay, beneath the wall.
1 100 feet. 5a. Climb a shallow grass-filled groove to a sentry-box. Move left below a little nose and take the deeper groove to a large spike. Finish on the left.

Throsher   135 feet   E1   (1970)
A much better climb. The long diagonal crack is an eye-catching feature of the wall. Start just left of the great quartz-topped flake embedded at the foot of the wall.
1 50 feet. 5b. Climb the rib and step into the bottomless groove on the left. From its top move up to a small stance on the rib on the right. Thread belay at the overlap.
2 85 feet. 5b. A deep crack has to be overcome before striking out leftwards along the slanting crack to reach the spike on Thrasher. Go up to the left to the top.

★Synapse   130 feet   E3   (1965)
A great climb that accepts the exciting challenge of the main line in the wall. Start at the embedded flake at the foot of the wall.
1 50 feet. 4c. Climb the groove with the long curving crack to a thread at the overlap, then take a stance on top of the rib on the left.
2 80 feet. 5c. Take the shallow groove on the right, then climb more directly to a recess; a further 30 feet leads to twin cracks and relief.

★Insidious Slit   130 feet   E4   (1979)
The triple overlapping nose on the front of the buttress will only yield to a daring assault. Start where a steep sweep of slab runs up to the overlaps.
1 130 feet. 6a. Climb straight up the slab towards the daunting overlaps but dodge into the crack of Synapse where it curves to the left. Go directly up the groove to the first overlap, peg, turn this on the

right, and climb the steepening wall to the second overlap. A groove on the left has to be reached in order to make an escape.

★Yob Route   135 feet   Very Severe   (1957)
A good climb in a nice position. It takes a leftward-facing corner a little lower and to the right of the overlaps. Start at the gangway that runs up to the corner from the right.
1 60 feet. 4c. Go up the easy gangway and a little groove. Swing onto the face and climb the square corner to a small ledge, which is quite an airy perch.
2 75 feet. 4c. Ignore the original way, off to the right, and continue up the corner crack, pulling out to the right. Make a long step to a small ledge on the right, and follow two steep cracks to join Slab Climb. Strenuous.

The Derelict   120 feet   E3   (1979)
The slab to the right of Yob Route is guarded by a steep lower wall, which gives concentrated climbing. Start at the foot of the gangway of Yob Route.
1 120 feet. 5c. Take a thin crack in the wall and move into a shallow scoop on the left. Climb this with difficulty to a good pocket. Reach to the right and gain the slab, which is climbed directly and pleasantly to the top.

★Llyn   100 feet   Hard Severe   (1931)
A wide crack curves up to enter a deep V-chimney. It looks most encouraging, but this excellent pitch is fraught with hidden difficulties. Start just to the right of Yob Route.
1 100 feet. 4a. Go easily rightwards and tackle the ever-steepening crack, until a few layback moves allow the rib on the right to be mounted. Climb up and regain the crack, now in the V-chimney, to reach Slab Climb.

★Diadem   90 feet   Hard Very Severe   (1979)
A little gem of a crack-climb on this short steep face. Start 20 feet right of Llyn.
1 90 feet. 5a. Traverse easily up to a ledge on the right to reach the thin but delightful crack running directly up the wall.

Sweet Sorrow   80 feet   Hard Very Severe   (1960)
A tough pitch tackling the deep crack in the remaining rock. Start at its foot, between Diadem and the slab, which is best reached by an approach from the left, below Diadem.
1 80 feet. 5a. Fight up the vicious initial crack to the ledge. Coming

Clogwyn Y Tarw: East Buttress

Photo: Simon Car

1. Throsher	E1	5. The Derelict	E3
2. Synapse	E3	6. Llyn	HS
3. Insidious Slit	E4	7. Diadem	HVS
4. Yob Route	VS	8. Street of Crocodiles	E2

in from the left, as for Diadem, is more reasonable. Regain the crack, now wider, but it is still very awkward.

Sorrowful   60 feet   E3   (1990)
Takes the bouldering wall left of Slab Intermediate Route's first groove.
1 60 feet. 6a. A short technical wall on dubious rock leads to a pleasant wall and overhanging flake. Using the flake, join the slab climb at the crevassed stance.

★**Slab Climb**   170 feet   Difficult   (1912)
The best of the slab routes. It is nicely situated over the steep face and so it enjoys the added exposure. Combined with pitch 1 of Slab Intermediate Route it forms an excellent way up the cliff. Start at the right-hand side of the slab.
1 50 feet. Climb the slab for a few feet and make a long rather uneasy traverse, in a shallow scoop near the edge of the slab, to reach a sandy corner on the left.
2 35 feet. Take the slab on the left to a crevasse stance.
3 25 feet. Go over to the exposure on the left edge.
4 60 feet. Climb the rib and the slab edge to the top.

Slab Intermediate Route   180 feet   Very Difficult   (1936)
Only the first pitch has any difficulty; the route then takes the dislocated slab above the previous climb. Start below a steep groove 30 feet left of Slab Climb.
1 40 feet. Climb the groove which leads to a sandy corner.
2 50 feet. Take the worn crack on the right of the slab and climb a steep groove to an immense belay.
3 50 feet. Good holds in the corner lead to a rock nose. Delicately cross the slab on the left to a quartz knob.
4 40 feet. Finish straight up the little wall.

Recess Monkey   50 feet   E4   (1988)
Start from Pitch 3 of Slab Intermediate Route.
1 50 feet. 5c. Climb the V-shaped arête that juts out above the slab routes.

Slab Recess Route   135 feet   Moderate   (1923)
The main slab looks quite impressive but the climbing is extremely simple. Start at the bottom right-hand corner of the slab.
1 60 feet. Climb straight up the main slab, then follow cracks diagonally leftwards to a good stance.
2 55 feet. Continue up the slab, slightly left at first, then go up to the foot of a rib and move right to a quartz belay.

3 40 feet. Cross the slab on the right, then follow a shattered groove between the enclosing walls to the top.

Slab Direct Route 90 feet Very Difficult
A pleasant pitch for the more ambitious. Start 25 feet up Slab Recess Route, where it goes off left.
1 90 feet. Climb the crack which runs directly up the slab, about 10 feet out from the retaining wall, to rejoin Slab Recess Route near the top.

Street of Crocodiles 170 feet E2   (1982)
A rising girdle of this part of the cliff.
1 70 feet. 4c. Start up Slab Direct, then go left along the traverse line past Llyn. Move up and belay in the next break.
2 100 feet. 5c. Move up, then go diagonally across the steep wall to gain the crack (possible belay) of Yob Route. Move left then up onto a rib. Climb this and the continuation to the top.

Ledge Lizard 40 feet E1   (1988)
At about 15 feet up and left of Peglegs is a hanging green corner.
1 40 feet. 5b. Ascend the corner to a large ledge. Then move up and right to gain a rightwards traverse below the prominent roof to finish at the top of Peglegs.

Peglegs 30 feet E3   (1987)
Start beneath a thin crack in the retaining wall right of Slab Direct Route.
1 30 feet. 5c. Ascend the thin crack to a big roof. Climb the cracks trending right to a good jug.

★**The Last Starfighter** 80 feet E3   (1983)
A good route up the steep groove above Slab Climb. Start below the groove.
1 80 feet. 5c. Ascend the thin crack to the start of the groove, which leads to an airy finish up the arête.

Bubbling 30 feet E6   (1987)
Short but fingery climbing. Start below the pocketed wall left of Rocking Chair Ridge.
1 30 feet. 6b. Grab the first pockets and climb the wall past two poor sky-hooks and two poor spikes to a peg. The top is more positive.

★**Rocking Chair Ridge** 40 feet E6   (1988)
Ascends the fierce-looking prow left of Rocking Chair. Start at the ledge above Pitch 1 of Rocking Chair.

1 40 feet. 6b. Gain the top of a flake, peg, to reach some pockets; then climb the arête past two pegs moving onto the right-hand face to finish.

Rocking Chair   100 feet   Very Severe   (1958)
A short but quite enjoyable climb up the lower groove. Start where the groove comes down to the right-hand end of the slab.
1 100 feet. 4c. Climb the groove to a good ledge on the right. Continue up the main corner above. It is steep and the moves are precarious for a few feet. The angle then eases and one can finish more pleasantly.

Le Fin   30 feet   E7   (1988)
A 30 foot climb of high technical difficulty with an 80 foot fall potential. Start at a ledge beneath the arête right of Rocking Chair pitch 2.
1 30 feet. 6b. Ascend the arête utilising two mysterious gaseous holes/pockets.

Couteau   30 feet   E6   (1988)·
A short and escapable arête just right of the descent routes.
1 30 feet. 6b. From the base of the wall climb leftwards with difficulty to gain a rest on the left arête. Continue boldly up the arête to finish.

Pocket Knife   25 feet   E1 5b   (1988)
The projecting arête just right of Couteau.

Central Buttress

This is quite striking, with its towers and great blocks cleft by deep cracks, which promise muscular exertion.

A narrow tower, high up, is the first clean feature. Playtime and the not very obvious Pinnacle Route are here. To the right a huge bastion abuts the cliff, behind which the classic Angular Chimney can be found. Farther right a massive monolith leans crudely against the cliff; the deep crevice of Monolith Crack up to the left leads to a quartz-marked slab which intersects this part of the buttress.

Grab and Flash It   70 feet   E4   (1990)
Climbs the left edge of the narrow tower above Pitch 1 of Playtime.
1 70 feet. 6a. From the Playtime belay step gymnastically off the tree and ascend the arête strenuously to where a swing right gives access to good holds and the top. Small wires protect.

Playtime   100 feet   Hard Very Severe   (1959)
A short, sustained route, with a good feeling of isolation, on the final
crack in the front tower. Start at a 15-foot spire standing just above
the broken ground at the left-hand end of the buttress, and below a
big tree.
1 40 feet. 4b. Step right, round the rib, and climb a greasy groove
on the arête to another tree.
2 60 feet. 4c. Tiptoe rightwards along a line of flakes round the arête
to swing into the crack, and climb it manfully to the top. The square
furrow from the ledge is a softer option.

Variations
Foreplay   30 feet   E1   (1990)
Start at a ledge right of Playtime.
1a 30 feet. 5b. Climb the thin crack to the flakes. It is then better to
continue up Pitch 2 of Playtime rather than:
2a 60 feet. 5a. Continue in the groove on the left side of the tower to
a ledge and finish up the steep crack.

Pinnacle Route   140 feet   Severe   (1948)
Relies entirely on the pinnacle pitch for interest, though this does have
a strong traditional flavour. Start at the lowest rocks at this end of the
buttress.
1 35 feet. Take the broken groove on the right. The 15-foot spire of
rock is now on the left.
2 35 feet. A small chimney leads to the foot of the tower.
3 70 feet. The corner crack is energetic and the chimney behind the
pinnacle is no relief. From its tip a tantalising step is made to the
steep rock beyond.

Various cracks in the vegetated area left of Angular Chimney have been
climbed and could be used as an alternative approach to the Pinnacle,
but they have little merit.

Angular Chimney   105 feet   Very Difficult   (1898)
One of the grand old routes of the crag, and it still retains a touch of
seriousness. Start by scrambling up to the corner formed by a tall
bastion on the right. A curious rock cannon projects from the chimney.
1 80 feet. Climb straight up the corner crack to a recess, then
continue upwards to reach a traverse left onto the slab. Delicately
work back right into the narrow chimney. It is tight but one can
wheedle away upwards and exit onto some sloping ledges.
2 25 feet. The normal way is to finish over easy blocks to arrive at
the top of the chimney. But this avoids the natural line, which is a

Clogwyn Y Tarw: Central Buttress

1. Playtime (Alt. Finish)
2. Playtime   HVS
3. Pinnacle Route   S

4. Pinnacle Route (Alt. Start)
5. Angular Chimney   VD
6. Centrally Heated Big Top   E5

7. Trouble With Lichen   E1   10. De Selincourt's Variation
8. Travelling People   E3   11. Stonehenge   E2
9. Monolith Crack   S   12. Zig-Zag Climb   S

fitting climax. Re-cross the sloping ledge and squirm up the final section of chimney passing through a hole at the top.

Centrally Heated Big Top   80 feet   E5   (1987)

A direct line left of Trouble With Lichen taking in its 'harder finish'. Start as for that route.

1 80 feet. 6a. Ascend the pinnacle, just under the traverse right of Trouble With Lichen, pull up leftwards via a thin flake to a small spike. Move up and right in to T.W.L. then traverse left on quartz to gain a flake. Step up, crux, to reach better holds and protection, continue to the top

Trouble with Lichen   145 feet   E1   (1976)

A thrilling route on the face of the bastion right of Angular Chimney. Start well down, amongst the tumbled blocks. It is also possible to start the route at the foot of Angular Chimney.

1 70 feet. 4b. Go up the front of a large pinnacle, traverse right and zigzag up via a corner.

2 75 feet. 5b. Layback a crack to gain the rising fault leading to the crack in the bastion. Climb this directly to the top.

Travelling People   90 feet   E3   (1988)

The hanging arête left of the crack of Monolith Crack. Start at a crack below the overhanging arête.

1 90 feet. 5c. Climb the arête to a ledge on the left, then move right with difficulty to another ledge. Step delicately back on to the arête and go up to the next break, small Friend runner. Step up and move back right to continue up the arête in an exciting position.

★Monolith Crack   130 feet   Severe   (1905)

A unique and legendary climb that requires both strength and a particular fighting spirit to succeed. The Monolith is massive and has fallen from the cliff. Up to the left twin chimneys lead to what appears to be a deep corner. Start on the right-hand side of the Monolith.

1 30 feet. Go up through a cave beneath the Monolith.

2 30 feet. Climb the awkward chimney ahead, or its harder twin on the left-hand side of the tall block.

3 40 feet. Face right and force yourself into the dank claustrophobic depths of the cavity. Hopes do brighten, so make a bid for the daylight with a sort of vertical crawl and caterpillar-like movements. The originators were bolder; they climbed straight up! The second can be ignominiously stuffed into the tightest part of the cleft, then by clambering on top of him a wider part can be reached and completed on the outside, passing over the chockstone.

Lew Hardy making the first ascent of *Get Close* (HVS), Glyder Fach.
Photo: Ray Wood

Chris Parkin making the first ascent of *Hyndsight* (E4), Glyder Fach.
Photo: Ray Wood

4 30 feet. Climb the quartz slab and re-enter the continuation chimney and work up and out from its back.

De Selincourt's Variation
Avoids the issue altogether by crossing the wall on the right.
3a 50 feet. Step from the pedestal onto the edge of the wall and climb up to the right, where an awkward mantelshelf brings one out on the quartz slab.

Stonehenge 120 feet E2 (1988)
Left of Zig-Zag Climb is a face with a shallow groove leading to an overhang. Start at the base of the groove.
1 70 ft. 6a. Climb the groove to a hard move left to the arête. Climb the overhang and V-shaped groove to a protruding flake. Move easily up the slab to a tree belay.
2 50 ft. 4c. Continue up the crack behind the tree to finish.

★ Zig-Zag Climb 140 feet Severe (1912)
An entertaining route, but the groove, which is deceptive and treacherously smooth, has been many a proud leader's downfall. Start on a rock step just right of the Monolith.
1 70 feet. Climb the angular corner, which changes to a crack, and go along to the right-hand end of the sloping ledge. The groove must be climbed in a positive fashion. It cuts up into the quartz slab, where there is a good belay higher up.
2 70 feet. Carry on up the slab to a pair of cracks. The right-hand crack provides good strenuous exercise, whereas the left is savage until good holds arrive.

Variation
Direct Start Hard Very Severe
1a 40 feet. 5a. Start 10 feet right of the ordinary start and climb the corner crack past an overlap, with difficulty, to join the ordinary way.

Hippy Invasion 45 feet E1 (1988)
Ascends the groove above the sloping ledge of Zig-Zag Climb. Start right of Zig-Zag Climb and gain a ledge from the right.
1 45 feet. 5b. Interesting moves up the groove on the left leads to a tree belay.

Blue Smartie 40 feet E2 (1988)
Pleasant climbing up the cracked arête 20 feet right of Zig-Zag Climb. Start beneath the overhanging base of the arête.
1 40 feet. 5c. Scramble up to the overhang, surmount it and climb

the crack above to a quartz ledge, move right to finish on the slab above.

Headmaster's Climb   80 feet   Very Severe   (1990)
Start 30 feet right of Blue Smartie at the base of a small rib with a layback crack on its right-hand side.
1 80 feet. 4c. Climb a bulge to gain the crack which is followed to an area of slabby rock. Continue up a steep crack above to a large quartz flecked slab and belay ledges.

Gully and Slab   160 feet   Difficult   (c.1923)
An interesting climb taking the deep rock recess. Start about 20 feet left of Wooded Gully.
1 50 feet. Some splendid holds lead up to the recess. Go up the back until an intrepid swing is made onto the right wall.
2 80 feet. Climb the nose above and a quartz-speckled slab to a perched block. Go up and belay by a cave on the right.
3 30 feet. Go over a block and climb a shattered crack in the wall to the top.

Senior's Climb   130 feet   Very Difficult   (1923)
Not as good a climb as the previous one. Start between Gully and Slab, and Wooded Gully.
1 65 feet. Go up into a recess behind a bollard, by a tree. Climb the corkscrew crack a few feet left of the corner-chimney. Scramble up leftwards to a spike in a hollow.
2 30 feet. Take the awkward scoop behind the spike.
3 35 feet. Pass through the tunnel on the left and go up to the right, where a steep crack leads to the top. A number of variations to the last two pitches can be taken.

The buttress is bounded by Wooded Gully, which with great care provides a descent.

West Buttress
Though diminutive and rambling there are several short, sharp pitches on steep rock. It is a secluded spot. The elegant sliver of the flake stands poised against the sky.

Don't Just Stand There   40 feet   E1   (1982)
1 40 feet. 5a. Ascends the crack in the right wall of the gully and left of Née Langley.

Née Langley   90 feet   Hard Very Severe   (1956)
Gives some steep and interesting crack climbing. Start a little left of

the base of the flake.

1 50 feet. 5a. Climb the groove that leads directly to a dead tree, or make a diversion on the right.

2 40 feet. 4b. Continue up the crack behind the tree and make a hard move into the crack on the right to finish.

★**Flake Crack**   80 feet   Very Severe   (1909)

An exciting little route. The flake does wobble perceptibly under pressure. As Colin Kirkus said, 'The prospect of finding a sheltered chimney transformed into an overhanging face by the sudden departure of one of the walls is alarming!' Start on a platform to the right of the flake.

1 45 feet. 4c. Gain a mantelshelf and climb to a ledge with a holly. The cleft behind the flake is now approached by a tenuous rising traverse moving from one crack to the next.

2 40 feet. 4b. Bridge up the chimney behind the flake and bravely step from its tip to finish slightly right.

★★**Herford's Crack**   70 feet   Very Severe   (1912)

An excellent vertical crack in the remaining rock. Start just beyond the block right of Flake Crack. Large Hexes or Friends are useful.

1 70 feet. 4c. Get up to the crack in the right side of the block. It is a superb jamming pitch.

★**Arkwright's Reward**   50 feet   E4   (1990)

A ferocious little route. Right of Herford's Crack is a ledge with a holly tree; start directly behind this bush.

1 50 feet. 6b. Climb up to the overhang, then utilising a wobbly and downward pointing spike it may be surmounted. Continue via a technical series of moves up a faint crack to finish on awkward jams then easier ground above.

Bonfire of the Vanities   50 feet   E2   (1990)

The next crack, six feet right of the holly forms a pillar of rock below the small overhang.

1 50 feet. 5c. Boldly ascend the front face of the pillar to reach good jams and protection. Superb and sustained jamming leads to the top.

Far West Buttress   100 feet   Very Difficult

The right edge of the buttress offers some pleasant climbing. A suggested route is to start up the slab and crack to a ledge left of a large leaning rock. Climb its left edge or a short chimney, then a groove above and layback to a flake on the left. Farther left a short crack ends the climb.

Girdle Traverses. There is no natural line, but the whole cliff can be girdled at about Severe standard. Any route is bound to meander. Some prior knowledge of the anatomy of the cliff will help.

Cwm Cneifion   (Cwm of the Flocks or Clippings)

OS Ref. 656 587

This secluded cwm, sometimes known as the Nameless Cwm, is tucked in way above Cwm Idwal, nestling between Y Gribin and the Seniors' Ridge of Glyder Fawr. At the head of the cwm looms the massive dark profile of Clogwyn Du; a high mountain bastion of Glyder Fawr that can raise a shudder in travellers passing along the summit ridge. The opposite slopes are bounded by the untidy rock landscapes of the West Face of Y Gribin, whilst beckoning at the entrance to the cwm stands the Sub-Cneifion Rib, an elegant stairway to the delights above.

★★**Sub-Cneifion Rib** 410 feet Very Difficult   (1931)
Positively idyllic, either as an approach to Cwm Cneifion or on a sunny evening when returning from a route on the Slabs. Apart from the easy break the climbing is delicate, and on marvellously firm rock. Start at the foot of the main rib.
1 70 feet. Step onto the rib from behind a pointed block. Climb the well-worn cracks and grooves on the crest to a crevasse stance. The rib beyond the grassy gully on the right can be climbed to join the normal way at 140 feet.
2 60 feet. A bulge, climbed on the left, proves interesting and interest persists with a crack running straight up the front of the rib. A good ledge soon arrives.
3 170 feet. An area of terraces now intervenes, offering excuse enough to sit back in idle contemplation. Scramble past a standing spike to the final section or take the rib on the left.
4 110 feet. Gain a shelf on the edge of the nose on the right and move delicately up a shallow groove. This leads back onto the front of the rib, where a crack cutting the crest leads to the top.

A fine little pitch has been climbed up and left of the base of Sub-Cneifion Rib.

★**Scimitar Crack** 80 feet Very Severe   (1980)
Start at a grassy bay under the short rightwards facing corner

half-way up the left-hand side of the buttress.
1 80 feet. 4c. Ascend the corner and the diverting jamming crack in the wall above. Finish up Sub-Cneifion Rib.

South Climb 80 feet Hard Severe   (1947)
Not a very good climb, but it can be done after the rib. Start below the steep south wall of the upper rib.
1 80 feet. 4a. Use a flat step to get beneath a nose, move into a steep recess and gain a mantelshelf on the right wall. A tricky move round the edge leads to a groove and rock finger. Continue up the groove in the right of the rib above.

The chimney to the right of the previous route can be climbed at Severe.

About half-way between Sub-Cneifion Rib and Idwal Slabs is a small slab.

Tooty Frooty 60 feet E1   (1989)
Start at the centre of the slab.
1 60 feet. 5b. Ascend directly to a small rowan, traverse delicately leftwards then go up again along the obvious line.

Angharad 50 feet E3   (1989)
A direct version of Tooty Frooty at 6b starting 15 feet further left.

West Face Y Gribin

Scree and cliff mix uneasily above the Sub-Cneifion Rib, but from this area three rocky arêtes, affording pleasant climbing and scrambling, reach up to the crest of the Gribin Ridge. The left-hand arête is small and nondescript. A scree-slope separates it from the central arête, **Pinnacle Edge** (170 feet, Moderate, 1936); this gives some simple climbing by keeping strictly to the crest. Beyond the next double scree-shoot the most prominent ridge forces through to give:

★★**Cneifion Arête** 450 feet Moderate   (1905)
A profusion of pinnacles, and the heady exposure of the steep scarp wall, give a route that is reminiscent of the Alps. Start at a shallow groove in the wall just right from the arête.
1 80 feet. Climb, moving around left into a short open chimney. Belay on ledges above this.
Above this the difficulties gradually ease but it is a delightful scramble for 370 feet.

Clogwyn Du Ymhen Y Glyder

1. The Crack   E1
2. Travesty   E1
3. Var. Finish
4. Stratosphere   E2
5. Hebenwi   E1
6. Var. Finish
7. Manx Wall   HS
8. Pillar Chimney   D
9. Clogwyn Du Gully   S
10. Finish, as described
11. Right-Hand Branch

Photo: Malcolm Griffiths

Higher up, **Tower Rib** (200 feet, Moderate, 1936) rises from the chaos. The route takes the left edge, where a crack at half-height offers some resistance.

Clogwyn Du Ymhen Y Glyder

(Black Crag at the top of the Glyders)   OS Ref. 646 582

This high mountain crag rises impressively from the head of Cwm Cneifion. It can play with the imagination; its sudden appearance, in swirling mist, plunging into the cwm creates an impression that it is a cliff of much greater scale. The routes are concentrated and absorbing, and the outlook is magnificent. From the top of the Upper Cliff of Glyder Fawr, you can easily drop into this quiet cwm to round off the day. The more single-minded can opt for the long flog up the contour path past the Sub-Cneifion Rib.

The lower right-hand side of the cliff has two obvious gullies. The main one, on the extreme right, is Clogwyn Du Gully; this is separated from Pillar Chimney by a buttress topped by a slender pillar. To the left of this the terrific main face dominates the cliff. It seems hardly feasible that Manx Wall pushes a route below the top barrier of overhangs, and that Hebenwi gets round the lower band striving for a way up the wall. On the left side of the wall a slanting gutter is the objective of Travesty, which first has to do battle with the overhanging band, and farther left the fierce Crack has a similar problem. Then the cliff becomes short; there is a chimney and gully before it merges with the hillside.

The Crack   200 feet   E1 (2pts. aid)   (1969)
A fierce, steep crack with a difficult entry which is rather prone to damp, slimy conditions. Start at a large spike up to the left of Travesty.
1 100 feet. 5b. Climb steeply up left and then right to join Travesty. Use a peg to get up to a small grass ledge on the left and then a sling on a spike to reach the crack. Climb the crack to the grass terrace.
2 100 feet. Go easily to the large ledge at the back wall. Climb the crack in the wall above, and the groove above that.

Travesty   280 feet   E1   (1943/1984)
A bold route which tackles the slanting chimney/crack dominating the left side of the cliff. A direct approach is barred by overhangs, so more devious tactics are adopted. Start at the cave beneath the

overhang.

1 60 feet. Take the parallel grooves to the left and belay in a luscious corner.

2 50 feet. 5b. Gain a rock ledge, traverse right into a corner and climb strenuously up to good spikes. Go down and round the overhanging nose to an old peg. Continue rightwards, in an airy position, to a niche then move up and right to belay at the foot of the chimney.

3 50 feet. 4a. Follow the chimney, which narrows to an overhanging crack. Belay in the bed of the chimney.

4 120 feet. Little more than an easy gully to finish.

Variation

3a 90 feet. 4b. An alternative finish takes the broken wall left of the chimney.

★★**Stratosphere** 250 feet E2   (1982)

An absorbing and airy climb up some steep ground between Hebenwi and Travesty. Start at the lowest point of the cliff.

1 30 feet. 4c. As for Hebenwi to the grass ledge.

2 50 feet. 5c. Ascend the obvious diagonal ramp on the left to gain a foothold, with difficulty, on the lip of the overhang. Climb the wall above until it is possible to hand-traverse to a sentry box stance.

3 130 feet. 5a. Make an exposed traverse to the arête and move up to a ledge on its right. Start up a groove but step right onto the steep wall; now trend up leftwards to the grassy ledges. The crack from the sentry box can be climbed to join Travesty.

4 40 feet. Climb the chimney, though the last pitch of Hebenwi is more appropriate.

Variation

4a 60 feet. 5a. From the lowest grassy ledge take the wall just left of the chimney of Travesty, passing a small overhang on the left.

★★**Hebenwi** 250 feet E1   (1969)

The main face is a powerful challenge amidst steep surroundings and with considerable exposure. Start at the lowest rock left of the foot of the easy rake slanting up to Pillar Chimney.

1 30 feet. 4c. Climb the steep initial rock, trending right to a large grass ledge.

2 90 feet. 5b. Traverse right for 15 feet then climb straight up the steep wall and the intimidating bulge above. Take the thin crack ahead then go right to a grassy bay.

3 40 feet. 5a. Climb the shallow groove, passing over the looming block, and continue more steeply, making a difficult pull onto the slab on the left. Belay farther left.

4 90 feet. 4c. Get onto the arête above and climb to the top, turning the overhang on the left.

Variation
4a 100 feet. 4b. Traverse back to the slab, go round the corner and climb directly to the top on splendid holds.

★★**Manx Wall**   180 feet   Hard Severe   (1942)
An exciting route. Well-positioned and interesting throughout, despite being so short. Start by scrambling up the chimney/rake to the Pillar.
1 45 feet. Move out left along lines of weakness leading to a stance and good belay.
2 35 feet. 4a. Climb the groove to the right, on small but good holds, to a tiny stance with belays on the left.
3 35 feet. 4a. Climb a tricky corner and go left to a narrow grassy ledge and thread belay.
4 65 feet. 4a. Crux. Cross the delicate slab to a crack. Traverse left beneath the imposing overhangs and escape, on big holds, to a ledge up on the left. Take a steep crack farther left to finish. All very exposed.

Chastity   330 feet   Hard Severe   (1943)
A high-level traverse that continues the line of the last pitch of Manx Wall instead of breaking out to the top.
1,2 & 3 115 feet. As for Manx Wall.
4 40 feet. 4a. Climb the delicate slab to a crack then make an exposed traverse left to a large block.
5 45 feet. Descend the easy upper chimney of Travesty.
6 60 feet. 4a. Traverse out to a perched block then climb up left to reach the long grass rake. Spike belay.
7 70 feet. Continue horizontally along the grass until a scoop provides the last bit of climbing to easy ground.

Pillar Chimney   180 feet   Difficult   (1907)
An unusual route, about as different as possible from the previous very open ones, being an enclosed rift in the rock. Start at the chimney/rake slanting up to the pillar.
1 50 feet. The easy introductory chimney leads to a loose landing in the rubble bed, then scramble up to the pillar.
2 60 feet. Squeeze into the tight chimney and tunnel up to reach the top of the pillar. A superb viewpoint!
3 70 feet. Descend 10 feet on the right and step onto the slab beyond. The difficulties soon disappear.

The **Pillar Face** can be climbed (75 feet, Very Difficult).

Clogwyn Du Gully   300 feet   Severe   (1895)
This makes quite a good climb, though it is escapable at several
points. Difficulties may depend on the quantity of water you are
prepared to tolerate. Start at the obvious Y-Gully on the right side of
the cliff.
1 120 feet. Easily up the gully bed, to the divide.
2 80 feet. Take the crack to a ledge on the left wall. Climb a greasy
slot, then pass a difficult chockstone on the left to an easier part of the
gully.
3 40 feet. Continue up easy steps and a mossy chimney.
4 60 feet. Go round the long rib on the left and climb a strenuous
chimney/crack to the top. The original way is the natural gully bed on
the right.

The right-hand branch of the gully is undistinguished and very
disappointing.

Cwm Idwal

Idwal Slabs and Walls

OS Ref. 645 591

Cwm Idwal provides some of the grandest mountain scenery in North Wales; the initial impact is enhanced by its being a mere 15 minutes walk from the bustle of Ogwen Cottage. The fine mountain of Y Garn, bold and angular, exposes a craggy flank to the Cwm, Clogwyn y Geifr, riven by the Devil's Kitchen, glowers over the waters of Llyn Idwal. The Slabs themselves rise in a glorious sweep, from the far side of the lake, to meet the Upper Cliff of Glyder Fawr. The Slabs are the major attraction of Cwm Idwal. They are supported on the left by the East Wall, and terminated on the right by the West Wall escarpment. These steeper sections augment the modest angle and languid grace of the slabs. Holly Tree Wall makes a fine headwall, and a more serious challenge. Many will prefer to scramble round this and, if they wish, follow the crest of the Seniors' Ridge in an easy ascent to the summit of Glyder Fawr.

The area offers a wealth of climbing of every standard of difficulty. Yet its best feature is the way in which a combination of routes can be easily linked to produce an irresistible continuous ascent. From Llyn Idwal to the summits, via the Slabs, the Walls, then on to the Upper Cliff and perhaps Clogwyn Du.

East Wall

The wall is quite complex in character and takes some time to appreciate; a subtle combination of alluring ramps and bulging walls pitted in profusion with bubbly holds which are a joy to use. The climbs are equally subtle, involving balance work, where the sequence of moves is important, especially because of the exposed position and limited protection.

A series of inset slabs defines the lower area, the cleanest of which is taken on the Girdle Traverse of the wall. Most climbs start high up above the broken area, from a large grass terrace at the foot of a broad section of quartz slab. Heather Weakness and Heather Wall start up the apron of slab coming down from the right. The narrow ramp of Rake End Chimney can be seen slanting up to the left from this. Between the chimney and the wide undulating slab of Ash Tree Wall stands the proud face of the Tower. The wall then becomes divided by a terrace; the top pitch of Grooved Wall shows up clearly above the grassy bay of the Meadow. Beyond this is the start of the Suicide Wall area. The climbs are described from RIGHT to LEFT, starting at the lowest part of the wall.

★★ Game, Set and Match   130 feet   E6   (1987)

The narrow wall slanting up leftwards beneath the first two pitches of Tennis Shoe provides an entertaining route with continuous interest and good protection. Start as for Tennis Shoe.

1 130 feet. 6b. Gain the leftwards slanting crackline in the middle of the wall. Progression is increasingly difficult and the final section enigmatic.

Hargreaves' Slab and Wall   145 feet   Very Difficult   (1930)

Low down, a large rectangle of slab abuts the flanking wall of the Slabs. The slab is entertaining, the wall optional. Start at the foot of the slab.

1 80 feet. Climb the left edge of the slab, or in the corner.
2 25 feet. Follow obvious holds to a stance on the wall.
3 40 feet. Climb the quartz slab and go rightwards up a short wall to reach Tennis Shoe. Another way follows the slab along a curious quartz seam and reaches Heather Weakness to finish.

Y Grug   180 feet   E2   (1991)

A bit of a filler in, but reasonably independent, with some bold climbing. Start at a dirty corner, gained by going round and down to the right of Heather Wall, below a line of bulges.

1 100 feet. 5a. Ascend the corner for a few feet to a line of holds leading up diagonally left to a weakness on the left-hand side of the bulges. Pull through the bulge, then go up the slab, keeping right of the vertical crack of Heather Wall. Belay at the obvious stance, as for Heather Wall.
2 80 feet. 5b. Ascend the groove above the belay to a large grassy ledge. Launch out horizontally leftwards from the ledge along a break, passing a crucial Friend 2½ placement, to a footledge at the base of a slim groove. A couple of difficult moves now gains some good flat holds and a larger groove trending rightwards; finish up this to belay on the slabs.

Heather Weakness   140 feet   Very Difficult   (1931)

A nice climb, but it evades the main challenge. Start at the large grassy terrace below the apron of slab about 200 feet up from the base of the cliff.

1 100 feet. Climb up the gangway on the right on pockets towards a

Idwal: East Wall

1. Route 5	VD	5. London Lady	E1
2. Ash Tree Wall	VS	6. Rake End Chimney	VD
3. Stepped Corner Start	VS	7. Heather Wall	VS
4. The Tower	E2		

grass patch. Staying on the right, continue up the slab until a traverse can be made to a small ledge on the low wall to the right. Step round a corner to reach a good ledge.
2 40 feet. Cross the rib on the right to join Tennis Shoe.

★★**Heather Wall**   170 feet   Very Severe   (1929)
A really good route that brings out the fundamental qualities of the wall. The climbing is exposed and honest, on holds which are small and secure. Start at the foot of the gangway, as for Heather Weakness.
1 100 feet. 4b. Climb up the gangway but trend more steeply leftwards once the slab is reached, to a small stance at its apex.
2 70 feet. 4c. There is a bulging rib on the left beyond the 'holdless corner', which can only be considered as escape routes. Traverse left and go up the rounded arête to a bulge; pull over this to reach an easy groove, which connects with Tennis Shoe.

London Lady   150 feet   E1   (1980)
The delicate virtues of directness and elegance lead on to a finish in a very open position, thoroughly enjoyable. Start just left of the gangway of Heather Weakness.
1 50 feet. 4c. Take the rounded rib to a triangular grass ledge at the foot of the ramp of Rake End Chimney.
2 100 feet. 5b. From the ramp, climb close to the edge of the curving arête to reach the traverse of Heather Wall. Above this lies a shallow groove, which must be approached from the left. It makes a very pleasant finish.

Rake End Chimney   200 feet   Very Difficult   (1929)
A route with a difference; it has a solid mountaineering feel. Start as for Heather Weakness.
1 50 feet. Climb straight up the wall, past a rock ledge, to the triangular grass stance at the foot of the rake. The belay is poor, so it might be best to continue.
2 80 feet. Follow the rake leftwards up to the chimney.
3 70 feet. The V-chimney itself is easy, but the walls soon close in and one is persuaded to escape by a traverse to the right over slabs made appreciably more difficult by drainage.

Rake End Wall   130 feet   Hard Very Severe   (1965)
Some interesting and rather nice climbing but somewhat overshadowed by the more powerful surroundings. Start at the upper end of the retaining wall of the rake. Approach across a slab from the foot of Ash Tree Wall.
1 60 feet. 5a. The wall on the right is taken on small holds to gain

the comfortable stance below Rake End Chimney.

2 70 feet. 5a. A pocketed groove on the right leads to a bulge, above which a further groove slants to the top.

★**The Tower** 165 feet E2 (1981)

This is obvious, in a staunch position above Ash Tree Wall. The route skilfully deals with its steep face. Start at the top right-hand corner of the approach slab.

1 45 feet. 5b. Go up the groove, over a bulge and exit right to the stance at Rake End Chimney. Bold.

2 80 feet. 5c. Climb the front of the Tower, moving onto the sharp edge left of the Chimney and continuing up the right-hand of the twin cracks to a lofty perch.

3 40 feet. 4c. A slab and a knife-edged flake lead to the scoop below the perched block that tops the Tower.

★**Ash Tree Wall** 180 feet Very Severe (1929)

Another very good climb with considerable exposure. It ventures up the undulating slab to finish on the side of the tower, the crux being reserved for the final few moves. Start at the left corner of the slab below the tower.

1 100 feet. 4a. Move along to the right and go straight up, pushing boldly through the bulge to where the wall eases. The climbing, on bubbly rock, feels very steep. Move up left again to a small ledge beneath a steep wall. There are two spikes above its left end.

2 45 feet. Go round to the left and climb past two grassy ledges to a stance just left of the Tower.

3 35 feet. 4a. Ignore the easy ground and go up to the tower. Move across its face to a corner, where a difficult exit brings one out on the polished slab below the perched block of Tennis Shoe.

Variation

The Stepped Corner Start 100 feet Very Severe

Takes the left edge of the slab above an obvious rock blade.

1a 100 feet. 4b. Climb an awkward groove to gain the steps in the blade. Continue up delicately until one can move right to join the ordinary way just below the stance.

Route 5 180 feet Very Difficult (1930)

The easiest way up the wall, of little merit or exposure. Start on the stony terrace left of Ash Tree Wall.

1 90 feet. A long steepening groove leads up to the Meadow.

2 40 feet. Cross a little slab at the foot of the next buttress to reach an edge on the right, above a low wall.

3 50 feet. Either of the cracks above will do, but the best finish is by

The Eaves. Move left onto the narrow continuation ledge, and climb on awkwardly spaced holds until the corner is rounded and a ledge arrives. Finish up the crack or groove.

Grooved Wall 160 feet Severe   (1929)
An excellent top pitch, set at a fair angle and situated above a more awe-inspiring part of the face. Start at the groove 10 feet right of Route 5.
1 90 feet. Go up the groove, staying out left where it is cleanest. Belay at the top of the Meadow.
2 70 feet. Climb up to a flake in the centre of the slabby wall. Then go round the corner to the left, where a long shallow scoop calls for steady progress, especially towards the top. This can also be approached by the exposed left edge.

★★★ **East Wall Girdle** 530 feet Very Severe   (1931)
A very fine rising traverse, sharing the characteristics of both the Slabs and the Walls. The situations are enthralling and though the climbing is not too difficult, it is sustained, so steadiness is of paramount importance to the whole team. Start left of the edge of the Slabs, as for Tennis Shoe.
1 90 feet. 4a. Climb the subsidiary slab of Tennis Shoe.
2 70 feet. Continue on the easy quartz slab.
3 80 feet. 4a. Take the crack in the edge of the next slab to a shallow cave. Move delicately round to the left onto the slab of Heather Wall. Climb to a small stance at its apex.
4 60 feet. 4b. Traverse left across a groove and move up the blunt arête towards the bulge, as for Heather Wall. Continue horizontally on widely-spaced holds until obliged to step down to the stance below Rake End Chimney.
5 70 feet. 4b. Get onto the slab on the left and cross it, moving through the slight undulation, to reach the small ledge on the skyline. Two spike belays farther up.
6 90 feet. A narrow terrace leads leftwards to the Meadow.
7 70 feet. 4b. The last pitch of Grooved Wall is most appropriate.

About half-way up the descent path, but away from the main walls is a little buttress with a steep, thin crack on its left-hand side.

Slim Pick Long Flap 30 feet E4   (1992)
A very trying little route, start below the obvious crack.
1 30 feet. 6b. A series of gymnastic moves past some small wires lead to a wider upper section protected by Friends. Belay on the edge, lower off, then scuttle up to retrieve one's gear. All very odd!

Suicide Wall

The continuation of the East Wall now assumes a serious countenance. It presents a long, grey face, water-stained and forbidding. The slanting break of Suicide Groove is obvious low down on the right. Capital Punishment forges a line boldly up the centre; to its right is Route 2, which comes out of a recess to skirt the blankest section. The famous, original line of Route 1 is on the streaked wall farther left; the twin grass patches of its ledge form a hopeful feature.

The climbing is steep and uncompromising, and clearly needs a confident approach.

Suicide Groove   150 feet   E1   (1948)

By far the least intimidating of the Suicide Wall routes. A good natural line with a tough finish. The big leftward-leaning groove forms a wide ramp on the right-hand end of the Wall. Start at a flake at its foot.

1 110 feet. 5b. The slab just left of the groove leads quite pleasantly to a small ledge, 15 feet below a sharp overlap. Climb the scoop and boldly overcome the overlap. Cross to a notch on the right wall, or layback up the remainder of the groove.

2 40 feet. 4c. Walk over and take the rightmost groove.

Variation

The Direct Finish   80 feet   E2

A hard, though very much better, finish.

3a 80 feet. 5c. Climb the obvious groove just on the left, and its shallower left-hand continuation.

Jailbreak   70 feet   E3   (1979)

A short fierce problem on the wall overlooking the Groove. Start left of the start of Suicide Groove.

1 30 feet. 5b. Climb straight up into a diamond-shaped scoop and exit right, to a grass patch in Suicide Groove.

2 40 feet. 6a. Make some difficult moves to reach the steep crack in the right wall. Climb this directly to the top.

Suspended Sentence   90 feet   E3   (1971)

The steep slab left of Suicide Groove is open and inviting. A few exquisite moves past the overlap provide the thrills. Start at a squat pedestal left of Suicide Groove.

1 90 feet. 5c. Go directly up the slab to the overlap, peg. Move up and climb diagonally rightwards to reach the top of Suicide Groove. This is all quite hard. The Direct Finish of Suicide Groove makes an appropriate continuation.

Idwal: Suicide Wall

Last Rites   140 feet   E3   (1976)
A desperate start leads to delectable climbing. Start 20 feet farther up
from Suspended Sentence where a high step at the base of the wall
provides a comfortable grassy platform.
1 140 feet. 6a. Take the thin crack, or the rib on the left at 5c, which
leads up to the enticing flakes above the bulge on Route 2, peg.
Move left to a brown scoop and climb steeply to the upper slabs.
Follow the edge of the slab, past a pocket, finishing up a thin crack.

★**Suicide Wall Route 2**   140 feet   E2   (1963)
The climb skirts below the very blank area, crossing Last Rites, to
reach the more slabby ground on the right. Start below a
crescent-shaped recess a short way up the wall.
1 90 feet. 5b. Get up into the recess. Climb round a blunt rib to gain
a line of flakes leading away to the right. There is a peg runner and a
few awkward moves before a ledge arrives.
2 50 feet. 5a. The groove ahead, escaping over its right edge.

★★**Penal Servitude**   150 feet   E4   (1977)
A very serious route providing some fine climbing, on a steeper
section of the wall. Start as for Last Rites, on the grass-topped step.
1 40 feet. 6a. Take the slight ramp leading up leftwards to the
crescent-shaped recess on Route 2; poorly protected.
2 110 feet. 5c. A thin crack shows the way but peters out early,
leaving a steep stretch before the girdle ledge. An awkward thread
gives some protection. Take the water-streak on the right to reach the
edge of the slab, where a thin crack leads to the top.

★★★**Capital Punishment**   160 feet   E4   (1971)
The best climb here, sustained and delicate. A rounded low relief rib
tapers to infinity; its right side makes an open groove with the wall to
provide an exciting challenge. Start as for Route 2.
1 20 feet. 5a. Climb into the crescent-shaped recess.
2 140 feet. 6a. Climb to the left across an intricate triangular slab.
Go on up the steep groove. It is not easy, but a good thread beckons,
and better holds then lead to the girdle ledge. Continue on the steep
ramp, delightful; Route 1 comes in from the left, though it is possible
to avoid this by climbing the overlap on the right and finishing more
directly.

Death Row   100 feet   E3   (1977)
A hard alternative way to the ledge on Route 1. Start where a
shallow grassy bay runs into the wall left of Route 2.
1 100 feet. 5c. Take a vague brown depression up to the left, it

steepens at 30 feet to a tiny scoop. Delicately climb to the ledge of Route 1 and follow the rest of this to the top.

★★ **Mur y Meirwon** 110 feet E5   (1979)
The initial crack sees many failures but leads to the fine rubescent upper wall. Start directly beneath the ledge of Route 1.
1 110 feet. 6b. A straight, desperately thin crack leads up the bulging wall to the ledge. From its right-hand end climb up, then trend left across the steep red rock, passing a stacked pair of pegs, to an undercut. Better holds on the right lead to the top.

Y Meirwon Byw 110 feet E5   (1991)
A technically easier but scarier start to the route above. Start below the shallow groove just up and to the left of the crack of Mur y Meirwon, below the grassy ledge.
1 110 feet. 6a. Ascend the open groove, not without trepidation, until it is possible to gain the right-hand end of the ledge. Move round to the right then up leftwards as for Mur y Meirwon.

★ **Suicide Wall Route 1** 100 feet E2   (1945)
An extraordinarily bold lead for its day. It marked a significant leap in standard for wall climbing and still remains a serious proposition. Start below and just left of the two grass patches.
1 100 feet. 5c. Start straight up the wall; a hard move is made to pass a tiny spike recessed in a pocket. The difficulties ease quickly towards the ledge. Go to the right, descending a little, then climb a difficult scoop. Now move rightwards, following improving holds, to where a slab leads up beneath the diagonal overhang to the top.

Zero 100 feet E6   (1979)
An uncompromising test-piece, direct, and destitute of the comfort of protection. Start as for Route 1.
1 100 feet. 6a. Start up the first moves of Route 1 but stay on the wall on the left to cross the girdle. Move up right and then left to finish up a faint groove in the upper wall. This is no more than a shallow indentation between the finishes of The Garotte and Mur y Meirwon.

Solitary Confinement 130 feet E2   (1978)
Escapes the isolation of its position to gain a 'Reprieve'. Start left of Route 1, beneath the final groove of The Garotte.
1 90 feet. 5b. Go up leftwards into a hollow in the wall. The bulge above gives a moment's excitement before a ledge intrudes.
2 40 feet. 5b. Climb the left edge of the obvious leaning corner.

The Garotte   290 feet   E4   (1971)
The girdle traverse of the Suicide Wall area is a sustained and exacting undertaking.
1 80 feet. 4b. Pitch 1 of Suicide Groove.
2 90 feet. 5b. Climb diagonally leftwards, crossing Route 2, to reach a narrow gangway leading to the ledge at the top of the crux groove of Capital Punishment.
3 50 feet. 5c. A difficult and slightly descending traverse has to be made to reach the ledge of Route 1. Problematic belay.
4 70 feet. 6a. Make a further short descent before moving round into a shallow groove. This is very steep, giving some thin bridging, and is a fitting finale.

Variation
Start as for Zero and step left to continue as for Pitch 4 of the Garotte. This makes a good one pitch climb in its own right at E4 6a.

Rhiwiau Caws   (Cheese Slabs)
or Idwal Slabs

The Idwal Slabs are by tradition a proving ground for those taking their first steps in the sport; however, they may not be suitable for total beginners. A smooth slab, unbroken for 450 feet, its many holds present themselves in all manner of shapes, but they are not large; many are merely excrescences on the rock surface, and are now well-burnished from years of traffic. Openness gives a notable impression of exposure, and ledges are few and a considerable distance apart.

The slabs are arranged in a progression of low-relief overlaps, which give definition to each of the climbs. The most natural lines are described, but there is no need for stubborn adherence and several delightful variations can be discovered.

It is to be hoped that establishments using the slab routes for instruction will refrain from using their initial pitches for abseil practice; it often hinders other parties who wish to climb the routes. Other sections of cliff would seem to be more suitable, for example Idwal Buttress.

Idwal Slabs

1. Game, Set and Match   E6
2. Tennis Shoe   HS
3. The Direct Route   HVS
4. The Ordinary Route   D

5. Charity   VD
6. Hope   VD
7. Faith   VD

Before embarking on the Slabs it is essential that the newcomers are aware of the ways off, as all the climbs end at the terrace below Holly Tree Wall. There are two ways:

Easy Way
Follow the terraces and cracks to the left of Holly Tree Wall by a devious but well-worn route. At about 300 feet above the slabs a rock shoulder is crossed and a steep gully descended to the vegetated slabs that guard access to the Nameless Cwm. Either descend the water-worn slabs below the East Wall or move out on to the hillside path.

West Traverse
From the right-hand end of the terrace go along the ledge below Javelin Buttress to a corner. Climb the corner, or the short exposed crack on the right (Very Difficult), to a block and easy ground, then descend the hillside beyond Idwal Buttress. It would be better to remain roped up for this traverse as fatalities have occurred here.

★★Tennis Shoe   475 feet   Hard Severe   (1919)
This really enjoyable climb has more atmosphere than the other slab routes, thanks to its superior position above the East Wall. Start just left of the main sweep of the slab, where a narrow subsidiary of steeper slab runs up to a rock ledge.
1 95 feet. 3c. Climb this slab. The holds close to the edge are now quite smooth and rounded.
2 50 feet. Go round to the right, where a groove leads to a crack in the edge of the main slab.
3 60 feet. Continue on the edge of the slab to a small stance level with a gully on the left.
4 120 feet. Take the delightfully airy rib and quartz slab to the left of the gully to a good rock stance.
5 100 feet. Go easily up the remaining slab to a grassy terrace.
6 50 feet. 4a. This last pitch brings a welcome note of exultation. Take a stance beside the tower, on the left. Climb the steep face of the tower to a scoop then move up the slab beneath the perched block. As a final touch one can pull over this.

Variation
The Direct Route   150 feet   Hard Very Severe
This is the more aesthetic start to the route; there is some very thin climbing and the protection is not over-generous.
1a 150 feet. 4c. Take the long scoop in the edge of the main slab. This steepens, so one is forced to move right onto the slab and climb directly to the stance of Pitch 2.

The Other Direct Route   150 feet   Severe
Start just right of the scoop on the very edge of the main slab.
1a 150 feet. 4b. Friction moves lead to the base of a crack which
descends from the shoulder. Follow the crack to its end, move left for
10 feet to gain another crack which leads to the stance of Pitch 2.

★**The Ordinary Route**   475 feet   Difficult   (1897)
This is the original route on the Slabs. It goes quite easily though
strangely it has little actual slab climbing until high up, where it opens
out. There are frequent places to belay and the route is thus suitable
for beginners. The route follows the deep furrow, 20 feet in from the
left edge of the main slab. A cosy niche is reached at 150 feet.
Above this is the hardest bit of the climb. The slab steepens slightly
and it is easiest to follow the crack that leans to the right before
moving back into a polished scoop. Good holds now lead up easily
and eventually the route narrows down to a polished crack below the
final steepening in the slab. Step right from the top of the crack onto
this slab and follow good holds to a large ledge on the right. Either
sidle off to the left or climb the rocks on the right to the terrace above.
The more ambitious will enjoy climbing the final nose directly to the
block on the terrace (Very Difficult).

Quartz Eliminate   100 feet   Very Severe
A blatant eliminate and any deviation will lessen its potency. Start at
a rib right of The Ordinary Route directly under a 'letter-box' at 35
feet, where a Friend will be useful.
1 100 feet. 4b. Smear up the slab to the 'letter-box'; follow rock
blisters to a thin horizontal crack, continue on the same line to reach
quartz and a belay on Charity. Bold.

★★**Charity**   470 feet   Very Difficult   (1916)
An excellent and delightfully varied climb. It lies up the attractive
quartz-sheeted slab in the central area. Start about 30 feet right of
The Ordinary Route, below a scoop in the next layer of very polished
slab.
1 140 feet. Climb to the scoop; continue carefully up this to where it
steepens before delicately escaping to the right. Go easily up through
the quartz region on the left, then go up rightwards to a grassy ledge
in a corner.
2 80 feet. The corner leads to the quartz slabs, which is climbed until
it narrows. An overlapping edge forces one to veer to the left then
take a stance in a slot.
3 60 feet. Move back onto the quartz, staying close to the overlap,
and climb to a small ledge at the foot of a corner.

4 100 feet. Climb the corner, which can be greasy.
5 90 feet. Various ways lead to the block on the terrace.

Central Rib 450 feet Severe (1929)
An overlapping layer of slab forms a plausible rib running straight up the middle of the slabs. This makes a long and entertaining climb for those who have done the regular routes. It is a continuous exercise on tiny holds, but the temptation to stray is ever present; keep to the rib as closely as possible and use stances on Hope and Charity. Start at the base of the rib just right of Charity.
1 150 feet. Follow the rib to a bulge, just left of the V-slot of Hope. Pull through the bulge on quartz holds to regain the rib above and reach the first stance of Hope.
2 100 feet. Step left past the 'Twin Cracks' to reach the pocketed rib, continue as near the edge as possible. After 80 feet the angle eases and a thin vertical crack is reached. Move left to belay on Charity.
3 100 feet. Continue up the rib until it is impossible to keep off the polished holds of Charity.
4 100 feet. The rib has faded away, but reappears for a short while as a steep nose above a band of quartz; follow this to the terrace.

★★★**Hope** 450 feet Very Difficult (1915)
A great climb and justifiably famous. The pitches are long and elegant, up beautifully clean rock in comparative isolation. Start at the foot of Central Rib or just to the right.
1 150 feet. Take the quartz slab, or the rib, or groove on the left, to the long rock ledge. From the right climb a diagonal crack to the inverted V-slot which cuts through the undulation on the left. Above, a slab of quartz veneer ends at a large platform.
2 80 feet. The perilous Twin Cracks. It is not unusual to grab the jug at the top just as the feet fly off! It is then best to move delicately left and make for a small ledge where the overlap comes in.
3 70 feet. Continue up on fine holds in the slab ahead to a small stance in the overlapping corner.
4 90 feet. Climb the corner, turning a steep bit to the left. There is a ledge in the broken area higher up.
5 60 feet. Climb direct through the quartzy ground until steep rock forces the line round to the left to gain the terrace.

Geography 200 feet Very Difficult (1929)
Although the route is contrived it does have some pleasant climbing and serves to liberate parties from entanglement in a queue on Hope. Start at the first stance of Hope, right of the 'Twin Cracks'
1 110 feet. Move on to a small slab just right of the corner, a swing up right gains the rib. Keeping to its edge go up to a ledge with a

crack above. Step left to gain the base of another wide crack, from here tiptoe left above the lip of the overhang to reach a smaller rib and ascend this to a belay.

2 90 feet. Climb the bulge, then go leftwards to the rib (do not continue up the wide, original, crack line of Faith); strut along the catwalk instead. Finish as for Faith.

Slabs Eliminate   150 feet   Very Severe   (1970)
A thin pitch which follows the pale streak in the slab right of Hope. Start directly beneath the streak under the first stance of Hope at a long ledge 40 feet above the base of the slabs.

1 150 feet. 4b. Step right and move up to gain the streak; follow this, boldly, to a ledge right of the Hope stance. Ascend the corner above, passing an overlap at its left-hand end, then up the rib of Geography. Faith West Finish or Sinner's Corner are the obvious continuations.

★★Faith   440 feet   Very Difficult   (1916)
Takes the remaining wide slab. A good climb, particularly near the top, though it suffers from a lack of individual identity. Start below the left edge of the final sheet of slab.

1 120 feet. Follow the curving edge of the slab all the way up to the left end of the big grassy terrace.

2 100 feet. Move leftwards along quartz veins and gain a crack. The slab above can then be reached.

3 50 feet. An easy groove leads to a stance at the West Wall where Faith West Finish rises steeply.

4 90 feet. Take the diagonal line to a ledge on the left, and climb the small holds on the very edge of the rib. The crack in the slab can be climbed but this has not the finesse.

5 80 feet. Climb up across the broken quartz bands to reach a crack, which leads round left to the terrace.

Subwall Climb   340 feet   Severe   (1925)
A more serious route with a moody feel compounded by the closeness of the West Wall and the dampness of the situation. Faith West Finish and Saint's Wall are recommended as welcome escapes. Start below the same plaque of slab as Faith.

1 120 feet. Follow a line of holds leading leftwards until a crack leads up the centre of the slab to the terrace.

2 90 feet. Climb the narrow pocketed slab on the right until forced to make a thin traverse below the impending West Wall. Make a hard move round a corner to a grassy ledge.

3 40 feet. Continue leftwards under the West Wall until it turns uphill to the start of Faith West Finish.

4 90 feet. Follow the slabby gutter to join Faith.

Holly Tree Wall

This steep barrier rears over the slabs so suddenly after the gentle angle below that it seems impervious to assault. Indeed, it took the best climbers of the day, to force its fine routes, for although the wall is short it is not juggy, nor are there many ledges. The climbing is concentrated, with a need for technique and a strong measure of boldness and there is a marvellous 'above it all' exposure. On the whole the wall is quick to dry; this is due to the perfect rock and an almost total lack of vegetation. Even the holly tree which once flourished at the foot of the chimney on Original Route has been plucked from the face, the occasion of a serious accident.

The wall is very broken on the left, where it merges with the Easy Way off the Slabs, but the grey tower of The Rampart soon stands out. Right of this, Original Route takes the crescent-shaped slab, which rises out of a recess in the main face and curves up to a wide crack on the right. Piton Route lies close to the edge of the next rib. The big natural break is Javelin Gully, its walls being at right-angles to each other. Lazarus cuts out across the left wall, and is a good introduction to the climbing. To the right of the gully is Javelin Buttress, smooth, sheer and grey; the face then joins the West Wall.

Cinderella's Twin 160 feet Severe   (1942)
A broken and artificial route. Start at a broad grassy crack at the left end of the wall.
1 70 feet. Climb the slab and pick a way up on the left to the heather belt. Spike belay.
2 90 feet. Move along the ledges and climb the crack and slab in the left edge to a quartz-topped ledge. A groove again on the left gives a steep finish with a hard pull out.

Cinderella 180 feet Hard Severe   (1929)
Quite a good climb. The damp conditions which usually prevail temper the approach, but it is still good fun. Start beneath the prominent buttress of The Rampart.
1 90 feet. 4a. Pass through a notch on the left to a short corner and an overlap. Pass this to the left, where pockets lead up to a narrow ledge in a corner beside The Rampart.
2 90 feet. Climb the rib on the left to reach a steep corner. This is the start of a weakness, which is followed to the top of the wall.

The Rampart 145 feet Very Severe   (1947)
Gives some very good climbing, but misses the main issue. Start at the boulder at the foot of Original Route.
1 75 feet. 4c. Climb into the groove of Original Route, then take the little overhung slab on the left out onto the face. Traverse left and

climb a crack to the stance of Cinderella.
2 70 feet. 4b. Take the wall on the right, on flat holds, to a groove then cross to the edge of The Rampart to finish.

★★**Rampart Corner** 120 feet E1 (1977)
A hard pitch taking the leaning corner right of The Rampart. Start as for The Rampart.
1 120 feet. 5b. Climb The Rampart but after the 15 foot traverse, break through the overhang to reach the corner crack. This is now followed to the top of the wall.

The thin crack between the top section of Rampart and Rampart Corner has been climbed at E2 5c, but with very little independent climbing.

Gobagape 120 feet E3 (1984)
A difficult route utilising the steep rock Between Rampart Corner and Ordinary Route. Start as for Original Route.
1 120 feet. 5c. Ascend the short pod-like groove, then the wall above to a ledge. Easier climbing leads to the terrace above.

★★**Original Route** 130 feet Very Severe (1918)
This is the route of the wall. A fine old climb that has fascinated generations of climbers, and it remains a worthy challenge to the aspirant hard man's ability. Start where a gangway curves down the centre of the wall to end at a deep groove, just above the terrace, on the left.
1 90 feet. 5a. Getting into the groove is the first problem. There must be a trick; some try for ages; some see it right away. The Crescent Slab is now a delight. It leads up beneath the overhang to a narrow chimney on the right. Insert an arm into the chimney, then a leg, and heave without dignity in a struggle to reach the rock bay above.
2 40 feet. 4b. The continuation crack is much easier, though the wall on the left can be taken in several places.

★★**Wall Variations**
1a 90 feet. 5a. Firstly, the Crescent Slab can be reached from the quartz-capped pinnacle on the right, where a line of holds leads up the initial wall. Then, instead of a chimney, the wall can be climbed. Go out left by a narrow ledge; a little below the chimney, a long stretch and a mantelshelf bring better holds and the rock bay within reach. An impressive pitch.

★**Piton Route** 120 feet Very Severe (1929)
A low-relief rib slants down the face right of Original Route; its left edge is square-cut. This gives a well-maintained and open climb that

is characteristic of the wall. Start at the corner on the left-hand side of the rib.

1 30 feet. 4a. Climb the corner and move across the rib to a stance on the right; sometimes too slippery to contemplate.

2 90 feet. 4b. Go up the crack; this relents at a meagre stance – the site of the historic, long-removed piton. The polished holds of Lazarus offer an escape, but the correct way lies up the crack in a steep little nose above.

Other Kingdom   120 feet   Severe   (1922)

Very contrived but pleasing climbing nevertheless. Start at the corner right of the rib.

1 30 feet. Ascend the corner to a stance.

2 90 feet. A semi-circular excursion; right then up to join the Lazarus traverse, left to the small 'piton' stance, then move up and out rightwards onto the easy slabs.

★Lazarus   140 feet   Severe   (c.1922)

This is the easiest route on the wall and it gives a welcome opportunity for parties who have completed Tennis Shoe to take to steeper ground. The crux is in an exciting position. Start at the foot of Javelin Gully.

1 55 feet. Climb the three steps of Javelin Gully and belay where it opens out into a bay.

2 85 feet. Traverse out across the wall, making for a rock nose way over on the left-hand side. Escape up a slabby groove just to the right of this; the way is barred by a steep little wall, which requires a moment's thought.

Karabiner Route   130 feet   Hard Severe   (1941)

Despite being very artificial there is some good climbing; it also broadens the options available. Start in Javelin Gully.

1 130 feet. Traverse horizontally left to the rib of Piton Route, descend a little and go over ledges and then up to a niche. Climb the wall to the right of the crack and continue directly trying to avoid the other routes

Javelin Gully   125 feet   Hard Severe   (1922)

An energetic little climb, which becomes more exposed than one would suspect. Start at the gully which cuts off Javelin Buttress.

1 55 feet. 4a. Climb the three pronounced steps in the gully and belay in the open bay.

2 70 feet. Climb the groove above and swing up to a mantelshelf on the left wall; a bold approach pays dividend. Step back right and

Ed Stone on the first ascent of *Grab and Flash It* (E4), Clogwyn y Tarw.
Photo: Ed Stone Collection

East Wall Girdle (VS), Cwm Idwal, George White climbing.
Photo: Paul Middleton

Rusty Baillie on *Suicide Wall Route 1* (E2), Suicide Wall, Idwal.
Photo: John Cleare

Dave Alcock and Martin Boysen making the first ascent of *The Garotte* (E4), Suicide Wall, Idwal. Photo: Ken Wilson

climb to the top. In dry conditions it is possible to bridge up the corner on the right of the bay.

★★**Javelin Blade** 120 feet E1   (1930)
A remarkable route for its time. The crux comes at the end of a long run-out, yet one has to be relaxed enough to commit oneself with confidence. Start as for Javelin Buttress.
1 120 feet. 5b. Follow Javelin Buttress, or a variation start coming into the groove from the right, to the thread. Cross the pock-marked slab to the left edge of the buttress. The Blade is the narrow pointed scarp that forms a little corner on the right. Climbing this feels very precarious; the difficulties are based on delicacy and uncertainty as one pulls onto the right edge. Finish direct, more easily.

★**Javelin Buttress** 120 feet Very Severe   (1925)
A fine pitch. It presents an intriguing problem on the smooth grey face of the buttress. The buttress to the right of Javelin Gully has a groove up its centre, giving the route.
1 120 feet. 4c. Climb the groove to where a slab breaks out to the left. Move up this to a scoop and a unique thread. Continue up past a series of mantelshelves to where the difficulties ease and so does the angle.

Wavelength Touch 85 feet E2   (1979)
A fiercely thin, but contrived, line running parallel to Javelin Buttress. Start on the ledge of West Traverse, below the buttress.
1 35 feet. 5c. Follow a vague crack left of Balcony Cracks. Move left on pockets and go over the bulge to the Balcony.
2 50 feet. 5c. Take the tapered corner on the left, then keeping in its line climb up to an easier crack on the right.

One More Calorie 50 feet E7   (1984)
Desperate climbing up the wall between the top pitches of Wavelength Touch and Balcony Cracks, starting at the latter.
1 50 feet. 6b. Very thin and precarious climbing leads to slightly easier ground.

Balcony Cracks 90 feet Very Severe   (1931)
A short route, which is interesting and not at all easy. Start at the narrow grass ledge of West Traverse.
1 40 feet. 4c. Climb the left-hand of the twin cracks until a line of pockets leads off left to reach the Balcony.
2 50 feet. 4a. Climb the crack on the right of the smooth wall, then ignore the easy way for the groove on the left.

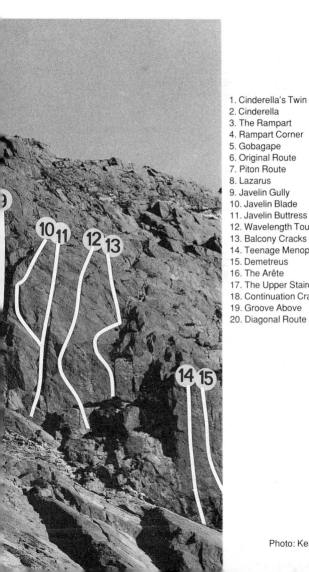

1. Cinderella's Twin   S
2. Cinderella   HS
3. The Rampart   VS
4. Rampart Corner   E1
5. Gobagape   E3
6. Original Route   VS
7. Piton Route   VS
8. Lazarus   S
9. Javelin Gully   HS
10. Javelin Blade   E1
11. Javelin Buttress   VS
12. Wavelength Touch   E2
13. Balcony Cracks   VS
14. Teenage Menopause   E7
15. Demetreus   E3
16. The Arête   VD
17. The Upper Staircase   D
18. Continuation Crack   HVS
19. Groove Above   S
20. Diagonal Route   VS

Photo: Ken Wilson

★ **Girdle Traverse of Holly Tree Wall**   340 feet   Very Severe
(1929)
This is a very exciting girdle, involving a descent of Original Route to
cross The Rampart. A higher line can be taken at this point though,
and if started from the Balcony will reduce the difficulties to Severe.
Start as for Balcony Cracks.
1 40 feet. 4c. Climb Balcony Cracks to the Balcony.
2 40 feet. 4a. Traverse round a rib to the thread on Javelin Buttress.
Move across onto the edge of the pock-marked slab, and from a little
higher step into Javelin Gully.
3 60 feet. 4b. Do the long traverse of Lazarus but at its end continue
round the base of a steeper rib to reach the rocky bay. The easier
finish continues leftwards from here.
4 60 feet. 4c. Slither down the chimney of Original Route and
reverse the Crescent Slab. Belay beneath the overhang.
5 50 feet. 4c. As for The Rampart, across the front of the face to the
ledge on Cinderella.
6 90 feet. 4b. Finish up Cinderella or Cinderella's Twin.

Continuation Wall
This is a similar, but much smaller version of Holly Tree Wall, which forms
the next tier. It adds a good pitch on the way up to the Upper Cliff of
Glyder Fawr, or to while away the time if the day is almost done.

★ **The Arête**   80 feet   Very Difficult   (1929)
A really good pitch, which will complement the routes on the slabs.
Start at the corner that leads over the slab on the left-hand end of the
facet. Quickly move out onto the left edge of the slab and finish
delicately up this.

The Upper Staircase   70 feet   Difficult
The obvious steep staircase formation in the centre of the face. This is
flanked by a pock-marked wall.

★ **Continuation Crack**   60 feet   Hard Very Severe 5a
The thin crack running straight up the face left of Groove Above gives
a good hard pitch with a cracking finish.

★ **Groove Above**   80 feet   Severe   (1926)
This is the obvious V-groove, which cuts deeply into the wall. The
entry is a perplexing problem (4b), the groove more reasonable;
where it steepens, escape to the right.

Diagonal Route 50 feet Very Severe 5a
This takes the twin cracks 30 feet farther to the right. Climb to a
scoop, then climb leftwards crossing Groove Above.

Scrutiny will produce other boulder problem type pitches, as will many
of the little walls on the terraces leading to the Upper Cliff of Glyder
Fawr. The best of which is **Lava Slab** (Very Severe) reached by an
amble over to the right and up two tiers; 80 feet of good rough rock that
is well worth finding.

West Wall

The West Wall rises over the main sweep of the slabs, bringing them to
an abrupt termination, before merging with Holly Tree Wall. It is not
continuous, but it is divided into separated facets; each faces forward.
The climbs are only short but they are given a vitality by their elevated
position and steepness.

The highest facet is a wall, square and bold. The vague crack in the
centre marks the line of Demetreus. Below, Faith West Finish takes the
more amiable triangular section. The slanting rectangle of Rowan Tree
Slabs is obvious from its sharp left edge; this is the longest route on the
wall. Just to the right and a little lower, stand the two short towers of
Penthouse and Last Exit.

The upper routes are best approached from Faith or Subwall Climb; one
can descend from these via Idwal Staircase, the long black slot that cuts
deeply into the base of Idwal Buttress.

★**Teenage Menopause** 80 feet E7   (1984)
A difficult and bold route taking the wall, pillar and crack left of
Demetreus. Start at a grassy bay right of Faith Pitch 4.
1 80 feet. 6b. Climb leftwards to the blunt pillar, where a tenuous
series of moves may gain the crack above, follow this to the top.

★★**Demetreus** 80 feet E3   (1979)
The uppermost facet is smooth in definition but shows a faint
weakness in its centre, which gives this superbly sustained pitch. Start
in the bay, as for Saint's Wall.
1 80 feet. 6a. Move up left where the semblance of a crack requires
a series of intricate manoeuvres to gain ground; then it gives out just
short of the top.

Saint's Wall 70 feet Very Difficult   (1930)
Takes the same wall as Demetreus but well to the right, towards the
corner. Start in the grassy bay at the foot of the wall, which is best

Idwal: Rowan Tree Slabs Area

Photo: Simon Car

1. Rowan Tree Slabs   E2
2. Thinking of the Girl   E2
3. Penthouse   HVS
4. Bread Line   E2
5. Ryvita   HVS
6. Summer Pudding   E1
7. Last Exit   VS

reached by a short traverse from pitch 4 of Faith.
1 70 feet. Move out from the corner to gain the first of three deeply carved niches; these form the route and require mild mantelshelf tactics.

Faith West Finish   100 feet   Severe   (1929)
An excellent pitch on the triangle of steep rock. It naturally stands alone, though it can be combined with other routes. Start from the third stance of Faith.
1 100 feet. Move to the top of a little pillar and climb the wall, trending leftwards to avoid the less-presentable rock. Clean and incut holds lead up to a horizontal block, where one can drop down the easy corner to take in Saint's Wall.

Sinner's Corner   90 feet   Very Severe   (1961)
The featureless corner right of Faith West Finish is well-guarded, but once reached makes a worthwhile pitch. Start from the second stance of Subwall Climb.
1 45 feet. 4b. Move diagonally right up the steep wall to a junction with the corner just below its upper continuation.
2 45 feet. 4c. Climb the corner above by bridging to the bulge, then move rightwards to easy ground.

Wrong Route   190 feet   Very Difficult
A wandering route that searches for the easiest way up Rowan Tree Slabs, but it has some fair moves and gives good views of the main slab on a busy day. Start in the corner 40 feet above the first stance of Subwall Climb at a detached pinnacle.
1 90 feet. Gain the left-hand end of the sloping 'gangway' on Rowan Tree Slabs, continue rightwards to the crack above the grassy rake. Ascend the crack to the large ledge.
2 100 feet. Move left to an airy step across the corner and so gain further slabs, trend diagonally leftwards to reach ledges and easy ground to a belay. A descent leftwards is possible to gain the foot of Saint's Wall.

★★Rowan Tree Slabs   155 feet   E2   (1929/1963)
The bold original route has been much improved to make an ascent of the slab in its entirety. The defects of a variation start and escape are thankfully discreet. Start from the first stance of Subwall Climb.
1 110 feet. 5c. An easy groove leads to the steep slab. Gain a smooth little gangway; it is thinly coated with quartz and runs back left. Carefully balance along this until the grassy rake can be reached (possible belay). Climb the slab, working up as far leftwards as possible. It gradually gets harder, the final move past a curious

pocket up to the ledge being very thin indeed. The original way sneaked off at about 80 feet.
2 45 feet. 5b. Climb the steep groove in the arête on the left to a ledge. Finish in a good position on the arête again.

Thinking of the Girl   50 feet   E2   (1984)
A strenuous but well-protected route that climbs the straight thin crack right of Rowan Tree Slabs pitch 2. Start at the base of the crack
1 50 feet. 5c. A series of awkward reaches up the crack gains a ledge and an easier crack above.

Penthouse   130 feet   Hard Very Severe   (1973)
A good climb, with a hard finish on the front of the steep tower right of Rowan Tree Slabs. Start at the right-hand end of the main sweep of the Slabs.
1 80 feet. 4a. Climb the damp corner on pockets and work left through a gap in the bulge to reach a broken slab. Climb this to a sloping stance.
2 50 feet. 5a. The foot of the tower offers no easy way. Firstly climb the crack on the left, then make a long stride to its edge. The groove and crack on the right are difficult to reach and lead up to the Penthouse.

★**Bread Line**   50 feet   E2   (1984)
The thin crack in the left wall of the deep groove right of Penthouse top pitch gives a good pitch. Start from the sloping stance of Penthouse.
1 50 feet. 5b. Steep and precarious crack climbing leads to easy slabs and a belay.

★**Ryvita**   50 feet   Hard Very Severe   (1984)
A fairly pleasant climb, though occasionally damp taking the deep groove right of Penthouse top pitch. Start on the sloping stance
1 50 feet. 5b. Float up the groove in a series of layaways and bridging moves.

★**Last Exit**   100 feet   Very Severe   (1973)
This makes the best use of the final facet of the West Wall. Start on a grassy ledge just above the right end of the Slabs.
1 60 feet. 4a. Climb a rather dirty quartz slab, then move steeply up the pock-marked wall on the right. Step left to a stance above the slab. Flake belay 10 feet higher.
2 40 feet. 4c. Go back to the flake and follow a rising traverse, which leads neatly to a shallow corner on the right. Climb the corner; be respectful when finishing.

★**Summer Pudding**   40 feet   E1   (1984)
1 40 feet. 5b. The crack and groove system left of Last Exit top pitch
gives some pleasant climbing.

Idwal Buttress

Further over to the right, beyond the West Wall, the black watercourse
of Idwal Staircase (previously known as Introductory Gully) cuts deeply
into the base of a heavily pock-marked wall.
The first two routes start high up on the Staircase, just to the right of an
arched overhang, at a seemingly wet (it often isn't) black and orange
streak.

Sluice Juice   50 feet   E4   (1992)
Quite a bold little route and the smaller sizes of Friends would be
found useful. Start about 50 yards up Idwal Staircase below a peg at
15 feet.
1 50 feet. 5c. Lean across the gulf and pull up onto a block to reach
the peg. Traverse boldly leftwards along the obvious line to gain a
huge pocket, then go up and left (Friend slots) to reach a hidden peg,
continue straight up.

Thorfinn Skullsplitter   50 feet   E4   (1992)
A fairly serious variant to Sluice Juice, start as for that route.
1 50feet. 6a. Follow Sluice Juice to the Friend slots, then undercut
right to reach a sloping shelf (a peg on the right is difficult to clip)
then finish direct.

The next routes start at the very base of Homicide Wall.

★**Homicide Wall**   125 feet   E3   (1971)
An exciting route following the diagonal line of huge pockets in the
wall overlooking Idwal Staircase. Start at the foot of the buttress.
1 80 feet. 4c. Follow the pockets up to a quartz gangway. Continue
round a blunt rib to a heathery stance.
2 45 feet. 5b. The wall above is very steep. Move up left, past two
old pegs, onto a small slab. Swing up boldly to a curious horizontal
spike in a pocket and climb steeply leftwards to reach an obvious jug.
Finish more easily.

★**The Hangman's Return**   120 feet   E4   (1986)
An interesting pitch up the wall right of Homicide Wall. Start as for
Homicide Wall
1 120 feet. 6a. Follow the Homicide Wall gangway until it is
possible to step right onto a steep pocketed wall at about 65 feet.
Ascend past two pegs and a thread to a small overlap, move right

and then up on spaced holds to reach large finishing holds. Belay well back.

Llofruddwyr 150 feet E4   (1990)
A series of delicate and entertaining moves up the blunt arête. Low in the grade. Start as for Homicide Wall.
1 150 feet. 5c. Follow Homicide Wall for 15 feet to a flake, then move out rightwards past a porthole to reach pockets and a crack. Step back left past a peg to a scoop, a series of fingery moves up the blunt rib gains easier ground above. Trend up leftwards to quartz seams and pull up on to the easier slab above. Belay well back.

Pocket Wall 75 feet Severe   (1963)
A very worthwhile little pitch, which takes the line of smaller pockets that leads to a groove in the front of the buttress. Start about 20 feet right of the previous route.
1 75 feet. Climb up, rather on the right, then follow the pockets. The final moves are awkward.

Idwal Buttress 300 feet Difficult
A pleasant route which follows the edge of the blunt rib, where the steep wall and easy-angled slabs join. A good place to escape to when the main slabs are heaving with climbers. Start at the foot of the rib.
1 150 feet. Keeping to the crest of the rib, steep at first, good rough rock leads to an easing of the angle. Continue past a large ledge to a heathery stance.
2 150 feet. The crest of the rib is now broader and slabbier. Wend a way up past ledges and a square recess to reach easy slopes and fine views of the bottlenecks on the classics.

Red Slab 300 feet Difficult
Scrappy climbing leads to a fine upper slab. Start at the foot of an easy angled rib 20 feet right of Idwal Buttress.
1 100 feet. Follow the broken rib to belay at a large grassy stance.
2 100 feet. Move right onto the slab, climb past twin diagonal cracks to reach a stance under a blocky overhang.
3 150 feet. Gain the slab and follow a series of rightward slanting cracks to reach ledges and easier ground. Was all Idwal rock like this before nails?

The diagonal slab to the right has also been climbed at Difficult.

A little to the right is a straightforward descent gully with a slab to the right, this is:

Goat Slab   200 feet   Difficult
A diverting piece of climbing. To the right of the gully a grey slab
tapers down to a point. Start at the base of a vertical crack.
1 100 feet. Follow the crack/seam on excellent incuts to belay at a
shattered stance.
2 100 feet. Continue directly up the slab.

To the right of the top stance are two ribs, both of which provide
entertainment at about Difficult standard.

Glyder Fawr   (The Big Mound of Rocks)

OS Ref. 644 585

The Upper Cliff

High up, and splendidly situated close to the summit of Glyder Fawr, this
cliff is the culmination of the grand sweep of the Idwal Slabs, and is part
of a continuous line of cliff that surrounds the head of the cwm.

Its slanting strata are built about the massive East Buttress, the deep-set
corners of each overlay forming the gullies. The Upper Cliff is a quiet
place, at its best when bathed in evening sunlight.

The rock types vary considerably, from rough grey to slaty smooth.
Nowhere is it more marvelously firm or massive than on the Grey Group.
The elegantly pointed Grey Rib on the left, and the long, narrow Grey
Slab, overlooked by the lofty Grey Arête, are all superb climbs. The
broad East Buttress stands to the right of this, in the centre of the cliff,
bounded on the left by East Gully and with Central Gully on the right.
Central Arête is a good mountaineering route on the next big buttress;
it has a sharply-toothed ridge on its crest.

With an early start and good intentions, the arduous stretches of screes
on the approach can be avoided by choosing a combination of routes
on the Slabs and Walls to suit ability and mood; this gives a most
satisfying day.

Above the conspicuous quartz seam, called Llwybr y Caws (the cheese
path), coming from Seniors' Ridge on the left, are a number of rather
out-dated routes. Oblique Gully slants up leftwards from the quartz ledge,

Glyder Fawr: The Grey Group

Photo: Malcolm Griffiths

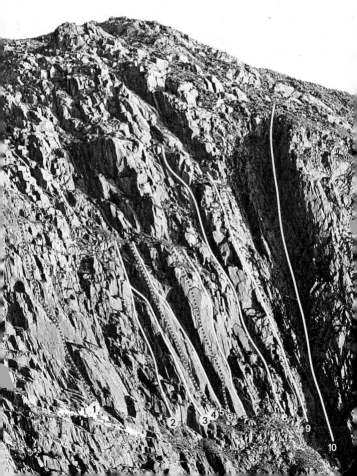

with steeper rock on the right separating it from **Three Pitch Gully** (200 feet, Moderate and interesting). Next are the **Square Slabs** (150 feet, Moderate), which are steep to start. **Narrow Gully** (250 feet, Moderate) rises in a series of chimneys, and 80 feet farther right **Square Furrow** (300 feet, Moderate) all 1895, marks the start of the main part of the cliff.

The Grey Group

Grey Rib 160 feet Hard Severe (1895)

This fine tapered rib is the leftmost and smallest feature of the Grey Group. The route rises with such deceptive ease that the top, by contrast, seems embarrassingly thin. Start at the foot of the rib, just right of Square Furrow.

1 100 feet. Climb the rib. Stay close to the edge until a ledge, which is too sloping for comfort, is reached.

2 60 feet. 4b. Go back out on to the slabby front and climb to a scoop cut into the edge. The few moves above this become progressively harder. Finish up Square Furrow.

Grey Gully (150 feet, Moderate) runs up the right side of the rib and is only tricky near its junction with Square Furrow.

Grey Eliminate 270 feet Hard Very Severe (1967)

This route is on the left side of Grey Slab. Its character develops considerably where the edge becomes more defined. Start towards the left edge of Grey Slab.

1 120 feet. 4c. Take a narrow slab that leads up onto Grey Slab and climb to the stance below the bulge.

2 150 feet. 5b. Climb over the difficult bulge on the left and head straight up, touching the normal route at 60 feet. Finish up the edge with some very thin and bold climbing.

★★★ **Grey Slab/Lost Boot Climb** 270 feet Very Severe (1932)

This long narrow slab is a route with classic qualities, and should not be treated too lightly. Its rough, textured surface is deeply indented with holds, but these are only thinly spread, and the top pitch is a bold lead, particularly the upper stretch where water is often encountered when one is thoroughly committed. Start in the corner on the right of the slab.

1 120 feet. 4a. Climb the corner for 50 feet, then trend leftwards across the slab on pockets and move up a slight rib to a sloping stance beneath the bulge. Good belays under this.

2 150 feet. 4b. Pull over the bulge and carefully move up the shallow rib on the left. Above, the right wall comes in, making the slab much narrower. Pockets lead up right then back left beneath this overlap and one can get round it by a groove on the left. Reaching the line of holds leading to the top is the last serious problem. A harder variation keeps close under the right wall after the bulge, rejoining the original line at the overlap.

★★**Grey Arête** 270 feet Hard Very Severe   (1959)
The clean arête that rears above Grey Slab confirms its promising appearance, and is a compulsive climb. Perfect rock in a perfect position, which succumbs to a bold approach. Start where the arête falls to the corner below Grey Slab.
1 120 feet. 4c. Climb a scoop in the arête until it is possible to swing onto the slab on the right. Go on easily to the horizontal break and belay on the right.
2 40 feet. 4c. Climb to a small stance on the arête by taking the pock-marked wall on the exposed left edge. This is sustained and has no protection.
3 110 feet. 5a. The steep crack in the arête above is the climax of the climb; it becomes a little awkward where it curves over to the right just before the top. There is a short wall to finish.

Eminence Grise 70 feet E4   (1984)
A precarious climb on the steep slab between the top pitches of Grey Arête and Grey Wall. Start at the small stance above the second pitch of Grey Wall.
1 70 feet. 6b. Climb to a small ledge. The final slab is hard and can be proteced by a runner on Grey Arête and another on the right, placed by an awkward hand-traverse.

★**Grey Wall** 260 feet E3   (1981)
The direct line on a smooth wall bold and quite exacting. Start beneath Grey Arête down at the foot of a slab.
1 130 feet. 5a. Steeply at first on the left edge of the slab, then follow the thin central crack to the break.
2 130 feet. 5c. Take the small groove in the middle of the wall to a narrow ledge. Place some protection on the right before proceeding on a wall, through a slight trough, to some decent holds. The straight crack on the right is now much less frightful.

Procrastination Cracks 230 feet Very Severe   (1932)
A good climb, and appealing to the intellect. It tackles the parallel cracks which cut down the right-hand part of the wall. Start at the foot of the slab below Grey Wall.
1 110 feet. 4b. Take the open corner on the right and easy ground to a ledge 20 feet below the cracks.
2 120 feet. 4c. Climb the left-hand crack, then move along a small

Glyder Fawr: The Grey Group, Central

1. Grey Arête	HVS	8. High Pasture	Mod
2. Grey Wall	E3	9. Central Arête	VD
3. Procrastination Cracks	VS	10. West Groove	VD
4. Twisting Gully Buttress	D	11. Great West Slab	HS
5. East Gully	VD	12. Western Passage	HVS
6. East Arête	Mod	13. West Gully	S
7. Central Gully	S	14. Grass Route	S

uttress and West Buttress

Photo: Ken Wilson

ledge to the right-hand one. Go up this and, where it narrows, pull out to regain the left-hand crack. This is funnel-shaped, and barred at the top by a smooth plaque of rock. Climb the crack, or its right edge, according to taste.

Above looms a tall grey tower, into which the cave pitch of Twisting Gully disappears. In its left face **Tower Groove** (70 feet, Very Severe) is a great pitch, well-worth staying roped up for.

There is quite a good **Girdle Traverse of the Grey Group** (300 feet, Severe, 1932). Climb Grey Rib then cross Grey Slab below the bulge, and descend the corner until it is possible to get round onto the horizontal break across Grey Arête. Easier climbing leads to Twisting Gully.

Twisting Gully 220 feet Difficult   (1895)
This is not a gully at all, but an easy open corner which defines the right end of the Grey Group. It is quite good though. Start by scrambling to where the gully is more obvious, at 120 feet.
1 120 feet. Climb in the corner; this has alternating steep sections and scrambling. Belay in the bed.
2 40 feet. Climb a last step before the gully disappears.
3 60 feet. Cross the hillside to the left for the finale. Here a cave is formed under an enormous jammed block. A struggle with a greasy corner leads into this. Climb through a hole in the roof, enter another hole into the second storey, and escape onto the rib on the left, all very entertaining.

Twisting Gully Buttress 350 feet Difficult   (1915)
This takes the narrow, low-relief rib between Twisting Gully and the big dark flank of East Gully. Its sharp left edge gives it some definition, and marks the proper route. Start straight up the middle of the easy ground. When the buttress steepens, the holds are excellent, and there is a strip of good grey rock before the rest, which is sprinkled with grass.

East Buttress
East Gully 600 feet Very Difficult   (1895)
There are two big open gully features in the central part of the cliff. This is the left-hand, and most prominent. The entrance to the gully is a stiff problem. Either take the sharp groove above the cascade which is the proper way or, if one has a thirst for these things, go directly up the watercourse. The subsequent passage in the gully bed is an adventure in a wealth of moist moss and dense atmosphere.

East Arête 700 feet Moderate (1907)
The East Buttress is broad, with a heavy rounded appearance, and is set between the East and Central Gullies. Only the lowest section has any angle; once on the crest one is free to wander. Start straight up from the foot of the buttress, or more easily by coming in from the left, and climb to two thin quartz ledges on the body of the ridge. Follow the skyline arête and little pinnacle buttress away on the left, and then your fancy.

Central Gully 690 feet Severe (1894)
This is the right-hand of the two big gullies on the cliff. It is a long and surprisingly open climb, but enjoyment will largely depend upon your attitude towards the torrents indigenous to these places. Start below the slabs just left of the watercourse.
1 120 feet. Climb the long shallow groove in the slab, in preference to the nasty grass in the gully bed.
2 70 feet. Continue up the runnel in the same line until it is possible to veer over to the right into the messy bed.
3 80 feet. Climb the gully, to the chockstone, which is ample to sample its delights.
4 20 feet. The huge chockstone bridges the gully forming an imposing obstacle. The hardy pioneers were forced to surmount this with some gymnastic jiggery-pokery and stolid persistence. Today a through route is much more acceptable. Nevertheless, the traditional way remains for those who wish to repeat the performance out on the slab on the left either close to, or a few feet out from, the chockstone; usually wet and Very Severe.
5 400 feet. The gully continues in a similar vein giving several short pitches, but the best is over.

Variation
Central Gully Slabs 700 feet Very Difficult
The broad acres of slab on the left can be climbed without the need to go into the gully and by-pass the chockstone. Instead of veering into the gully on Pitch 2, stay on the slabs and the rock on the left. They continue more pleasantly all the way to the top.

Central Buttress

Just right of Central Gully, above a low retaining wall, is the **High Pasture** (700 feet, Moderate, 1932). A tall narrow rake, clothed in a mantle of green, where only goats will wish to browse.

★**Central Arête** 650 feet Very Difficult (1909)
A good mountaineering climb, smooth and steep at first, then a toothed ridge to finish. Its character is strengthened by the position

high up above Cwm Idwal. This is an excellent choice after the Slabs. Start beneath the large buttress right of High Pasture.

1 150 feet. Climb the slabby base rocks to a good grassy platform.
2 110 feet. The arête now steepens. Take to the slab on its right edge. The holds feel too tiny for the vastness of the surroundings, but they never give out. Belay in a groove.
3 50 feet. Continue up the crest on the left.
4 340 feet. Entirely on the edge, where a parade of thin gendarmes lines the way.

West Groove   250 feet   Very Difficult   (1932)
This runs up the left side of the great recess. It certainly starts off well. Start on a terrace at the back of the recess, 120 feet above the broken lower rocks.

1 120 feet. Move down into the wide groove on the left and climb directly up this on shelving holds.
2 130 feet. Continue in the groove. When this becomes broken, work across left and finish on Central Arête.

Great West Slab   130 feet   Hard Severe   (1937)
The back of the recess is a steep slab sandwiched between Central Arête and the West Buttress. Start towards the left end of the terrace.

1 130 feet. 4a. Follow the shallow groove in the left edge of the slab. This has a line of pockets on either side, it tends slightly leftwards and the rock feels insecure. Near the top an awkward traverse is made to join West Groove.

Western Passage   290 feet   Hard Very Severe   (1975)
A challenging route that takes the slab more directly. It stands up well against the routes on the Grey Group. Start in the middle of the terrace.

1 140 feet. 5a. Follow a faint weakness straight up the slab to pock holes. Climb over a bulge to a shallow light-coloured groove at 70 feet. Move left towards a grassy tongue before making a rising traverse to the right edge.
2 150 feet. 4c. Continue more steeply, on big holds on the left, until some perched blocks in a very open position are reached. Move round the arête on the right to a pleasant finishing slab.

West Buttress
West Gully   265 feet   Severe   (1895)
This is quite obvious on the right of the recess. It is split by a narrow rib. The route takes the left-hand branch. A trifle athletic to start, but it then retires to a more respectable gully climb. Start by scrambling up below the right wall to the terrace.

1 85 feet. Climb the clean overhung corner on the right and belay in the grassy bay above.
2 40 feet. Move into the greasy bed of the left branch and step across to a crack on the left. Good stance above the slab.
3 40 feet. Continue in the gully with much steep grass.
4 100 feet. Little more than scrambling remains.

Grass Route   230 feet   Severe   (1933)
A tough route. 'Those who don't like grass will probably class it at the end of the Frankly Boring or at the beginning of the Definitely Unpleasant'. Thus commented the originator, so be warned. Start by scrambling up to the terrace as for West Gully.
1 90 feet. Descend a little and tackle a curious groove in the right wall. It looks impossibly steep. The grassy tufts which sprout from it at all sorts of angles are of little help.
2 20 feet. Move left into the hollow bay of West Gully.
3 80 feet. The right branch of the gully now hangs above. This is no easy prospect; it becomes quite exposed before sloping back in inevitable lushness to a small stance.
4 40 feet. Straight ahead, or the arête on the left.

The rocks of the remaining buttress continue down to the right, but this is very broken up. **West Arête** (350 feet, Moderate, 1910) makes the best of the ribs and furrows close to the gully edge.

Clogwyn Y Geifr   (Cliff of the Goats)

OS Ref. 639 589

Stretched across the head of Cwm Idwal, brooding in the subdued light, is Clogwyn y Geifr; these strange and mysterious cliffs provide an impressive backdrop to the cwm. With nothing to disrupt the tortured and twisted layout, the evidence is plain enough that some powerful forces have been at work. These smouldering forces remain, to fire the imagination of the student of geology, the sightseer, the naturalist and even the occasional wayward climber who becomes caught up in their spell. There are three large cliffs, on which the climbing is made serious by the uncertain nature of the rock. But a sympathy for this is quickly acquired, along with a fascination for the plant-life that flourishes

Clogwyn Y Geifr: South Cliff

1. South Nose	VD	6. The Trident	HVS
2. South Gully	S	7. Devil's Appendage	HVS
3. Botany Bay Climb	VD	8. Devil's Pulpit	HVS
4. Piece by Piece Climb	VD	9. Devil's Pipes	HS
5. Pluto	VS	10. Little Corner	S

Photo: Ken Wilson

wherever there is moisture. Grass is strongly represented, but this should not be taken as indication of any slackening of angle; it is essential to some routes.

Set within the huge synclinal fold is the Central Cliff, its towering bastions split by vertical clefts; the deepest and darkest of these by far is known as Twll Du, or the Devil's Kitchen. Through this dark cavern rushes a mighty torrent; the outfall of Llyn y Cwn, a tiny lake on the grassy plateau of Bwlch Blaenau Cwm Idwal. It is here that the eccentricities of the rock occur, one moment solid, perhaps pitted with pockets, the next an unstable purgatory resembling stiff mud. There are two segments of cliff lodged beneath the fold, one on either side. The South Cliff is on the left with the South Syncline, the main path to the plateau, running over it. By comparison the North Cliff, on the right, displays some exceptionally clean features.

Finally these cliffs are habitat and stronghold for several species of rare flora. Please respect their presence, and do not disturb their delicate existence.

South Cliff

On the far left the cliff is too easy-angled to be of any interest. Except South Nose that is, the steep arête which overlooks a disagreeable hollow of rotten gullies and grooves down which water cascades in copious quantities. To the right things become steeper; overhangs are predominant. The clean rib is Pluto and the crack cutting through the overhangs is The Trident. At the base of the cliff a huge flat tower buttresses the columnar organ pipe structure of Devil's Pipes. The rest quickly diminishes to insignificance.

South Nose   335 feet   Very Difficult   (1933)
The arête does have a steep, reasonable pitch despite the loose nature of the rock. Start just left of the watershed of South Gully.
1 70 feet. Follow grass ledges that lead out and up to the nose. Move back round the arête to a bay. Thread belay.
2 75 feet. The nose overhangs on the right, so take a little pillar, then a groove on the left, until the edge itself can be climbed. A narrow gangway then leads left to ledges.
3 70 feet. Zigzag up grassy steps close to the gully.
4 120 feet. Easy ground over on the left leads to the top.

The South Bay is definitely not an attractive area. It is composed of a series of depressingly rotten ribs separating channels which are constantly awash.

South Gully 80 feet Severe   (1933)
The tall wet left-hand corner of the Bay. Start at its foot.
1 80 feet. Climb the right-hand wall to a watery hollow, then escape
rightwards to join Botany Bay. This avoids the smooth steepening rock
and the worst of the water.

Botany Bay Climb 210 feet Very Difficult   (1933)
Beautifully named! Nevertheless it does hold some interesting, but
nerve-racking rock-climbing. Start at the first groove right of South
Gully.
1 110 feet. Go up the groove or the rib to the narrow terrace.
2 100 feet. Climb onto, and up, the flimsy rib overlooking South
Gully, until forced to step right into a groove at steeper rock. Follow
this groove to the top.

Central Groove 220 feet Difficult   (1933)
An easy route, remarkably sound and straightforward. Start at the
shallow runnel in the centre of the Bay.
1 100 feet. Ascend directly up the open groove.
2 120 feet. Go left and right at the step, then continue easily in the
bed to finish.

Piece by Piece Climb 200 feet Very Difficult   (1933)
The rib left of the deep-cut gully. It rises in two steps and is thoroughly
rotten, and quite exposed. Start at its foot.
1 100 feet. It is best to follow the rib.
2 100 feet. Continue on the rib, moving right at a steeper bit. The
rest is steep vegetation.

The deep-cut gully completes the South Bay and it contains one very wet
pitch. The main area now quickly develops, with steep walls and
interrupted lines of overhangs.

Pluto 290 feet Very Severe   (1971)
A good climb in a secluded spot. It takes the clean rib to the
overhangs, then works its way rightwards. Start beneath the rib.
1 20 feet. Go easily up to a ledge on the left.
2 90 feet. 4c. Step down onto the rib and climb it, passing a jammed
flake, then get into a bottomless groove, which is followed to a small
ledge.
3 30 feet. 4b. From a bit higher, make a neat little traverse between
the overhangs to a belay perch on the right.
4 50 feet. 4b. Take the rather loose groove on the left until it is
possible to pull over onto the slab above. Climb this, and belay in a

little corner on the right.
5 100 feet. Scramble up easy rocks and grass.

The Trident 170 feet Hard Very Severe   (1971)
The gaping chimney/crack, guarded by a steep wall, is the dominant
feature of this side of the cliff. Start at a blade of rock below the crack.
1 90 feet. 4c. A steep, narrow gangway is the only weakness, and
leads to a small ledge under the crack. There is still an awkward
move before lodgement can be effected and one gets stuck into the
objective. Follow the crack to a grassy ledge.
2 80 feet. 5a. The crack soon closes but there are prospects on the
broad rib on the right, which is followed to the overhang. Then an
escape is made to an easy corner on the left.

Devil's Appendage 170 feet Hard Very Severe   (1975)
A rather loose route with a steep finish. Start up to the left of the great
tower at the base of the cliff, below two similar miniatures.
1 90 feet. 4a. Climb to the top of the leftmost tower, take the
shattered groove, and arrange a belay round the column supporting
the overhang.
2 80 feet. 5a. Climb over the bulge to finish in a good position.

Devil's Pulpit 235 feet Hard Very Severe   (1972)
A quite serious route of steadily improving situations. Start below the
small towers, as for Devil's Appendage.
1 55 feet. 4a. Go up the chimney between these towers to the grassy
top of the left-hand tower.
2 65 feet. 5a. Climb diagonally right up to the overhang; skirt round
this by a short exposed traverse to a small ledge round to the right,
The Pulpit, and a poor belay.
3 45 feet. 4c. Take the short, slimy groove, and go a little way left on
a slab before climbing steeply to a tiny open ledge on the front of the
buttress. Good thread belay.
4 70 feet. 4c. Bridge up the corner above until one can cross the
black water streak to the right edge. A pleasant groove and slab lead
to the top.

Devil's Pipes 290 feet Hard Severe   (1933)
A serious and airy climb in a superb position. The crucial column at
the 'Organ Pipes' is becoming increasingly unstable; its collapse
would destroy a classic climb. Start at the base of the great tower
which is the lowest point of the cliff.
1 100 feet. Climb pleasantly up the face of the tower.
2 50 feet. 4b. One is now confronted by the vertical columns, or
'Organ Pipes', above which is an ominous bulge. Scale the most

detached column. This must be executed with extreme care. From its top, boldly attack the bulge by moving up to the left, where the angle is easier; then move back right above it, on improving holds, to a large grassy bay.

3 60 feet. 4a. Follow the edge of the rib on the left, then the groove on its left to a small grass ledge.

4 80 feet. 4a. The exposed left-hand rib is of good rough rock. Climb it all the way to the top. The middle bit requires most thought.

Little Corner   155 feet   Severe   (1933)
From the smaller right-hand section of the cliff a deep corner emerges from the steep banks of heather. Start below the right-hand side of the corner.

1 40 feet. Go easily along wet ledges to a good platform.

2 35 feet. Rock and steep heather lead up to the corner.

3 80 feet. Climb the prominent right edge of the corner, on small holds, to another grassy finish.

Redemption   375 feet   Hard Very Severe   (1972)
A long and interesting traverse of the main part of the South Cliff. Start just right of the deep-cut gully in South Bay, below a smooth slab.

1 80 feet. 4c. Climb a little way up the crack in the slab to a tiny niche. Make a couple of thin moves to the rib on the right, then continue across some poorer rock to belay at the lowest grassy ledge.

2 40 feet. 4b. Reach the horizontal fault in the steep wall and follow it round, under the crack of The Trident, to some tottery pinnacles. A vast belay can be arranged around the column supporting the projecting overhang.

3 35 feet. Descend the shattered groove beyond the column.

4 65 feet. 5a. As for pitch 2 of Devil's Pulpit.

5 34 feet. 4b. Take the short slippery groove then cross wet ledges to the grassy bay. Belay in a corner.

6 110 feet. 4c. Climb diagonally over a series of narrow ribs to the flat spikes on the skyline. Go round the arête and traverse the wall on the right, making some difficult moves into the top of Little Corner.

Central Cliff

The awesome, cavern-like rent of the Devil's Kitchen is the unique attraction of this cliff. Walkers and climbers alike make the long pilgrimage here to view its black, bulging inner walls. Stationed on each side of the Kitchen are towering bastions divided by dark deep clefts. To the left there are three cracks in an N-formation, though the luxuriant vegetation is the stronger representative. The right-hand side is much more prodigious. Tall mysterious buttresses are built of strange contorted rock, richly seamed with exotic plant life and herbiage. There is even a waterfall cascading down the cliff.

All factors make climbing here a unique experience. Holds are plentiful, well-weathered, though occasionally prone to crumble with violent use. Moisture and vegetation flourish everywhere. The first narrow cleft in the right-hand section is that of Devil's Staircase. To its right there is the pronounced Devil's Bastion, before the huge, vertical corner of Devil's Appendix rises above the overhanging, black, base wall. The last obvious feature is the corner gully of Hanging Garden Gully, before the cliff breaks up.

Goat's Groove 50 feet Difficult
This heavily vegetated groove can be found at the extreme left end of the cliff. It starts from the track and joins the ledges of Goat's Walk.

Goat's Walk Moderate   (1933)
This exposed grassy ledge slants up leftwards from the N-cracks and runs above the track to the left end of the cliff. The ledge can be reached from a rib beneath the left-hand N-crack and from there it is only really an airy walk.

Devil's Pasture 220 feet Moderate   (1933)
The grass-filled left-hand N-crack. Start just to its right.
1 30 feet. A grassy staircase to the wider trough.
2 90 feet. The bed soon steepens and requires climbing for a few feet before more scrambling leads to a good platform.
3 100 feet. Easy climbing leads to the top.

Hothouse Crack 230 feet Very Difficult   (1933)
The slanting and less-enclosed crack of the trio. Start at the top of the grassy ramp below the crack.
1 90 feet. Climb the slab and an open corner, break out right past a large block then cross a further slab to the bed. A more direct but harder approach is possible.
2 50 feet. The path can now be glimpsed above the overgrown glade. Go up the crack, without incident, to a stance.
3 90 feet. Continue straight up into a deep part, which soon leads to the pinnacle between the crack and the Pasture.

Dump Crack 220 feet Severe   (1933)
The right-hand and most formidable of the N-cracks. It retains the hallmark of this area: dispensable rock and remarkable plant life. Start in the wider part of the gully on the left.
1 110 feet. Move on up to a skinny tree on the ledge on the right,

then follow the crack and overhang to a lush bay.
2 50 feet. Return to the crack, to the final chimney.
3 60 feet. Enter the cave, then climb straight up behind the outer chockstone.

Devil's Dump 230 feet Severe   (1933)
The dilapidated buttress of very melancholy appearance standing on the left of the Devil's Kitchen. A long ledge crosses the broken rocks before the steep part. Go along this from the left; or more interestingly, climb a corner crack behind a short tower just in the Kitchen.
1 60 feet. From a pinnacle, climb the steep right edge, on uncertain pockets, to the comforting grass tufts. Follow a slight heather rake leading left.
2 70 feet. Zigzag up ledges on the front.
3 100 feet. The buttress falls back; proceed easily near the right edge.

Twll Du (The Black Pit) or **The Devil's Kitchen**
The steep inner walls of the Kitchen are an intriguing place to climb. The sheer intensity of effort to cope competently in the chill damp climate of the confines, with rock which is slippery and sometimes loose, leaves one awed. However, this feeling is quickly forgotten in the wave of elation and relief which successful escape brings.

The entrance walls are wide apart and bristle with overhangs. You can easily clamber up the cascades and steps, dodging the rock-pools in the gully bed. At about half-height the chasm is blocked by a big boulder, over which the water once flowed; it is known as the Waterfall Pitch and can be tackled on the right, underneath, or by its left corner. The first way is the easiest, the latter the driest. The cavern continues at a higher level; a huge pinnacle is seen leaning against the right wall, but the walls close in, cutting out the light; it now earns its Welsh name. The cul-de-sac ends in a tall, roofed cloister. The torrent rushes over the great capstone, pounding the gully floor and overwhelming the senses to the point of panic. The effect is magnificent and awe-inspiring.

Pilgrim's Progress 165 feet Hard Severe   (1948)
A good pitch coming out of the Kitchen to join the chimney defining the Dump. The rock is good but the traverse can seem quite insecure in slippery conditions. Start well inside the Kitchen, but before the Waterfall Pitch.
1 100 feet. 4a. Make a long and delicate diagonal traverse up left into the chimney, where a chockstone is soon reached.
2 65 feet. More easily now up the chimney.

Clogwyn Y Geifr: Central Cliff, The Band,

North Cliff

Night Moves   150 feet   E3   (1980)
A serious outing on the daunting left wall. Start about 15 feet before
the leaning pinnacle.
1 150 feet. 5c. Climb directly for 30 feet, then move left and go up
steeply to reach a good small thread. Continue up to a wall of more
compact rock on the right, then traverse left and climb to the obvious
double bulge. Traverse right with difficulty for 15 feet, then move up
to a leftward-slanting break leading to easy ground.

★**Devil's Kitchen Route**   80 feet   Very Difficult   (1898)
This is the original escape from the great chasm. Start a few feet past
the leaning pinnacle.
1 80 feet. Climb the slanting cracks in the left wall to the level of the
capstone. The first is easy; the second steeper but on big holds. There
is then an awkward move onto the spiky block on the right before a
long traverse left leads to the top of the capstone.

Variation
Direct Finish   Very Severe
It is possible to climb straight up from the top of the second crack.

Waterfall Climb   70 feet   Very Severe   (1957)
Will douse the ardour of the keenest enthusiast. Start beneath the
shelter of the capstone.
1 70 feet. 4c. Climb the straight crack rising up the left wall to a cave
beneath the capstone. Quit this, making a difficult finish round the left
edge of the capstone.

Right Wall Route   90 feet   Very Severe   (1934)
Usually very greasy, but a much drier proposition than the previous
route. It is sustained, and it requires great efforts of concentration to
overcome the intense background noise. Start a few feet in front of
the downfall at the very back of the Kitchen, at a steep crack in the
right wall.
1 90 feet. 4c. Climb the crack and a little way up the wall on sloping
holds. Now make a very precarious traverse over a mantelshelf to
reach the capstone.

★**Hell's Teeth**   140 feet   E3   (1987)
Pleasant climbing on small sharp pockets up the wall left of Gehenna.
Start below the leaning pinnacle before the big waterfall pitch.
1 140 feet. 5c. Step off the top of the pinnacle moving left at first,
then right, before climbing directly to finish via the prominent clean
wall.

On Holly Tree Wall, Idwal. Photo: Eric Byrom Collection

Central Arête (V Diff), Glyder Fawr. Photo: Eric Byrom Collection

Twll Du: The Devil's Kitchen

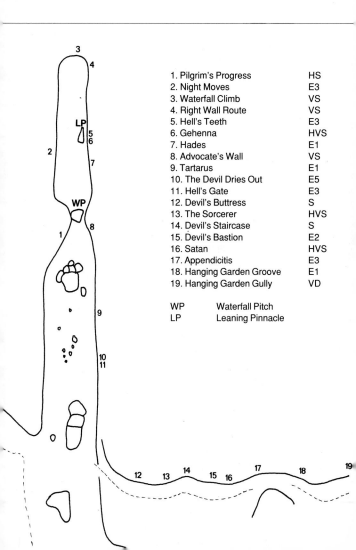

1. Pilgrim's Progress	HS
2. Night Moves	E3
3. Waterfall Climb	VS
4. Right Wall Route	VS
5. Hell's Teeth	E3
6. Gehenna	HVS
7. Hades	E1
8. Advocate's Wall	VS
9. Tartarus	E1
10. The Devil Dries Out	E5
11. Hell's Gate	E3
12. Devil's Buttress	S
13. The Sorcerer	HVS
14. Devil's Staircase	S
15. Devil's Bastion	E2
16. Satan	HVS
17. Appendicitis	E3
18. Hanging Garden Groove	E1
19. Hanging Garden Gully	VD

WP	Waterfall Pitch
LP	Leaning Pinnacle

★**Gehenna** 140 feet Hard Very Severe   (1972)
A good little route with a much more pleasant atmosphere than one would expect from the inside of this chasm. Start from the top of the pinnacle against the right wall.
1 40 feet. 4b. Climb the steep wall, trending to the right to gain a good ledge.
2 100 feet. 5a. Traverse left to where a shallow vertical corner leads nicely through the bulges to the top.

Hades 200 feet E1   (1969)
A steep route on an inhospitable part of the right wall. Start about 30 feet right of the leaning pinnacle.
1 100 feet. 5a. Climb straight up the wall into a dark hollow. There is a bewildering selection of very temporary holds. The art is to climb the wall without dismantling it.
2 100 feet. 5b. Continue up a little, then move over to the left where a vague depression runs steeply upwards.

Advocate's Wall 220 feet Very Severe   (1945)
A rather oppressive route, as the opposite wall closes in. The crux is set in a good position, however. Start below the right wall, just before the Waterfall Pitch.
1 60 feet. 4a. Start in the corner and climb the black slab until it curves over to form a ledge.
2 70 feet. 4b. Go up the corner on the left, make a decisive swing to gain a steep little wall on the front, and climb up into the chimney farther left.
3 90 feet. Continue in the chimney, which soon runs into a grassy gully leading to the top.

Tartarus 200 feet E1   (1976)
Makes an interesting escape between the overhangs. Start well before the Waterfall Pitch, where a tall tapered slab faces the entrance to the Kitchen.
1 70 feet. 5b. Climb the steep corner crack between the slab and the right wall, then the slab itself to a ledge.
2 130 feet. 5b. Above the first band of overhangs a vague gangway can be traced, leading to the right. Go up a small steep corner, then work along this, with little let-up, to a ledge. Step awkwardly up in to a steepening hollow to finish on a horizontal break.

★**The Devil Dries Out** 260 feet E5   (1969/1987)
Spectacular and strenuous climbing based on the old aid route The Devil Rides Out. Start at the entrance to the Devil's Kitchen. A crack comes down from the overhang to form a mossy groove in the

right-hand wall. Start 20 feet left of this at a better groove of detached blocks.
1 130 feet. 6a. Climb the groove to the overhung ledge. Over this to enter a groove which leads to a peg on the left. Ascend a layback crack to the roof then go over this, peg, thread, and continue steeply up flakes to a hanging stance. Nut and thread belay.
2 130 feet. 4c. Climb the overhanging chimney above to easy ground. Stake and large thread belays well back.

Hell's Gate 250 feet E3   (1982)
A fine line giving good exposed climbing. It takes the obvious grooves in the buttress forming the right side of the Kitchen, immediately right of The Devil Dries Out, starting as for the latter.
1 50 feet. 5a. Climb the groove, cross the bulging wall and belay in the niche in the crack leading up to the roof of The Devil Dries Out.
2 150 feet. 5c. Traverse right for 15 feet, then move up into the shallow groove. Climb past the first overhang and follow the deepening groove above, sustained and strenuous, until it ends at a band of overhangs. Traverse right beneath the overhangs and move up to a ledge around the arête (possible belay). Climb up and leftwards onto the slabby arête, and follow it to a poor belay.
3 50 feet. Climb the slabby rock above, then scramble to the top.

Central Cliff Right-Hand Section
Devil's Buttress 260 feet Severe   (1932)
The buttress is immediately right of the Kitchen. It is a distinctly exposed route, most suited to those willing to expend energy overcoming the adorning vegetation. Start above easy rocks, at about the middle of the buttress.
1 100 feet. Start up a short wall on the left, then a corner. Persevere over the ledges that break up the left side of the buttress, until a large terrace overlooking the entrance to the Kitchen is reached.
2 60 feet. Above is a grassy oblique break, running from left to right, fortunately having a crack behind its steeper parts. Climb the break, and belay after the first step.
3 100 feet. Take the next step, by a similar crack, to a broad grass patch. Climb fairly directly to the top.

The Sorcerer 235 feet Hard Very Severe   (1971)
This is a quite good climb. The steep, open groove is where the main difficulties are concentrated. Start to the left of the foot of Devil's Staircase.
1 60 feet. 4b. Take the diagonal slab and groove, below the overlap, up left to reach the first ledge. Walk along this to the right until beneath a white tree.

2 35 feet. 4c. Climb the crack on the right to the next ledge.
3 140 feet. 5a. Climb the groove. It has two overhangs, which now seem to have grown considerably and hamper progress. Pass the first on the left and the other more to the right. The right edge is then followed to the top.

★★ Devil's Staircase   295 feet   Severe   (1899)

The dark narrow cleft splitting the cliff to the right of the Kitchen. A magnificent route with a grand finale, one of the best Welsh gully climbs. Start where the gully is not very pronounced at the bottom but is really just a rocky slot.
1 85 feet. The first section of the box-like chimney is smooth, but good holds soon appear, followed by a ledge on the right. Continue to another ledge.
2 40 feet. More steeply now on rather looser rock, until the foot of an obvious cave pitch is reached on the left.
3 70 feet. Climb the dank chimney until under the capstone, then exit unexpectedly up the wall on the left. Scramble to the back of the gully below the final impressive section.
4 100 feet. The right-hand exit is the normal route. Climb a little wall and rib to gain the main chimney, then squirm up into its deep recesses, The Drainpipe, and fight to gain the top of a chockstone. Climb up into the daylight, where a few more feet of steep chimney leads to the top of the cliff.

Variation
4a The left-hand direct exit is harder and more strenuous than the original. It takes the steep crack from the back of the gully bed. A specialist's pitch, for those who enjoy a long struggle with wet conditions.

★ Devil's Bastion   280 feet   E2   (1965)

A superb climb, always interesting, on the sound buttress to the right of Devil's Staircase. The lower wall is smooth and grey. There is a pedestal towards its right side. Start by scrambling from the right, to the top of the pedestal.
1 90 feet. 5c. Above the initial slab is a groove. Climb this past a peg to move round a bulge, then take the slab ahead to a large, shaky flake. Go to the left, where some excellent holds allow a long swing left. Climb easily up to the horizontal break, where there is a spike belay over to the right, or threads in a cave on the left.
2 40 feet. Step up above the spike and go right to a grass ledge. Belay in a corner of the final wall.
3 150 feet. 5a. Get up into a grassy niche and climb more steeply, trending left by a bulge, to an obvious traverse left to the arête. This gives a very thrilling finish.

Satan 250 feet Hard Very Severe   (1971)
Before the great black concave area in the lower cliff is a reddish
groove where the wall is still slabby and smooth. Start near the
pedestal at the bottom of Devil's Bastion.
1 70 feet. 5b. Climb the groove, which slants to the right, and move
onto the rib on its right when nearing the top.
2 50 feet. 4a. Go straight up the steep wall then traverse right into
the huge corner of Devil's Appendix.
3 130 feet. 4b. Move out left onto the arête and climb this, with
increasing exposure and diminishing difficulties.

★**Devil's Appendix** 140 feet Very Severe   (1937)
An impressive climb in a very exciting part of the cliff. It is the
conspicuous black corner in the upper half, and between the
Staircase and Hanging Garden Gully. Normally wet and rather
slippery, being just left of the waterfall, though in dry conditions it
becomes considerably easier. Start below the corner, which is best
reached by doing the first pitch of the Staircase and traversing right
along ledges.
1 20 feet. Go up either of the two short chimneys.
2 120 feet. 4c. Climb the slabby corner, which gradually gets
harder, to a small ledge below an overlap. Continue up the
ever-steepening corner and make an escape by a timely traverse to
the left.

Variation
2a 140 feet. 4c. From the small ledge below the overlap, go up the
corner for five feet, before traversing right into the groove where the
waterfall usually flows. Follow this over a little overhang to the top.

★**Appendicitis** 300 feet E3   (1984)
A route based on the winter line Devil's Appendix gives one of the
best expeditions on the crag; unfortunately it is rarely dry. Start
directly below a rightwards facing corner at 50 feet which tapers into
the wall above. The home of many a rusty peg, placed during winter
ascents
1 100 feet. 5c. Climb the mossy lower wall to the base of the corner,
peg, step back down and move out left and go up the slabby rib,
crux. Move back right to the corner and continue up the obvious
groove above to a large ledge.
2 50 feet. Walk 20 feet right and up to an easy corner to another
ledge below another rightwards facing corner.
3 120 feet. 5a. Follow the corner above to a weakness/crack on the
left-hand side of some bulges. Pull through these, both steep and

exposed to belays.
4 30 feet. Easier climbing leads to the top.

Hanging Garden Groove   260 feet   E1   (1976)
A good route, finishing in the groove left of the gully. Immediately left
of Hanging Garden Gully is a clean wedge of buttress. Start at the
foot of this.
1 150 feet. 5c. Climb up the front, close to the right edge, to the
overlapping fringe. An awkward mantelshelf and a thin crack on the
left lead to a tiny tree on easy ground. Go up to a square block at the
final wall.
2 110 feet. 5b. The groove is now obvious, but cut-away at its foot.
Luckily the retaining wall is furnished with a narrow ramp. Go along
the ramp and climb the groove. It is steep but holds magically appear
on demand at the finger tips.

Hanging Garden Gully   260 feet   Very Difficult   (1899)
The obvious corner gully in the right-hand part of the cliff. A botanist's
paradise, only the last pitch has any climbing merit and that is
surprisingly open. Start at the poorly-defined foot of the gully; a wet
runnel in the back of the corner leads to the more pronounced upper
storey.
1 120 feet. Go easily up the broken grooves to a stony amphitheatre,
then scramble up to the narrows.
2 40 feet. Climb the slimy rift on the left to gain a scree-filled bay.
Belays are sought after with some difficulty.
3 100 feet. The original route now forsakes the gully for the Great
Pitch, a steep crack in the right wall. Climb a little wall to reach the
crack, which quickly steepens to a vertical exit into a grassy gully.

Variation
The Main Crack   110 feet   Severe
The natural route of the gully; steep and messy but fascinatingly
exposed, despite being climbed as far in as possible.
3a 50 feet. From the scree-filled bay, continue up without much
trouble to a stance in the deep cleft.
4a 60 feet. The final crack, which is quite taxing.

Staircase Traverse   Difficult   (1933)
A pair of parallel ledges cuts a curving path across the whole of the
right-hand section of the cliff. The lower of these begins just inside the
Kitchen, and gives an easy and exhilarating diversion. Some of the
ground covered will be wet and loose, so care should be taken.

The Band

On the northern side of Clogwyn y Geifr two synclinal terraces cut up through the cliff. They are broad, and provide useful descents for all the routes on this side. Between these terraces is a steep section of cliff, The Band. Its most prominent feature is the curving gash of Devil's Cellar.

Cellar Buttress 125 feet Difficult   (1933)
A poor climb, almost all on grass and heather. Start below a vague depression at the lowest rocks.
1 50 feet. Follow a grassy line into the hollow, then go left to a stance beneath a dripping nose.
2 45 feet. Steeper now, straight up right of the nose to the main grassy ledges. Spike belay.
3 30 feet. Climb a small gully and groove, then exit left.

★**Devil's Delight** 205 feet E1   (1966)
A good open climb on the pocketed buttress left of the gash of the Cellar. Start 30 feet left of Devil's Cellar at an orange rock scar.
1 95 feet. 5b. Ascend steeply at first, utilising elongated pockets and move across to a ramp. Climb a steep ramp rising to the right. Belay at a wedged flake.
2 110 feet. 4c. Continue up to the overhang, then go to the right to just beyond a rockfall scar. Go up and slightly left to gain an amazing slab. Stay close to its left edge.

Devil's Cellar 210 feet Very Difficult   (1927)
The wet, curving gash is narrow at the start, but it soon becomes slabby and open with two distinct finishes. Start at the gash a little way up the Lower North Syncline.
1 110 feet. Enter the slot and climb it, avoiding the loose rock of the bed for the more delicate slab. Eventually a shallow groove leads to an area of ledges. (One can continue in their line indefinitely.)
2 100 feet. Above is an open gully, the back of which is quite steep. Climb this, avoiding the first part on the right wall.

Variation
Coal Chute Exit 100 feet Severe
The direct left-hand corner of the gangway makes a much better finish than the original route.
2a 50 feet. Go down a little to where the retaining wall is only low. Move left over this into the corner, which becomes steep and quite strenuous. Good stance and belays.
3a 50 feet. Continue in the corner, which is loose, or up the detached line of blocks in the middle of the right wall.

North Cliff

There is a totally different character about this steep cliff. Its smooth, lofty walls are of a quality unsurpassed anywhere on Clogwyn y Geifr, and are almost free of the usual undergrowth. In the centre of the cliff are the two V-chimneys of Devil's Fissure and Devil's Doghouse. To their left a peculiar square recess is the distinctive feature of Devil's Nordwand. Up to the right, under a gaunt hanging wall, is a grand terrace which is the sanctuary of Devil's Dive. Farther to the right, round the foot of the cliff, is a band of slabs running steeply uphill, and presenting a fiercely undercut lower edge.

Easy Slab 110 feet Very Difficult   (1966)
The small triangular buttress at the left end of the cliff. Start down to the left of Easy Gully.
1 110 feet. Climb the middle of the buttress; at a small crack it is steeper. Now continue more delicately to easy ledges and the Lower North Syncline.

Easy Gully 90 feet Moderate
The slanting rake on the left before the steep part starts. The only difficulty is a narrow bit near the bottom.

God's Little Acre 200 feet Hard Very Severe   (1963)
Not too difficult a route, nice and open, and quite delicate in places. Start above the rock band 30 feet right of Easy Gully.
1 50 feet. 4b. Climb straight up to a green ledge below a shallow depression of horizontal hexagonal ribs, then go up a low-relief rib to a second larger grassy ledge.
2 110 feet. 5a. Gain a small rock ledge up on the left. A difficult move up the wall, left of a thin crack, leads to a precarious traverse into a scoop farther left. This becomes easier and ends on a heather ledge with a spike belay.
3 40 feet. 4c. Climb the steep exposed rib on the left.

Junior Slab 285 feet Hard Very Severe   (1960)
A good route that attains the small, sloping gangway only vaguely discernible on this smooth section of cliff.
1 50 feet. 4b. As for God's Little Acre.
2 85 feet. 5b. Go up a little way to a peg. Make a short hand traverse, then climb up a shallow groove past a perched flake to the gangway. Follow this to a ledge at its right end, where a crack leads to a stance farther left.
3 20 feet. Go easily up to an overhanging groove.
4 60 feet. 4c. Climb the groove, or the right-hand rib.

5 70 feet. Go up right, staying on the face, and climb diagonally to the top.

★**Devil's Nordwand**   310 feet   Hard Very Severe   (1959)
A very fine and surprisingly steep route, taking the cliff at its full height, it makes the obvious square niche at 60 feet its first objective. Start directly below the niche.
1 80 feet. 5a. Shallow grooves and cracks form the only weakness running down the steep wall to the left of the niche. Ascend these until level with the niche and make an awkward step right into it. A less sustained and less serious alternative is to climb the wall by following a rampline slanting up rightwards to the top of a pedestal. When level with the niche, make an awkward traverse left to reach it.
2 110 feet. 5a. From high on the left, pull out of the niche and climb to a grass patch. Above, a steep narrow corner should be taken direct to gain a large terrace.
3 120 feet. 4b. Finish up the back wall (the holds grow in proportion to the steepness) moving right at the top.

Hell-Bent   290 feet   E2   (1981)
The steep upper wall slashed by a pair of diagonal cracks gives a brisk piece of climbing. Start at a sort of pedestal standing flat against the cliff.
1 110 feet. 5b. The easy ramp of the left side of the pedestal leads to a straight crack. Climb this and belay on the right.
2 80 feet. 5b. Gain a tiny oblong niche from the right before climbing straight up to the diagonal cracks. Follow these, then move up and left with difficulty to reach a groove.
3 100 feet. 4c. The chimney beside the pillar on the next tier, then easily to the top.

★**Devil's Fissure**   290 feet   E1   (1971)
An exhilarating and very direct route, which takes the left-hand of the twin V-chimneys and the steep crack in the wall above. Start beneath the chimneys.
1 110 feet. 5b. Move into the left-hand chimney and climb it past a small overlap, before making an insecure traverse into the top of the other chimney. Go up a slab to a small stance.
2 80 feet. 5b. Take the awkward broken wall on the right to a small ledge. Climb the crack, where astonishing jams allow a flamboyant ascent until it thins, then some airy pulls are needed to reach a comfortable grassy ledge.
3 100 feet. 4b. The corner on the right and a short wall lead to easy ground and the top.

Devil's Doghouse 300 feet Hard Very Severe   (1964)
A good climb, which tackles the difficult hanging corner right of the
Fissure. Reasonable care will avoid disturbing the blocky nature of the
rock. Start at the foot of the right-hand V-chimney.
1 100 feet. 5a. Climb the chimney, making a short excursion to its
right arête at about half-way. Then go up the slab to a small stance.
2 30 feet. 4a. Go diagonally right to beneath the corner.
3 90 feet. 5c. Climb directly up the corner to a convenient ledge
below a bulge. Go up left of this, and continue with difficulty close to
the left edge.
4 80 feet. 4b. Just a short wall, then finish easily.

Faustus 280 feet E2   (1972)
An exposed route that focuses its attention on the hanging wall above
the huge hollow in the upper right-hand side of the cliff. High in the
grade. Start just right of the twin V-chimneys.
1 130 feet. 5a. Go along grassy ledges to the right; they rear up to a
groove. Climb the slabby wall, staying on the left where a vague
groove leads to the extreme left-hand end of the long terrace beneath
the overhangs.
2 150 feet. 5c. There is a little capped corner on the left. Go up this,
and get out left onto a small slab. Climb smartly up the overhanging
groove and go on up the wall, moving steeply left to an easier
groove. Finish easily.

Devil's Dive 300 feet Very Severe   (1933)
A serious undertaking, both in position and execution. The initial
steep vegetation is part of the strong character of this route. Dry
conditions are advisable. Start at the right-hand corner of the face.
1 80 feet. 4a. From a grass tongue carefully climb the left edge of a
tall sliver of rock partly detached from the cliff. Make an awkward
ascending traverse left to a grassy rake. A belay can be arranged in
a small corner.
2 100 feet. 4b. A steep pitch involving poor-quality grass. Climb
straight up then make a traverse right beneath an overhang, where a
groove and slab lead to the large terrace. Belay right of a sapling,
which should be cherished.
3 70 feet. 4b. Around the corner to the right, a narrow rock
gangway slopes up beneath a section of steep wall comprised of
hexagonal blocks. Get onto this gangway, which is quite exposed,
and climb to a ledge in a corner.
4 50 feet. 4a. Traverse awkwardly down to the right into a steep
damp dyke. Complete the climb up this.

Pete Evans on *Homicide Wall* (E3), Idwal Buttress. Photo: Bob Lewis

Ann and Paul Edwards on *The Ordinary Route* (Diff), Idwal Slabs.
Photo: Bob Lewis

'A perfect position' high on *Grey Arête* (HVS), Glyder Fawr. Photo: Alan Leary

Inferno   190 feet   Very Severe   (1970)

The route follows the left-hand border of the undercut slab round on the right side of the cliff. Start at an overhung groove at the lowest part of the slab.

1 100 feet. 4c. Climb the groove to the overhang of shattered blocks. Move right and up a short smooth groove to a ledge beneath the impending line of overhangs.

2 90 feet. 4b. Follow the ragged crack below the overhangs, to finish up a short chimney.

North Slabs   130 feet   Very Severe   (1933)

This is a smooth and delicate climb on the boldly undercut slab that runs up the right side of the cliff. Just on the left the base wall is only vertical. Start below a perched block on the edge of the slab.

1 90 feet. 4b. Climb over the block onto the slab, then move up to where it steepens in a shallow scoop. Climb up to the right then make a precarious traverse right, to the lower of two grass strips. Go along this to a tree belay.

2 40 feet. 4c. Up to the left, above the slab, is an inverted V-niche. Reach this by climbing below an intimidating block, then finish easily with a short chimney.

Tranquillity   480 feet   Hard Very Severe   (1970)

A girdle traverse, taking the reasonable passage of weakness crossing the whole cliff at half-height. Start 60 feet up Easy Gully, where the right wall steepens.

1 130 feet. 4b. Swing up the wall on a flake and traverse to an obvious short crack. Continue to a series of ledges then go down a ramp to a good ledge and belay.

2 80 feet. 4c. Descend the groove on the right before climbing diagonally along a narrow band of slab to a small stance near its end, at the top of Pitch 1 of Devil's Doghouse.

3 120 feet. 4b. Go horizontally right, round the edge, to pick up a long thin heather ledge, which ends at a bottomless groove.

4 60 feet. 4c. Step across the groove and climb the edge of the steep rib to a thread. Bridge across the corner on the right, and go beneath the overhangs to the stance of Inferno.

5 90 feet. 4b. As for pitch 2 of Inferno.

Index

Mountain Rescue

In the event of a serious accident where assistance is required, a message giving all the factual information about the person(s), location (crag, climb, pitch etc.) should be passed on to the North Wales Police by dialling 999.

The Police will contact the respective Rescue Team and as co-ordinators will obtain further assistance (e.g. helicopter) as directed by those effecting the rescue.

After an accident, please report in writing directly to the Hon. Secretary, Mountain Rescue Committee, 18 Tarnside Fold, Simmondley, Glossop, Derbyshire, SK13 9ND, giving particulars of: date of accident, extent of injuries, name, age, and address of the casualty, details of the M.R.C. Equipment used and the amount of morphine used (so that it can be replaced). Normally this will be done by the local Police and/or the Rescue Team involved, who will also require the names and addresses of the persons climbing with the injured party.

Avoid making rash or unconsidered statements to the press; refer any journalist to the mountaineer who has overall charge of the rescue.

Helicopter Notes

In the event of a helicopter evacuation ALL climbers ON and OFF the cliff should take heed. A helicopter flying close to the cliff will make verbal communication between climbers difficult, and small stones will be dislodged by the rotor downdraught. All loose equipment must be secured and climbers in precarious positions should try to make themselves safe. A smoke grenade may be dropped from the helicopter to give wind direction.

The persons with the injured party should try to identify their location. No attempt should be made to throw a rope to the helicopter, but assistance should be given to the helicopter crew if requested.

A helicopter will always be flown into the wind to effect a rescue and on landing there are three danger points; the main rotor, the tail rotor and the engine exhaust. The helicopter should not be approached until directions to do so are given by the air crew.

Mike Jones in *Great Gully* (V Diff), Craig yr Ysfa. Photo: Alan Leary

Ed Stone on the first ascent of *F-stop Fitzgerald* (E5), Craig Blaen y Nant.
Photo: Ray Wood

Contents

List of Photodiagrams

Guidebook Disclaimer

This guidebook attempts to provide a definitive record of all existing climbs and is compiled from information from a variety of sources. The inclusion of any route does not imply that it remains in the condition described. Climbs can change unpredictably: rock can deteriorate and the existence and condition of *in situ* protection can alter. All climbers must rely on their own ability and experience to gauge the difficulty and seriousness of any climb. Climbing is an inherently dangerous activity.

Neither The Climbers' Club nor the authors and editors of this guidebook accept any liability whatsoever for any injury or damage caused to climbers, third parties, or property, arising from the use of it. Whilst the content of the guide is believed to be accurate, no responsibility is accepted for any error, omission, or mis-statement. Users must rely on their own judgement and are recommended to insure against injury to person and property and third party risks.

The inclusion in this guidebook of a crag or routes upon it does not mean that any member of the public has a right of access to the crag or the right to climb.

Before climbing on any crag in this guide please read the appropriate access and conservation notes.

The West Side of Nant Ffrancon

Castell Y Geifr   (Castle of the Goats)

OS Ref. 637 594

This is situated on the southerly flank of the north-east ridge of Y Garn and is clearly seen from Cwm Idwal. It appears impressive from a distance but fails to sustain its promise on closer inspection. The cliff is a long wall with a rock pimple on a step in the ridge. The pimple is The Pinnacle: it offers small problems on all its flanks, the south side being Very Severe. Over to the left the wall has a buttress, where **The Brace and Bit** (170 feet, Very Difficult, 1938) turns the square cut-off to the right '... with pleasurable ease'. A verdant shelf leads left from the gully to a little grassy saddle supported by a horn of rock. Above, a scooped rib has two steps on its right edge. The **Original Route** (100 feet, Difficult) goes left of these and then gains the arête on the right. The shelf continues, slightly downhill, to a rock rib which is just above a tilted block. Here **Groove Route** (90 feet, Very Difficult, 1943) is obvious. Up round the corner, a crack with a rowan tree growing from it starts **Rowan Route** (80 feet, Very Difficult); it then goes up the back wall of a shallow amphitheatre. **The Runnel** (60 feet, Very Difficult) takes the groove left of this. The mountainside beyond offers little more than scrambling, but the odd pitch can be found on the ridges before the Kitchen Cliffs.

Drws Cwm Clyd

(Door of the Sheltered Cwm)   OS Ref. 635 596

This is a tiny north-facing cliff which overlooks Llyn Clyd held within the embracing ridges of Y Garn. It has two or three steep grooves and a deep chimney, **Flat Chimney** (90 feet, Severe, 1935). More can be found on the broken crags just above the lake and on the tower at the foot of the spur that drops from the summit. This gives a 100 foot Severe.

The Pinnacle Crag of Cwm Cywion

OS Ref. 634 603

This crag, in the 'Cwm of Young', stands silhouetted above the screes on the northern slopes of Y Garn. The cliff which, is about 200 feet high, boasts a fine pinnacle and a number of reasonable climbs; they, along with others in the cwm, help to satisfy the deeper passions of an exploring instinct.

The inspiring pinnacle is cut off from the main cliff by The Gully, which was the original route here. The steep main section is taken by two direct routes and the surprising Little Woodhead. The great corner on the right is The Crack.

The easiest approach is to walk in from the northern end of Llyn Idwal, otherwise one can take the minor road past Idwal Cottage Youth Hostel for about half a mile, before following a stream up into the Cwm.

Fallacy   130 feet   Very Difficult   (1943)
The obvious weakness in the front of the pillar. Start by coming in from The Gully to a good ledge, though the true approach is more direct.
1 60 feet. Take the natural break to a V-recess.
2 70 feet. Turn the overhang on the left, where an inclined slab makes a fitting climax.

The Gully   240 feet   Very Difficult   (1932)
Vegetated and entertaining, as tradition dictates. Start at the foot of
the gully, at about the centre of the cliff.
1 80 feet. Climb a scoop, two steep steps, then a crack on the left to
get established in the gully.
2 50 feet. A grassy slope leads to the neck of the pinnacle.
3 50 feet. It is best to descend a little and attack a slab on its left
edge. It does improve. Belay on the left wall.
4 60 feet. Go rightwards over a block resting on a ledge, then climb
across to reach the right edge of the slab.

The Chicken Run   190 feet   Very Severe   (1970/1977)
Makes the best use of the centre of the main buttress. Quite good and
sustained in the middle section. Start just left of the lowest part of the
buttress.
1 60 feet. 4a. Climb a short wall to a bilberry ledge. Now the
chimney-like slot then lands one on a terrace.
2 50 feet. 5a. Gain the slab from either side, and pass a peg to
reach an overhang. Pull round this to enter a steep groove. When it
steepens, swing round the arête on the left.
3 40 feet. 4c. Climb the crack above and the chimney of Little
Woodhead. A traverse right, around a rib, then brings one to a
stance at the foot of a steep groove.
4 40 feet. 4b. Laybacking is the solution, to better holds.

Little Woodhead   190 feet   Severe   (1932)
An interesting climb up seemingly difficult ground. Start by the
quartz-splashed wall at the foot of the cliff.
1 50 feet. Climb the wall and a miniature rib, then take a cracked
groove, and step right onto a long ledge.
2 35 feet. Ascend the corner on the right.
3 55 feet. Make an awkward stride onto the exposed gangway that
slants up leftwards to a perched block. Cross a groove and climb the
steep chimney just beyond a spike.
4 50 feet. Climb the slabs, moving right to a finishing groove.

The Broiler   210 feet   Hard Very Severe   (1971)
A tough, direct line that crosses Little Woodhead. Start as for Little
Woodhead, at the quartz wall.
1 50 feet. 4b. Follow Little Woodhead to the long ledge.
2 60 feet. 5a. A crack splits the small overhang. Climb this and the
prominent V-chimney to a perched block.
3 100 feet. 4c. Step right and go up three small ledges, then climb a
shallow corner and final wall in a little bay.

The Crack 220 feet Very Severe   (1932)
The big open corner is an appealing feature of the cliff. Start below
the corner, right of the quartz wall.
1 100 feet. 4a. Climb the corner crack; it gets gradually harder as it
approaches a good belay on the right wall.
2 90 feet. 4c. Bridge awkwardly to the bend, moving silently past a
doubtful chockstone, only to find the way barred by the final
overhang. So traverse right and climb a difficult crack in the arête to
escape.
3 30 feet. A staircase on the left leads to the top.

★**Poultry in Motion** 130 feet E4·   (1987)
The prominent arête between The Crack and The Groove. Start a few
yards up to the right of the start of The Crack below the arête.
1 60 feet. 5a. Ascend the blocky arête to a good stance.
2 70 feet. 5c. Gain the arête from the left and ascend directly,
climbing to the left in its upper half. Good Friend protection in the
halfway break provides the only protection. An excellent bold pitch.

The rest of the cliff is rather scrappy but three short routes have been
found: 60 feet to the right of The Crack is the chimney/groove line of
The Groove (150 feet, Very Difficult); another chimney further right,
gives **Wide Chimney** (110 feet, Severe 1949); **Finale Groove** (60
feet, Very Difficult 1964) is the last main feature of the crag.

There are some crags in the upper part of Cwm Cywion. The first is a
series of steep walls, with the obvious **Slanting Chimney** (90 feet,
Very Difficult, 1911) about halfway along. There is another cliff higher
up, but so far routes have only been made up the three steep gullies
between the leaning tower-like buttresses. These are: **Six Pitch Gully**
(250 feet, Very Difficult, 1911); **Gubben Gully** (170 feet, Severe,
1964) and **Petrous** (135 feet, Severe, 1964). The climbs barely justify
the walk but they are worth investigation in good winter conditions.

Craig Blaen Y Nant   (Head of the Valley)

OS Ref. 641 609

A very steep little crag above the old Bangor road, a little beyond the
Venture Scouts Hut and above the farm Blaen y Nant, now boasts a
difficult route. DO NOT PARK DIRECTLY BELOW THE CRAG AS THIS IS

THE TURNING POINT DOWN TO THE FARM! There is adequate parking just 100 yards up the road.

★**F-stop Fitzgerald**   100 feet E5   (1990)
Much of the ironmongery sported by this route dates from its previous existence as an aid climb. Start directly below the overhanging and central V-shaped groove.
1 100 feet. 6b. Go up to a hanging spike, then make a long reach up left to gain two pegs. Desperate moves past the pegs allows access to a leftwards slanting crackline containing rust and a peg. Step back right in to the centre of the groove, climb the groove to a large 'biscuit-like' hold where another step leads to easier ground. Belay well back in a grass niche on the left.

Carnedd Y Filiast

(Cairn of the Greyhound Bitch)   OS Ref. 623 627

The eastern slopes of Carnedd y Filiast fall into Cwm Graianog, the north side of which is dominated by a vast expanse of layered slab, known locally as Creigiau'r Rowlar. Several routes here give 1,000 feet of continuous climbing.

The best climbing is on the edges of each overlapping layer; these run up the slabs and are generally of an easy angle. The rock low down is slatey and smooth, making climbing very awkward; high up however it becomes more massive and gritty. It can be dangerously loose, particularly if one strays onto the blocks lying in the runnels. Despite this the routes have a very serious feel because of an almost total lack of protection and complete isolation. It has not been unknown for pegs to have been used at the stances.

Climbing has gone on here since the earliest days by parties who have, from time to time, come seeking the solitude the mountain gives, or perhaps more recently as an escape from the vexation and disciplines of a modern crag. A number of new routes have been climbed since the last guidebook, even a 2,000 foot girdle.

The approach is easy, directly up the hillside from the old Nant Ffrancon road. Once in the cwm the ridge opposite the slabs provides a good position to familiarise oneself with the layout. The main area of slab with its rough-hewn edges commands the view, but just down to its right is the seemingly diminutive, but radiant Red Slab. A route on this is a sheer delight before the sterner stuff to come.

Russet Slab 400 feet Very Severe
High up on the left a smooth narrow slab has been exposed by a rockfall; this becomes progressively finer as one ascends.

Altantic Slab

This is a vast expanse almost too large to comprehend; it is waved with a gentle undulation, and the run-outs are so long that you can suffer from loneliness when trying to choose a way.

The Runnel 1,000 feet Moderate
This runs up the left side of the slab, below a retaining wall. It is best left as a winter climb when a ribbon of firm snow can extend down its length.

Central Route 1,000 feet Difficult
This is just one of the many possibilities on the slab itself. Start down to the right of The Runnel and aim for a perched block on the skyline of The Ridge, at half-height. Then go back out onto the slab along a grassy gangway before climbing for the top. Stay well in from the crests.

The Ridge 1,000 feet Moderate
A long outing on the right edge of the slab which is made more interesting by the interconnecting of crest and little slabs. Start from the lowest part of the slab and climb the broken steps to a perched block at half-height. Continue on the ridge; the main crest, on the right, of the upper section is the best.

Next are two narrow slabs, the crests of which are fairly clean and give some very open climbing. The routes start from the left end of a slanting boulder terrace.

Broken Edge 700 feet Very Difficult
The central and upper sections of the left-hand slab are quite enjoyable; stay off the broken and loose stuff in the gully bed.

Jagged Crest 800 feet Severe
The lower edge of the right-hand slab is cut away sharply into a line of overlaps, which adds some spice to the climbing. The route follows

Carnedd Y Filiast

1. Russet Slab   VS
2. The Runnel   Mod
3. Central Route   D
4. The Ridge   Mod
5. Broken Edge   VD
6. Hawkwind   S
7. Gothic Slab   VD
8. Waved Slab   Mod
9. Jay Route   VD

Photo: Simon Cardy

the edge above the overlaps, the majority of which is on good gritty rock.

On the right now is a huge triangle of smooth slab, the right-hand side of which offers the possibilities.

Hawkwind 1,000 feet   Severe   (1979)
The route is typical of the climbing here. The initial rock is smooth, slaty and friable, higher up it is better. The edge comes down to the left of the Tower. Start on the edge moving left at the first difficulties, move up the crest curving leftwards on a finely-rippled slab near its apex. Break through the overlap onto the Jagged Crest, which makes a delightful finish.

High Corner 1,000 feet   Hard Severe
Round to the right of the upper half of the slab a big corner capped by massive red overhangs comes part way down the face. Start as for Hawkwind but stay on the sharper edge on the right and go into the bay beneath the corner. Climb the corner and escape to the right by a slanting crack below the overhangs.

The Tower 160 feet   Difficult   (1921)
This is black, and an obvious feature standing quite erect amongst so much sloping ground. The route starts on the left and zigzags up the breaks in its front face. It is steep and makes a welcome change.

Tower Chimney (180 feet, Moderate, 1916) is on the left and is said to turn out better than one would expect.

Tower Continuation 800 feet   Very Difficult
Makes an ascent of The Tower less futile as it takes one away from the bottom of the cliff! After some messy scrambling from the top of the tower, take a steeper slab going left at a stuck-on tower-like piece. Take the leftmost of the three crests over to the right. Sheer delight, on good rough rock.

Gothic Slab 500 feet   Very Difficult
The more broken slopes below and right of The Tower show a smooth rib that quickly broadens to a clean slab. Avoid the heathery cracks and use the cleanest section, keeping parallel to the crest. This finishes level with the top of the tower, so one can scramble up and join Tower Continuation.

A big, wide gully now separates the next portion of slab.

Seagull 450 feet Very Difficult   (1986)
Take the extreme left of Waved Slab, climbing on the edge, avoid
easier ground to the right. As the slab becomes more heathery
traverse left above the grassy gully to finish.

Waved Slab Goodbye 600 feet Difficult   (1986)
Start at the lowest point of the V-shaped slab and climb a very direct
line to the top of the crag. Near the top heather and loose blocks
have to be negotiated. No stances.

The Waved Slab 500 feet Moderate   (1921)
This quite remarkable slab forms the back of a wide recessed area to
the right of the gully. It is ascended as if it were some giant's staircase.

Jay Route 500 feet Very Difficult
This takes the edge of the narrower slab inset between Waved and
White Slabs. Begin easily, low down, stick to the slabby crest and
overlap onto the Left Edge to finish.

★★**Left Edge** 600 feet Very Difficult
A light and airy climb on the edge of the White Slab that runs up to
bound the right-hand side of Waved Slab. Stay on the very edge,
where the rock will be found perfect.

White Slab 600 feet Difficult
Climb the face of the slab and finish on its right edge to where it
converges with the Left Edge and forms a point.

The main body of slabs now dissolves into a hillside of heather and
perched masses. Low down on the right stands Tree Slab. A diminutive
but steep block splashed with quartz on its left edge.

Friction 100 feet Very Difficult   (1983)
Ascends the left edge of the slab past an overlap.

White Lightning 120 feet Severe   (1983)
Takes the second quartz crack left of the tree with a step left at about
half height.

Bracken Corner 85 feet Severe   (1983)
The first quartz crack left of the rowan, finishing up a corner.

Dog Leg 100 feet Very Difficult
Takes the quartz-lined crack from behind the tree and finishes with a
choice of cracks, the right one being favoured.

Perchover   200 feet   Difficult
High above Tree Slab is a loose slaty slab. Choose your own route,
finishing left of the perched overlap. This is not very pleasant but
fortunately on the right there is the fabulous:

★ **Little Tree Edge**   300 feet   Moderate
This starts up the steep cracked slab with a little flying buttress just to
the right. Superbly juggy on rough rock.

The Red Slab

The massive slabs on the left have the height and grandeur but none
could match this 300 feet of perfection. This is the focal point of the area,
its colour being that of the true rock without lichen. The friction on the
slab is marvellous, the holds are small but always on hand. The problem
is finding stances; there are so frustratingly few that one is driven to
abandon the rope and enjoy the pure exhilaration.

These are some of the better lines here; other ways exist and their beauty
lies in their discovery.

Red Edge   210 feet   Very Difficult
Climb just in from the extreme left edge on friction. There is a poor
stance with a good spike at half-height.

Route One   240 feet   Very Difficult
A large block at 80 feet looks useful, and is something to aim for;
take the broad trough or subsidiary slab on the left to reach this.
Trend leftwards across smoother rock to a poor stance before
finishing more easily.

★ **Central Route**   280 feet   Severe   (1924)
An impressive test of confidence. A slight depression marks the way;
a belay can be arranged at a tiny scoop at 120 feet. The easy way is
rightwards to a perched block belay though one should continue, in
the grand manner, more or less directly, and belay just before the top.

★ **Underlap**   260 feet   Very Difficult
A lovely route starting 20 yards left of the big overlap crack, where
two small overlaps face each other across a groove. Climb to the
perched block at 150 feet, on the ledge formed by the big overlap
curving over. Climb the left corner where the overlap turns vertical
again.

The perched block can be reached more directly and, after an awkward
start, the upper slab is climbed. The easy corner of the big overlap and

heathery crack going up rightwards from the ledge gives **Route 2** (160 feet, Moderate).

Gina's Traverse 2,000 feet Severe   (1986)
This girdle traverse links the lowest slabs with the highest. Starting on Red Slab climb the right-hand edge of the broad trough on Route One, climb to the top of that route. Traverse down and left through heather and scree, then across slabs and ribs making for the base of Tree Slab. Climb the quartz crack on the left of the tree, hand-traverse left to the shoulder of the triangular slab, stance. Traverse upwards over loose and slatey rock, making for the overhanging ridge of rock on the left. Climb the chimney with a chockstone to a good stance. Descend two steps to White Slab and climb diagonally up to join up with Left Edge. Descend the steep quartzy step to The Waved Slab, traverse this by using a 'wave' and descend Seagull. Climb the steep blocky step above The Waved Slab. Traverse slatey overhanging ribs and join Gothic Slab, follow this to the top. This is the top of The Tower, follow Hawkwind to where it joins with Jagged Crest, traverse left horizontally, climbing three steps in the slabs crossing Broken Edge, The Ridge and finish up Central Route on Atlantic Slab. A fine mountaineering day out, but care should be exercised in respect of the large amount of flakey and fragile rock encountered.

Finally, when looking up from Tai Newyddion, the Naval hut on the old road five ribs can be seen standing out from the first shoulder of Carnedd y Filiast. These give several pitches of no more than Difficult, and make the approach to the Red Slab more interesting.

Cwm Marchlyn Mawr   OS Ref. 615 616

A crag where previously solitude and isolation were added attributes to the selection of good climbs available. The construction of a dam for the Pump Storage scheme, with its access road, does detract from the beauty of this once remote spot. However, the scars are healing slowly and still one will rarely find others on the crag. This quietude plus the fact that the quality of the climbing is good should be enough to satisfy anyone and justify the walk.

Craig Cwrwgl or The Pillar of Elidir clutches the north east slopes of Elidir Fawr. Elidir Slabs form a band on the mountainside up to the west; just inside the entrance to the cwm is Elidir Tower. The cwm then opens out to the north and near the old quarry workings east of Deiniolen (597 631) there is ample parking and an access road. The approach up the tarmac road is tedious and takes about 45 minutes. However, a roller coaster descent may be made in a few minutes if a cycle has been made available (beware of cattle grids and melting brake blocks). A far more traditional approach may be made from Nant Ffrancon via Foel Goch and over Bwlch y Brecan.

Craig Cwrwgl (Coracle Crag)
or **The Pillar of Elidir**

The face of the pillar is steep and bold, demanding a certain alacrity in ascent. It is cut off from the hillside by a deep brèche with gullies down either side. This means the summit can only be reached by climbing, and that the descent is made awkward. This is best achieved by slithering down The Rift then climbing or abseiling down West Gully.

Elidir Rib   250 feet   Very Severe   (1967)
Quite a good 'alpine style' climb – T.D.Sup? It ascends the sometimes loose and vegetated rock to the left of The Pillar. The crux is reserved for the top and is quite serious. Start at the rib, 50 feet left of the East Gully.
1 130 feet. 4b. Go straight up the rib and groove above, then get onto a delicate slab. Belay at the top of the grassy ledges, in the right-hand corner of a square-cut buttress.
2 120 feet. 4c. Climb the crack past a chockstone and go over two small overhangs. Take a groove on the right-hand edge and delicately reach a traverse line across two wobbly blocks. Go over these, or by-pass them on the left, and turn the top overhang on the right.

East Gully and Rift   115 feet   Difficult   (c.1900)
A deeply interesting old-fashioned climb. East Gully separates The Pillar from the hillside.
1 65 feet. Climb the gully to the brèche.
2 50 feet. Move over the lower boulder bridge and into the rift behind The Pillar; you can become lost in its depths, but a light appears above, and leads to a sudden landing on the summit.

Nick the Neck   150 feet   Very Difficult   (1973)
A useful continuation up from the brèche, it avoids the rather odious
descent from The Pillar. Start behind a huge boulder in the brèche.
1 150 feet. Climb a groove, stride round the arête and go up a
corner until an obvious turvy traverse leads across right to a grassy
bay. Ascend this to easy ground.

The first of the routes on The Pillar itself is:

Siesta Cracks   120 feet   Hard Very Severe   (1982)
No gentle layback this, but a series of steep cracks rising out of East
Gully. Start in the gully.
1 40 feet. 5b. Climb the first steep crack breaking the impending
right wall, by strenuous fist jamming, to a large ledge.
2 30 feet. 5b. Climb the corner/crack to the next ledge.
3 50 feet. 5b. Gain the groove on the left, by a trick move! A wide
bridge and a swing then allow the remaining crack to be reached.

Mexico Cracks   110 feet   Hard Very Severe   (1960)
The more obvious cracks and corners of the east face are surprisingly
exposed. Start in East Gully, where a little gangway leads out right.
1 30 feet. 4b. Move along the gangway and go over the blocks.
2 40 feet. 5a. Climb the deep jamming crack; its flake top thankfully
relieves the pain. Belay on the left.
3 40 feet. 5a. Now take the corner and wide crack above.
Hand-traverse right to another crack to finish.

★**Corrugated Cracks**   150 feet   Hard Severe   (1937)
The route of The Pillar, strenuous and quite thrilling. Start on the
terrace on the east face of the Pillar.
1 70 feet. A grassy corner leads to the prominent crack.
2 40 feet. 4a. The narrow corrugated chimney is hard to start, and
taxing to the utmost. Pull over a chockstone into the wider part, and
thrutch violently up to the next chockstone and a ledge. A mortifying
pitch.
3 40 feet. 4a. The chimney now opens out and looks ever more
intimidating; the climbing is spectacular. Work up and use a crack on
the right to gain a terrace to finish.

The Arête   150 feet   Difficult   (c.1900)
This makes for a hanging curtain of rock high up. Start on the right of
the terrace, above the lower slabs.
1 100 feet. Easily climb beside the steep flank to the curtain.
2 50 feet. Climb the awkward crack behind the curtain, then finish up
the steep right wall.

Craig Cwrwgl

1. Mexico Cracks   HVS
2. Siesta Cracks   HVS
3. Corrugated Cracks HS
4. The Arête   D
5. North Chasm   S

Photo: Ray Wood

North Chasm 50 feet Severe   (c. 1900)
The obvious cleft which cleaves the front of The Pillar is a short, stiff
problem made exciting by the exposure. Start as for The Arête, on the
right-hand end of the terrace.
1 50 feet. Start up the easy rock of The Arête then approach the
Chasm across a steep slab, step into it and climb it, helped by a pile
of dubious blocks.

West Wall
The smooth West Wall of The Pillar enjoys a very open aspect. It is a
large rectangle of good rough rock, providing several climbs that are
well-maintained in technique.

Coelacanth 130 feet E1   (1982)
An intricate route passing through the obvious wedge-shaped bite
missing from the edge of the wall. Start at the lowest end of the wall.
1 60 feet. 5a. Climb a crack close to the edge moving awkwardly
left to a ledge.
2 70 feet. 5c. Continue delicately upwards before stepping left into
the bite. Move across and exit to a shallow corner on the front. This is
hard to start and to finish; several large blocks add to the interest.

★**Living Fossil** 100 feet E2   (1982)
An excellent pitch taking the thin central crack of the wall. Start from
the foot of the crack.
1 100 feet. 6a. Gaining the grotto and reaching the halfway ramp
are merely preludes to the perplexities of the upper part of the crack,
though all is quite hard.

Antediluvian 100 feet E5   (1987)
Start at the third, very thin, crack from the left edge of the wall.
1 50 feet. 6b. Ascend the crack and then the wall above to reach a
stance.
2 50 feet. 6b. Gain the leftwards slanting crack and continue to a
finger snapping finish.

Primordial 110 feet E6   (1987)
Start at the left-leaning crack/ramp on the right-hand side of the face,
as for Manana.
1 50 feet. 5c. Follow the leftwards slanting ramp, and at the first
opportunity, move directly up the wall to reach a crack and a stance.
2 60 feet. 6b. Climb another crack slanting leftwards past two pegs,
to gain a resting niche. Traverse horizontally right and then go up to
a crack and a block.

Manana   150 feet   Hard Very Severe   (1982)
Follows the left-leaning crack before going round the right edge. Start
at a small ramp.
1 60 feet. 5b. Go up the ramp, then it is best to take a vertical crack
to the halfway ramp. This is delicately linked to a grass ledge on the
right.
2 70 feet. 5a. Move right, round the corner, and climb a shallow
groove to a crack on the crest.

Raj Path   120 feet   Severe   (1966)
A steep but surprisingly easy route. Start below a large boulder in the
bed of West Gully.
1 65 feet. Get into a little triangular cave, pull out of this and climb a
crack, moving right at the top to reach the other end of North Chasm.
2 55 feet. Climb the crack on the right until a hole enables one to
enter The Rift and squirm to the top.

West Gully is the best descent from The Pillar itself.

Sundowner   200 feet   Hard Severe   (1972)
A reasonable climb on the slopes above The Pillar. Start at an
obvious groove in the wall below and to the right of the steep part of
West Gully.
1 100 feet. 4b. Go up the groove and the right edge to a stance.
2 100 feet. 4a. Carry on in the same line to the top of a flake. The
crack in the wall above leads to the top.

Elidir Slabs

These are obvious, lying a few hundred feet up the mountainside west
of The Pillar. Though often wet, and appearing quite difficult, the slabs
are quite reasonable, with excellent friction when the good holds
disappear.

Sospan Bach   275 feet   Severe   (1966)
A not-too-difficult, mountaineering route that follows the low-relief rib
just left of the main area of slabs. Start by scrambling up a grassy
gully to the rib proper.
1 55 feet. Mainly grass but there is some rock in a groove.
2 65 feet. A slanting crack leads to the top of a block; gain the rib
and climb to a belay in the grass on the left.
3 65 feet. Continue more or less directly on the rib.
4 90 feet. Go on up to the overhang and turn it on the right. The rib
now fades into broken ground.

★**Armour**   220 feet   Very Severe   (1967)
This develops into quite an excursion; it deserves popularity. Start
where a lip of the slabs curves to the right of Sospan Bach; two broad
quartz streaks mark the wall above the gully.
1 55 feet. 4b. The wall is steep but the key is just right of the
right-hand streak. Climb to a small stance and a peg.
2 65 feet. 4c. Traverse left beneath the overlap to a corner. A steep
move on the right leads to easier ground.
3 100 feet. 4c. Climb up then diagonally left of the overlap. Step
back right and finish more directly. A great pitch.

★★**Janos**   265 feet   Very Severe   (1967)
A first-class route, quite hard and sometimes serious. The upper part
gives some delightfully open climbing. Start just left of the lowest
slabs, by a quartz vein.
1 25 feet. 4a. Climb directly to the right end of the large overhang
and step round the block on the right to a stance.
2 75 feet. 4b. Move off the block onto holds above the overhang,
turn to the next overlap on the right, and climb to a stance.
3 60 feet. 4b. From up on the right, traverse leftwards across a steep
groove, making a long step onto its left rib. Follow this to a grass
ledge and peg belay.
4 45 feet. 4a. Climb up to the left of the overhang, cross the groove
on the right. Peg belay beneath a roof.
5 60 feet. 4a. Work up, on the left of the groove, to the top.

The Yazar   190 feet   Very Severe   (1966)
Makes the best of the right-hand slabs, taking a smooth slab below
the obvious overhang. Unfortunately it is often wet. Start halfway up
the right-hand gully, as it opens out.
1 95 feet. 4c. Climb the easy-angled rock to a niche. Traverse left
then go straight up to the black overhang. Move left with more
difficulty to a grass ledge and peg belay.
2 95 feet. 4b. Go up the rib and its continuation on the left to a
second overhang. Climb steeply to the right and exit right. A further
buttress gives two easy pitches.

The rather broken buttress to the right of the gully does have some
interesting climbing. **Raven's Groove** (120 feet, Difficult, 1966) is on
the right side of a pillar on its upper tower.

Elidir Tower
Lower down the hillside on the right is a sharp tower with a steep left
side and a rippled slab on the front face.

★★**The Laxative** 165 feet Very Severe (1967)
The keen left edge is quite magnificent. Start at the cut-off base, by an overhanging wall.
1 25 feet. 4a. The jagged corner crack to a stance.
2 140 feet. 4c. Go up the corner on the right, then take the slanting crack across the slab to the exposed edge. Follow this to the top. A fine pitch, sustained and serious.

★**Cricklewood** 80 feet E2 (1988)
Climbs the steep left face of the 'sharp tower'. Start at the base of a thin crack.
1 80 feet. 5c. Ascend the wall below the groove via a crack on the right then move left and climb the overhanging groove and crack past a peg. A series of wild moves leftwards provides an exit on to easier ground and the upper slab of Laxative. Belay well back.

There are some cliffs above the small lake of Marchlyn Bach. The lower rocks are of no consequence but on the main buttress there are two routes. These serve either as a pleasant evening's outing, or to relieve the tedium of a tarmac ascent in to the Cwm.

White Horse 185 feet Hard Severe (1966)
Although artificial it does provide some good climbing. The main cliff is divided into two buttresses by a central grassy depression. Start at the lowest point of the left-hand arm, just left of the depression.
1 90 feet. Difficult moves lead up to a ridge, move left and climb a groove to a stance.
2 95 feet. Ascend the crack on the left to a ledge then the ridge above to a step leftwards. The crack above leads to another ledge at 60 feet. The corner crack proves difficult at first until it is possible to move right into a groove.

Auspice 150 feet Severe (1966)
Another obscure offering. Start to the right of the central depression at the foot of a rock groove.
1 90 feet. Ascend the groove on good holds to reach grass and a move up right to blocks. Follow the crack on the left to go back right again to a stance.
2 60 feet. Continue up the groove strenuously to finish up a final wall.

Lawrie (top) and Les Holliwell, major Carneddau pioneers; Les went on to write the 1975 guidebook. Photo: Ken Wilson

Carneddau (Mountains of the Cairns)

Introduction

Whosoever ventures into the Carneddau shall certainly realise that they have entered an arena where climbing sometimes takes second place to enjoyment and a feeling for mountains. They shall also find that high crag routes can also be found in North Wales away from Clogwyn Du'r Arddu. Many of the routes are brilliant mountain climbs of high quality and historical value. Indeed these cliffs rank with Lliwedd and Ogwen as being the original areas for the development of rock-climbing in Wales. However, the area's reputation for traditional routes should not mask the fact that there are many excellent modern routes. The atmosphere at some of the crags is stark and intimidating, and has contributed to their lack of development; but it is a part of the climbing and should be savoured as such.

The Carneddau is the largest mountain mass in North Wales and it has a unique and compelling character, comprising undulating mountains and pleasantly secluded cwms. It is a wilderness with few reminders of the twentieth century. The crags are widely scattered and are usually remote from main roads. They are often sufficiently far away to ensure relative peace and are quiet even in the height of summer; a great attraction for those who seek solitude.

There are seven major summits within the Carneddau area. The topography of this range is fairly complex with a greater area above the 900 metre contour than Central Snowdonia. The highest peaks are Carnedd Llywelyn 684 644 and Carnedd Dafydd 663 630. Two long, parallel ridges lead north west, one from each of the Carneddau to form Cwm Llafar, at the head of which are the huge cliffs of Ysgolion Duon and Llech Ddu. Yr Elen 674 651 is part of the northern ridge. Pen yr Ole Wen 656 619 is to the south-west of the two principal summits, and is the only one reasonably close to a road; it throws a spur southwards to Ogwen Cottage, which contains the cliffs of Braich Ty Du. On the opposite side of the mountain is Cwm Lloer with its secluded cliff. To the south east of Carnedd Llywelyn a ridge leads to Pen yr Helgi Du 698 629; on the eastern flank of this ridge is the sprawling mass of Craig yr

Ysfa. Pen Llithrig y Wrach 716 624 is the farthest east while Foel Grach 688 658 is the most northerly and remote of the major peaks, and has Craig Cwm Dulyn to its north east. All of the summits are linked by a series of high ridges. Most of the crags are best approached from various points along, or close to, the A5. Some of the more easterly crags can also be reached from the Conwy Valley. Access points will be described in the preamble to each cliff.

In the main, Llech Ddu and Craig yr Ysfa are of the greatest interest. The minor crags, Craig Lloer, Carreg Mianog, Craig yr Ogof and Braich Ty Du are worthy of a few visits. The remainder can probably best be described as acquired tastes. Creigiau Gleision is indeed rather poor while Craig y Dulyn, the most remote of all the cliffs, is set above a tranquil cwm with a truly black lake and is a desolate place.

Llech Ddu which is north-facing, black and usually wet, can hardly be described as a friendly crag. It is a cliff for the improvement of fortitude and character.

Ysgolion Duon is a huge cliff, with a vast amount of scope for the seekers of adventure. The scale is such that cliffs that would attract attention elsewhere are lost among the maze of buttresses and rock walls staggered on different levels. Much of it is steep, usually extremely wet and with grooves and ledges choked with lush vegetation.

Craig yr Ysfa is also a very large crag, yet almost the antithesis of Ysgolion Duon. The general angle of the rock is low with large areas virtually buried beneath fields of heather. However, the Amphitheatre redeems the cliff with large sweeps of steep rough rock. The Right Wall has some stunning routes, comparable to the best on Cloggy! This apart, only the classic routes Great Gully and Amphitheatre Buttress are outstanding objectives.

The grading of the routes on these cliffs reflects their tradional style, the determination of the pioneers and the resolve required. Moreover, the climber must allow for the fact that the weather, vegetation, poor rock and lichen can compound the difficulties. Certainly there is no shame in retreat when adverse circumstances dictate. Routes are usually described from left to right, and as free as is possible, or is known. The pegs, which have been placed over the years should be treated with the utmost distrust, even on the more popular climbs. Furthermore, one should not use the mention of pegs either as a belay or a waymark as a measure of their worth. In all cases pegs should be backed up with other forms of protection. It must be stressed that rock-climbing is potentially a dangerous activity, any directions or information contained in this guidebook is acted upon at the reader's own risk. The standard preamble explaining adjectival gradings, technical gradings, stars et cetera can be found in the Ogwen Introduction.

Finally, one must remember that the cliffs of the Carneddau lend themselves to powerful and committing climbing, often in impressive or sombre surroundings; the antithesis of many Ogwen cliffs. The skills developed on such mountain routes, as well as the thrills, will be remembered for many years. The routes are for connoisseurs with a more discerning taste; who may relish the seclusion and bask in the fact that few 'Cafe Heros' could manage the walks in!

Cwm Llafar   (Valley of Echoes)

This classic glaciated valley runs south-east from Bethesda towards the two principal Carneddau summits. The gentle lower reaches contrast well with the rugged head of the cwm which is dominated by huge and impressive cliffs.

Ysgolion Duon   (The Black Ladders)

OS Ref. 670 632

This cliff is remote from all roads, and about one and a half hours should be allowed for the walk. By far the least strenuous and most straightforward(!) approach is from Gerlan, OS Ref. 634 665, above Bethesda. A narrow surfaced road leads to the uppermost bridge over Afon Llafar to Ty-slatters and the water treatment works, here is the start of the path. However, getting to this point needs the skill of an RAC rally navigator.

On entering Bethesda from the Ogwen Valley take the first turning on the right 626 660; this is Braichmelyn. Continue along the road and over a bridge, then go steeply leftwards to a junction. Turn sharply right and continue along a narrow road to a Post Office and chapel, it is best to park in this vicinity. Parking is very limited further along the road.

Walk along through farmland to where the road drops down to a small bridge across the Afon Caseg. It then rises back up to reach a fork, take the right-hand fork to gain the bridge over Afon Llafar, cross this, then bear left to gain the water treatment works. A stile immediately right of the gate takes one around the water treatment works to a ruined farm and an ancient trackway. If one approaches Bethesda from Bangor, it is still better to reach Gerlan from the Braichmelyn turning; which now becomes the last road on the left before the Ogwen Valley. Otherwise, ask for directions; you can only be sent the wrong way!

Once at the ruined farm, behind the water treatment works, a track leads over an ancient bridge to a stile. Marshy enclosures then give access to open moorland and the mouth of the valley; where, due to old explorations for Manganese, a better track is attained. This follows the south west bank of Afon Llafar to a point beyond Llech Ddu, where it peters out altogether. An ill-defined path then leads into the upper cwm. Boulder screes and water-logged ground provide options leading to the final steep incline. From the south, the best approach is from Glan Llugwy, OS Ref. 683 613. A little to the west of Carreg Mianog a stream bed is followed on to the ridge. An easy walk then leads up to Cefn Ysgolion Duon.

The eastern ridge is cairned and provides a scrambling descent to the foot of the cliff. Easy descents can also be made at the extreme western limit of the cliffs. Central Gully may be descended, but this is not recommended for inexperienced parties.

Ysgolion Duon is really a whole complex of cliffs, forming an immense cirque below the summit of Carnedd Dafydd. Fortunately, three principal gullies provide good points of reference and the Pyramid Face is easily recognised. The remainder of the cliff is more confusing. The Y-shaped Eastern Gully is obvious; then Central Gully, slanting up to the left, is well left of centre. Western Gully, rising one cave pitch above another is approximately in the centre. The Pyramid Face is defined by Pyramid Gully on the left, and Central Gully on the right. Each of the buttresses is associated with an adjacent gully. There are three buttresses to the west of Western Gully; Western, Mid West and Far West.

Although the Ysgolion Duon cliffs are over 750 feet high and close to three quarters of a mile long, very few continuous lines exist. Tedious approaches and exits detract from the enjoyment of otherwise worthwhile climbs. The structure is of alternate ribs and grooves, the latter invariably choked with luxuriant vegetation encouraged by perpetual drainage. This, combined with the high angle of many buttresses and inaccessibility, accounts for the limited exploration that has taken place. The initial steep black walls and bands of overhangs quickly give way to broad undulating terraces traversing the cliff at various levels. These are known as Ysgolfeinciau (benches or ledges of the Ladder), and are largely responsible for the discontinuity of the climbs. Most routes are escapable, due to the broken character of the crag, yet the 'escapes' seldom prove to be easy.

Apart from the classic gullies and the routes Flanders, Cannon Rib and Cannon Ball, very few climbs can be recommended, most provide a little interest in what is otherwise a long scramble to the cliff top. It seems unlikely that this will ever be a popular rock-climbing crag; north-facing, wet and high on the mountain, it seldom provides comfortable climbing conditions. However, some people revel in these very conditions. They won't be disappointed, as ascents are usually eventful and have a less predictable nature than most; having more of a mountaineering than rock-climbing character. It is not a place for beginners or those who hanker after safe 'sport' climbs; indeed, many seasoned climbers have departed more respectfully than they came. Moreover, it may be wise to carry a selection of pegs and a hammer on an ascent of some of the harder routes as many belays are sometimes difficult to arrange and ancient pegs have rusted away. Here is a truly redoubtable cliff!

Route finding can be a problem, but precise lines are of little consequence here, as the climber can be left to devise one to suit his own abilities and the time available. With this point in mind some climbs have been described in outline only. The climbs are described from Left to Right as are the buttresses.

The Eastern Ridge   Moderate   (Before 1895)
This somewhat vaguely defines the left-hand edge of Eastern Gully. It is gained above the initial pitch of the gully and provides an ascent or descent.

Eastern Gully   Moderate   (Before 1895)
After an initial waterworn pitch, the main gully is little more than a walk. The right-hand branch is slightly harder and steeper. It is gained via a vegetated rake leading diagonally right from the largest terrace some 250 feet above the steep black rocks at the base of the cliff. It is not particularly obvious.

The Eastern Buttress

The buttress is situated between the two branches of Eastern Gully. It is broken, but more continuous on the left-hand side overlooking the main gully. Three routes have been made here:

Pegasus   190 feet   Very Difficult   (1947)
A poor climb, artificial in line. Start in the Eastern Gully. About 250 feet above the steep black lower rocks is a distinctive pile of large blocks, fringed with grass, on the left arête (Eastern Ridge) of the gully. A hundred feet higher and on the right of the gully is a slabby buttress. The slabs lead up to, and pass either side of, a large overhang. The lower edge of the slabs is defined by two short ribs.
1 30 feet. Climb either rib or the groove between them, to a ledge with flake belays.
2 100 feet. Climb a series of slabs, with grassy breaks, to a chimney groove, to the right of a large overhang. Swing out left when the chimney closes and gain a ledge awkwardly.

Tom Leppert on The Red Slab of Carnedd y Filiast. Photo: Margaret Hankey

Unknown climbers high on *The Great Corner* (E2), Llech Ddu.
Photo: Chris Jackson

3 60 feet. Step on to a block above the stance, then go right, and follow a grassy groove. Exit right then belay well back.

Variation
Chimera   120 feet   Difficult   (1949)
A rather pointless alternative. Start from about 40 feet up pitch 2 of the original route, where a grassy rake on the right can be gained. A little rib defines the right-hand edge of the upper slab. Start immediately right of the toe of the rib.
1 120 feet. May be split. Gain a flake on the left, then take a cracked corner and mantelshelf to a boulder garden. Go up blocks and then cracks on the left which lead to the buttress crest.

Mare's Nest Climb   190 feet   Severe   (1947)
A pleasant climb, more accessible than most. Start about 50 feet above the pile of blocks mentioned for Pegasus. The largest of the grass terraces leads right beneath the Eastern Buttress. A further 40 feet up the gully bed a rake leads up diagonally right; a short way up is a fallen block, above is a 20-foot rib with a groove on its right.
1 60 feet. Climb the groove and step left, then follow a little ridge to a broad grass ledge. Belay below a slab.
2 130 feet. Climb the slab 10 feet from, and parallel to, its left edge. Traverse right where it steepens into a wall, and go up a short vegetated groove, then back left on to a rib. Ascend the rib and a slab above, awkward at first, then continue on better holds to a ledge. Finish easily up a 20-foot block to a pile of rocks.

Pyramid Gully   280 feet   Very Difficult   (1961)
A rather open gully, not easy to protect. It defines the left edge of Pyramid Face. Start from Eastern Gully. Above the initial steep wall a grass terrace is traversed rightwards. Another 100 feet of scrambling then leads into a gully. This entry avoids the uninviting chasm, which provides a direct start and a positive means of identifying the gully from below.
1 120 feet. A curving waterworn groove steepens. Climb first on the right, then on the left, to a possible belay. Step on to the right wall above then make a couple of awkward moves back in to the gully bed.
2 100 feet. Scramble, then climb a little wall and continue past a flat block. Climb 10 feet of rock and then go easily to the foot of a tower on the right.
3 60 feet. Climb a crack near the left-hand edge of the tower, with increasing difficulty. A few more feet then the angle eases. About 200 feet of scrambling and easy rocks lead to the summit.

Variation
Direct Start   110 feet   Very Severe
This is the obvious chasm below the gully; it is invariably wet, with a dangerously loose exit.
1 100 feet. A broken groove leads to a wide chimney, widening still further into the chasm, which is strenuous and insecure. This gives direct access to pitch 1 above.

Pyramid Face

This is the most easily identified section of the cliff, bounded on either side by Pyramid and Central Gullies. The base is guarded by jutting overhangs that are black with algae which thrive on perpetual drainage.

Jacob's Ladder   470 feet   Hard Severe   (1935)
Invariably wet and greasy. The route breaks through the initial overhangs impressively, but there is an unfortunate break above where a large grass terrace interrupts. The line is apparently the easiest available, but it is not well defined. Start about 100 feet right of the chasm at the base of Pyramid Gully where there is a large block lying against the crag, about 40 feet above the terrace. A line of overhangs are immediately above the block. Start 25 feet left of the block at a flake belay.
1 50 feet. Two mantelshelves lead to an obvious traverse ledge, which is followed to the right to a corner formed by the block. Climb the corner to the top of the block and move right to belay at the far end.
2 80 feet. 4b. Continue traversing, round a bulge, to a crack. Climb it and awkwardly gain a slab on the right. Go diagonally right up the slab, then traverse left along a line of vegetation beneath an overhang, to a large flake belay.
3 120 feet. Ascend a rake on the left to a broad belt of steep grass which leads to a belay by a small cave.
4 110 feet. Descend left for 30 feet to a large spike. Go over the spike and climb a rib above. Climb the left-hand of two grooves until forced right to grass ledges, which lead to a block belay.
5 50 feet. Directly above the belay leads to a small grass platform. Gain a groove awkwardly and follow it more easily.
6 60 feet. Make an exposed traverse right, over a hanging rib. Move right again and climb a groove and rib beyond to a spike. Thirty feet higher where an obvious traverse leads right into Central Gully, or scrambling direct to the top.

Hoyland's Route   500 feet   Difficult   (1934)
This route follows the fairly well-defined ridge on the left-hand edge of Central Gully. It is gained above the reed rake mentioned for the

Gully. The line can be modified almost at will, and if a pitch leads inevitably into the Gully a short traverse left will find another. Higher up, an overhanging tower is best avoided on the right. Higher again, a monolith is passed.

Central Gully 500 feet Difficult   (1879)
This gully is situated well to the left of the centre of the crag; it is easily identified as the one slanting left and defining the edge of Pyramid Face. The route really comes into its own in winter conditions, and ranks high among snow and ice routes in Wales. All the pitches can be climbed direct but the unpleasant introductory section is best avoided by following a reed rake, over on the right of the main gully line; this is gained via a 10-foot chimney. Only one pitch, a tall chimney with a large jammed chockstone, is worthy of detailed description and this can be avoided on the left; it starts some 250 feet up the gully:
1 60 feet. Climb the back of the chimney to a stance at 30 feet, level with the first chockstone. Back-up and work outwards until an exit can be made above a block. A few moves then lead to the stony gully bed.

Central Buttress

This is a rather ill-defined area of rock situated high up and to the right of Central Gully. Although it extends to Western Gully, it is broken yet steep, and is interrupted by broad vegetated ledges and barriers of overhangs. Only a very small section, known as Central Gully Wall, has been climbed on and even this is not very inspiring.

The Central Gully Wall is, in fact, a series of ribs, situated close to the gully and about 100 feet above the main chimney pitch. The next three routes all commence high in Central Gully and are very close together. The key to the starts is a short chimney on the right of a large jammed boulder in the bed of the gully, approximately 300 feet from the top. Some 40 feet directly above the short chimney, is a long wedge-shaped block on the right wall. All three routes are artificial in line and somewhat disjointed, but the rock is excellent. Long pitches may be split.

Jupiter 220 feet Very Difficult   (1949)
Quite sustained and probably the most interesting of the three. Start about 20 feet above the short chimney and directly below the wedge-shaped block, where there is a narrow grass ledge leading horizontally right. Traverse this to a block belay.
1 100 feet. Gain a square chimney and climb it to a capstone. Exit right and go up to a grass ledge. Step left awkwardly on to a rock ledge and move along it for a few feet. Go up a rib above, keeping

just inside its left edge, to grass. This is followed to a large block belay on the left.
2 120 feet. Step from the belay block and climb a rib directly above trending right into a scoop, then scramble up grass. Continue up twin cracks to a steep wall, with an awkward exit to grass. A crack and groove on the left lead to vegetation, then another short groove leads to broken ground.

Juno   160 feet   Very Difficult   (1949)
Difficulties are short lived and some of the rock is loose. Start at the wedge-shaped block.
1 100 feet. Squeeze behind the block and continue traversing right across a groove, around a rib to a large detached spike in another groove. Climb a knife-edged rib on the left and then three blocks to a short grass rake trending right. Move left to another rib and go up to a flake on its left. Boldly go up the flake (crux), to a grass platform and low spike belay.
2 60 feet. Trend slightly right to a little recess, past loose flakes and blocks to a summit rib. Belays and easy ground.

Jason   190 feet   Difficult   (1950)
This route enjoys more exposure than its neighbours as it emerges on to the face of the buttress. Start as for Juno.
1 95 feet. Ascend Juno for 30 feet then go up a short groove on the right, then a little slab on its right to perched blocks. Continue diagonally right until it is possible to step across the top of a groove. A few feet higher is a stance and belay.
2 95 feet. Move left and climb a slabby arête on superb holds, spiralling right to a ledge. Step left across a groove and go up to more broken ground to finish.

★Flanders   715 feet   Hard Very Severe   (1969)
An excellent mountaineering route. Most of the difficulties are concentrated in the first two pitches, but interest is well-maintained. The line follows the left arête of Western Gully. Start by scrambling up to the foot of Western Gully. Follow the initial easy pitch to the highest of the grass terraces on the left, and traverse it for 30 feet. A shallow groove is above.
1 100 feet. 5a. Climb diagonally left for 10 feet before ascending rightwards to gain a shallow groove. Go delicately up the groove, to a small ledge on the edge of a rib. Continue up to a spike belay at the right-hand end of a grass ledge.
2 70 feet. 5a. Move left across grass for a few feet then go up into a steep groove trending left. Climb the groove and pull over a roof on good holds. Ascend another groove to a good ledge below a line of

overhangs.

3 110 feet. 4a. Traverse a few feet left and break through the overhangs trending left. Step left and climb a thin crack in a slab until it is possible to move back right to good holds at the top of a shallow groove. Climb up to a small grass ledge and continue up a groove above to a small platform on the left.

4 20 feet. Scramble right through the hole behind a large flake to a good stance and chockstone belays at the foot of a huge groove.

5 140 feet. 4a. Climb the groove direct. Finish over broken rock to a fine ledge overlooking the gully

6 60 feet. 4a. Step down past a flake on the left, then continue on to the edge of a rib. Climb this direct on good holds to a small ledge.

7 30 feet. 5a. Climb the right-hand edge of a smooth wall above, with a delicate finish. Belay around the top of a pinnacle.

8 60 feet. 5a. Scramble across a horizontal ridge to the foot of a narrow chimney on the right of the ridge. Climb this to a broad grass terrace.

9 25 feet. Walk along the terrace to the foot of a grassy groove left of a short pillar.

10 100 feet. 4a. Climb the grassy groove to a small bay, ascend a corner on the left, then a short crack in the final wall. A short scramble along the ridge leads to the summit.

Central Buttress is defined on the right by the most distinctive feature of the cliff, a steep gully with cave pitches one above the other. This is:

★★★ **Western Gully** 760 feet Severe   (1901)
One of the great Welsh classics. It is sustained at a high standard with an inescapable line, and is more serious than Great Gully on Craig yr Ysfa. In less than perfect conditions it will prove harder than its grade. Although the line is very obvious, the lower section is less well-defined. The water course is the best guide.

1 250 feet. Eighty feet of unpleasant waterworn grooves lead to grass and the gully bed, which is followed past a couple of short rock walls to the first of the jammed stones. Alternatively a line to the east of the main gully bed, via a little chimney at 60 feet with a jammed stone, leads to the same place.

2 130 feet. Pass the chockstone on the right, then move across it and into the gully. Ascend the gully past a smooth section.

3 85 feet. Bridge into the bottom of a narrow chimney. Face left as it narrows, and exit left to a large platform with a belay on the right. Continue to the stony bed of a large mossy cave.

4 40 feet. Either traverse out right, over and behind piles of blocks to the foot of a groove above a large rushy terrace, or climb the cave direct, at Very Severe standard.

5 70 feet. Make an awkward entry into the groove and follow it to a grass platform on the right. Vegetation and rocks on the left then lead to a belay just outside the gully.
6 35 feet. Traverse easily left along a rock ledge to the right-hand side of a large jammed boulder which leads to the floor of another huge cave.
7 50 feet. The crux. A slab on the right provides a clean and difficult pitch to reach scree above. Poor belay immediately, or continue.
8 100 feet. Walk into a little amphitheatre where a chimney on the left provides the best exit. Grooves on the right are less pleasant and more difficult. Scramble up to a boulder bridge, which is taken on the right, or the slim may squeeze through. About 200 feet of scrambling leads to the ridge.

Western Buttress

To the west of Western Gully there is a vast expanse of rock, which eventually peters out and merges into the mountainside. There are three fairly distinct sections, the first of which is the largest and is known by the above title. Here the terraces are larger and extend right across the cliff at approximately 250 feet above the scree. The routes described commence at this level.

The boundary between this buttress and the next is ill-defined, but the Mid West Buttress has an impressive barrier of jutting overhangs at about one-third height.

Cannon Ball   430 feet   Hard Very Severe   (1973)
About halfway between Western Gully and Mid West Buttress is a tall, broad rib, the most continuous piece of rock hereabouts. When approaching from the west (right), a very distinctive stone 'cannon' protrudes at about two-thirds height. Directly below the 'cannon' are two grooves. A short scramble leads to a grassy ledge below the grooves. Start on the grassy ledge below the right-hand groove.
1 150 feet. Scramble up to a ledge beneath the first groove of Cannon Rib. Traverse left into the left-hand groove and crack system and follow this past wobbly blocks to a large flat ledge on the right.
2 50 feet. From the left-hand end of the ledge, climb up to a small overhang, then traverse left with difficulty to a short groove. Cross this, to a crack which is climbed to easy ground. Belay well back.
3 150 feet. Scramble over steep grassy rock (very loose in places). This leads to a corner/groove forming the left-hand side of a prominent rib on the right.
4 80 feet. Climb the corner for 20 feet, then the right wall to reach a short chimney above and thus gain a ridge. Scrambling remains.

★★**Cannon Rib** 500 feet Hard Very Severe   (1971)
A route of sustained interest. Start as for Cannon Ball, below the
right-hand of the two grooves.
1 150 feet. Follow the groove until it divides, move up right then go
back left to reach a crack in the left-hand groove, or continue up the
original groove, this leads to a large ledge and spike belays as for
Cannon Ball.
2 80 feet. Traverse right with difficulty on undercuts, (tiny spike runner
above a bulge); this leads back to the original groove line, which has
been climbed direct. Continue up the groove and across grass to a
large spike belay on the right.
3 120 feet. Move back left for a few feet, then climb up into a long
groove which becomes a flared chimney at half-height, and leads to a
long ledge with spike belays.
4 150 feet. Move up left across large flakes to a groove in the centre
of a rib, then follow it to the top.

Mid West Buttress

This is a steep, compact crag with jutting overhangs. It is even wetter
and more repulsive than its neighbours.

Far West Buttress

Here there is a change of character, with less drainage and
coarse-textured rock. It is the extreme right-hand buttress alone that is of
any significance and this is easily distinguished by the sloping terraces
which divide it into three tiers. About a third of the way along the base
from the left-hand end, is a detached block 'The Turnstile'. Step left off
the block to gain a grass ledge, which is traversed for 50 feet, where
an awkward break gives access to the lower terrace, from which the next
two climbs start.

Roughcast Wall 260 feet Severe   (1937)
Vegetated, but the proportion of rock and the difficulty increases with
height. Start by ascending the lower terrace past a clean little slab to
another with a small pinnacle at half-height. Thread belay.
1 130 feet. Climb the slab on increasingly steep vegetation, until a
platform on the left can be gained. A poorly protected pitch.
2 80 feet. Move up on to some blocks, traverse right along a ledge
for a few feet, then climb a narrow grassy groove and wide crack
behind a pinnacle to its summit. Continue up a slot to a terrace.
3 50 feet. Ascend a steep little wall behind the stance, then follow
another more delicate wall, to complete the serious climbing.
Scrambling remains.

Roughcast Flutings   190 feet   Very Difficult   (1937)
A less worthy route than its companion. Start at the upper end of the
oblique terrace, 30 feet beyond the previous climb, by some large
detached blocks.
1 70 feet. Climb a grassy groove, then traverse slabs on the left to
belay on a ledge.
2 80 feet. Up a bubbly groove until a delicate traverse can be made
right, to a sloping shelf. This leads to another groove which is
followed to a grass terrace and large belay.
3 40 feet. Move over to the left and climb a steep slab to a large
block. Scramble to the summit.

West End Buttress   Moderate   250 feet   (1911)
Well over to the right are the final rocks, gained via a little green col.
Follow an obvious line up the edge of the buttress.

Llech Ddu   (The Black Slab)

OS Ref. 666 636

This crag is situated at the northern end of Crib Lem, the ridge running
north west into Cwm Llafar from the summit of Carnedd Dafydd.

The most straightforward approach is from the village of Gerlan, OS Ref.
634 665, above Bethesda, taking the route as for Ysgolion Duon but
striking up the screes to the base of the crag after about one hour. Refer
to that section for a detailed description.

Descents can be made to the east or west of the crag; use the nearest,
both are fairly long but easy. However, loose scree is potentially a serious
hazard to those below and care should be exercised.

Llech Ddu is a magnificent crag of great character, its size and steepness
are not immediately apparent. Moreover, there is an unique atmosphere,
stark, sombre and rather intimidating. A band of vegetation traverses the
cliff at half-height and, in conjunction with steep central grass chutes,
tends to exaggerate the discontinuity of the buttresses. Some of the routes
are seriously affected by this vegetation.

The crag has a northern aspect and seldom gains advantage from the
sun; this, combined with the vegetation and moisture-harbouring summit

screes, make it slow to dry. The structure is complex and difficult to comprehend on first acquaintance, and as there are relatively few good points of reference it is more than usually important to locate the more obvious features before approaching the crag too closely. The 'skylight' of Iota is well to the left and at the summit of a prominent arête; Skid Row chimney is obvious at the left-hand end of the Central Wall; The Great Corner is approximately in the centre of this wall; and The Groove divides the most continuous buttress, steep and bulging below. Well over to the right on the West Flank is Y-Chimney, a forked groove. The West Flank is well-featured with a series of ribs and grooves.

Routes are described from east (left) to west (right). Those which commence at the base are dealt with first, then those from The Pillar Traverse. The routes on the upper and lower sections of the cliff can be coupled together to provide continuous climbing. The state of the pegs on this cliff is a cause for concern, they should all be considered as suspect. Many climbers have 'burnt their boats' in reaching a peg only to find it crumbling to dust in front of their eyes. Moreover, they are sometimes used in the text as waymarks, but appear and disappear regularly; they should not therefore be taken to be permanent features. One thing must be borne in mind when climbing on this cliff – all pegs should be backed up!

East Flank

Cave Route   370 feet   Moderate   (1918)
A diagonal traverse of the upper part of the cliff's east end. To provide a route of some interest, The Corridor, a narrow horizontal slot, has been described with the original two pitches. Start at the extreme left-hand end of the cliff, on its east flank a mountain ash tree grows from a short rock wall. On its right is a scree gully. Some 40 feet up on the right is a poised slab which forms the roof of the cave.
1 50 feet. Scramble up, and where the true gully line trends left, enter the cave. Exit through a skylight to a platform.
2 50 feet. Climb a rib on the right edge, then a little groove where the rock is loose, and on to a broken area of cliff.
3 60 feet. The Corridor is obvious farther right. Follow the line over to it, past the top of one groove and down into the next. This is the top of Corridor Gully. Belays.
4 90 feet. Go up the opposite branch of The Corridor. It becomes lost in vegetation, but reappears blocked by a boulder. Belays at the foot of the right-hand of two cracks.
5 120 feet. Climb either crack. The line is obvious, but there are no real features until a 25-foot chimney leads to the summit.

Llech Ddu: East Flank

1. Meibion Glyndwr	E2	7. Askant Chimney	D
2. Far East Chimney	D	8. Skid Row	VS
3. Corridor Gully	VD	9. Herostratus	E3
4. Iota	VS	10. Endor	E2
5. The Ribbon	S	11. Venom	E3
6. Gytrack	E1	12. Great Corner	E2

Photo: Iwan Arfon Jones

Meibion Glyndwr   130 feet   E2   (1989)
A line up the buttress left of Far East Chimney. Start as for Far East
Chimney and scramble 30 feet to a belay below the wall proper.
1 130 feet. 5b. Ascend up and rightwards past a horizontal break.
Arrange protection then work back leftward to gain the arête. Climb
the arête to finish.

Far East Chimney   180 feet   Difficult   (1919)
There is very little clean rock on this climb, and even this can be
avoided. An unsatisfactory route. Start below the extreme east end of
the crag where a scrappy broken rock buttress drops down into the
cwm. On its right is a scree chute, above which are two gullies. This
climb takes the least distinguished left-hand one.
1 100 feet. Scramble up vegetation. There are several equally
pointless alternatives, all of which manage to avoid the rock. Poor
tree belay.
2 80 feet. Walk left along the base of a wall, to a point where it can
be climbed on small holds to an arête, which is followed to scree at
the top. The arête can be taken direct, but this robs the route of its
only virtue.

Corridor Gully   190 feet   Very Difficult   (1917)
A virtually inescapable line, but it is rather vegetated. A serious route,
especially in wet conditions. Start as for Far East Chimney. This is the
right-hand of the two gullies at the extreme left-hand end of the cliff.
Belay on the right of the gully.
1 110 feet. Follow a grassy rake easily left into the gully. Make a
move on the left wall, then step right and continue up the gully bed to
a short rib on the left which leads to a little slab. Go past a jammed
block and belay on another higher up. This pitch can be split.
2 20 feet. Pull over the block and scramble up to a good flake belay
on the left.
3 40 feet. Walk into a corner and climb the left wall on good holds.
Exit right up grass to a large spike belay. Here The Corridor crosses.
4 20 feet. Climb the left-hand branch to the top, or, follow The
Corridor, as described for Cave Route.

Iota   260 feet   Very Severe   (1966)
Two grassy and serious pitches lead to a worthwhile finish in a fine
position. Start towards the eastern end where high up on the cliff is a
prominent pointed arête with a 'skylight' at its summit. Belay at the
front of the buttress, directly below the arête.
1 60 feet. 4a. Climb a shallow groove on the right, move left
beneath a small overhang, and continue up to a grassy ledge on the
left. Good spike belay.

2 60 feet. 4a. Move back right on loose flakes then go up, bearing left, to a ledge and large spike belay.
3 140 feet. 4c. Climb up, trending left, to a grass ledge. Continue in the same line to gain an obvious groove to the left of an overhang. Climb the groove, keeping right where it forks, to a crack, which is followed to the top. Large chockstone belay well back.

The Psychlist 320 feet E2 (2 pts. aid) (1972/1976)
A serious and exposed route; requiring resolve and good ropework; its quality is only marred by the grassy break where Ribbon Route crosses. It follows the overhanging buttress to the right of lota. Start at a groove in the left-hand arête at the start of Ribbon Route.
1 70 feet. 5a. Climb the groove and traverse right 15 feet below the overhang on dubious flakes to a block on the arête. Go straight up to a small stance on a flake.
2 80 feet. 4c. Go directly over the roof behind the stance to a chimney, then on to the ridge. Follow this through vegetation to Ribbon Route and a belay at the foot of a groove in the Upper Tier.
3 130 feet. 5c. Climb the groove, then swing left round the overhang to a steep wall and two thread runners. From the right-hand thread go straight up to a huge roof, peg. Gain a ledge which leads right to a scoop. Continue diagonally, two peg runners and one aid peg, to a sling. Tension from this to a rib on the right. Follow this to a constricted stance in the gully.
4 40 feet. 4b. Climb the slab behind and then the gully.

The Ribbon 330 feet Severe (1970)
The route is continuously vegetated with the exception of the last pitch. However, it has some merit, as it reaches a comparatively inaccessible section of the crag. Start just to the left of the diagonal rake which gives access to routes on the Central Wall where there is a thin line of vegetation with a small tree at 60 feet. Belay below the tree.
1 60 feet. Climb the thin ribbon of vegetation to the tree.
2 130 feet. Continue in the same line, trending left, to the top of the buttress. Spike belay below a huge bulging overhang. Sparse protection.
3 40 feet. Traverse easily left.
4 100 feet. Move up into a recess and turn an overhang on the left. Step right and go up a rib, then into The Corridor, exit on the right.

Primitive Route 270 feet Moderate (1917)
This route takes a diagonal line across the steep vegetation below the Central Wall. It is not recommended. A rock is embedded just above the path along the foot of the crag. Twenty five feet to its left is the

grass-topped bollard of Cupid's Inspiration. Farther left is a
pyramid-shaped rock, where the climb starts. Climb a tortuous track of
vegetation diagonally left to the foot of Askant Chimney. Belays may
be found.

Cupid's Inspiration   260 feet   E2   (1968/1987)
Pleasant climbing in good situations. The line completely avoids the
copious vegetation on this section of the cliff. Start in the centre of the
cliff, from a grass-topped bollard leaning against the rock wall, about
100 feet left of Central Route.
1 130 feet. 4a. Climb diagonally right on to a slab, which is
followed to the bottom of a big open groove, the principal feature on
this part of the cliff. Ascend the groove to an obvious exit right, move
across a wall and go up to a grass ledge. Belay at the far end.
2 130 feet. 5c. Traverse right across a slab and go up to overhangs,
step left and continue upwards. The angle eases and a groove is
followed. Move right at a bulge to avoid unpleasant vegetation, then
go straight up to peg belays on the terrace. Finish either up the final
pitches of Central Route or reverse Pillar Traverse to the west end of
the cliff.

Variations
Yr Wydd Grug   120 feet   E2   (1984)
A direct finish to Cupid's Inspiration at about 5b.

The Straight to the Heart Start   120 feet   E3   (1989)
A direct start to Cupid's Inspiration. Start 30 feet right of the
grass-topped bollard of the original route.
1 120 feet. 5c. Go straight up for a few feet then trend rightward
over a bulge then go up again with a difficult move to gain the big
open groove. Continue as for Cupid's Inspiration pitch 1.

★★ **Central Route**   420 feet   Very Severe   (1946)
A good route, which gets easier as it rises. This slight fault can be
rectified by including pitch 3 of Scarface and pitch 4 of The Groove,
to give a route of consistent standard and quality. The rock is clean
and the situations fine. If the Scarface variation is included, the route
is one of the best in the Carneddau. Start to the right of the cliff's
centre at a prominent light-coloured, open groove with a V-chimney
below. Two boulders, lying one below the other are a further guide;
the path passes just above them and a few yards to the left is the
recess.
1 110 feet. 4c. Climb the V-chimney to a large loose spike at 40
feet. Leave the chimney and move left for a few feet. The wall above
overhangs and an awkward diagonal traverse right leads to a high

step, easier rocks, then a stance and belay. A harder alternative, usually climbed in error, is to follow the line of the initial chimney almost to the stance of Scarface at the top. Then traverse left to reach the same stance and belay, as above.

2 100 feet. 4b. Climb a slab and corner crack to a recess below a steep wall. The right-hand retaining wall gives way to a short slab with belays at the top.

3 30 feet. 4a. The flake crack on the left leads to a field and a large belay at the foot of a chimney on the right.

4 90 feet. Easily ascend the chimney, to the Pinnacle.

5 90 feet. 4a. Continue up to the left or right of an obvious overhang, or anywhere.

Variation
★★**Scarface/The Groove Finish**

3a 80 feet. 4b. Climb the diagonal crack on the right (pitch 3 of Scarface).

4a 60 feet. 4b. Climb a wall on the right (pitch 4 of The Groove) then scramble up the bed of the chimney to the Pinnacle. Finish as pitch 5 above.

The next four routes take different facets of the Pinnacle, and terminate at its summit. The Pinnacle is not immediately recognisable as such, when seen in elevation. It is in fact a huge flake separated from the rest of the crag by Pillar Chimney. The Pillar, is at the right-hand summit of the Pinnacle, best seen from the west. There are two separate summits.

★**Scarface** 450 feet E1   (1967)
The climbing is varied and always interesting, with the hard moves concentrated on the second pitch, but the final few feet of the fourth pitch demand thought. The rock on the initial part of the second pitch requires care. Start 30 feet right of Central Route at the base of a clean groove leading right. The second pitch takes a slim groove immediately left of the huge bulging overhang above. Higher up the route goes across the face of the Pinnacle in a superb position.

1 110 feet. 5a. Ascend the clean groove, step right and go up a slab to a grassy ledge. Traverse easily left and stride on to a rock projection. Move delicately into a scoop, go diagonally left for a few feet, then move back right into a corner.

2 120 feet. 5c. Climb the steep rock immediately left of the corner groove for a few feet, then step into it. Continue until the groove terminates on a sloping ledge. Broken cracks now lead to a grassy ramp. Traverse left into a corner and belay, as for Central Route.

3 80 feet. 4b. Go up a diagonal crack on the right, and continue until a shallow groove is reached. Follow this to a grassy stance at the

top of The Groove.
4 50 feet. 5a. Climb a wall on the right for a few feet, then step left
to a wide crack. Ascend this, with an awkward exit, to a grassy bay
and belays in the chimney beyond.
5 90 feet. 4a. Scramble up the bed of Pillar Chimney to the top of the
Pinnacle and finish as for pitch 5 of Central Route. Alternatively,
reverse The Pillar Traverse to the west end of the crag.

Marathon   350 feet   E3   (1976)
This route takes a line left of The Groove. Start at a grassy bay below
a rightward curving groove between Scarface and The Groove.
1 80 feet. 5c. Climb to the groove and follow it until a traverse right
leads to a crack. From a small ledge above, step left and climb steep
rock to reach a grassy bank. Peg belay below a right-slanting ramp,
just right of a bulging overhang.
2 70 feet. 5b. Climb the ramp, then move up and left to a groove,
which leads to a peg at the end of the traverse on The Groove.
Traverse left for 20 feet to a grassy stance.
3 70 feet. 5a. Climb the depression above the stance for 20 feet,
then move left to the arête and follow it to a ledge. Traverse 15 feet
left to a stance.
4 80 feet. 5a. Climb the steep wall on the left to join and finish up
pitch 3 of Scarface.

★★★The Groove   450 feet   E1   (1961)
An excellent climb taking the most obvious feature of the cliff. Interest
is sustained, but the difficulties are not great for the grade. Start some
30 yards right of Central Route, where a withered and weak
Y-shaped tree remains on a terrace at 80 feet. This terrace
commences just to the right of The Great Arête, which is to the right of
The Groove. Directly below the tree is a narrow groove; belay at its
base.
1 80 feet. 5a. Climb the groove to the grass terrace, rather awkward
at about 50 feet.
2 60 feet. 5a. Go up the corner behind the tree, turning the first
bulge on the right. Take the right wall for a few feet, then step back to
a small ledge and peg belays, good nut higher up. When wet a sling
may be required for aid at the first bulge.
3 70 feet. 5a. Move down left from the stance and traverse delicately
down left into The Groove. Go up this for 30 feet to an uncomfortable
stance.
4 100 feet. 5a. Climb the groove direct to a ledge. An excellent pitch.
5 50 feet. 4b. Trend right up the wall on the right to a grassy bay
and belays in the chimney beyond.
6 90 feet. 4a. Finish straight up as for Central Route.

Dave Shaw climbing *The Great Corner* (E2), Llech Ddu. Photo: John Darling

Mary Niklas on the first ascent of *Mother Earth* (Diff), Craig Ddaear.
Photo: Dave Basford

Eric 'Spider' Penman climbing *Biceps Wall* (VS), Carreg Mianog.
Photo: Ken Wilson

Bob Junkinson in *The Groove* (E1), Llech Ddu. Photo: Tom Leppert

Llech Ddu

1. The Groove — E1
2. The Great Arête — E4
3. Blitzkrieg — E1
4. Shrapnel — HVS
5. Elliw — E1
6. Commuter's Crack — HVS
7. The Jester — HVS
8. Y-Chimney — S
9. Y-Chimney Direct — VS

Photo: Ken Wilson

★★★ The Great Arête   440 feet   E4   (1969/1975)

A brilliant and very exposed climb on the edge of nothing, takes the hanging arête between The Groove and Blitzkrieg. This has much technical bridging and is quite strenuous. Many small wires protect the main pitch. Start as for The Groove.

1 80 feet. 5a. Pitch 1 of The Groove.

2 60 feet. 5a. Go up a difficult wall immediately right of the second pitch of The Groove, out of balance, into a tiny groove. Then go back left to belay as for The Groove. Poorly protected.

3 120 feet. 6a. The pitch! Move left for a few feet, then go up to a very thin peg. Trend slightly left and go up with difficulty to a very poor resting place below a small deep hole (difficult to see from below). A series of precarious moves is then made up a groove to the first overhang, (thread, and semi-rest). Move right beneath the overhang to reach a peg and crack above then surmount the overhang. Continue with difficulty into a groove on the right of another overhang and go up to a peg. Ascend the narrowing groove until it is possible to swing right on good holds where the angle eases. Fifteen feet higher is an uncomfortable belay on poor pegs. Better to use these as a runner, and traverse right to a secure belay and good stance on Blitzkrieg.

4 90 feet. 4c. Follow the left arête in superb position to the top of the Pinnacle

5 90 feet. 4a. Finish as for Central Route.

★ Blitzkrieg   440 feet   E1   (1968)

A route of character, taking an intricate line up the steep broken wall right of The Groove. It trends left above the principal overhangs and goes up a prominent groove leading to the top of the Pillar. Start 40 feet right of the start of The Groove, near a little corner in the lower wall. A few feet to the left of the corner are two grooves which diverge slightly; the less distinct left-hand one is the first objective.

1 80 feet. Go easily up a shallow groove to a four foot high flake on the left. From the top of the flake, move up a steep wall and enter a groove, which leads to a large grass terrace. Spike belay above a small tree.

2 130 feet. 5a. Ascend diagonally left to an awkward little groove, climb this and step left to a resting place. Continue in the same line for a few feet, then move back right to an overhanging rib. Ascend this to easier grooves above. Keeping to the left of a small vegetated cave, continue on steep rock until it is possible to traverse left for 20 feet above the major overhangs. Small stance and peg belay below the final groove.

3 130 feet. 4c. Climb a wall to the groove, then go up it to the top of the Pillar. A fine pitch.

4 100 feet. 4a. Finish as for Central Route, or reverse The Pillar Traverse to the west end of the crag.

Shrapnel 220 feet Hard Very Severe   (1970)
Takes the more obvious right-hand of the two grooves at the right-hand end of the lower wall, then makes its way through the overhanging laminated flakes above. It is technically reasonable but loose in the upper part. Start as for Blitzkrieg.
1 110 feet. Go easily up a ramp leading right into the groove and continue to the top, with a diversion on to the left wall at mid-height. Large spike belay.
2 110 feet. 5a. From the right get on to a big spike and step left into a groove. Move up the slabby left wall then go back right. Continue to loose flakes beneath an overhang and step right on to an exposed arête, then go up into a niche. Climb an overhanging crack above. Rock and vegetation now lead to a block belay on The Pillar Traverse.

All the routes that follow (with the exception of Gytrack), start from The Pillar Traverse, and are described from east (left) to west (right). The part of the crag which lies above the Traverse, is divided into three sections. The Central Wall is above the grass chutes in the centre of the crag, and has a prominent terrace traversing below it. To its right and above the Pinnacle there is a fairly broken area of rock which provides exits for routes on the Pinnacle, and one independent climb, Central Slab route. Right again is the West Flank.

Central Wall

This wall is of fairly consistent height and is uniformly steep. It provides a high concentration of hard climbs. The most obvious features are the Skid Row chimney on the left, and The Great Corner approximately in the centre. The wall steepens left of Skid Row, but becomes more vegetated and broken. There are three approaches; a climb on the lower section of the crag, Cupid's Inspiration or Central Route for example, The Pillar Traverse itself, or an obvious, steep diagonal rake leading right up to the foot of Skid Row, which is probably the most straightforward, if a little frightening.

Sirius 270 feet Very Severe   (1976)
On Central Wall is an obvious groove left of Anubis and immediately right of the huge bulging overhangs. Start about 70 feet up the vegetated rake, at a good spike on the left.
1 120 feet. 4c. Trend leftwards up the lower wall for 40 feet then go straight up until a short traverse right, then a few moves straight up lead to a ledge. Move left and go up a short steep wall to the base of the main groove.

2 150 feet. 4b. Follow the groove to a cave than move out left to climb a second gully/groove to spike belays just below the top.

Anubis   270 feet   Hard Very Severe   (1976)
The central groove in the wall left of Gytrack leads to a V-groove on the skyline. Start up the vegetated rake to belay directly below the top groove of Gytrack at a rock step. An obvious traverse line goes left onto the wall.
1 120 feet. 4c. Traverse 30 feet left then step up into a shallow groove, which is followed until the wall can be climbed diagonally rightwards to the base of the main groove. Peg belay 15 feet up this.
2 150 feet. 5a. Climb the groove via a ramp to within 10 feet of the roof, then move out to the left edge. Step round and traverse left for 10 feet. Ascend a few feet then go diagonally rightwards to a ledge below the final groove. Surmount some shattered pinnacles and climb a V-groove to finish. No belays.

Cerebus   220 feet   E2   (1976)
A rather contrived line up the steep arête left of Gytrack, giving interesting and exposed climbing. Start as for Gytrack.
1 80 feet. 5a. Pull over the initial bulge and traverse 40 feet left. Go rightwards up the wall above to the arête and step right to belay in the groove on Gytrack.
2 140 feet. 5b. Climb the arête to a small overhang, step left and go up shattered cracks in the steep wall to a tiny niche. Move back right to the arête and move up, then go diagonally onto a ledge, which gives access to an exit ramp trending leftwards to the top. Belays 30 feet back.

Gytrack   170 feet   E1   (1968)
This route takes the line of the curving groove on the wall left of Askant and Skid Row chimneys. Some loose rock persists but this situation should improve with traffic. It is not high in its grade. Start from the diagonal rake leading to the foot of Askant Chimney. There is a peg belay some 60 feet below the chimneys, at the base of a shallow groove trending left.
1 150 feet. 5a. Step left and pull strenuously over a bulge into the shallow groove, which is followed to a steeper groove. Climb this, and move left at the top, then go back right above an overhang. Continue to a good ledge and peg belay.
2 20 feet. Climb a little corner to the top. Spike belays well back.

Askant Chimney   120 feet   Difficult   (1917)
A fine little chimney. Start by scrambling up the diagonal rake to the terrace of The Pillar Traverse. The start of the rake will be found on

the right of a little square bay at the left-hand end of the vegetated central area of the crag.

1 120 feet. The first feature, a chockstone, may be passed either inside or out, and at about 75 feet an excursion on to the left edge is advisable. The capstone can be turned on the left or right. Exit on to scree, where belays are scarce.

Skid Row   140 feet   Very Severe   (1968)

An apposite name! It is usually wet, and is graded for these conditions. A good pitch of mountaineering character. Start at the left-hand end of the terrace, just right of Askant Chimney.

1 140 feet. 4c. Climb the chimney direct to a grass ledge. A little slab on the left enables the chimney to be re-entered a few feet higher. Continue to the top.

★**Herostratus**   200 feet   E3   (1968/1978)

An impressive wall climb, very exposed and difficult to protect. Start at the left-hand end of the terrace on The Pillar Traverse, 20 feet right of Skid Row, the obvious chimney.

1 80 feet. 5b. Climb a rib for 25 feet, then an obvious diagonal break rightwards, to a grass stance in the centre of the wall. Peg and small spike belay.

2 120 feet. 5c. Continue in the same line for a few feet then ascend a broken groove until the wall begins to overhang. Make an awkward move up, sling on a tiny spike, to a peg about two feet above and to the right. Continue up the steep wall and move right to a roof. Pass a peg (on Endor), gain a good spike on the left, then climb straight up to finish.

★**Endor**   200 feet   E2   (1965/1981)

To the right of the wall of Herostratus and some 50 feet left of The Great Corner are two offset grooves, one above the other; they each form a diagonal slab facing west. The route is based on the slabs. Start at the highest point on the terrace, slightly left of the lower groove.

1 80 feet. 5a. Move diagonally right awkwardly to a peg and continue directly up the groove above. Trend left to an exposed stance and peg belay at the edge of the slab.

2 30 feet. 5c. Go up to an overhang and traverse right across a steep wall to the second groove, past pegs. Peg belay.

3 90 feet. 5a. Climb the groove by the slab to the roof. Move left on to an exposed arête, and climb a steep wall on very dubious holds, moving right above the roof at the top of the crag.

★**Venom**   200 feet   E3 (1 pt. aid)   (1966)
A line of roofed grooves immediately left of The Great Corner. Most of the loose rock has been removed, but some remains on the first pitch. Interest is well-maintained, and the finish is very exposed. Start by a small tree on the terrace just to the left of The Great Corner.
1 100 feet. 5b. Climb a shallow groove to a grassy ledge below a sloping overhang. Go up left over shattered rock to a spike on an arête. Ascend directly up a steep wall with increasing difficulty, until it is possible to move right to a ledge. Peg belay immediately below The Great Corner finish.
2 100 feet. 5c. Climb an obvious groove on the left, past a small overhang and continue to a peg. With aid from the peg gain a rib on the right and move up to a roof. Make a sensational move over the roof and go up a steep crack in the wall above, to finish on the left.

★★★**The Great Corner**   230 feet   E2   (1965)
A classic route. This is the most prominent feature on the Central Wall; a big corner capped by a huge roof. It provides good climbing on sound rock with excellent protection. Start directly below the corner, just left of a pinnacle on the terrace.
1 130 feet. 5a. The corner, with steadily increasing difficulty leads to a peg on the right wall. Continue into a niche. Stance and belay a few feet higher, under the roof on the right of a large detached flake.
2 100 feet. 5b. Traverse left across a wall on good holds to an arête. Move down five feet and step left into the right-hand of two grooves. Climb this with a hard move where it overhangs. Continue to a small overhang, surmount it and follow a groove to the top.

Zenith   150 feet   E1   (1968)
This route follows a groove which leads to an impressive double overhang. Unfortunately, it is a natural drainage channel, and is rarely dry. Start from a small pedestal some 30 feet right of The Great Corner.
1 120 feet. 5b. Climb the obvious groove to the overhang, move left beneath it and go up on to a steep wall. Continue with difficulty to a short broken groove and so to a good sloping ledge.
2 30 feet. 4a. From the right-hand end of the ledge, climb an arête to finish. Belay well back.

★**The Fourth Dimension**   430 feet   E5   (1971/1989)
An impressive and sustained girdle traverse of the Central Wall. It is amongst the most serious routes of its kind in Wales. It is difficult to safeguard the route for both leader and second. Start at the left-hand end of the terrace as for Herostratus.
1 70 feet. 5b. As for pitch 1 of Herostratus. A rising traverse right

leads to a belay on a ledge in the centre of the wall.
2 70 feet. 6a. Move up to a spike below the steepening wall (as for Herostratus), then descend rightwards for 10 feet to an arête on Endor. Traverse below roofs past two pegs to a stance (Endor pitch 2).
3 60 feet. 5c. Descend to a large spike. Traverse right across a steep wall for 10 feet, to the lower groove of Venom. Climb steeply, trending right, to the stance of Venom on the arête. Poor protection.
4 100 feet. 5c. Traverse right round the arête, then go across a wall to belay in The Great Corner. Climb down the corner for 40 feet, then traverse 30 feet right into a small chimney. Hanging stance.
5 90 feet. 5c. Descend 15 feet, to a small ledge. Climb right on to and across a steep wall to an arête. Ascend the arête then move round in to a groove (Zenith). Continue to the right, to reach an undercut chimney. Climb this for a few feet, then step right on to a steep slab and make a rising traverse to gain an obvious arête. Once again a hanging stance. Poor protection.
6 40 feet. 5c. Step up and left from the belay. Bridge across a groove to a peg high in a small niche. Pass this, then climb a groove above to a ledge, 10 feet of vegetation leads to the top. Belay well back.

The next climb starts at a higher level, above The Pinnacle.

Central Slab Route   290 feet   Very Difficult   (1921)
This climb provides a convenient way off routes which terminate on The Pinnacle and The Pillar. It follows more or less the original line. A good deal of vegetation and some rock. Start from the top of The Pinnacle, (see The Pillar Traverse pitch 2).
1 30 feet. Step from The Pinnacle on to a wall, then go easily up grass to belay at the foot of a rock rib beneath a big square overhang.
2 30 feet. Ascend grass and a little rock just by the rock rib to a belay.
3 35 feet. Traverse right to a mossy area and then go on with more exposure to a little niche and chockstone belay beneath an overhang.
4 30 feet. Step right on to a slab and climb it on small holds at first, to a grass ledge.
5 60 feet. Go up a weakness on the right, or better and harder, a slab. Continue up an easy-angled slab above, and a short wall on the left by some flakes, to a grassy bay beneath a huge quartz-marked overhang.
6 80 feet. Go up to the right-hand corner of the overhang and round it awkwardly then go straight up the wall above. Finish on lava 'eggs'.
7 25 feet. Easy rock leads to the top.

West Flank

This is a fairly well-defined section of the crag, bounded on the left by the Pillar Chimney, and ultimately petering out into the hillside on the right. The base is formed by the rising dyke line of The Pillar Traverse. It is further identified by its structure of alternate ribs and grooves. The nature of the climbing is slightly less steep and the lines are more obvious than on some other parts of the crag.

The Pillar Traverse 820 feet   Difficult   (1917)
A long and very often exposed expedition, involving vegetation, stones and a little rock. Recommended only to experienced parties. It provides an excellent opportunity to see the topography of the crag. Knowledge of the precise line will be of great assistance when trying to locate other climbs; it also serves as a convenient escape. Start at the west end of the cliff at a terrace of grass at about 60 feet. On its left is a rising dyke line.
1 270 feet. Follow the dyke, which is intermittently apparent, to the second of two large belays.
2 100 feet. Go up the stony bed of the Pillar Chimney, behind a huge detached flake which forms The Pillar.
3 40 feet. Continue to the next semi-detached flake, The Pinnacle.
4 90 feet. Descend a chimney beyond The Pinnacle.
5 200 feet. A steep undulating grass terrace is traversed to the foot of Askant Chimney.
6 120 feet. Climb Askant Chimney.

Witterer 200 feet   Hard Very Severe   (1970)
The climb takes a crack line to a conspicuous sloping overhang, then traverses beneath it. Start 30 feet right of the Pillar Chimney at two large spikes. Immediately right of the right-hand of these is a short sloping groove leading to the crack. Flake belay at the base of the groove.
1 70 feet. 5a. Climb the slabby left wall of the groove, round a little overhang to the crack. Continue up the crack and exit right. Go up diagonally right to a stance and belay, below the overhang.
2 80 feet. 4c. Traverse diagonally left across a slab beneath the overhang and step awkwardly around the edge into a groove. Climb a bulge above the groove trending left. Traverse left for a few feet, then go straight up pleasantly to belay in a little niche on Central Slab Route.
3 50 feet. 4b. Move into a short groove on the right and go up through a notch in an overhang. Continue trending slightly right, until a grass rake leads easily to the right. Finish easily up the final section of Central Slab Route.

Wit   290 feet   Hard Severe   (1953)
A rather indifferent route apart from the good second pitch. Start 70
feet right of the base of Pillar Chimney, and 40 feet right of two large
spikes. At the base of a grassy break between two fairly prominent
ribs, higher up the dyke than its neighbour Humour.
1 50 feet. Trend slightly right to a small rock rib, which is followed to
a good spike. Move back left into a square-cut corner. Good stance.
2 80 feet. Climb the corner and groove above using the slabby wall
(possible belay at 30 feet). Continue up the groove, facing left to turn
the overhang. Step back right above and belay at the base of a
pinnacle.
3 70 feet. Pull on to the top of the pinnacle and step across on to a
wall. Move right then back left, move right again and go up to grass.
Stance and poor belay.
4 90 feet. A gentle slab on the left leads to the final section of Central
Slab Route. Finish right of a big triangular overhang.

★**Humour**   300 feet   Very Severe   (1953)
A good route, varied and slightly easier than Central Route. Start 50
feet left of Y-Chimney and a little higher up the dyke, at a recess with
an open groove. It has a crack line on either side of it. This route
takes the obvious wide crack on the left of the recess.
1 70 feet. 4b. Climb the crack and follow grass to a spike belay at
the base of the left-hand of two grooves.
2 30 feet. 4b. Go up either groove, the right-hand one is harder.
Large spike belay and stance on the left.
3 80 feet. 4c. From the top of the spike step right, almost into the
groove of Elliw, then move up awkwardly to gain a crack, which is
followed to a flake at 40 feet. Traverse left and climb a superb crack
to a belay at the base of a pinnacle. Or move straight up from the
flake and climb a wall on excellent holds, trending left to the same
belay; somewhat harder.
4 80 feet. 4c. Traverse easily right for 20 feet and continue delicately
round into a groove, that of Elliw, which is followed until an exit can
be made to the right (the crux). A grassy ledge leads to a large spike
belay.
5 40 feet. Climb on in the same line as the groove to reach Central
Slab Route, or escape easily to the right.

Variation
The Laughing Finish   80 feet   Severe
A pointless escape.
4a 80 feet. Go straight up to the top of the pinnacle, junction with
Wit. Step on to the steep wall above and climb this, in a few feet the
angle eases.

Another variation climbs the wall and crack gained from the traverse on pitch 4 at Very Severe 4b.

★★**Elliw**   290 feet   E1   (1965)
An entertaining route up the open, light-coloured groove in the recess left of Y-Chimney, a distinctive V-chimney. The rock is clean and the climbing sustained and technically interesting. Start as for Humour.
1 140 feet. 5b. Enter the groove by a crack and climb directly to an overhanging wall. Follow the groove more awkwardly, move diagonally left and go straight up to an overhang. Poor stance on the left.
2 150 feet. 4c. Traverse right and follow the line of a slim groove. Step right at an overlap and scramble to the top of the crag.

★**Commuter's Crack**   310 feet   Hard Very Severe   (1966)
A good route, following the crack line in the right wall of Elliw. Start as for Humour.
1 90 feet. 5a. Climb a little wall diagonally right to the base of the crack. Pull strenuously over a bulge to get to the crack above. Follow this more easily until the last few moves are made on the left wall. Poor stance, chockstone and spike belay.
2 80 feet. 4c. Continue up to the steep crack until it gives way to a groove. Pleasant bridging avoids vegetation in the bed of the groove and leads to a niche. Exit left, step left again round a little arête and go straight up via a good spike (possible belay). Scramble up a runnel of vegetation to a spacious stance and fine spike belays.
3 140 feet. 4a. Scramble up a gully on the right and climb a slabby wall on its left. This provides a pleasant and contrasting finish, if artificial.

The Jester   200 feet   Hard Very Severe   (1967)
Between Elliw and Y-Chimney is a fine arête on the left wall of which lies Commuter's Crack. There are two routes on the arête, Jester and Trindod. Jester takes a groove immediately right of the arête, then a crack, finishing up the arête itself, in a good position. Start at the base of the arête.
1 70 feet. 5b. Climb a shallow groove just right of the arête with difficulty, until the angle eases and a rib on the right can be followed to a grass ledge. Belay as for Trindod.
2 40 feet. 4b. Climb a deep crack above to a ledge at 20 feet (as for Trindod). Continue up a crack leading back left on to the arête. Good spike belay but poor stance.
3 90 feet. 5a. Bridge up over a bulge, treating a large loose pinnacle with due respect. Then climb the arête to a ledge and the top. Scramble to the right to descend.

Trindod   230 feet   Very Severe   (1966)
A series of cracks and grooves in the left arête of Y-Chimney. It takes
a more obvious line than Jester but lacks the exposure. Start as for
Y-Chimney.
1 65 feet. As for Y-Chimney.
2 45 feet. 4b. Move back into the chimney and move out across the
steep left wall, then climb up to grass ledges. Belay.
3 40 feet. 4a. Go up to a chimney on the left and step right at 20
feet, then go up grass ledges to a belay.
4 80 feet. 4b. Ascend a shallow ramp until it widens into a deep
crack. Step left and climb a short wall to the top.

Y-Chimney   200 feet   Severe   (1917)
A good climb, more varied than appearances might suggest. Start
about 75 feet up the dyke line of The Pillar Traverse at the foot of the
obvious chimney/groove.
1 65 feet. The chimney is more awkward than it looks until an
opportune exit right leads to a platform and pinnacle belay.
2 55 feet. From the right-hand end of the platform a tricky little
groove is climbed. A series of grassy ledges overlooking the chimney
then lead to a good belay.
3 80 feet. The easy rib above is followed to the foot of a groove,
climb it and exit right. Broken ground leads to the top.

Y-Chimney Direct   180 feet   Very Severe   (1961)
The natural line. Start as for Y-Chimney.
1 65 feet. 4a. As for Y-Chimney.
2 115 feet. 4c. Re-enter the chimney which is followed easily for 50
feet. A strenuous bulge then leads to precarious climbing and the top.

West End   230 feet   Very Severe   (1970)
To the right of the obvious chimney/groove of Y-Chimney is a
light-coloured, water-worn depression. This is the objective. The route
is usually wet. Poorly protected, yet technically very reasonable. Start
as for The Pillar Traverse on a broad ledge, some 60 feet above the
base of the crag. Belay in a short corner with a wide crack in it.
1 70 feet. 4a. Climb a wall on the left, move into the crack and pull
over a block to a grassy ledge. Traverse right into and across the
water-worn depression, then go up a few feet to a large flake belay
on the right.
2 60 feet. 4b. Continue delicately up a groove, step right and go up
a further 10 feet, then diagonally left to a small stance and block
belay.
3 100 feet. Go easily up a rib behind the stance and into a

vegetated groove on the left. Climb this, and exit right at the top.
Finish up easy ground to good spike belays.

Craig Y Cwmglas Bach

(Crag of the Little Green Cwm)   OS Ref. 662 635

The approaches for this crag are identical to those for Llech Ddu, as it
lies in a subsidiary cwm, Cwmglas Bach, higher and to the west. Formerly
the crag was known as the 'Crag by Llech Ddu'.

Even by comparison with its neighbours, this is a poor crag; nevertheless,
it has 10 routes. A prominent cleft, The Gully, divides it into two sections:
on the left the steep, narrow Pillar Buttress and on the right the Main
Buttress; also steep to half-height but then degenerating into easy-angled
ribs. The climbing is varied and, vegetation is certainly prolific. The routes
are described from left to right (east to west).

Snuff   180 feet   Hard Very Severe   (1990)
The first pitch is wet, slimy and thoroughly unpleasant, the second
starts badly and gets worse, climbing tottering rock. A route for
irresolute suicides. Protection is poor, hardly worth bothering with as
the rock is unlikely to bear a fall. Approach Pillar Buttress over wet,
steep vegetated ground, peg belay below short shallow corner.
1 30 feet. 4b. Struggle, slip, fight and slide (upwards a help) in the
shallow corner, dislodging slime and moss may uncover holds.
Resorting to pulling on runners may thankfully shorten the struggle.
2 150 feet. 4c. Move right to the deep, wet chimney which bisects
the Pillar's face. Bridge this until it is possible to move left, via grassy
ledges, to a tottering pillar perched on the left bounding arête, care
required. From the top of the pillar step onto the arête and climb
directly up, keeping left to follow the arête. Belay when the rope runs
out. Scrambling remains to the top of Pillar Buttress.

The Gully   270 feet   Severe   (1936)
This wet, vegetated cleft separates the two buttresses. It has a very
awkward start but relents. Unpleasant and recommended only to gully
enthusiasts with a kink for poor belays. Start by scrambling to a point
below a mossy rectangular chockstone in the gully.
1 20 feet. Bridge up past the chockstone with difficulty.
2 100 feet. Climb the right wall for a few feet, then continue up a

groove and repulsive green ooze, where a little rock can be found, until the angle eases.

3 120 feet. Scramble up the gully bed, of no interest.
4 30 feet. Climb an obvious chimney in the centre of the gully. Scrambling remains.

Covent Garden   490 feet   Difficult   (1944)
A poor vegetated route. The backbone of the ridge immediately right of The Gully is reached by a rising traverse right, above the steep lower wall. Start in the bed of The Gully, 40 feet below the rectangular chockstone of the initial pitch.
1 150 feet. Make a rising traverse right across the right wall on a tufty ledge, rakes and go up grassy grooves to a vegetated saddle. Belay on a rib.
2 120 feet. Climb the rib direct to the top of a detached block. Step right, cross a little slab and go up to belays on the right. Various grooves on the right and left of the rib provide alternatives.
3 100 feet. Scramble up easily to belay 30 feet right of an overhanging nose.
4 120 feet. Climb over piled blocks, then scramble to a groove on the right; go up this. Continue via a flaky chimney, right of another overhanging nose, to the summit.

The next four climbs terminate well below the level of the vegetated saddle of Covent Garden, but in each case this can be gained by scrambling. The easiest and quickest way off from the saddle is to reverse pitch 1 of this route, or follow it to the summit tediously.

Low Wall   180 feet   Severe   (1949)
Not a worthwhile route, which takes a circuitous line up the steep lower wall on the left of the buttress. The route is forced well to the right by the impending upper section of the wall. Start immediately right of The Gully. Approximately 100 feet above the toe of the buttress is an isolated blade of rock protruding from the grass close to the crag. Just to the right is a recess with a line of grass leading out right. Above is a small triangular overhang. Scramble up the grass and a little slab to a block belay.
1 65 feet. Strenuously climb a little broken groove just right of the overhang to a heather ledge. Or, traverse right for 15 feet, then move delicately back left to the same place. Step left and follow a line of vegetation diagonally left to a ledge. Move back right and go steeply up rotten flakes to a belay.
2 45 feet. Descend for a few feet. Move right awkwardly across a rib to a grassy stance. Go up a little, then traverse right and descend to a triangular recess beyond another rib.

3 70 feet. Climb a groove above, taking the right-hand branch at 35 feet to a pleasant ridge. Scrambling leads to the saddle of Covent Garden.

Dead Calm   130 feet   Hard Very Severe   (1990)
Start as for Low Wall, the route is poorly protected.
1 90 feet. 5a. Move right along a wet grassy ramp, until it is possible to move back left below the steep wall. Climb directly up the wall to a small sloping ramp on the right (out of view), peg runner. Climb up left of the peg to a horizontal break, then hand-traverse the break leftwards stepping up to a grass ledge. Belay below a small overhang.
2 40 feet. 4b. Take a rising traverse right, below the small overhang and over a bulge. Climb straight up to a shallow corner and traverse right to a rib, belay as for Smithfield/EEC.

EEC   150 feet   Very Severe   (1990)
A direct line to the final corner of Smithfield, drier than that route. 150 foot ropes will make the belay with a little stretch. Start 20 feet left of Smithfield at a small spike belay.
1 150 feet. 4b. Follow a ramp rising leftwards, then climb direct to the final corner of Smithfield turning the overhang en route on the left. Care should be taken with loose rock whilst moving up into the Smithfield corner. Peg belay at the top of the corner on the right-hand side of the arête. Poorly protected.

Smithfield   210 feet   Very Severe   (1967)
The Main Buttress has three fairly distinctive sections; on the left a narrow sub-buttress, in the centre a recessed area and on the right a bilberry saddle with a barrier of overhangs above. Start just left of the toe of the sub-buttress.
1 80 feet. Scramble up to the right, go round a little arête, and climb a corner, slabby at first but steepening at about 60 feet. After a difficult move, good holds in a crack lead to a stance astride an arête.
2 130 feet. Step left from the stance and across a little wall. Go up for 40 feet until a traverse can be made right into a corner. Climb the corner to the top; belay ledge on an arête, junction with Low Wall. Scramble to the saddle of Covent Garden.

Billingsgate   220 feet   Very Severe   (1966)
Climbs the right-hand side of the sub-buttress, then moves left to the spine of the buttress where it joins Smithfield and Low Wall. Start a few feet right of the toe of the sub-buttress. Scramble easily up right over rock ledges and vegetation to a ledge at the base of a shallow groove.
1 80 feet. Climb the groove and continue in the same line to the level

of the first of two prominent bands of overhangs. Move right and belay on a heather terrace.

2 70 feet. Make a rising traverse left between the two bands of overhangs, round a little rib and up to a grassy recess belay as for Low Wall pitch 2.

3 70 feet. Move out diagonally right and follow the spine of the buttress, joining Low Wall higher up. Scramble to the Covent Garden saddle.

Petticoat Lane   280 feet   Very Severe   (1971)
This route takes the prominent corner between the right-hand section above the bilberry saddle and the recessed central section. It is usually wet and serious. Start immediately left of the little bilberry saddle abutting on the right-hand side of the crag, at the foot of a waterworn gully/groove.

1 110 feet. 4a. Easily go up the gully/groove, keeping to the right. Gain a broad boggy ledge on the bilberry saddle and belay.

2 40 feet. 4a. Traverse left on to a slabby rib and climb it diagonally right until it is possible to step right into the corner.

3 130 feet. 4c. Climb the corner direct, moving out steeply right at the top. Huge bilberry terrace and poor belay immediately on the left. Scramble 150 feet diagonally left to the vegetated saddle of Covent Garden.

Day-tripper   220 feet   Hard Very Severe   (1967)
Above the little bilberry saddle on the right of the Main Buttress is the big barrier of overhangs, with wet slabs leading up to them. This climb breaks through the overhangs on the right and takes a direct line above. Worthwhile after a bad start. Poorly protected. Start right of the little bilberry saddle, higher up the scree in a little corner leading to the wet slabs.

1 100 feet. Go up a little rib and move on to the slabs. Continue easily (there are several lines) to the overhangs and traverse to the right-hand end of them to a small stance.

2 90 feet. 5a. Step awkwardly left on to the lip of the overhangs, then go up slightly right to undercuts. Climb a rough flake and step left into a shallow groove. Follow this to a small heather ledge on the right, move back left and continue in the same line to a block belay on a broad grass rake.

3 30 feet. 5a. Traverse left on to an arête and climb an awkward flake crack to a bilberry terrace.

Straight Chimney   200 feet   Severe
This is the obvious chimney on the right of the crag. Belays are scarce.

Craig Dafydd   OS Ref. 664 633

High above and to the west of Llech Ddu is a small cwm, almost directly above Craig y Cwmglas Bach. At the back of the cwm a series of broken buttresses rise to the summit plateau of Carnedd Dafydd. The buttresses are close to 200 feet high in the centre. For those who have a yearning to escape their fellow beings, as yet only a single route awaits. There is scope for further development for those with the determination and the zeal.

Top Storey   160 feet   Very Severe (1 pt. aid)   (1969)
True enough there are not many other places as high as this to climb on in Wales. There are two gullies in the centre of the crag. This route traverses from the left-hand gully to a fault-line in the buttress. Start by traversing across vegetation above the lower rock band to the foot of a very small corner groove.
1 50 feet. 4c. Ascend the groove, with a sling for aid at 15 feet, then hand-traverse right on a ledge, and go up a corner crack to a good stance.
2 40 feet. 4c. Climb a wide groove by its right-hand edge to a stance just right of a prominent thin rock pinnacle.
3 30 feet. 4b. Climb the pinnacle until it is possible to step into a corner. Go up it, then traverse diagonally left to a good stance.
4 40 feet. 4b. Easily ascend a wall and crack to the top.

Pen Yr Ole Wen (Hill of White Light)

Craig Braich Ty Du (Arm of the Black House)

OS Ref. 650 606 – 651 626

This is a series of cliffs on the west flank of Pen yr Ole Wen lying approximately 300 feet above the A5 and extending for three-quarters of a mile north west from Ogwen Cottage and parallel to the road. The structure is extremely complex, with a maze of buttresses and rock walls separated by broad grass and scree-filled gullies, this really is a guidebook writer's nightmare! The previous guidebook sorted out the rather confusing nomenclature and this guide keeps to this clearer format. The buttresses have been numbered from right to left and the climbs, apart from Buttresses 3 and 8, similarly described; as most parties will start from Ogwen Cottage. Once over the Alf Embleton stile faint paths lead up diagonally leftward past three old pill-boxes to the rocks.

The rock strata are such that the crags are generally steep on the Ogwen flank and slabby on the other, with alternate ribs and grooves. In some areas the rock is friable but, if treated with care, should not detract from the climbing.

The area was first explored by Palmer who made 'No extravagant claims... but better climbing... than on the Gribin or the Milestone'. Perhaps he was being economical with the truth! However, Moulam then displayed his characteristic zeal for the obscure and found a number of reasonable routes. Meanwhile, others have shown some interest and a few routes have been added. There is still plenty of rock for many short hard climbs to be developed. The majority of the present routes are very artificial in line, many search for difficulty and comprise a series of short problems. All the really worthwhile climbing is concentrated on Buttresses 3, 7 and 8; apart from these, only Pinnacle Ridge Route can be recommended. Generally the buttresses are broken and vegetated. They nevertheless constitute the most easily accessible Carneddau climbing and provide an option for those who have tired of Cwm Idwal's polished routes and hordes of people.

Craig Braich Ty Du

Numbers marked correspond to Buttress Numbers in text

Photo: Simon Cardy

Areas for further exploration may be found farther along and up the hillside towards Bethesda on Clogwyn Castell 649 618, Clogwyn Grugog 648 622 and Clogwyn Twll Du 651 624.

Ogwen Pinnacle   OS Ref. 650 606

This is the obvious, but not true pinnacle above the bridge at Ogwen Cottage. It provides one route and several boulder problems on the very steep right-hand side, including a Joe Brown crack and an unprotected arête, **Saint Laurent** (1982).

Pont Pen y Benglog Buttress   200 feet   Difficult   (1924)
A pleasant route on sound rock, ideal for novices. Many lines of varying standard can be taken. Start just left of an overhanging nose, at the foot of the buttress.
1 75 feet. Climb a short crack and move left to slabs. Traverse right to more slabs; ascend these on enormous holds to a platform.
2 125 feet. Two short steep walls are surmounted, then scrambling leads to the top.

Buttress 1

This is the first piece of rock of any climbing significance to the left of the Ogwen Pinnacle. It is small but clean and sound. There is a corner crack leading to an overhang at the front and a steep wall on the right. The left-hand side is slabby. All the principal features have been climbed, between Severe and HVS, but there are no routes worthy of description. It serves well as a landmark, and just to confuse, one lost soul has misguidedly painted a figure 2 onto the rock!

Buttress 2

Higher up than the previous buttress, it is situated between a vegetated gully on the left and a wide stony gully on the right. The gullies converge to form a broad gully between Buttresses 1 and 3. On the right wall there are some peculiar vertical markings like 'organ pipes'. There is one route.

Introvert   150 feet   Severe   (1950)
A scrappy climb with an awkward finish. Start in the wet vegetated gully on the left, 30 feet above the toe of the buttress.
1 70 feet. Step from the belay spike and mantelshelf. Trend right and go up a curved chimney formed by blocks, or over the blocks. Scramble up heather, then a little groove leads to a gnarled tree.
2 50 feet. Traverse left on quartz, then go up vegetation to more trees. Belay on the right.
3 30 feet. Climb a chimney in an arête, move awkwardly out right around a huge chockstone then go up a crack above.

Buttress 3

This buttress is easily identified by the broken-down dry-stone wall leading directly up to it. It is larger than the preceding buttresses and is steep and compact. The cliff can be seen easily from the dry-stone wall, therefore from left to right are:

★**Widdershins**   150 feet   Very Severe   (1950)

A good route in spite of being blatantly artificial. About 100 feet above the foot of the crag, and on its left, is a stout tree among some piled blocks. Higher, on the buttress flank is a squat holly tree on a ledge. Start at a flake belay below the holly.

1 60 feet. 4c. Climb a crack to the tree, then bridge awkwardly up an overhanging crack, large Friends useful. Step out left and go easily up a slab to a long heather ledge. Embedded flake belay on the left.

2 40 feet. 4c. Step left into a grassy corner, then go up its right edge for five feet and make a long stride across to a crack on the left. Go up and left to the top of a detached flake. Stance and belay in a chimney beyond.

3 50 feet. 3a. Easily climb the chimney for 15 feet then step left on to a rectangular grassy platform. Ascend a hard corner to a small grassy bay and a little wall to finish.

★**Ring of Scorpio**   120 feet   E5   (1992)

The overhanging crack in the face left of Georgie Lad... over strenuous! Start in the gully beneath a shattered niche.

1 65 feet. 6a. Climb up over some loose blocks to gain the large spike in the niche. Swing left to gain the crack and follow it to where it fades, step right and finish up the slight groove with difficulty. Belay on a good ledge.

2 55 feet. 5b. The crack behind the belay, finish up the slabby arête above to block belays.

Georgie Lad the Bricklayer   130 feet   E3   (1981)

Although strenuous and difficult, not a very good route. Start below the obvious overhanging groove with a loose block and ivy at its base, down and right of Widdershins.

1 80 feet. 5c. Climb the friable groove and make a hard exit to a belay on the left.

2 50 feet. Climb the wall above and either finish up the arête on the left or the continuation chimney on the right.

A 20-foot cracked block above provides three little problems. The prominent wide chimney on the right at the front of the buttress, directly above the broken down wall, has also been climbed at Difficult standard.

Buttress 3

★**Time Served** 60 feet E2 (1981)
An entertaining route with a technically difficult but safe crux. It climbs the crack splitting the small neb. Start as for Apprentice's Route.
1 60 feet. 6a. Climb the cracks of Apprentice's Route, then the steep wall to the roof; jam up this. Friends are very useful. It is possible to climb the wide crack to the right behind the tree at about 5b.

★**Apprentice's Route** 100 feet Hard Very Severe (1959)
Still an interesting route. Start just above a subsidiary dry-stone wall on the right of the buttress, at some thin cracks above a small spike. There is a tree on a ledge above.
1 50 feet. 4c. Go up the left-hand crack to a sloping ledge, then ascend to the tree, either directly up a groove (5b) or easily on the right, but not as much fun.
2 50 feet. Ascend the wide crack to the left of the tree. The original finish fell down during the winter of 1991.

The steep crack to the right of the tree is **Let Your Feet Hang** E2 5b (1981) however, the block that forms the right side of the crack seems to be a prime candidate for joining its brother down on the A5.

Deasel 210 feet Very Difficult (1933)
A promising start gives way to scrambling. Start on the right of the buttress at a bay of rocks and heather. On its left is a steep wide crack.
1 60 feet. Struggle up the wide crack to a grassy ledge below a chimney. Gain the chimney awkwardly and climb it to a rift.
2 150 feet. Climb over rocks on the right, past a perched block, via a narrow cleft to a bollard. Scramble up heather to a short wall and pull over a block to finish.

Extrovert 90 feet Very Severe (1957)
Rather pointless. On the right of the bay facing Deasel's chimney, is a large block with quartz veins low down. Climb the right edge of the block, then a short V-groove and traverse to a little crack, which leads to a ledge at 40 feet. Continue straight up, stomach-traverse and climb the edge of a block to a slab. Go up another slab overlooking a gully and scramble to finish.

On the left of Buttress 3 is a broken area dotted with trees. Farther left again is another small squat buttress, separated from the next by a wide grass and scree gully. The squat buttress has a tall block on the skyline, with a tree on its right. The gully has a dry-stone wall built across it. Two routes have been made on this buttress, neither of which is good. The line described makes the best of the available rock.

F Sharp   130 feet   Very Difficult   (1951)
Start from the toe of the buttress. Climb a short steep crack to a ledge
and a large flake. Step off the flake and follow the nose directly
above to broken ground.

Buttress 4

This is much higher up than any of the other buttresses. Approaches are
best made via the grass and scree gully, with a dry-stone wall built across
it, right of Buttress 5, or from the summit of Pinnacle Ridge Route. The
water-course between Buttresses 5 and 6 is less satisfactory. It is a steep
and triangular little crag; on the right-hand side are steep walls and
overhangs. Both the climbs described start on the slabby left side.

Blue Sunshine   140 feet   E1   (1992)
Start at a slabby groove (10 feet left of the narrow slab that is the
start of Joyce).
1 95 feet. 5a. Ascend the slab, then ramp, to a steepening, then
follow cracks to a ragged overlap. Step left and go up to a ledge.
Follow easy slabs to a large block, move left to gain the top of a flake
from where a shallow groove and 'crevasse' stance can be reached.
2 45 feet. 5b. Climb the obvious steep jamming crack above the
stance; a subtle blend of delicate and brutal techniques required.

Joyce   140 feet   Very Severe   (1965)
A nice route with interest. The overhanging walls give way to slabs on
the left. On the right-hand side of the slabs is a narrow subsidiary
slab with cracked blocks on its right. Start at the foot of the narrow
slab.
1 70 feet. 4b. Climb the narrow slab, then move right to beneath a
little overhang. Step awkwardly right into a broken groove and
continue via small ledges to a big flake.
2 30 feet. 3b. Move left on to a rib and go up into a 'crevasse'.
3 40 feet. 4b. Step across the 'crevasse' and go along a horizontal
ridge, then up an obvious smooth groove. Swing out right to finish.

Tyromancy   140 feet   Hard Very Severe   (1992)
A quirky route which starts at the base of a slabby rib up and left of
Aaron, spaced protection.
1 100 feet. 5a. Climb the rib until a move left gains a clean
subsidiary slab. Follow this to an overlap, pull over this and scuttle up
the easier upper section to belay at the slim groove of Joyce.
2 40 feet. Finish either as for Joyce, or take easy slabs on the left.

Aaron   100 feet   Difficult   (1956)
Start 30 feet higher up the wet gully on the left of the buttress.

Scramble up heather to mossy slabs.

1 50 feet. Climb the lower of two slabs, then trend right along an obvious line and go up into a 'crevasse'. Stance on Joyce.

2 50 feet. Step across and go along the horizontal ridge, as for Joyce. Traverse left to heathery slabs and follow these to the top.

Buttress 5

This is distinguished by a ridge of prominent pinnacles forming a serrated skyline. It is further identified by a long, forked tongue of rock which descends from the base of the buttress almost to the road, terminating with a small rock wall on the left and a semi-detached block on the right. A Very Difficult route has been made on the left and a Severe on the block. There is obvious scope for other problems. On the main buttress above there are three climbs.

Gargoyle   110 feet   Severe   (1967)

Unsatisfactory. Start 40 feet below the dry-stone wall in the gully on the right of the buttress. A belay block leans away from a little wall. Climb easily straight up a series of steps to an obvious pinnacle summit at 70 feet. Swing right across an overhanging wall to a ledge on an arête then go straight up to a heather ledge. Escape into the gully.

The next route is about 100 feet farther left.

★★Pinnacle Ridge Route   330 feet   Very Difficult   (1950)

A fine route, the lower section is particularly good. Unfortunately there is some easy ground before the final amusing ridge. There are two distinctive ribs, with a stunted oak low down on the right of the left-hand rib. Between the ribs is a bay of broken rock and heather. The climb takes the clean slabby rib on the right; 'P.R.' is marked on the rock.

1 130 feet. Climb the slabby rib to an obvious block, then make a high step into a groove on the right, or there is an easy option on the left. The trough above leads to a heather terrace.

2 50 feet. Walk up an easy-angled ridge.

3 150 feet. Traverse right and climb the ridge above until it peters out; or follow a shallow chimney to a 'totem pole' belay, then take a tower on the left to the crest of the ridge. Good fun.

Digitalis Direct   220 feet   Very Difficult   (1957)

Only slightly better than it looks, but it deteriorates higher up. Start at the base of the left-hand rib, 60 feet left of the previous climb. On the right of the rib is the stunted oak, below which are some large cracked blocks forming the foot of the rib. A short crack leads to a flake edge.

1 20 feet. Climb the crack, swing left on to the edge and belay by a small tree.

2 90 feet. Go up a slab on the right, step left awkwardly into a groove and continue in the same line to a little wall. Make a long reach to a gorse ledge. Spike belay.

3 70 feet. Broken rocks and vegetation lead to an obvious pinnacle. From behind it, step left on to a crest and scramble up to a rock tower.

4 40 feet. Take the left edge of the tower. Escape left into the gully.

Buttress 6

This is an extensive crag with a watercourse on the right and a large blunt pinnacle on the skyline. The central area is very broken and vegetated. There is a climb on either side of the buttress, neither of which is particularly worthwhile.

Custodian's Creep   250 feet   Severe   (1951)

A series of varied problems, with escape into the gully a tempting option at several points. Start at the extreme right-hand edge of the buttress, immediately left of the water-course, at the foot of the rocks.

1 100 feet. Climb a rib then move easily up to a large spike. Go behind it and climb a short wall to an overhanging crack.

2 70 feet. Go up the crack to a huge block. Trend right across a gorse terrace, then go up a little chimney to a broad heather ledge.

3 30 feet. Traverse right, then move back left up ledges to a block belay. Or, much harder, climb a strenuous thin crack in a short wall direct to the same belay. Poor final pitches.

4 30 feet. Ascend a corner to a heather terrace, rather loose.

5 20 feet. Climb the right-hand of three breaks, just left of a little tree. Escape into the gully or scramble to a corner crack and climb it.

On the left-hand side of this buttress is a small, partially detached sub-buttress. It is lower and to the right of the gully right of Decameron Rib. This little rock wall has numerous overhangs and a stunted oak on a ledge 10 feet from the top.

Shelf Edge   90 feet   Severe   (1960)

Start above some vegetated ledges on the extreme right of the sub-buttress. There is a protruding overhang low down, immediately on its left is an open groove. Climb the groove with difficulty to a tiny ash tree. Move right then left to a shelf beneath a small overhang. Climb out right, up on to a bilberry rake and finish up a wide crack. The route may be continued on the wall above.

Buttress 7

Two diamond-shaped overhangs with a distinctive corner leading up to them help to identify this buttress. The left flank facing Buttress 8 across the gully, has a series of ribs.

★★**Decameron Rib**   170 feet   Very Severe   (1955)

A fine route for these crags. Start at the foot of a rib just left of the corner leading to the diamond-shaped overhangs on the left at the front of the buttress.

1 70 feet. 4a. Climb a crack splitting the rib to a small tree. Move up left to another tree. Continue up a crack, belay beneath the left-hand overhang. Or, climb the corner direct and move out left just below the larger overhang to the same belay.

2 70 feet. 4b. Move right into a bottomless chimney. Climb past a dubious block and continue up a crack, then move right to another crack. Go up it for 15 feet then escape left by a large loose flake. A steep slab leads to a belay.

3 30 feet. 4a. Climb up leftwards, then go easily to the top of a prominent pinnacle. Move left and scramble to the top.

Variation.

Boccaccio's Start   90 feet   Severe

A popular variant.

1a 90 feet. Climb the cracked rib right of the corner, stance and belay. Traverse left into the corner and go up it to join the original route.

Lazy Sunday   210 feet   Hard Very Severe   (1981)

An artificial route up the slabs left of the roofs. Start as for Decameron Rib.

1 70 feet. 4a. Decameron Rib Pitch 1.

2 70 feet. 5a. Trend up the slab leftwards to the arête. After a thin move up, traverse right to reach oak tree belays.

3 60 feet. 4c. Fight the tree to traverse leftwards back to the arête then go up to a crack for protection. Move back right to a wide bottomless chimney then climb this to an exciting exit rightwards.

The vegetated gully with trees left of the previous route has been climbed.

Another Route   140 feet   Difficult   (1927)

A rather unsatisfactory climb making the best of what rock there is immediately left of the vegetated gully. Start 30 feet left of the lowest point of the rib. Climb a slab to a heather terrace and traverse right, then step round an arête to a gorse stance on the edge. Continue up

Photo: Simon Cardy

a narrow slab on the right to a perched block, then take a knife edge to a heathery corner. Finish up a chimney on the right.

Temptation   130 feet   Very Difficult   (1960)
Takes a rib with a poised block, that is well-seen from higher up the gully between the buttresses. Start about 50 feet below the level of Route 1, on Buttress 8 opposite.
1 60 feet. Go straight up the rib to a heather niche. Belay on the left.
2 70 feet. Continue up the poised block. Avoid the obvious chimney and take a little corner on the right edge.

Patience   130 feet   Severe   (1960)
An intriguing route. Start at the foot of a rib 40 feet left of Temptation.
1 70 feet. Go up the rib to the foot of a wide open chimney. Climb it to an exposed stance on another rib to the right.
2 60 feet. Move left and climb to a heather ledge. Go straight up a shallow groove on the left of yet another rib, which is climbed. Step left and finish up a steep corner.

Buttress 8

This buttress faces Buttress 7, and starts 100 feet higher up the gully. It is smaller and its front is broken and not impressive. The hidden gully wall, however, is steep and clean. It proves to be the best of all the crags, with a high concentration of good little climbs. For convenience the routes are described from left to right along the gully wall.

Route 1   140 feet   Severe   (1927)
An interesting route, which emerges on to easy ground after each pitch. Start at the lowest point of the buttress at a detached pillar with a curved chimney on its right.
1 40 feet. Squirm up the curved chimney to the top of a huge flake. Move back on to the main part of the crag and a platform.
2 60 feet. Step awkwardly from the top of a pinnacle on to an overhanging wall and climb a little slot. Take a steep slab on the right to a heather ledge, traverse right and belay beneath a huge block on the skyline.
3 40 feet. Traverse left along a gangway on the face of the block. Broken rocks and scrambling to finish.

Pat's Crack (Keep Pullin' Cen)   75 feet   E4   (1990)
Start 20 feet right of Route 1 and five feet right of a dirty corner.
1 75 feet. 6b. Ascend the wall via a mantelshelf move, then traverse left to the top of the corner. Follow a ramp up leftwards to where a hard move right gains a niche below an obvious finger crack splitting the headwall. Climb the crack to a difficult move past a finger pocket

Photo: Simon Cardy

to gain a shallow groove on the right. Follow the groove to a roof where a long stride left allows access to a ledge and huge belay spikes.

K.C. Route   75 feet   E2   (1991)
Start as for Pat's Crack.
1 75 feet. 5c. Climb up to the ramp, as above; but continue up the ramp until a move right is possible to gain a fist-sized crack. Follow the crack diagonally rightwards to a hard exit, belay as above.

★**Route 2**   110 feet   Severe   (1927)
A fine direct line. Start 40 feet right of the chimney of Route 1, at the base of some big jammed blocks.
1 50 feet. Go steeply over the blocks, then pull into a niche. Climb on to a horizontal 'needle' and step awkwardly out right. Ascend 10 feet to a stance and belay.
2 60 feet. Go straight up a steep quartzy wall on good holds to a small tree. Move right and continue up the wall, a fine pitch.

★**Cuckoo Groove**   150 feet   Hard Very Severe   (1960)
An appealing and strenuous route. The main groove is the most prominent feature of the crag. Start about 20 feet right of Route 2 at a 10-foot bollard.
1 50 feet. 4c. Step awkwardly from the bollard into the groove and follow it to ledges on the left.
2 50 feet. 4b. Move down and right to a small ledge. Traverse right for a few feet, then go diagonally up to an arête. Swing down and round to a bilberry corner.
3 50 feet. 4c. Climb the corner break strenuously, trending left at first. Then pull into and up the final little corner.

Variation
2a 50 feet. 5b. A faint groove to the right of the main groove also leads to the arête.

Gwdihw   150 feet   E2   (1991)
Start as for Cuckoo Groove.
1 100 feet. 5b. Step awkwardly from the bollard into the groove for 20 feet. Now take the first of two diagonal thin cracks on the right wall of the groove, with increasing difficulty to the arête. A few feet up the arête brings a good stance.
2 50 feet. As for Cuckoo Groove pitch 3.

Alouette   110 feet   Very Severe   (1967)
A commendable route. Start 20 feet right of the Cuckoo Groove

bollard, at cracks leading to elongated blocks.
1 70 feet. 4a. Go steeply up over the blocks, then diagonally left across a quartzy wall, with a thin move to better holds and the bilberry corner of Cuckoo Groove.
2 40 feet. 4b. Climb a nasty, strenuous, slanting crack on the right to join the easy finish of Cluck's Nook.

Cluck's Nook   100 feet   Hard Severe   (1965)
Gratifying climbing with interest well-maintained. Eighty feet right of Cuckoo Groove is a chimney/crack-line with a holly tree above. Start below the chimney and either climb on to a spike and traverse to its base from Ring Ouzel, or scramble up vegetation of the left.
1 100 feet. 3b. Go straight up the chimney and cracks, then continue with an easy-angled chimney to a ledge on the left. Move along the ledge then pull over on to easy rocks and the top.

Ring Ouzel   120 feet   Very Difficult   (1960)
A fair climb. Start above another bollard, 90 feet up the gully from the Cuckoo Groove bollard – at the foot of a grass runnel.
1 90 feet. Climb a steep wall near the left edge on good holds. Step left to a bilberry corner at 70 feet.
2 30 feet. Ascend the short corner above, or more easily on the right, followed by scrambling to the top.

Stone Chat   110 feet   Severe   (1960)
Rather artificial and not as good as its neighbours. Start 15 feet right of the previous route.
1 110 feet. Go up the wall, keeping right of the fault line of Ring Ouzel, to the centre of a small bilberry ledge. A steep crack trending right is followed by a short corner. Scrambling remains.

Buttress 9

This is the final buttress and also the most extensive. It is seen on the skyline from Ogwen Cottage and is several hundred feet in length. Unfortunately it is very vegetated, often wet and discontinuous. In all a dangerous and unattractive crag.

The Lectern Grooves   230 feet   Difficult   (1950)
Frightening, mainly on loose rock! It follows the skyline when seen from Ogwen Cottage. At the right-hand edge of the buttress, about 20 feet above its foot, is an embedded spike. Higher are three holly trees. If you really want to climb it (!) start at the spike. Up broken rocks above the belay, then a little groove leads to a sloping ledge just above the hollies. Traverse easily left to a holly tree belay. Climb a cracked groove above and exit left. Go over more easy rocks then

pass another tree to the 'lectern'. Cautiously go out left to easy ground.

Farther left is a vegetated gully, which has been climbed, then more broken rocks divided by gorse and heather terraces. On the extreme left is a slabby wall with sharp-cut overhangs. At the right edge of the wall the cliff drops back into a black and usually wet recess. Two unsatisfactory routes have been made here. **Primrose** (Difficult), starts at the back of the recess. Climb an overlap, then a ridge is followed via a crack and scrambling. A corner leads to another crack and heather is avoided on the left. **Lining Crack** (Hard Severe), starts on the left of the recess and follows a vague crack-line up overlapping slabs to a slender chimney, the line of which is followed to the top.

Much farther north are two gullies, which are reached by ascending the hillside directly above the eighth Bangor milestone. In defiance of originality they are known as: **Right Gully**, which has a pitch of Difficult standard left of a cascade, which can be avoided farther left, and; **Left Gully**, easier, with one avoidable pitch. Both can provide good winter routes given suitable conditions.

Craig Lloer

(Crag of the Moon)

OS Ref. 661 619

This cliff is situated on the south side of the Cwm above Ffynnon Lloer (Spring of the Moon). The cwm has an easterly aspect, but the cliff stays in the sun until mid-afternoon. It has a delightfully secluded flavour despite its apparent proximity to the road; in short, a wonderful place to escape the crowds.

The cliff has an Eastern and a Western Buttress separated by a wide scree-filled amphitheatre. The Eastern Buttress is the short, steep left wall of the amphitheatre, and it offers comparatively few opportunities for routes. A band of strange oviform rock traverses the wall higher up. The other buttress is a fine piece of rock. Approximately pyramid-shaped, it consists of a series of steep ribs separated by grassy grooves which converge towards the top. When approached from the llyn the apparent right-hand edge has a prominent overhanging nose low down. Beyond this, the crag is more broken. A descent of the amphitheatre is the simplest way down, although there is an easy angled but stony gully to the far right of the crag.

Approaches are best made from Glan Dena, at the east end of Llyn Ogwen 668 606; there is ample parking along the main road. A track leads to Tal y Llyn farm. Just before the farm turn up right and walk along a wall to a stile, go over this and then an initially faint path zigzags up the hillside west of Afon Lloer to a stone wall. After the wall, the path eventually leads into the cwm and so the llyn. The crag is beyond the llyn, as is a small flat area of ground, on which to set up an idyllic campsite for the weekend.

Eastern Buttress
Central Route 150 feet Very Difficult   (1911)
This climb follows a rather unpleasant-looking water-worn groove, which is the first feasible weakness in the left side of the amphitheatre left wall. The line is direct and obvious.

Hhier 110 feet Very Severe   (1960)
A steep interesting route taking the next line of weakness in the amphitheatre left wall. Start from a grassy bay below a knobbly overhang, about 50 feet right of the previous climb.
1 50 feet. 4b. Climb a steep wall to the overhang, step right, and swing round a rib with difficulty to a small grassy ledge. Belay on a huge knobbly spike.
2 60 feet. 4a. Go straight up, then exit right on to a bilberry runnel, and continue up a rib to the right, then its right edge. Step left to finish.

Good Egg 120 feet Hard Very Severe   (1976)
Start higher than Hhier, and 50 feet to the right at a light-coloured groove below the highest part of the crag. Belay at its base.
1 120 feet. 5a. Step left and climb the groove to a ledge at 30 feet. From its right-hand end go up on suspect holds to an arête. Move back left and go up to a small bilberry ledge. A short corner crack leads right to a large pinnacle. Step right from its top into a short, bottomless groove. A few feet higher easier climbing leads to the top.

Moonrise 170 feet Severe   (1954)
Quite a good route, although the rock needs some care. It takes the line of least resistance through some impressive terrain. Start 70 feet right of Hhier, level with the top of the scree, directly below a huge pinnacle with an undercut base, high on the wall. The pinnacle is better seen from higher up in the amphitheatre.
1 80 feet. Ascend a broken groove to shattered blocks. Step out right

and go up to grassy ledges. Climb a knobbly wall and a steep crack to a grassy niche and pinnacle belay.
2 90 feet. Traverse left across a steep wall to an obvious crack by the pinnacle. Step down and continue traversing for a few feet, then go up to finish.

The wide scree amphitheatre separating the two buttresses has three branches all of which have been climbed, but only the left-hand one provides anything more than scrambling.

Western Buttress
The Eastern Arête   160 feet   Difficult   (1911)
A pleasant first pitch. Start at the base of a shallow groove, just to the left of the lowest point of the amphitheatre's right retaining wall.
1 80 feet. Climb the groove to a large heather platform, then go up to the foot of the next rock.
2 80 feet. Continue over the gendarme to an easy ridge and belays. Tedious scrambling above is possible.

On the right of the previous climb is a wide grassy bay with two little gullies. Right of this the true Western Buttress commences.

★★Kirkus's Route   280 feet   Very Severe   (1928)
One of the best routes on the crag, and worthy of its originator. Varied climbing on clean rock. Start immediately right of the bay at an easy sloping chimney.
1 90 feet. 3c. Climb the chimney to a platform on the right. Move up right towards a groove, then climb back leftwards to the edge of a slab. Climb it delicately to a heather ledge.
2 50 feet. 5a. Surmount a little rib above by an awkward pull, then mantelshelf on to a sloping ledge. Thrutch up the obvious crack to good finishing holds and a thread belay.
3 90 feet. 3c. From a heather shelf traverse right to a rib. Climb this, and a little groove that leads back to the top of a square furrow. Bridge up and climb a slab to a large spike belay directly above.
4 50 feet. Pleasant scrambling leads to the finish.

Farther right is a large recessed area with three parallel, vegetated grooves commencing from a large grassy ledge at 30 feet. The left-hand and central grooves are fairly continuous, whilst the third is shorter and less obvious.

First Trinity Groove   270 feet   Very Difficult   (1937)
Very vegetated, not well-protected and loose at the top. Just to the right of the chimney of Kirkus's Route is a shallow depression with

heather ledges. Start on its left below the first groove.

1 90 feet. Climb a mossy wall then a square-cut shallow groove to the terrace. Scramble up to the main groove, and go up it for 20 feet. There is a large spike belay on the left, small stance.

2 80 feet. Climb grass in the groove, with a diversion on to the right wall higher up, to a ledge and spike belay.

3 100 feet. Continue up the right wall of the groove, almost to a sloping overhang. Traverse left to an overhanging block, which is apparently detached. Move round it cautiously and go up a groove above to easy ground.

★**The Rib**   260 feet   Severe   (1971)
The obvious rib between the First and Second Trinity Grooves provides delightful climbing superior to both grooves. Start at a detached block leaning against a rib at the lowest point of the buttress.

1 80 feet. Climb to the top of the block, then step left into the chimney, where difficult moves lead up to the heather shelf. Scramble to the flake belay on the previous route.

2 120 feet. From the bottom of the groove, traverse right on to The Rib. Follow it direct, awkward where it steepens, to belay in the right-hand groove.

3 50 feet. Move back left on to an arête, go up it, then a little groove to finish.

Second Trinity Groove   260 feet   Severe   (1937)
A fairly disgusting route, not to be commended! Belays and protection are scarce. Start on the right-hand side of the leaning block under the right-hand chimney/crack, at the lowest point of the crag.

1 60 feet. Climb a wall trending right, then the short crack with an awkward move on to the terrace. Scramble up heather to the base of the second groove.

2 130 feet. Can be split. Go up vegetation in the groove until it steepens. Move left on to The Rib for 20 feet, then step back into the groove. Continue more easily to a stance below a small chimney.

3 70 feet. Either, go up the chimney then broken rocks and vegetation, or better, trend right up grass and a slab, then go back left and easily to the top.

Third Trinity Groove   240 feet   Hard Very Severe   (1950)
Really just one pitch, very scrappy low down. Start 20 feet right of the blunt rib at the lowest point of the buttress at a shallow stepped groove.

1 40 feet. 4a. Ascend the groove to the terrace. Harder than it looks.

2 100 feet. Scramble diagonally right up the terrace to a shallow

Craig Lloer

Photo: Iwan Arfon Jones

groove.

3 100 feet. 5a. Climb the groove awkwardly to a jug on the left, step right and up a mossy little slab to a rib, which leads to an overhanging niche. Exit awkwardly right from the niche to a good grassy ledge, no belay. Step back left and follow a crack-line to the top. Usually dirty, greasy and grassy!

★**Central Ridge** 250 feet Hard Severe   (1953)
A good climb with varied problems. A worthy companion to Kirkus's Route. The line follows the pinnacled lower ridge, then the centre of a compact wall. Forty feet right of the nose mentioned for the previous route is a grassy break leading up to some large blocks. Start at the foot of an obvious ridge, directly below the blocks.
1 100 feet. 3a. Climb over the blocks to a 10 foot-crack in a corner. Ascend the crack, then another shorter one, step out left and follow ledges to a terrace. Blunt spike belay just above.
2 50 feet. 3b. Go up a V-groove on the left of the ridge. Move up right behind a huge flake, and from the top of it go up a wall on good holds to a juniper ledge.
3 100 feet. 4a. Climb a rib on the right, then traverse 10 feet left on a narrow ledge. Go up steeply to a grassy bay on the right. Enter and continue up a smooth groove with difficulty. Exit left to easy ground.

Grooved Ridge 260 feet Difficult
Fairly interesting, taking an obvious narrow ridge. Start down and left of the start of North Arête at a slightly recessed slab with a grassy groove on either side. The right-hand groove is taken, below and to the left of a seven foot high block.
1 70 feet. Climb the grassy groove to a terrace, then cross it to a fine 'horn' belay.
2 90 feet. A slab above is gained as soon as possible from the right. Climb it with a long move on the left to a stance. Follow a groove above to a capstan on the left. A short wall leads to a small grassy cave.
3 100 feet. Climb a narrow chimney on the left, then scramble and take any one of three short grooves. A steep bubbly wall leads to the top.

★**North Arête** 220 feet Difficult   (1911)
Quite entertaining. It takes the apparent right arête of the cliff, which has a distinctive overhanging nose low down. Start slightly left of the overhanging nose at the left-hand of two chimneys.
1 70 feet. Ascend the chimney and exit rightwards. Easy rocks lead to a stance and belay by quartz-marked rocks.

2 100 feet. Climb the arête, broken at first. Move left where it steepens, step up onto a slab and move back right to the rib. Grassy ledges and belay a few feet higher.
3 50 feet. A crack on the left leads on to the ridge, then go up a groove and easier ridge above.

Right of North Arête the buttress becomes more broken and vegetated. Several routes have been made but none can be recommended. The best is described.

Bivouac Buttress 220 feet Difficult   (1937)
Two hundred feet to the right of the nose of North Arête, the steep lower wall terminates with a grassy choked chimney with spikes at its foot. Thirty feet farther right there are some big blocks. Start at the foot of the chimney.
1 75 feet. Climb the chimney to a grassy terrace, trend right on to the crest of the buttress and follow it to beneath a nose with a zigzag crack in it.
2 45 feet. Move up left to a short chimney with a large chockstone, climb it and exit right.
3 100 feet. Go straight up above with decreasing difficulty.

Farther right there are two undistinguished routes of Moderate standard, each starting at an easy break. The buttress ends with an easy-angled stony gully. Right of the gully is a compact slabby little wall of good rock.

Slab Route II 150 feet Very Difficult
Quite a pleasing route to finish off the day. Start 15 feet left of the right-hand end of the slab beneath a groove.
1 150 feet. Climb the shallow groove below the edge, steep at first, curving over leftwards as it rises parallel to the edge.

Slab Route I 150 feet Moderate
The edge of the slab is fairly pleasant, and on good rock.

Up and right is a scrappy route.

Chimney Buttress 160 feet Difficult   (1937)
1 50 feet. Start in a slabby corner and climb up to the crest of the ridge.
2 50 feet. The chimney is higher up on the left of the buttress. The exit is awkward; then swing up right to the edge.
3 60 feet. Cross to a corner on the left. Climb it and move right again to the top.

Craig Ddaear

(Crag of the Earth)

OS Ref. 659 623

Across the scree to the right of Craig Lloer lies the recently discovered Craig Ddaear. Never reaching more than 150 feet in height the cliff extends for several hundred yards. The right-hand end is laid back and provides the easier routes, whilst the left-hand end, by contrast, is deceptively steep. Good rock, solitary surroundings, and a south-facing aspect makes a visit worthwhile.

★**Sweating Peat** 80 feet E3   (1992)
Start at the arête bounding the left side of the very steepest part of the crag.
1 80 feet. 5c. Hard moves to leave the ground lead up the arête to better holds and a spike runner. Continue slightly left past another spike and swing right to a rest. Follow the short ramp rightwards to a ledge and a large block. Stretch up to gain a good hold on the arête above, swing left to a peg runner and sprint up the flakes past another spike runner to the top. Steep.

★**Surrogate Soils** 100 feet E3   (1992)
Start to the right of Sweating Peat by an obvious small pinnacle.
1 100 feet. 5c. Step off the pinnacle and climb an easy blocky groove. Step left to gain a left leaning and very innocent-looking left slanting crack. Follow this strenuously to a delicate move onto a blank sloping shelf. An airy step right gains a wide groove to finish.

The crag now drops temporarily in height, past a water course, and becomes less defined. Further down to the right stands a large flat-faced obelisk split by a finger sized crack. The next route begins below the crack.

Wet Roots 50 feet Very Severe   (1992)
Start in the bay 30 feet right of the water course.
1 50 feet. 5a. Climb the left slanting crack out of the bay and follow the obvious line into a deep groove to finish.

Moving Moss 100 feet Severe   (1992)
The pinkish wide slab 50 feet left of the obelisk.
1 100 feet. Climb the cracks in the slab, and a steep flake. Trend left and finish up through some large blocks to easy ground.

Earth Summit   150 feet   Very Severe   (1992)
Start below the obelisk
1 100 feet. 4c. Avoiding the thin crack step up and follow a flake left
to a protruding block on the left. Gain the wide crack above and
follow the slab to the ledges (possible belay). Climb the slab above to
a left slanting crack. Climb this and the easier slabs above.

Whole Earth   30 feet   E2   (1992)
1 30 feet. 6a. The thin crack which Earth Summit avoids provides a
skinny well-protected problem.

Salt of the Earth   130 feet   Very Severe   (1992)
Start at the right-hand side of the crag at its lowest point below a
stepped pillar.
1 130 feet. 5a. Climb the short wall to a large grass ledge (it is
possible to walk off or start the route from here). Tackle the crack in
the next wall above with difficulty and follow the line leftwards. Finish
up the groove, or harder, the unprotected wall to the right.

Mother Earth   150 feet   Difficult   (1992)
1 80 feet. Start just right of the last route. Climb the cracked bulge, a
slab, and a groove to the right of the rib above to belay on good
blocks.
2 70 feet. Walk back then climb the rib above.

Carnedd Dafydd

Carreg Mianog

(Angular Cliff)

OS Ref. 687 619

A steep compact little crag situated on the south-east flank of Carnedd Dafydd. It can be easily seen from the A5, and with the exception of Braich Ty Du is the most accessible of the Carneddau cliffs. The best approach from the main road is to follow the access road to Ffynnon Llugwy as for Craig yr Ysfa to the leat or watercourse which traverses the hillside, and follow this to a footbridge just before Afon Llugwy; then take a direct line to the boulder slopes below the crag, about 30 minutes from the road. **On no account should the private road to the farm at Glan Llugwy be used**. Moreover, the access road serves both the farmer and the Mountain Rescue teams; therefore, DO NOT PARK IN FRONT OF THE LOCKED ACCESS GATE.

There are two steep buttresses with a rather vegetated central bay. The climbing is usually strenuous and on sound abrasive rock. The routes in the intermediate grades provide the best climbing, whilst some of the recent additions are good. A variety of short walls and boulders in the vicinity are also entertaining. The routes are described from left to right commencing with the West Buttress. In general a fine little crag which receives sunshine most of the day.

★ **Zip Wall**   90 feet   Hard Severe   (1944)
An absorbing climb, with one hard move, on the left-hand side of the West Buttress. There is a small cave at the foot of the buttress. On its left a clean steep arête, then a groove. Start 10 feet left again.
1 90 feet. 4b. Climb the wall trending left. Make a long reach past a bulge to a ledge, step right to a crack then ascend a blunt arête to another ledge, finish up a steep thin crack above.

★ **Zip Groove**   100 feet   Very Severe
A reasonable route with some good moves. Start at the groove immediately left of the arête mentioned above.
1 90 feet. 4b. Climb the groove easily at first, then more awkwardly

to a ledge. Jam up another short groove to a ledge. Ascend a thin crack, as for Zip Wall, or, much harder, another crack 20 feet farther left.

★★The Cracked Arête   110 feet   Very Severe   (1945)
Very enjoyable. Start at the foot of the arête left of the cave, on the left-hand side of the buttress.
1 110 feet. 4b. Go straight up a thin edge to a ledge. Step left and climb a pleasant curving crack, then go up and left to another curved crack, a little harder. Finish up a wide crack in a corner, The Crawl Climb pitch 4.

★Zippo   115 feet   E3   (1989)
A steep little number. Start right of Cracked Arête under a line of overlaps slanting up left.
1 120 feet. 5c. Climb the corner for a few feet until it is possible to move left at the overlaps. Some hard moves gain a small foothold on the edge then go up a little corner to the ledge on Cracked Arête. Move down and right to gain the overhanging crack which is followed to the ledge on Crawl Climb. Follow the arête again to a large ledge. Follow the top section of The Cracked Arête to finish.

Moss Wall   110 feet   Severe   (1962)
A poor start leads to a good jamming crack. Start in a corner right of the small cave.
1 50 feet. Easily ascend the gorse-overhung corner. Continue up a short groove then go left on to a mossy wall and the traverse of The Crawl Climb.
2 60 feet. Jam a steep crack immediately above, then make a rising traverse around the right arête to finish.

The Crawl Climb   160 feet   Very Difficult   (1944)
A rather circuitous route, which includes a few good moves. Start immediately right of another cave at the front of a little buttress, right of the first cave.
1 65 feet. Step from a large block on to a rib above the cave. Climb this, then a steeper rib and groove left of a bilberry chute. Scramble up to a heather shelf on the left.
2 70 feet. Continue traversing left, crawling round an airy arête and on to the upper part of Zip Wall.
3 25 feet. Climb the blunt arête of Zip Wall, just left of the stance then traverse right to a large platform. Finish up a wide crack in the corner.

Carreg Mianog

1. Zip Groove   VS
2. The Cracked Arête   VS
3. Zippo   E3
4. Pectoral Wall   HVS
5. Biceps Wall   VS
6. Knee Cap   VS

Photo: Ray Wood

Crack and Corner 130 feet Very Difficult   (1944)
A reasonable route despite a broken central section. Start 20 feet
right of the second cave, at the foot of a steep crack with a rowan
tree above.
1 80 feet. Ascend the crack! Pull over a bollard on the left to a
detached flake. Move up a wide crack, swing on to the flake and go
up to a ledge.
2 50 feet. Climb a sharp-edged crack into a corner, which is taken
direct, or a ledge on the left for an easy finish.

Redstart 115 feet E2   (1984)
Steep interesting climbing. Start between Crack and Corner and
Central Route, below a steep wall.
1 50 feet. 5c. Climb the wall direct to a ledge and a huge pinnacle
belay.
2 65 feet. 5b. Move up a short wall to a ledge and then climb the
thin crack in the wall left of Crack and Corner. Finish via a shallow
groove.

Central Route 80 feet Very Severe   (1958)
A deep groove left of the trees leads to a prominent square-cut
overhang with the corner of Crack and Corner climb on its left, and
the crack taken by this climb above on its right. Start at the foot of the
groove.
1 80 feet. 4b. Grope up the vegetation in the groove to a ledge
beneath the overhang. Go up the right wall to gain the crack above
the overhang and climb it with difficulty to a large ledge. Finish
awkwardly up a steep little wall.

Carreg Mianog Pinnacle is really a perched block just left of the top of
Angle Gully. The west side can be climbed via a short traverse and
corner.

Angle Gully 80 feet Severe   (1944)
This very obvious gully is the left-hand limit of East Buttress. Start by
scrambling to the bottom of the gully.
1 80 feet. Climb vegetation and little rock to a cave. Flakes on the left
lead to a very steep crack, then boulders with a thread belay
beneath. Continue and exit right.

The East Buttress is another attractive section of rock. A wall on the left
is interrupted by horizontal ledges, but the central part, which is the
highest, has bold features. The right flank is steep but rapidly loses height,
and is terminated by a short, yet very obvious chimney.

Tramline Traverse 90 feet Very Difficult (1948)
The obvious line from the hollies high on the left of the buttress. Quite pointless!

Pectoral Wall 110 feet Hard Very Severe (1971)
A mossy start leads to good rock. Start 20 feet left of Biceps Wall directly beneath a ledge full of hollies, left of a 'cannon'.
1 60 feet. 4a. Climb a steep wall between two cracks, move right at 20 feet and go up to a terrace. Traverse easily left until directly below a large perched block.
2 60 feet. 5a. Climb a shallow groove and move up right to an overhang. Surmount this then trend right and climb a crack on the right of the perched block to the top.

★**Temper** 100 feet E2 (1963/1982)
Good climbing on some steep ground. Start 10 feet left of Biceps Wall directly under a 'cannon' on a ledge.
1 60 feet. 5b. Climb the wall and crack to a ledge step right then follow the thin crack in the wall to end up just left of the 'cannon'.
2 40 feet. 5c. Move up leftwards, easy but prickly, to surmount the overhang direct.

★**Biceps Wall** 100 feet Very Severe (1948)
A good strenuous climb. Start 20 feet left of the edge of the lower wall below the little niche.
1 70 feet. 4c. Climb directly up a steep wall awkwardly into the niche. Move on to a ledge and go up a wall on the right to a grass terrace . From a block step right on to a slab above an overhang, then continue to another grassy ledge with a 'cannon'.
2 30 feet. 4c. Fight past a holly tree on the left and go up the right wall of a shallow groove. Or, better, go straight up the wall above the 'cannon'.

★**Funny Bone** 110 feet Very Severe (1959)
Rather devious, but a route with real character and it is at the upper limit of the grade. There are two entertaining mantelshelves. Start below the front of the buttress, in a groove just right of the arête right of Biceps Wall.
1 30 feet. 3b. Go easily up the slabby right wall of the groove to a ledge and thread belay.
2 30 feet. 4c. Move up right, then hand-traverse on a poor edge and mantelshelf on to a ledge. Belay on the 'cannon' of Biceps Wall.
3 50 feet. 4c. Step back right and mantelshelf precariously into a grassy niche. Step right again and go up a little groove to a ledge. Layback into a wide crack above and continue to the top.

Funny Bone Variation 50 feet E2   (1982)
3a 50 feet. 5b. From the mantelshelf on pitch 3 climb an obvious leftwards-curving flake crack and finish over a small roof.

Knee Cap 80 feet Very Severe   (1959)
Pleasant climbing. Start by scrambling up broken rocks and vegetation to below a greenish central groove at the front of the buttress (the most prominent feature).
1 45 feet. 4c. Go straight up to an overhang, then gain a ledge above and to the left. Bridge up the groove to another ledge.
2 35 feet. 4b. The steep flake crack above leads to another ledge. Step right and pull over a little wall.

Mitre 80 feet Very Severe   (1950)
Not very good. Start at a large spike below a tree on the right of the buttress.
1 80 feet. 4b. Move left on to a large ledge, then climb cracks to some grassy ledges. Finish up a steep broken groove on the right. Awkward.

Jane (If she doesn't mind) 70 feet Severe   (1950)
Below and to the right of the buttress, is a short wall at right-angles to the main section. On its left is a conspicuous bracken ledge with small trees. Start at the base of the wall.
1 70 feet. Pull onto a little rib and scramble across the bracken ledge to a corner. Climb the corner, then the right wall to a ledge on the right arête. Move right on to another arête and so to the top of the cliff.

Right Chimney Moderate   (1940)
An amusing chimney well to the right approached over broken rocks. Face right.

Upper Tier

At the back of the main cliff is a smaller upper tier. On closer inspection a 60 foot pinnacle is revealed in the middle of the tier.

Pinnaclissimo 60 feet Severe   (1990)
Entertaining. The climbing is about Very Difficult, the jump isn't. Start at the back (East) of the pinnacle.
1 60 feet. Climb up on to the saddle, continue *à cheval* to a step left to gain the summit. Stand up, take a deep breath and jump to the safety (!) of the heather ledge opposite.

Carnedd Llywelyn

Craig Yr Ogof

(Cliff of the Cave)

OS Ref. 687 634

Originally, the cliff was inaccurately known as Craig y Tri Marchog (Cliff of Three Knights), hence the names of the three original routes. Then the cliff was named Craig Eryl Farchog (Cliff of Eryl the Knight) after the bwlch above. It now has its correct name; hopefully! The crag lies in the cwm to the north west of Ffynnon Llugwy and is approached by traversing hummocky moraine from the path to Craig yr Ysfa. About 40 minutes from the road.

At a distance the crag appears slabby, but this proves to be an illusion as it is very steep in places with some excellent rock. Most of the climbing is situated on the roughly triangular buttress to the left. The first obvious feature is the large overhang on the far left of the cliff. To its right is a bottomless groove and a steep lower wall with a small pinnacle at its right-hand end; the start of Gawain. Above this wall are a series of ramps, cracks and walls. Farther right is a larger pinnacle, in fact a huge detached flake, with a steep arête to the left, a vertical crack on its front face and a vegetated slab to the right. Farther to the right of the slab is a final slanting buttress with the magnetic offwidth chimney of Morgan La Faye. The easiest descent is above this final buttress.

The cliff has a pleasant sunny aspect, in fact the sun remains on the face until late afternoon. This factor, coupled with good rock and an air of isolation, except for a few mountain ponies, make this crag worth a visit.

Llywelyn Ein Llyw Olaf   200 feet   E1   (1989)
A varied route with an intimidating start. Start on the left directly beneath the chockstone in the chimney.
1 60 feet. 5b. Climb straight up the clean area of slab. Boldly pull through the overlap then move left and up over the chockstone.
2 40 feet. 5a. The wide chimney continuation.
3 100 feet. 4c. Take the breezy arête over to the left, a complete contrast in two stages.

★**Pentangle**   160 feet   E2   (1989)
The pod-shaped groove right of the chimney. Short but exciting due to
the surprising steepness. Start at the foot of the overhung chimney
crack.
1 100 feet. 5c. A steep but awkward break gives access to the
groove from the left. Ascend the groove until barred by an overhang,
then swing across rightwards to reach a wide crack leading to the top
of the large detached flake.
2 60 feet. 4a. Finish up pitch 3 of Gawain.

★★**Broadsword**   150 feet   E2   (1989)
A very direct way up the central area, perhaps the most satisfying
route on the crag. Start at the poised lozenge-shaped rock, an
obvious feature on the low terrace.
1 70 feet. 5b. Ascend the hanging left edge to gain the point then
hand-traverse the diagonal quartz crack to a bay. Climb the corner
forcing its cap to the right.
2 40 feet. 5c. Delicately now on pockets in the arête ahead. Small
threads.
3 40 feet. 5b. Power up the big layback crack in the headwall.

Gawain   150 feet   Very Severe   (1943)
A wandering route wending its way through some steep rock. Just left
of the lowest point of the buttress, walk up to the left, then traverse
easily back right through ferns to a corner behind a pinnacle boulder.
1 40 feet. 5a. From the top of the pinnacle boulder, make a long
awkward stride left on to a sloping ledge or layback into the corner,
harder, and go up to a vegetated ledge, then take an easy crack to
rowan trees. Small wires protect the start.
2 50 feet. 3b. Traverse left along a ledge, above a crevasse, then go
up a short chimney to belay on top of a large semi-detached flake.
3 60 feet. 4a. Move right and go up a steep little wall, then climb
leftwards up an easy mossy slab to a large bilberry terrace. Go back
right to easy ground.

Launcelot   130 feet   Very Difficult   (1949)
A scrappy route. Start below the pinnacle boulder of Gawain.
1 40 feet. Go leftwards up an easy slab then move up and traverse
right to a corner behind the boulder.
2 40 feet. Squeeze right behind the pinnacle boulder then go up a
thrutchy chimney, junction with Mordred.
3 50 feet. Traverse right for a few feet, then go up a steep mossy
wall to a groove and broken rocks.

Craig Yr Ogof

1. Llywelyn Ein Llyw Olaf	E1	6. Gwynhyfryd	E4
2. Pentangle	E2	7. Cadwaladr	E3
3. Broadsword	E2	8. Morgan La Faye	E3
4. Gawain	VS	9. Clustfeinydd	E2
5. Gawain Direct	E2		

Photo: Iwan Arfon Jones

★**Gawain Direct**   190 feet   E2   (1969/1990)
Much better than the original route, it provides an enjoyable and
absorbing way up the cliff. Start at the foot of the lower tier.
1 50 feet. 5c. Climb the overhanging corner and take a quartz ramp
to the top of the pinnacle boulder.
2 50 feet. 5a. The mossy V-groove (pitch 1 Gawain), then climb the
rightwards-sloping ramp to the foot of the open central corner.
3 50 feet. 5c. Follow the big slanting corner, past an awkward bulge.
4 40 feet. 5b. The last pitch of Broadsword, which seems more
appropriate than the original wide crack on the right.

★★**Gwynhyfryd**   150 feet   E4   (1990)
Something of a test-piece. A leaning arête that reaches down to the
very toe of the crag.
1 90 feet. 6b. Scale the initial sharp section of the arête then gain the
sloping perch on the right in as dignified a manner as possible. Now
the round edge is hard for a step before relenting.
2 20 feet. 4a. Go diagonally left across the slab to rowan tree.
3 40 feet. 5c. The thin crack and steep groove returning to the crack
complete the climb.

★★**Cadwaladr**   140 feet   E3   (1989)
Right of the arête a long slim crack runs up the face. Start below the
crack.
1 80 feet. 6a. An overlap in the damp recess gives a trying start and
the crack is quite strenuous and reachy. Where it merges with the
edge step right and climb straight up a steep wall and a slab.
2 60 feet. 5b. Continue up the slab and dark groove above to finish.

Mordred   130 feet   Difficult   (1947)
To the right is a tree-filled crack; farther right is a grassy recess with
another crack filled with loose flakes and blocks.
1 130 feet. Climb the crack to a pinnacle, step left and go up a wall.
Possible belay by rowans on the left. Traverse right on good holds,
across vegetation and a little slab. Block belay on the edge.

A Girdle Traverse of Difficult standard takes the first half of Mordred,
then follows a line of huge flakes to an easy exit on the left of the cliff.
The line is obvious.

To the right of the bay is a slabby buttress with a steep slanting face. Set
in the face is an offwidth leading up to a groove.

Meillionydd   100 feet   Hard Very Severe   (1990)
A short corner and ramp below the gash of Morgan La Faye. Start

below the corner.
1 100 feet. 5b. Step into the corner and climb the ramp. Where this steepens pull over rightwards to good holds. Finish on the open rib above.

★★**Morgan La Faye** 100 feet E3   (1990)
A fine example of its genre, and a real bitch if not treated properly! Start at a slab under the bottom end of the offwidth chimney.
1 100 feet. 5c. Climb directly to the base of the sloping chimney, squirm, or otherwise, up this to reach the V-groove. Undercut blindly round the overhang to the left then follow the open groove to the top. Friend runners would be useful.

Clustfeinydd 100 feet E2   (1990)
A steep start leads to pleasant slabs. Start at a ledge under a steep bubbly wall to the right of Morgan La Faye.
1 100 feet. 5c. Climb the wall on pockets to a small ledge, surmount the bulge above and sidle up the slab diagonally leftwards.

Pen Llithrig Y Wrach   OS Ref. 717 617

Translates literally into Slippery Head of the Witch; probably because the word Grach (witch) has been misused. Crach (poor or barren ground) is perhaps the correct word; however, the former is much more fun!

High above the head of Llyn Cowlyd, on the south-east ridge of the mountain, this steep compact little outcrop juts from the hillside. Only 70 feet high, it gives an impression of greater stature. Two routes have been made and there is obvious scope for harder problems on somewhat loose rock. Approaches are as for Creigiau Gleision, but it seems hardly worth the effort.

Staircase, 60 foot, Difficult, follows a series of steps on the left-hand arête, and **Puffin**, 70 feet, Very Difficult, takes a scoop near the right-hand side, starting on its left.

Creigiau Gleision

(The Verdant Crags)

OS Ref. 727 615 – 738 628

This extensive complex of crags stretches across the hillside for almost a mile above Llyn Cowlyd and is opposite Pen Llithrig y Wrach.

The approach from the Ogwen valley is via a boggy, ill-defined footpath from Tal y Waen OS Ref. 717 594 to the head of Llyn Cowlyd. An alternative approach is from Trefriw in the Conwy valley; a long, gated road leads almost to the Cowlyd dam. Although not immediately apparent, there is a good low-level track traversing the south-east bank of the llyn. It is only from this track that it is practicable to locate the crags. Once among the maze of buttresses, scree slopes and steep heather it is very easy to get hopelessly confused.

Eight routes are described on four widely spaced buttresses. The broken and vegetated nature of the climbs, coupled with their remoteness make a visit of questionable value. For ease of identification the crags have been divided into four groups of buttresses, which are described from right to left. The routes are similarly described with the exception of the Central Group.

Southern Group

This is the most extensive section, over a quarter of a mile in length. On the left is a series of clean-cut little buttresses leading to Castle Buttress, larger, square and also clean. A column of blocks some 40 feet high, leans against it on the right, and on the left-hand side is a sharp-cut overhang.

Anvil Cracks   140 feet   Severe   (1931)
A fine little route on sound abrasive rock. Start on a grassy shelf, left of the column of blocks, below an obvious crack. Just to the right is the 'anvil', a squat block with a spike.
1 70 feet. Ascend the crack, past a platform to a ledge. Move left to another crack and layback. Or, take a mossy slab via a pointed flake, harder and less pleasant, to the same heather stance. Awkward thread belay low down.
2 30 feet. Go up a V-groove on the left and walk to a belay in a corner.
3 40 feet. Climb the obvious bowed-Y cracks to finish.

Climbs of about Difficult standard have been made on the crags either side of Castle Buttress, but they are undistinguished. The Southern Group continues, becoming increasingly broken and vegetated, although higher.

A quartz-flecked scree chute, with a quartz crag at its head, is the next easily recognised feature. Both the Central and Northern Groups are best located from this landmark as it forms the boundary between them.

Central Group

Only two buttresses are of climbing interest, the routes are described from left to right. Immediately right of the quartz-flecked scree chute is a double buttress, which is somewhat larger and more continuous than others hereabouts. It is divided by a deep cavern. Some 40 feet below and to the left of the cavern is a little inset slab, on the right edge of the left-hand section of the buttress:

Bird's Wing Buttress   180 feet   Severe   (1937)
Start at the inset slab.
1 100 feet. Ascend the slab, then move right and climb a pocketed wall to a ledge and flake thread belay on the left.
2 80 feet. Go straight up over a small fallen block and follow a series of broken grooves to the top.

Variation
A much harder initial pitch has been climbed, starting up a short steep wall, 40 feet to the left, and trending diagonally right to the same stance.

Trident Route   170 feet   Severe   (1937)
Takes a groove from the deep cavern. Start in the cavern.
1 60 feet. Follow a gully and chimney to a grassy stance.
2 60 feet. Traverse right and climb a steep slab just inside the right edge, or, the slab direct leads to the same stance.
3 50 feet. Climb a rib or loose gully to the top.

Well to the right of the cavern and at a higher level, a wet rock gully defines the right edge of the buttress.

Black Chimney   170 feet   Difficult   (1937)
A poor climb. Start by scrambling to the foot of the gully.
1 102 feet. Follow an easy rib then a chimney. Continue up an easy-angled gully to a spike belay.
2 50 feet. Climb an obvious groove, awkward at the top, or, take the left wall after 20 feet.

About 100 yards to the right, beyond an area of broken rocks divided by wide vegetated gullies, is a buttress at the back of an amphitheatre. It is of fairly uniform height with a narrow slab to the left of centre.

Amphitheatre Slab   150 feet   Hard Severe   (1937)
The grade is for the line described, but there are several alternatives. The original route avoided both difficulty and interest by skirting the steep upper section on the left. Pleasant climbing on sound, abrasive rock. Start at the foot of two thin cracks at the lowest point of the narrow slab.
1 70 feet. 3b. Climb between the cracks and continue in the same line to a heather patch and belay.
2 80 feet. 4a. Go up for a few feet, then make a delicate rising traverse right, almost to a grassy ledge. Climb an awkward little groove and move back left to a small ledge. Diagonally right up a short wall, spike belay a few feet farther back.

Northern Group

On the left of the quartz-flecked scree chute is a two-tier buttress, and on its left a small scree-floored amphitheatre with a prominent quartz band traversing the back wall. On the lower tier is:

Autumn Buttress   140 feet   Very Difficult   (1937)
At the right-hand end of the buttress, a shallow-angled shaley rib extends to a lower level than the sound rock. Immediately left of the rib, a little scree runnel leads up to the foot of the crag. Start here.
1 90 feet. Climb broken slabs to a heather ledge. Continue over loose spikes and mantelshelf into a V-groove left of a steep nose. Go up the groove and exit right or straight up. Belay high on the left by loose blocks.
2 50 feet. Cautiously pass the blocks into a groove on the left. A rib on the right leads to a platform, from which a groove in the left wall is followed to the heather backbone of the ridge.

Band Stand   140 feet   Severe   (1964)
A poor climb with much scrambling. It takes a broken rib with a pinnacled summit on the left of the scree-floored amphitheatre. Start in the centre, at the base of the buttress, at an ill-defined crack in a square wall.
1 30 feet. Ascend the crack to a grass terrace. Traverse right for 20 feet to belay.
2 60 feet. Pock-marked rock on the left leads easily to a stance. Climb a steep crack above and move strenuously out right. Finish over a perched block to slabs and a small pinnacle. Scramble up the ridge, across the quartz band and past a pile of rocks. Continue to

the final arête.
3 50 feet. Finish up the crest of the arête, or just on its left.

Far North Group

Several hundred yards north of the quartz-flecked scree chute, there is a discontinuous dry-stone wall running up the hillside, giving way to a scree tongue higher up. A little to the south there is a sheep pen at the lakeside. Although this group is extensive, only a very small section is worthy of attention and even this leaves a lot to be desired.

Sheep Pen Buttress   170 feet   Very Difficult   (1949)
The rock is very loose low down, and the climb gains its length by traversing to the right. The remnants of the dry-stone wall reach the cliff, and about 30 yards to the right there is a diagonal break in a line of overhangs. Start by some large blocks, directly above the sheep pen and just right of the diagonal break.
1 70 feet. Move cautiously right on to a ledge. Trend diagonally right via a crack and traverse a heather ledge to a pile of loose blocks. Go up a little wall to a spike belay by a small rowan tree.
2 60 feet. Climb another short wall slightly on the left, and follow an obvious vegetated rake up to the right. Thread belay at the foot of a leaning pillar.
3 40 feet. Ascend a groove left of the pillar and slabby rocks to finish.

Craig Llethr Gwyn

(Crag of the White Slopes)   OS Ref. 721 612

Opposite Pen Llithrig y Wrach and at a lower altitude stands a small cliff overlooking the southern tip of Llyn Cowlyd.

Y Blaidd   80 feet   E4   (1991)
The centre of the crag is characterised by a large overhang at two thirds height. This route takes the clean wall to the left. Start below the roof at an obvious groove. Protection is good when needed, with the crux reserved for the final 20 feet.
1 80 feet. 6a. Climb the groove, two good flake runners. Move left, past a peg, and surmount a small overhang, peg. Climb the wall above passing another peg until a series of difficult moves gain good holds and the top. Belay well back on a natural bollard.

Ysgyrnygu   70 feet   Severe   (1991)
The arête which bounds the extreme right hand end of the crag is
pleasant enough.

Foel Fras and Foel Grach

(Rough Hill and Barren Hill)

The four crags described in this section are situated in the very heart of
the Carneddau, and are remote from all main roads. A minor road from
Tal y Bont in the Conwy Valley leads almost to Llyn Eigiau, beyond this
is a rough track to the dam, and another continues to Melyn-llyn (Yellow
lake). Alternatively they may be approached on foot from the Ogwen
Valley. None of the climbs can be recommended, but for those who seek
the rare solitude of the mountains and enjoy long walks, they are
interesting to visit.

Craig Eigiau   (Crag of the Flocks)

OS Ref. 718 657

Above the west side of the Llyn is a series of crags; wet, vegetated and
discontinuous, but also compact and overhanging. At the northern end
of the Llyn, about 15 minutes up the boulder screes is a small two-tier
buttress. Close to the base of the buttress is a 20-foot isolated pinnacle.
This summit is easily attained by the south face.

Premiere   200 feet   Severe   (1959)
It makes the best of what rock there is. Start 30 feet right of the
pinnacle. Climb a dirty groove for 20 feet, traverse delicately left from
a flake, go up and mantelshelf on to a big block. Step down right,
then go up to an overhang, move out right and up parallel cracks.
Walk 10 yards to a wall with rowans. On its left is an arête. From the
right, go up over large loose blocks, then a crack. Traverse left round
the arête and continue via cracks to finish.

Vin Ordinaire   190 feet   Very Difficult   (1959)
On the left of the pinnacle is an obvious easy-angled slab, often wet.
Start at its right-hand edge. Pleasantly climb the slab, passing beneath
a gnarled holly, then back diagonally right up a vegetated gangway
to a silver birch tree. Climb a chimney round to the left, traverse left
and scramble up to finish.

Craig Fawr   (Big Cliff)

OS Ref. 699 657

A very unsatisfactory, slabby buttress rises above Melyn-llyn. It has a
very wet gully.

Yellow Chimney   220 feet   Difficult   (1942)
Start from the left-hand side of the crag at about water-level. Go up
the left rib of the gully for a few feet, then follow the gully bed to an
open groove and easy chimney. Finish up a narrow 40-foot chimney.

Craig Y Dulyn   (Crag of the Black Lake)

OS Ref. 698 668

This enormous crag rises straight from a truly black llyn, which is
estimated to be 50 feet deep only a few feet from the edge. So awe
inspiring is this secluded mountain hollow that the dam and other
evidence of man's presence do not detract from it over much.

There are two principal buttresses, of entirely different character. The one
on the right is clear of the llyn. It is very steep in the upper third but
marred by prolific vegetation in rakes sloping up from the right. At
two-thirds height, easy ledges encroach beneath jutting overhangs. The
ledges lead across the cliff, finally dipping below an impressive 80-foot
wall. The features are bold but discontinuous.

A number of routes have been made on this section, mainly graded Very Severe and Hard Severe; they are all seriously affected by vegetation and none of them seems worthy of detailed description.

The area between the buttresses has four steep water-courses, the two on the left have been climbed and are reported to be rather unpleasant. All four of them have been done and are in the winter guide and provide hard winter climbing given the right conditions.

The left-hand buttress is very large, also vegetated but is usually dry. Features are less well-defined. In general it is pyramid-shaped, rising vertically from the lake and it lies farther and farther back as it gains height. Above the steep lower nose a diagonal rake leads up from right to left; this has been climbed and is Moderate vegetation. Starting from a grassy depression on the left of the nose, a diagonal gully rises intermittently to the top of the rake; this has also been climbed. Above the lines are coincident, with route finding hampered by a scruffy buttress and a complex of heather ledges. The gully is about Very Difficult standard, mainly vegetation.

Waterfall Gully is obvious, in the centre of the big amphitheatre between Craig y Dulyn and Castell Dulyn. About Difficult standard, it is loose and usually wet.

Castell Y Dulyn   (Castle of the Black Lake)

OS Ref. 701 663

This scruffy little cliff is completely overshadowed by its neighbours. From the dam a path skirts the left edge of the llyn. Follow it, up steps beneath a large chockstone (The Needle's Eye), and continue for about 100 yards to the foot of the cliff.

Garden Cracks   180 feet   Very Difficult   (1949)
Towards the right-hand end of the cliff, there is a broad ledge at 25 feet, with a large boulder on it. Below is a block pinnacle and on its right a short overhanging groove.
1 50 feet. Climb the groove and the slot above to a ledge. Take a short mossy groove to a heather ledge and continue to the foot of a steep V-chimney.

2 30 feet. Strenuously follow the chimney.
3 40 feet. Traverse right from a tree and go up a short groove to a ledge.
4 60 feet. From a terrace right of some overhangs, climb a crack to a slab, which is taken direct to finish.

Garden Wall   110 feet   Severe   (1961)
Start 20 feet left of the edge of a steep little wall at the right-hand end of the crag at a vegetated groove.
1 60 feet. Ascend the groove to an overhang, then move out right to a good ledge.
2 50 feet. Climb diagonally left to beneath a small overhang. Go up a wide crack to the overhang, then on to a large flake on the left. A steep slab leads to the finish.

The right edge of the crag gives another 100 feet of climbing.

Craig Yr Ysfa   (Cliff of the Gathering)

OS Ref. 694 637

The word ysfa does translate to mean a craving or itching. However, a much more likely explanation is that our ysfa is derived from the old Welsh word hysfa. This was where a shepherd would collect his sheep from the high pastures. Because of the previous errors, one can enjoy such morsels of writing as ...

'Experience, bitter experience, has proved that the simple literal translation of the name must be accepted. A party in 1916 entered the dark recesses of one of its gullies as cheerful and with as great a craving as any that had set out from Pen-y-Gwryd. Hardly had they roped up when they were attacked by myriads of small, but active and virulent gnats. The battle was fierce and long. No sooner had one cloud been added to the heap of slain that littered the bottom of the gully than other and still other clouds appeared. Climbing with desperation and haste, clinging with one hand and with the other endeavouring to slay their ten thousands, the members of the expedition finally emerged into the upper world, but at what cost! They have however the satisfaction of knowing that they have torn from the dark recesses of these cliffs the fearful secret of their name'.

The crag has many classic and/or historical routes which, combined with their remoteness, can rekindle the enthusiasm and energy of the most jaded of climbers. Archer Thomson and his friends first explored these huge cliffs and Great Gully was a tremendous discovery for its time. Many others, of differing eras, have come to the cliff and left some stunning climbs of equal quality. Furthermore, there are now a number of difficult routes of a modern mode.

A few hundred metres west of Helyg on the Capel Curig to Bangor road, the A5, is the start of a tarmac access road (687 603) which strikes directly up the hillside northwards. Parking is available at Gwern Gof Isaf, some 200 metres towards Bangor. Rapid entry is required to the access road by Mountain Rescue Teams and the farmer; therefore, DO NOT PARK IN FRONT OF THE LOCKED GATE! Follow the tarmac road tediously, through several gates, to a fairly level section. Just where the road bears left fork off right along a narrow footpath over a rise to contour above the llyn, this is Ffynnon Llugwy, Spring of the Conwy (Lucovium). The path then strikes up the hillside to zigzags and Bwlch Eryl Farchog, Pass of Eryl the Knight. Either follow paths down to the base of the crags or continue up the ridge above the cliff to the top of the Amphitheatre. About one hour from the road to crag top.

Alternatively the long ridge of Pen yr Helgi Du (Hill of the Black Hound) may be gained from Tal y Braich on the A5, and followed to a large quartz cairn above the llyn. From this point a poor path contours round to the saddle above the crag.

From Tal y Bont in the Conwy Valley an unsurfaced, gated road leads to the dam of Llyn Eigiau. A good track traverses the llyn side, crosses the river beyond and continues to some quarry buildings. Marshy ground and a steep incline then lead to the foot of the cliffs. This is not a very satisfactory route for those based in Central Snowdonia but quite good for those coming in from the East.

Climbs in the Amphitheatre may be approached by descending the loose broken area in and about C and D Gullies, but this is not recommended for inexperienced parties.

Directions to the various sections of the crag are dealt with under appropriate headings.

Craig yr Ysfa is a large, complex cliff. There are two principal crags with a large Amphitheatre separating them. Despite its size there are relatively few long routes, and even these are generally of poor quality. Amphitheatre Buttress and Great Gully being notable exceptions. Much

Norman Elliot on the upper section of *Pinnacle Ridge Route* (V Diff), Buttress 5, Craig Braich Ty Du. Photo: Terry Gifford

Roland Perkins high on the popular *Amphitheatre Buttress* (V Diff), Craig yr Ysfa.
Photo: Simon Cardy

Simon Cardy on *Aura* (E2), Craig Yr Ysfa. Photo: Andy Orton of the South Crag is easy-angled and almost buried in heather. There are four gullies, which are for the most part poor; nevertheless they serve to divide the crag into well-defined sections.

Small steep buttresses tend to emphasise the discontinuity and are responsible for inconsistencies in the standard of the climbs. This erratic quality is only partially redeemed by a few good short climbs in The Cirque.

The Amphitheatre has three facets. The Left Wall is steep but comparatively short and The Back Wall is broken, but The Right Wall compensates for all the crag's shortcomings. The exposure of The Lower Amphitheatre Right Wall is striking in spite of its being enclosed.

The North Crag is an anti-climax being initially steep, then falling back sharply at one-third height. Beyond Great Gully it becomes even more broken.

From the bwlch the two crags are barely visible, and The Amphitheatre is not recognisable as such. However, good views are obtained from Cwm Eigiau and the ridge of Pen yr Helgi Du opposite.

The climbs are described from left to right beginning with South Crag.

South Crag
Truant Rib   300 feet   Difficult   (1938)
On the extreme left-hand side of the crag, left of Pinnacle Gully, a buttress emerges from the heather. The route follows the less vegetated upper section and although entirely artificial it provides some pleasant little pitches. Start where a flaky staircase commences and traverse right from the descent path, across the buttress towards Pinnacle Gully. The start is at the level of a substantial tree with a grass-topped bollard on its right and immediately above a small mountain ash tree. Scramble up easily for 50 feet to a flake belay.
1 100 feet. Take a pleasant slab to a bollard on the right, then another short slab to a bilberry platform.
2 90 feet. Continue up a broken rib to a bollard at its top and a ledge, then climb a slabby rib on good holds, just right of a vegetated groove.
3 60 feet. Gain a steeper rib on the left and follow the edge, with a delicate finish, to a heather terrace.
4 50 feet. Go up the edge of a rib, then step left into a scoop and so to the top. Scrambling remains.

Pinnacle Gully   600 feet   Easy
Not really a climb, but the very distinctive rotten flake pinnacle serves
well as a landmark, both from above and below. Its summit is easily
attained. All obstacles in the gully can be avoided, leaving only
stones and vegetation. It serves as a descent to gain access to The
Cirque.

The Banister   150 feet   Severe   (1949)
A scrappy route, entirely artificial but it makes the best of what rock
there is. Start at the level of the pinnacle in Pinnacle Gully. A bilberry
saddle on the right is easily gained. There is a vegetated groove to
the left of a large leaning pillar on the little buttress above the saddle.
Left again is a tiny triangular niche with a broken groove above.
1 60 feet. Climb awkwardly via the niche to a grassy ledge, then
another short awkward step, taken on the left, leads to a fern terrace.
Large spike belay on the left.
2 40 feet. Go up a little groove directly above, then make a tricky
traverse right beneath an overhang to an ash tree ledge, The
Landing. Alternatively a short wide crack some 30 feet right leads to
the same stance. Harder with less character.
3 50 feet. Follow a spiky weakness leftwards to the final mossy slab.
Scramble to finish.

The Cirque

This is a small high-level amphitheatre. Of the three walls only the least
impressive left wall provides climbing. The other routes described under
this heading skirt the edges of The Cirque and Arch Gully goes right
through it. There are three alternative approaches;
(a) a long, easy, but rather exposed traverse can be made from the paths
descending from the saddle. Take the flaky staircase as for Truant Rib,
continuing in the same line to Pinnacle Gully. Ascend this to the level of
the pinnacle, over a bilberry saddle on the right and descend the first
pitch of The Staircase into The Cirque.
(b) Bending Gully and its left-hand branch, which is preferable to Arch
Gully.
(c) Descend Pinnacle Gully and continue as for (a) above from the
pinnacle. Probably the easiest.

The Staircase   180 feet   Very Difficult   (1938)
This route follows the left-hand edge of The Cirque. Rather broken and
vegetated. Start at a broken and usually greasy groove defining the
edge of the left wall of The Cirque. Belay 15 feet to the left.
1 40 feet. Climb the groove to a ledge with numerous spike belays.
2 50 feet. Go easily up a grassy groove to a platform and large
spike. A short crack leads to The Landing and gnarled ash trees.

3 90 feet. A slab is climbed on good holds at first. Then step left into a scoop and go up to an easier slab leading to a bilberry terrace. Finish up slabby rock left of a nose. Scrambling remains.

Originally the above route started some 50 feet lower down, 20 feet left of the jammed boulder of Arch Gully, at the toe of the rib between Pinnacle and Arch gullies. This adds length and difficulty, but not merit. Either of two vegetated grooves may satisfy the purist and avoid pitch 1 above.

The next three climbs are on the left wall of The Cirque. They all have some merit.

Gomorrah 150 feet Severe   (1938)
A pleasant slab climb on good holds. It is often greasy, when it is harder than graded. Start a few feet right of the groove of the previous route, level with the end of a quartz tongue leading up to the back wall. The line is obvious.
1 80 feet. Trend slightly right at first. Continue direct avoiding most of the grass tufts, then traverse left to a notch on an arête and belay.
2 70 feet. Move back right and go up a short curving crack to rejoin the arête. Step from a big flake on to a rib and continue delicately to easy ground.

Spiral Route 120 feet Very Severe   (1938)
A fine route which is delicate and not easy to protect. It takes a rather indirect line to a large grassy ledge, with the remnants of a small tree on it, in the centre of the wall. Similar in character to Gomorrah. Start a few feet above the toe of the quartz tongue leading to the back wall of The Cirque, 15 feet left of the corner of Angle Groove and lower down. Poor belay low down.
1 70 feet. 4a. Climb a shallow diagonal groove to a small ledge and spike, just a few feet left of Angle Groove. Follow a curving depression back left; the line is marked by a thin crack. (Gomorrah is easily accessible on the left). Move right over a bulge and then left again. A delicate slabby rib leads direct to the centre of the grassy ledge. Poor flake belay.
2 50 feet. 4a. Go straight up a cracked wall above, trending left to reach the easy section of the arête on Gomorrah.

Angle Groove 120 feet Very Severe   (1944)
A strenuous climb in contrast to its neighbours. Start by scrambling up a corner formed between the left and back walls of The Cirque. Belay at the base of a chimney level with the small ledge on Spiral Route.
1 90 feet. 4b. A few easy feet lead to awkward bulges, surmounted

by bridging. The right-hand crack is followed where the chimney divides. Exit left and climb pleasant slabs via a grassy ledge to a large belay in a groove above.

2 30 feet. 4a. Climb the groove. Not without incident.

Arch Gully 820 feet   Difficult   (1901)

The lower part of this gully is a rather smooth, water-worn groove, which gives way to heather scrambling, leading in turn to two jammed blocks guarding access to The Cirque. Beyond The Cirque it becomes a deep cleft of considerable character. Start approximately in the centre of the South Crag at a deep recess from which two gullies rise and diverge. Low down they are separated by a narrow grey rib. A distinctive light-coloured scree chute spews into the cwm from the base of the gullies. This is the left-hand gully; the other is Bending Gully.

1 250 feet. The smooth groove. Slabs on the right give relief from the difficulties in the groove.

2 200 feet. Vegetated scrambling until the two jammed blocks give access to The Cirque.

3 150 feet. Walk up and into a deep cavern on the right.

4 100 feet. Ascend a steep chimney with good holds on the left, continue to a capstone and squeeze behind, or harder pull over left or right outside. From the capstone, the arch itself can be gained by 20 feet of hard delicate climbing.

5 120 feet. Go easily up the gully bed and over jammed blocks. A groove on the left gives way to easy ground or the gully bed may be taken direct.

A small buttress high on the cliff, defined by the two branches of Bending Gully, is known as Y-Buttress. It is split by a broad heather terrace leading out right from The Cirque. The next route commences from the terrace and Arch Wall crosses it farther right.

Cirque Rib 180 feet   Hard Very Severe (3 pts. aid)   (1963)

Not a good route, but the climbing is exacting. Start some 15 feet right of the left edge of the right wall of The Cirque at a stepped corner capped by a roof. There is a small tree at 30 feet.

1 60 feet. 5a. Climb the corner to the roof and traverse left to a small ledge on the arête, using a peg and a sling for aid. Step left across a groove (flake runner), and go up a little rib until it is possible to move back right to a juniper ledge.

2 60 feet. 5a. Use a shoulder to gain a groove on the left with a thin crack in its left wall. Ascend the groove then more easily go up grassy rock to a stance on the edge of The Cirque (junction with Arch Wall).

3 60 feet. As for Arch Wall pitch 5, go out right, scramble to a block, step left to cracked ledges and go up to the top.

The next two routes start from Bending Gully.

Arch Wall 340 feet Hard Severe   (1937)
The lower half of this climb is vegetated and often wet, whilst the section above the heather ledge is more open and cleaner. The route is rather disjointed. Start almost immediately above the bend in Bending Gully and a little below the level of some distinctive overhangs above the main (right-hand) branch of the gully, where a wet and rather unpleasant groove rises.
1 100 feet. 3b. Climb the groove until it begins to overhang, then escape left and follow bilberry ledges to an easy-angled slab.
2 90 feet. Go up the slab, or the vegetation on its right to the heather terrace. Continue up a vegetated rake to a platform in the centre of wall.
3 30 feet. 4a. Mantelshelf awkwardly on to a quartz ledge and gain a little groove on the left. Ascend the groove with a tricky exit.
4 60 feet. 3a. Over broken blocks to a short groove on the left. Climb the groove until the steep left wall leads to an airy stance overlooking The Cirque.
5 60 feet. 3a. Move out right and scramble to a huge detached block. Step left from the block to cracked ledges and go up to a bilberry saddle and the top.

Cobweb Wall 180 feet Severe   (1948)
Not a very distinguished route. It commences from Bending Gully some 80 feet beyond the start of the previous climb and follows a vegetated groove rising towards the left-hand end of the distinctive overhangs above, then curves right for 50 feet to avoid them.

Bending Gully 600 feet Difficult   (1900)
Other than providing access to the two previous climbs and a moderately interesting approach to The Cirque, this is an unsatisfactory climb. The left-hand spur leads to The Cirque and the main gully peters out amongst broken rocks and heather. Start in the deep recess, as for Arch Gully. This is the right-hand of the twin gullies.
1 300 feet. After passing a diagonally jammed monolith on the right, continue easily to two short parallel chimneys. Here the branches diverge.
2 300 feet. The main gully. A few obstacles before the bend are turned mainly on the right. Beyond, the gully becomes a deep V-groove. Pass left of some wedged splinters, then an easy slab on

the right avoids a jammed stone. A groove is smooth at first and
another slab is taken. Scrambling remains.
2a 250 feet. The left-hand branch. An initial difficult crack, then
water-worn rocks and scrambling leads to The Cirque.

Bending Gully Reach

This section of the cliff is defined on the right by Bending Gully and it
extends across the cliff virtually to Avalanche Gully. It consists of an area
of broken overlapping slabs, which are set back from the main line of
the crag and rise from a field of dense heather. Higher up the slabs
steepen into a wall with a distinctive band of overhangs on the left. The
whole of this area is seriously marred by vegetation, the rock is mossy
and the two slab routes are serious undertakings in the wet.

The approach and frustrating exits detract from the merits of these routes.
The least unpleasant way off is to traverse left to the edge of Bending
Gully then scramble straight up, or better, traverse back right to join
Avalanche Buttress above pitch 3.

Low down on the left, a shoulder abuts onto the slabs. This may be
climbed by a cracked slab on the right or via a short groove from Bending
Gully. It gives access to the next climb.

Heron Slab 260 feet Hard Severe   (1965)
Vegetated, but may well improve with traffic. Not easy to protect.
Start from the top of the shoulder. Poor belay.
1 40 feet. 3a. Climb delicately diagonally left to a spike then
continue up a heather rake to a better spike. Belay.
2 90 feet. 3b. Go diagonally left for a few feet, then traverse back
right and continue diagonally right until a thin quartz traverse can be
made beneath an overlap. Step down and go right round an edge, to
a vegetated break, which is followed to a pulpit and huge belay.
3 130 feet. 3a. Step out left and traverse left for a few feet, then
trend diagonally right up a slab to a line of overhangs. Traverse right
and go up a break in the overhangs to a broad ledge. Awkward
belays just right of a little rock nose.

The Slab Climb 350 feet Very Difficult   (1909)
The easiest line up the heather slabs. There are approximately equal
amounts of rock and vegetation. Belays are scarce. Start to the right
of the shoulder at a step in the slabs. Farther right, about 150 feet
from the shoulder, scramble up 40 feet to belay. This is directly above
a distinctive quartz-marked boulder, which is immediately above the
path.
1 150 feet. Trend left over vegetated rock, crossing an overlap at

100 feet, to a rib, which is climbed to a comfortable stance at the level of an obvious traverse right.
2 80 feet. Traverse right across a slab to a short square chimney, then go up this to another chimney. Thread belay.
3 30 feet. Ascend the chimney, awkward entry, to small trees and a spike belay.
4 70 feet. Continue easily in the same line until a slab on the right can be gained. Climb it diagonally to more trees. Stance and belays.
5 20 feet. Go awkwardly up an obvious break in a wall above or avoid it on the right.

Birch Tree Chimney   180 feet   Difficult   (1909)
An unsatisfactory climb, with much vegetation and little rock. The final little chimney is the sole attraction. High on the right-hand side of Bending Gully Reach is a small twisted chimney, with a track of vegetation leading up to it. Start at the foot of the track of vegetation.
1 120 feet. Little more than a vegetated scramble leads to a leaning bollard on the left.
2 60 feet. Go up to a small cave and make an awkward exit on good holds over a chockstone. Climb the final chimney, loose.

Avalanche Buttress   670 feet   Very Difficult   (1950)
The first two pitches of this route are considerably more difficult than those that follow. However, the upper section does provide the best exit from the Bending Gully Reach climbs. Start in Avalanche Gully. Just beyond the last of the difficulties in the gully, a small shallow-angled rock rib divides the gully bed, with grass on the left and stone on the right. In the left wall of the gully a crack fails to reach the base, and on its left is a line of overhangs at 15 feet.
1 30 feet. Make a hard move over a small overhang, or use a shoulder, and mantelshelf to gain the steep crack. Climb it to a stance and belay.
2 60 feet. Climb a slab on the right to a little V-recess, then go out left across a wall and step round to a grassy bay in a groove.
3 80 feet. Climb the groove or either of its bounding ribs to a heather platform with a lying block. Exits from the Bending Gully Reach climbs join the route here. Above is a grass-filled groove with a small tree at the top. The line follows the very edge of the gully.
4 100 feet. A little grass, a slab and an avoidable crack, lead to a broad shelf at the base of a wall.
5 100 feet. Go up the wall to a crevasse behind a block. Scramble and trend right to a detached block. Belay on a small terrace.
6 300 feet. Take the edge of the gully, exposed to a distinctive platform. Continue up a series of mossy ledges and some optional

rock. Avoid a chimney on the left and traverse right above it. Slabs and broken rocks lead to the top.

The Untidy Buttress

Towards the top of Avalanche Gully a subsidiary gully or break bears away to the left. Between it and the main gully is The Untidy Buttress. There are numerous wide fissures, cracks and tumbled blocks, giving an impression of serious instability, which is apparently well-founded to judge from the gully's name. All five routes are on the right flank and are best approached from above, either by descending the vegetated top section of the gully, or descending Amphitheatre Buttress and crossing the gully bed. Care should be taken to locate the correct gully, Avalanche Gully is the last before the amphitheatre. The climbs are broken into short sections, often of unequal quality and standard. None can be recommended, but Troglodyte and Enigma are probably the best. The rock is very mossy and treacherous in the wet.

Original Route   170 feet   Very Difficult   (1938)
Undistinguished. Start at the lower end of the buttress. The initial 50 feet are steep and avoided by a rake on the right.
1 40 feet. Trend left up the rake to the crest of the buttress.
2 80 feet. Can be split. Continue easily to a large flat-topped block. Go up a wall above to another ledge. Scramble up left to a poised flake, go up it, or pull over it. Platform on the right.
3 50 feet. Go up left over tumbled boulders. A gangway now leads left round a corner to a short wall. Or scramble to the second pitch of Beaumont's Chimney and climb it (much harder).

The next four routes are best located from the region of the two gendarmes and knife edge of Amphitheatre Buttress, pitch 4. Immediately opposite the big gendarme are two wide chimneys.

Beaumont's Chimney   110 feet   Severe   (1938)
Start at the foot of the left-hand chimney, by a large flat-topped bollard.
1 60 feet. Go up the chimney, behind and between huge blocks, to emerge on a terrace of broken blocks. Pinnacle belays beside a rotten tree stump.
2 50 feet. Climb another narrow chimney immediately above the stump. Struggle up facing right or awkward bridging to start. Above a cave, then a short wall and easy rocks lead to the top.

Troglodyte   100 feet   Hard Severe   (1949)
Part of this climb collapsed, but it has been reascended. All the difficulties are concentrated in the second pitch. Start at the base of

the right-hand chimney, with debris spewing out and a large jammed stone above. It is 25 feet right of the previous climb and at a higher level.

1 50 feet. 3a. Scramble up through the chimney, behind the stone and up a gangway on the left to pinnacle belays and the rotten stump of Beaumont's Chimney.

2 50 feet. 3b. Step awkwardly right from the top of the left-hand pinnacle on to a mossy slab. Move up right to a steep, sharp-edged crack. Climb this strenuously with an awkward exit right to a good ledge. Ascend a wall to finish.

Variation

2a 50 feet. 3a. Most of the difficulties can be rather pointlessly avoided by moving right at the top of the chimney, up rust-coloured slabs and into a dangerously loose chasm. Pot-holing leads to a ledge, then go up a short wide chimney to finish.

Sigma 100 feet Difficult   (1949)
Start some 50 feet right of and higher than the chimney of Troglodyte at a smooth grey wall, set forward from the main part of the buttress. At the very bottom edge of the wall is a spike belay; above is a series of grassy steps overlooking the grey wall.

1 45 feet. Ascend the steps and trend slightly left to a cave formed by jammed blocks.

2 55 feet. Climb cracks in the wall above the cave, taking either branch to a crevassed ledge. Ascend a short wall to finish.

Enigma 110 feet Severe   (1949)
Start the smooth grey wall mentioned for the previous route which is terminated at its upper end by a large rib. In the corner between the corner and rib is a vegetated stepped cleft, with a triangular recess in its left wall. Start inside the cleft.

1 50 feet. Go up the cleft for a few feet then traverse left just above the recess to a shallow broken groove, which is followed to a ledge and belay on the left.

2 60 feet. Move back right and go up to an obvious diagonal break. Follow it right via two jammed stones to a good ledge. Ascend a short wall to the top.

Avalanche Gully 750 feet Difficult   (1905)
All the climbing is concentrated in the lower part of this unsatisfactory gully, which was once notorious for the danger of falling rocks, a point still not to be ignored. Except as an approach to Avalanche Buttress this route cannot be recommended. If taken direct the pitches are considerably harder than the grade given, especially when wet,

but all the difficulties can be skirted on the right. The narrow cleft which leads into the gully is somewhat concealed amongst heathery slabs to the left of Amphitheatre Buttress, but the line is quite obvious.
1 250 feet. A rib lower on the right avoids a capped chimney. Stony scrambling leads to a wet cave with a very awkward rounded capstone, or take the right wall on good holds. Another short cave pitch and a wide mossy chimney are both turned on the right.
2 500 feet. Unpleasant vegetated scrambling leads to the finish.

★★★ **Amphitheatre Buttress**   960 feet   Very Difficult   (1905)
A classic mountaineering route, not high in its grade, which is undoubtedly one of the very best at this standard in Wales; justifiably popular. The exposure provided by the Amphitheatre amply compensates for the unfortunate break midway. Archer Thomson described it perfectly as a 'very entertaining but not seriously difficult climb'. Start some 50 feet above the toe of the buttress formed between Avalanche Gully and The Amphitheatre, at the level where The Amphitheatre Left Wall peters out.
1 400 feet. Pleasant pocketed slabs, easy climbing and scrambling lead to a large platform below a steep wall. This can be split into short pitches. At about 200 feet a groove provides the principal obstacle.
2 70 feet. The crux, mainly due to polished holds. Go up a well-worn corner on the right to a huge detached block. Now go up again, with rounded holds to finish.
3 200 feet. Vegetated scrambling and paths!
4 100 feet. Climb the crest to a gap, two gendarmes and a knife edge leading to the main mass of the mountain. Exposed but not difficult; the knife edge can be taken *à cheval* by traditionalists.
5 180 feet. Continue up a good ridge on the right to the summit.

The Amphitheatre

This huge recess is the principal feature of the cliff, and separates the North Crag from the South Crag. The left wall of The Amphitheatre is quite steep while the back is disappointing; there are four gullies separated by three easy ribs, the two on the left provide pleasant climbs, whilst the division between the right-hand gullies is broken and indistinct. The magnificent right wall is undoubtedly one of the most impressive pieces of rock in Wales. It is steep and compact. A broad, sloping, bilberry ledge divides the wall horizontally at two-thirds height.

If one is only climbing in the Amphitheatre it is usual to descend into the cleft from the cliff top, choosing the easiest line in or about C and D Gullies. This is not easy to find and although technically easy, care is essential. A good spot to leave 'sacks is directly above Pinnacle Wall;

just over a low stone wall. Here, one finds a sheltered spot to contemplate a good day's climbing. A long and rather humdrum approach can be made following the path down from Bwlch Eryl Farchog traversing the base of South Crag and scrambling up scree into the Amphitheatre. However, you'll only have to go back down to your 'sacks and climb up to the bwlch again!

Amphitheatre Left Wall

The routes on this wall are short, steep and terminate on Amphitheatre Buttress. The climbs are frequently greasy and consequently often harder than their normal grade.

Figure of Eight   110 feet   Very Severe   (1944)
A fairly good route to do if Mur y Niwl is busy. Start at the left-hand end of the wall where a grassy bay gives easy access to the lower part of Amphitheatre Buttress. To the right of the bay are two large diamond-shaped blocks (the Figure of Eight) projecting from the wall. Start on the right of the bay where a ramp leads up to the top of the lower block.
1 110 feet. 4b. Climb the ramp to a grassy ledge. Step left and go up a steep wall to a large flake. Move right and go awkwardly up to a ledge, step left and climb a curving crack strenuously, to easier ground. Continue trending slightly left, until an awkward swing can be make on to Amphitheatre Buttress.

Pieces of Eight   100 feet   Very Severe   (1949)
Another pleasant little climb. Some 40 feet right of the bay mentioned for the previous route are two parallel diagonal cracks leading left to the top of the upper block of the 'Eight'. Start at the base of the cracks.
1 70 feet. 4b. Go up the cracks and a little ramp to the top of the block. Trend slightly right up a steep wall to a perched block, then go up to a small overhang, lower and left of a larger one. Pull over this and step left to grass then scramble right to a pinnacle belay.
2 30 feet. Strenuously go up an obvious layback crack (the final pitch of Sentry Box Crack).

The most prominent feature on the next section of the wall is a huge bottomless 'sentry box', with a short block-choked chimney leading up to it.

Sentry Box Crack   100 feet   Hard Severe   (1950)
A rather disjointed climb. Start directly below the 'sentry box'.
1 70 feet. 3b. Scramble up vegetation to the short chimney choked with blocks, and climb it to a large sloping grass ledge. Go up a crack on the right of a large block to pinnacle belays.

2 30 feet. 3a. Descend a ramp leftwards to the foot of an obvious layback crack. Climb it strenuously to the top.

Dover Road   120 feet   Very Severe (A2)   (1955)
Start as for Sentry Box Crack.
1 70 feet. 4c A2. Climb to the blocks, then go up the crack on the right-hand side of the deep groove, cross left and go up to the roof. Aid across this then up to a small ledge above the overhang and step right to a stance.
2 50 feet. Step back left and climb the groove to reach the Amphitheatre Buttress.

Cockroach Crack   100 feet   Severe   (1944)
One of the better climbs on this wall, steep and enclosed, then more open. Start at the foot of an obvious recessed chimney/crack line to the right of the 'sentry box'.
1 30 feet. Scramble across vegetated ledges to the foot of the chimney.
2 70 feet. Ascend the chimney, awkward at first, then the continuation crack to a ledge. The block at the top of Reed Rake is climbed on the left.

Reed Rake   100 feet   Difficult   (1934)
An unsatisfactory vegetated break, to the right of the 'sentry box' and the previous climb is taken direct.

About 40 feet up and right of Reed Rake, opposite and level with the toe of Amphitheatre Right Wall is a large and roughly diamond-shaped rubescent sheet of rock. At about 10 feet above the floor of the Amphitheatre is a slanting ledge with two spikes.

★**Whirlwind**   150 feet   E3   (1989)
The hanging flake crack in the smooth wall right of Reed Rake. A powerfully compelling line. Start on a hump directly below the undercut roof of the crack at the lower spike, sometimes damp.
1 150 feet. 5c. Climb the steep groove to the right-hand end of the roof. Traverse left beneath this and layback the crack to a second roof. Move left to a slight niche before romping diagonally up the face to a short groove and lofty perch on the right. A hard high step remains.

El Nino   130 feet   E3   (1983)
Starts on the ledge at the upper of the two spikes beneath a blunt nose of rock
1 70 feet. 5b. Scramble up to the right, or directly and more boldly,

Craig Yr Ysfa: Amphitheatre Left Wall

1. Whirlwind   E3
2. El Nino   E3
3. Drought   E4
4. Coffin Scoop   HS

Photo: Simon Cardy

to reach a foot traverse leading leftwards to below a small overhang. Climb up to the overhang and surmount it using the obvious flake line to the grassy ledge.

2 60 feet. 6a. From the left end of the ledge, gain a small slab which leads to a short groove, climb this to good footholds. Traverse left to a pulpit then finish direct with a long reach.

Drought   140 feet   E4   (1983)

Start as for El Nino.

1 70 feet. 5c. Follow El Nino, but instead of traversing left, climb a steep slab to a tiny crack which in turn leads direct to a belay.

2 70 feet. 5c. Climb directly above the belay, then move right below some overhangs. Surmount an overlap via a crack and follow this for 30 feet until it is possible to gain the top of a quartzy flake. Move right to reach good finishing holds.

Coffin Scoop   150 feet   Hard Severe   (1944)

Rather vegetated especially in the upper part. Start to the left of an undercut slab shaped like a 'coffin', at the obvious weakness.

1 100 feet. 3b. Climb diagonally left, awkward to start, to the higher of two grass ledges. Trend right up the scoop, to the left of the 'coffin', a continuation groove leads to grass and belays.

2 50 feet. 3a. Move down to the right, and climb a chimney followed by a steep wall to the top, or escape easily left.

One Flew Over the Cuckoo's Nest   180 feet   Very Severe
                                                                   (1976)

A good climb on the buttress right of Coffin Scoop; the line follows the blunt nose opposite Mur y Niwl on the lower section and the prominent groove on the left of the upper section. Start 40 feet right of Coffin Scoop, at the foot of the blunt nose.

1 130 feet. 4c. Climb straight up past two bilberry ledges to a bulge with quartzy veins. Surmount this on the right, move left, then continue trending rightwards to a groove. Climb this for a few feet until a ramp leads to a stance.

2 50 feet. 4c. Go up a steep groove to a small ledge then swing out left to another groove. Move left round an overhang, then step right and follow a bilberry runnel to belay on Amphitheatre Buttress.

Cradle Chimney   110 feet   Very Difficult   (1944)

Rather unpleasant and usually greasy. Well to the right of the Coffin Scoop, at a higher level than the foot of the Nameless Rib, are some shattered blocks with a wide grass-choked crack leading to a very obvious chimney above. Start at the blocks.

1 40 feet. Go over the blocks and ascend the crack. Fortunately this

rubbish is avoidable on the right.
2 70 feet. Climb the chimney.

The Back Wall of The Amphitheatre

This section of the crag consists of a series of gullies with ribs separating
them. None of the gullies is worth climbing, except perhaps in winter
conditions, but two of the ribs provide pleasant routes. On the extreme
left a steep vegetated groove leads on to the upper part of Amphitheatre
Buttress; to its right is A Gully, continuously vegetated. The broken rib
between this and the next gully has a huge pinnacle at mid-height.

The Nameless Rib   430 feet   Difficult   (1905-8)
This is the left-hand of the two principal ribs. The line described is
entirely artificial and can be modified at will. There are three rock
sections separated by vegetation. Pitches can be split. The toe of this
rib projects farthest down into The Amphitheatre. Start some 60 feet
above the toe, and on the left flank at an overhanging block with a
short wall on its left.
1 100 feet. Climb the wall and continue to a pile of boulders. Go up
these to grass, which is followed to a slab and grassy groove.
2 130 feet. Ascend the slab and go on to a detached block on the
right. A few feet up the right-hand of two bilberry grooves, then a
delicate slab leads left to an arête. Walk to large belays on the right.
3 90 feet. Climb an arête pleasantly.
4 75 feet. Easy scrambling.
5 35 feet. Go up either side of the final nose.

B Gully   400 feet   Very Difficult   (1905-8)
Both unpleasant and unsatisfactory. This gully is in the centre of the
Back Wall between the two principal ribs. After the initial easy
scrambling a few nasty obstacles are surmounted or skirted on the
right with difficulty.

Amphitheatre Rib   260 feet   Difficult   (1931)
A good little route. It provides interest and a less dangerous exit from
the back of The Amphitheatre. The most reasonable line is described;
there are alternatives. Start at the lowest point on the right-hand of the
two principal ribs.
1 90 feet. Climb black slabs and trend right to an awkward corner.
Climb this, then traverse right and climb the edge overlooking C Gully
to a block belay and poor stance.
2 60 feet. Move left, then go diagonally up a pleasant slab. Traverse
left, then go easily up to the left-hand end of a grassy ledge. Fifteen
feet higher on the right are some spikes.
3 110 feet. From the top of a bollard traverse left along flakes. Climb

an awkward little groove, then traverse right to a ledge overlooking C
Gully. A little crack on the left and some scrambling lead to a final
easy slab. Scramble to the summit.

C Gully   120 feet of climbing   Difficult   (1905-8)
Very loose and prone to funnel debris dislodged at the summit. It
starts at the level of The Crack, in the Amphitheatre Right Wall. The
line is obvious, there are several obstacles to surmount, commencing
with a two-tier cave.

D Gully   200 feet   Moderate   (1905-8)
This is the least obvious gully as it diverges from the previous one
after the first few pitches, and is not very distinct. Unsatisfactory as a
route.

The whole area between C and D Gullies is very broken and can be
traversed easily at almost any level. As a consequence it provides the
best access into The Amphitheatre.

Amphitheatre Right Wall

An excellent sweep of steep solid rock provides the best climbing on
Craig yr Ysfa. There are two walls, one above the other; separated
horizontally by a broad bilberry terrace. The routes on the lower wall
can be combined with those on the upper or Pinnacle Wall. The lower
wall is dealt with first and the routes are described from left to right.

Lower Amphitheatre Wall

One of the finest walls in Wales, with tremendous exposure adding to
the feeling of remoteness. As the base of the wall descends the
Amphitheatre Screes, the height increases until it is almost 350 feet in
the region of Agrippa. Beyond that point the wall terminates abruptly,
giving way to a broken vegetated area. On the extreme left, high up, is
a tricky access line to the bilberry terrace, right of which is the obvious
cleft of The Crack. Down again is a short chimney low down, with a
large V-groove offset above and to the right, the line of Plumbagin. Below
this groove there is a step in the floor of the Amphitheatre, here a small
gully abuts the wall, and a line of holds leads out of the gully to a grassy
ledge. Aura starts in the gully while Mur y Niwl and Griseofulvin start
beneath the ledge. The large open V-groove above, which leans to the
right, is the line of the Mur y Niwl Direct. Beyond, the wall is even more
compact, where Agrippa wends its way.

★**The Crack**   90 feet   Very Severe   (1932)
A difficult and sometimes damp crack. Start at the base of the obvious

crack-line immediately right of the base of C Gully.
1 90 feet. 4c. Struggle up the crack, which eases after 20 feet, to a
grassy ledge (possible belay). Continue up a groove until a traverse
left on good holds leads to easy ground and a short scramble to
reach the bilberry terrace.

★★**Plumbagin**   150 feet   E1   (1965)
A fine route, with some blind alleys! It follows the next line of
weakness right of The Crack. Start below a distinctive V-chimney
capped by a roof a few feet left of a large shallow groove.
1 50 feet. 5a. Gain the chimney and follow it to the overhang, move
up left to a horizontal crack, then traverse right to a slender ledge.
Belay on poor pegs and small wires above.
2 100 feet. 5b. Move rightwards to the base of the shallow groove,
not without some interest, follow the groove to its top.

★★**Solid Air**   140 feet   E3   (1980)
A steep little number. Start just right of Plumbagin at a vertical crack
directly beneath the belay ledge.
1 40 feet. 5c. Ascend the crack to reach the belay ledge, both
strenuous and sustained.
2 100 feet. 5c. Follow the thin crack above the left end of the ledge
for 20 feet, trend left, then continue up the wall above to easier
ground. Scramble up to the bilberry terrace to finish.

★**Turn the Centuries, Turn**   180 feet   E3   (1981)
A little contrived, but with some good climbing. Start above the step
in the Amphitheatre floor directly under a triangular overhang below
the groove of Plumbagin. Belay to a rather loose flake.
1 130 feet. 6a. Move out right above a gully; go up right again then
back left over a bulge to reach a short groove, and a peg. Step back
down and move right, until difficult moves past a hole gain a thin
crack. Follow the crack to the Girdle Traverse. Continue up the crack
above to reach a belay.
2 50 feet. Scramble easily to the bilberry terrace.

★★★**Aura**   200 feet   E2   (1975)
An utterly brilliant main pitch which struts its way up the wall. Start
below the step in the Amphitheatre floor, where it forms a little damp
gully/alley, directly beneath a small triangular overlap at 30 feet.
1 150 feet. 5b. Climb directly to the overlap then diagonally left up a
crack, and move back up right to gain good holds at the base of a
slanting crack-line. Gain the crack (crux) and follow it to its top with
one tricky move right before the belay ledge.
2 50 feet. Scramble to the terrace.

Craig Yr Ysfa: Lower Amphitheatre

Photo: Simon Cardy

★**Griseofulvin**   240 feet   E3   (1964)
A route with good situations, but also a tendency for dampness. Low
in the grade. Start lower than the rock step, below the alley, directly
beneath the left-hand end of a grass ledge at 15 feet.
1 60 feet. 5c. Ascend the short wall to a grass ledge (as for Mur y
Niwl). Trend up leftwards with difficulty to gain a rib to the left, then
move diagonally back right to a small stance.
2 80 feet. 5a. Climb the awkward groove directly above and
continue straight up the wall, moving right near the top to a grass
ledge.
3 90 feet. 5a. A short steep corner leads to another grass ledge, then
a groove on the right is climbed to join Mur y Niwl.
4 10 feet. 4c. The cracked wall of Mur y Niwl provides the finish.

★★★**Mur y Niwl**   250 feet   Very Severe   (1952)
A truly tremendous mountain route, sustained, steep and exposed.
Near the base of the cliff, under a large but shallow groove in the
middle of the wall, is a ledge at 15 feet. Start under the left-hand end
of this ledge, as for Griseofulvin, below the damp gully.
1 40 feet. 4b. Gain the ledge, then traverse right to a belay. Harder
if wet. The ledge can also be gained by a traverse on flat holds from
the base of Aura.
2 100 feet. 4c. Go steeply up the wall to a niche, move right and
continue on good holds to the base of the V-groove (possible belay).
Hand-traverse right along the upper of two horizontal ledges, then
step down. Move right again and follow a rising 'staircase' to the
perch stance. Awkward belay.
3 60 feet. 4c. Step down, exposed moves now lead right beneath an
overhang to a ledge. Move back left and go up past a ledge, then an
arête to reach a grassy platform, belay.
4 40 feet. 4c. Climb the groove behind the stance, then more easily
ascend a glacis and go up left to the base of a short cracked wall.
5 10 feet. 4c. The cracked wall is harder than it looks.

★**Mur y Niwl Direct**   200 feet   Hard Very Severe   (1967)
Continually interesting and airy climbing make this route worthy of
attention. Start as for Mur y Niwl.
1 40 feet. 4b. As for Mur Y Niwl.
2 110 feet. 5a. The steep wall leads to a niche, then move right and
go up on good holds to the base of the V-groove (belay possible). A
difficult step up from the groove on to the lip of an overlap leads to
another move right then follow the blunt rib above on improving
holds. Move back left to gain a slab in the groove then go up to a
grassy platform.

raig Yr Ysfa: Lower Amphitheatre Right Wall

1. Plumbagin	E1	
2. Griseofulvin	E3	
3. Mur y Niwl	VS	

4. Agrippa	E1
5. Amadeus	E4
6. Mother of Mercy	E5

Photo: Simon Cardy

3 60 feet. 4c. Scramble up to join Mur y Niwl pitch 5, and so the terrace.

Faenaldo   180 feet   E3   (1992)
An absorbing and somewhat precarious addition. Start as for Mur y Niwl.
1 40 feet. 4b. As for Mur y Niwl.
2 80 feet. 5c. Move horizontally right to pull up onto the obvious ledge, about 10 feet away. A series of bridging and layaway moves, past a peg, leads to the 'staircase' of Mur y Niwl. Continue directly up the wall to a horizontal break, go up again and trend left to the rib of Mur y Niwl Direct. Finish as for that route.
3 60 feet. 4c. Scramble up to join Mur y Niwl pitch 5, and so the terrace.

★★**Amadeus**   250 feet   E4   (1980)
Exhilarating and absorbing climbing when clean; even more difficult if dirty. Start as for Agrippa.
1 50 feet. 4c. Follow Agrippa to a stance on a flat ledge.
2 90 feet. 6a. From the left-hand end of the ledge, move up to a small ledge then left to a crack on the left-hand side of a roof. Climb the crack to a V-groove and follow this directly to the perch stance on Mur y Niwl.
3 110 feet. 4c. Follow the top pitches of Mur y Niwl.

★★**Mother of Mercy**   140 feet   E5   (1991)
The groove between Amadeus and Agrippa provides a stunning and sustained outing up a very impressive area of rock. Start just left of Agrippa.
1 140 feet. 6a. Climb directly past a bulge to reach a ledge, go over another bulge to gain ledges and the rotten pegs of Agrippa. Follow the crack above, as for Amadeus initially, but continue in the same line to an obvious jam slot. Difficult moves lead to a pocket, then layback up the groove to an ancient ring peg. Move right to the sanctuary of the Girdle then up left to belay on the third stance of Mur y Niwl. Finish as for that route.

★★**Agrippa**   340 feet   E1   (1959)
A breezy route of considerable character. Start 50 feet right of Mur y Niwl where a series of grassy ledges leads up to the left.
1 100 feet. 5a. Climb bulges just left of the bottom ledge to gain a leftwards-slanting vegetated groove to a grass ledge at 40 feet, possible belay. Continue diagonally right up a steep wall to a long narrow ledge and from its right-hand end go straight up on good holds to another ledge with a flake on the right.

2 50 feet. 5a. Climb the steep wall directly above the stance and step left above the second of two overhangs. Climb the corner then make a rising hand-traverse to a grass ledge on the right.
3 70 feet. 5a. Descend five feet and traverse right to a ledge on a nose. Continue up left past sloping ledges and a block to gain large holds to a ledge and belay.
4 120 feet. 4c. Traverse right on to a steep wall, then pull up into a groove and follow this to easy slabs, up these to belay on the bilberry terrace.

★★★ Girdle Traverse of the Lower Amphitheatre Wall
500 feet   E1   (1966)

One of the best girdles in Wales; the climbing is superb while the situations become increasingly airy as the Amphitheatre screes drop away beneath. Start as for The Crack.
1 70 feet. 5b. Climb the crack for 30 feet until it is possible to step right to a good spike. Descend a steep diagonal crack with difficulty (crux) to reach the top of the overhang on Plumbagin then step right to the belay ledge.
2 100 feet. 5b. Move down and right awkwardly, then a hard move past a hole gains a horizontal crack. Traverse right along the crack until it is possible to step into a niche. Move right to another niche, then semi-hand-traverse for 30 feet almost to the arête, peg and old nut. Abseil 30 feet and swing into a stance on Mur y Niwl pitch 2.
3 70 feet. 4c. Hand-traverse right along the upper of two horizontal ledges, then step down and move right to reach a rising 'stairway'. Follow this up to 'the perch stance' of Mur y Niwl.
4 70 feet. 5a. Descend a groove, below the traverse right of Mur y Niwl. Continue down over a small overhang until it is possible to traverse right to a jug on the arête. It is more usual to use a sling for aid on the jug, but goes at 5c free, descend to the hand-traverse of Agrippa pitch 2, follow this right to a stance.
5 70 feet. 5a. Descend five feet, traverse right to a perch, then continue up left past sloping ledges to reach a ledge. Agrippa pitch 3.
6 120 feet. 4c. Move right on to a wall then go up a groove to easy slabs and follow these to belay on the bilberry terrace; Agrippa pitch 4.

The Amphitheatre Wall now degenerates into a series of short rock walls and ledges.

Limax   330 feet   Very Difficult   (1955)
This route has the distinction of being the worst on the crag. To the right of Agrippa is a prominent pillar with a wide crack on its left; right again, is a smaller grass-topped pillar with a projecting block.

Start on its left.
1 50 feet. Ascend grass and go over the smaller pillar.
2 150 feet. Trend diagonally right up or between rock walls and through lush vegetation.
3 130 feet. Traverse left into a gully chimney. Climb it to a cave then go up blocks forming the cave and take the left-hand gully rib to finish.

Carpet Baggers   230 feet   E1 (1 pt aid)   (1970)
Makes the best of what rock there is. The route covers similar ground to Limax but accepts the challenge of the short walls and includes the steep final wall. Approximately level with the Figure of Eight on the opposite side of the Amphitheatre is a little white slab right of a rib. Start at the top of the slab.
1 120 feet. 4b. Climb a greasy box-shaped chimney to a ledge, then go up a shallow groove to an awkward exit and a ledge. Climb straight up for a few feet to step left delicately past a large block to another ledge.
2 40 feet. 4a. Scramble up leftwards then go back right to the foot of the steep final wall.
3 70 feet. 5b. Climb the right-hand of three grooves, with a sling for aid, to a tiny ledge. Continue up a little corner to the top.

Pinnacle Wall

Slightly less impressive than the main wall; however, the climbing is equally good. The main face is highlighted by a horizontal quartz ledge, the 'pavement', with a cuneiform pinnacle above; the latter provides the name.

The next two routes start directly from the upper bed of D Gully. Just above the point where C and D Gullies begin to diverge, there are three short, parallel, grassy grooves up and left of the main wall. High above them is a prominent overhanging nose.

Clean Rib   120 feet   Very Difficult   (1944)
Pleasant enough once the rib is gained. Start at the foot of the left-hand of the three grooves
1 120 feet. Ascend the groove to a little bay left of a rib, step right and climb a little slab to the rib, then continue up the edge to a ledge. Belay possible, but it is best to continue pleasantly up the rib to finish left of the nose.

Skyline Chimney   120 feet   Difficult   (1944)
Not the obvious chimney high on the crag, but the one immediately right of the prominent nose. Start at the base of the right-hand of three grooves.

1 60 feet. Climb the groove to belay under a small square overhang on the left.
2 60 feet. Move right and climb an open chimney, then step left and go up a cracked wall just right of the final chimney, or strenuously climb the chimney itself!

The next routes start from a subsidiary recessed terrace just up and left of the main bilberry terrace. This is gained by a tricky traverse in from the gully. The terrace has three corners.

★**Gettysburg** 160 feet Hard Very Severe   (1969)
A strenuous route that takes an impressive line through some large overhangs. Start at the base of a steep slab below the overhang, between the left and central corners at a rib.
1 110 feet. 5b. Awkward moves up the slab lead to a step right into a niche beneath the first overhang. Surmount the overhang above with a struggle, continue to the second smaller overhang and pull round to a corner which is followed to a third overhang. Step left and go up to a stance.
2 50 feet. 4c. Climb a steep wall directly above the belay trending right to a ledge. Move left and go up two steps to the top.

★★**The Grimmett** 160 feet Very Severe   (1938)
A fine climb, taking in some steep ground. Start at the right-hand corner under a large sloping roof.
1 110 feet. 4c. Ascend an obvious corner groove to a cave, pull out left of the cave into another corner, then follow this until forced left to a narrow groove (crux). Bridge up past the overhang then climb easily and go out left to grass, belays up and right.
2 50 feet. 4b. Traverse left round an arête, go up a steep rough wall, then step left to a wide crack and follow this to the top.

★**Excalibur** 160 feet E2   (1981)
Reasonable climbing with one exciting swing round an arête. Start as for The Grimmett.
1 110 feet. 5b. Follow The Grimmett until it is possible to move right above the second overhang to the base of a shallow groove. Move up to a small overlap and pull round rightwards, in an exposed position, to reach a sloping ledge. Follow the crack above to a large grassy stance.
2 50 feet. 5a. Climb straight up to the obvious groove in the wall behind the stance, enter this and follow it to the top.

★**Spiral Scratch** 170 feet E2   (1983)
A good route up the slender pillar of rock right of Excalibur. Start as

Craig Yr Ysfa: Pinnacle Wall

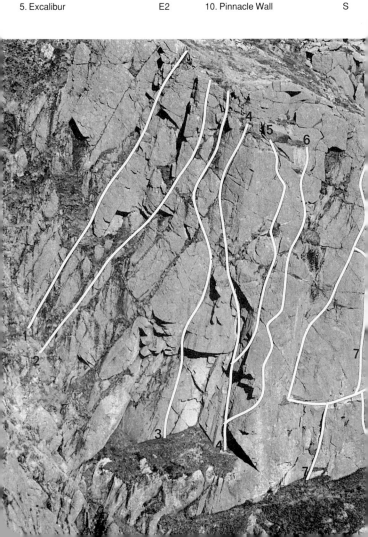

for The Grimmett.
1 120 feet. 5b. Follow The Grimmett for 12 feet and traverse right above the overhang to reach the arête; ascend this via a tiny ramp, hidden nut runner, to an overhang. Climb the overhang on the right to a ledge on the edge of the pillar, move up to a peg then go right and up the centre of the wall on good holds to a large stance.
2 50 feet. 4c. The arête on the right leads to easy ground.

The next routes start from the bilberry terrace, which is gained either by climbing a route on the lower wall, or a difficult access line below the left-hand end of the bilberry terrace.

★★**Pinnaclissima**   150 feet   E2   (1969)
Continually interesting climbing on superb rock makes this route one of the best on these walls. Start under the left-hand of the quartz pavement where a line of weakness leads up to a short left-facing corner.
1 50 feet. 5b. Surprisingly strenuous climbing up the corner leads to a difficult move to gain the quartz pavement; belay at the base of the corner to the right.
2 100 feet. 5c. Bridge up the corner, small wires protect, past an overlap to reach the base of a wide crack. Follow the crack, not without amusement, to reach a horizontal break 10 feet below the top of the pinnacle. Traverse left to join Pinnacle Wall and follow this to the top.

Ancient's Wall   170 feet   E3   (1962)
Artificial, but with some steep and absorbing climbing. Start 20 feet right of Pinnaclissima at a shallow right-facing corner under two overhangs.
1 80 feet. 5a. Climb the corner, then swing out left and go up the wall on jugs (bold) to reach the quartz pavement. Protection must be arranged for the second before moving right to belay at the right-hand end of the pavement.
2 90 feet. 5c. Move left and go up into a scoop, then step left and pull up to another ledge. Move right and swing on to the arête and so another ledge and a flake. Sidestep to the left end of the ledge and pull up and over a bulge to a crack and poor peg, wires beneath. Either traverse left with difficulty to enter a groove, or pull directly in to the groove, follow this to the top.

★★**The Haunted**   170 feet   E5   (1983)
An exacting route, both bold and technical. Start at the foot of the ramp as for Pinnacle Wall.
1 80 feet. 5c. Climb directly up the wall on good holds with one long

reach to gain the quartz pavement, unprotected. Arrange protection on the pavement for the second and move left to belay in the corner of Pinnaclissima.
2 90 feet. 6a. Difficult moves up a rib to the right of the corner lead to an overlap, surmount this and follow a flake crack rightwards to its end. Move left along a thin seam to reach a peg. Bold and sustained climbing up the thin cracks above prove to be the crux.

★★**Pinnacle Wall**   230 feet   Severe   (1931)
A great classic with an unusual indirect line. Start under the right-hand end of the pavement where a bilberry ramp/corner descends diagonally leftwards to reach the terrace.
1 40 feet. The ramp/corner leads to a stance.
2 90 feet. Climb up 10 feet to reach the quartz pavement and traverse across to its left. An awkward step past a crack leads to a good belay under a groove.
3 100 feet. Follow the groove for 30 feet, then trend diagonally up right to the apex of The Pinnacle, step left and finish up a slab.

Variation Finish   110 feet   Hard Severe   (1971)
3a 60 feet. 4a. Climb the groove above the stance then move a little awkwardly left into a small groove and go up it.
4a 50 feet. Go diagonally right up a grassy groove and take a mossy slab to finish.

★★**Sea of Dreams**   340 feet   E3   (1983)
An exciting right-to-left girdle of the Pinnacle Wall. Start as for Pinnacle Wall.
1 50 feet. Climb the ramp and short wall above to belay at the right-hand end of the quartz pavement.
2 90 feet. 5c. Move up and left into a scoop, step left and pull up past a ledge to reach another ledge with a flake. Descend from its left-hand end and traverse left with difficulty to reach the descending flake crack. Hanging stance in the corner of Pinnaclissima.
3 30 feet. 5b. Traverse left around the arête to join Pinnacle Wall at a good flake belay.
4 40 feet. 4b. Descend the slab to a stance and peg belay.
5 90 feet. 5b. Move out left and go up to a ledge. Continue left to the arête and step up and left again to a shallow groove. Continue more easily to the large corner of The Grimmett and belay on a grass ledge at its top.
6 50 feet. 4b. Traverse left round the arête and ascend the steep wall and a wide crack on the left to the top.

North Crag
The Great Buttress

Although this section of the cliff is very large, it is also very disappointing. There is a serious lack of continuity and both approaches and exits are frequently long and tedious. There are two major gullies; Vanishing Gully, which does, and Great Gully, which is.

The first three climbs all finish inconveniently short of the crag top, making long uninteresting scrambles inevitable. Experienced parties may prefer to traverse left at a convenient point and descend easily, if precariously, into the lower part of The Amphitheatre.

Low Climb   130 feet   Very Difficult   (1910)
A poorly situated climb. Approximately 100 feet above the toe of the ridge flanking the right-hand side of The Amphitheatre is a short kinked chimney between a detached block and the main part of the crag. Start some 40 feet below the chimney at a mossy glacis adjacent to the scree.
1 60 feet. Cross the glacis, go over a block and up a cracked slab and heather to the chimney, which is climbed.
2 70 feet. Ascend easy-angled slabs, then to a bollard. Continue to an overhang and turn it on the right, using small holds, to a poor grass stance. Continue 15 feet to a good ledge. Endless scrambling remains.

★**Nether Climb**   360 feet   Severe   (1938)
An absorbing climb, the best in this area of the crag apart from Great Gully. It takes a rib just to the left of Vanishing Gully. Start just right of the lowest point of the rib forming the left-hand wall of the gully, by a small tree.
1 100 feet. Ascend a short wall above the tree to an arête. Go pleasantly up the arête to the foot of a V-groove.
2 90 feet. Move out left and pull up on to a mossy little slab, go up it and step right across the V-groove. Continue to the edge and follow it, then move left and scramble up right to belay among boulders behind a prow of rock.
3 70 feet. An easy slab leads to a diagonal crack in a steep wall, follow it right to an arête and climb this to a ledge.
4 100 feet. Climb a clean groove on the right for 20 feet then go up the steep left wall, with good finishing holds, to a grassy rake leading right. From the rake, step down on to a mossy slab and traverse right below a steep wall to an easy break. Belay well back.

Vanishing Gully   350 feet   Very Difficult   (1904)
After quite a good start this gully fades out among the broken rocks
and vegetation of the upper part of the buttress. This is the first gully
to the right of The Amphitheatre and from most vantage points is
much more obvious than its neighbour, Great Gully. The cave on the
second pitch is easy to identify.
1 50 feet. Pass a grass-crowned jammed block on the right, and
continue up grass and ferns to a cave.
2 50 feet. Climb out of the cave and climb a grass ramp to a
comfortable hole.
3 60 feet. Climb a fine chimney, easily at first then more steeply. It
gives out on to a ledge on the left. Move back and go over some
chockstones.
4 60 feet. The gully narrows to a cleft and is steep. Either work up
the back of the recess behind the uppermost chockstone. Or, chimney
up outside and finish over the chockstone.
5 130 feet. The gully finishes. The easiest line above trends right,
then comes back to the centre of the Buttress.

★★★**Great Gully**   725 feet   Very Difficult   (1900)
A great classic, undoubtedly one of the best gullies in Wales, seldom
rivalled for atmosphere and character, culminating with a difficult
final pitch. From the base of Vanishing Gully ascend the scree to the
right for about 200 feet, to a cavernous gully entrance. Scramble up
the gully bed for about 150 feet, skirting the first mossy step on the
right to the initial obstacle.
1 90 feet. A short crack on the left, past a jammed stone, leads to 80
feet of scrambling.
2 120 feet. Another big chockstone is surmounted on the left, then
100 feet of scrambling lead to a belay under...
3 60 feet. The Door Jamb (without the help of a snow bank or a
Human Pyramid?). Then climb a short steep groove on the right,
passing a ledge on the left, to a larger one. Walk back left into the
gully bed.
4 35 feet. Go directly up the gully bed, or better, climb a deep
40-foot chimney and a crack on the right, moving out left into the
gully bed near the top.
5 45 feet. The Chimney. This is climbed awkwardly facing right until
a platform on the right is gained, or go direct to the top.
5a 45 feet. Ascend a crack in the right wall of The Chimney.
5b 65 feet. Avoiding The Chimney is much easier. About 20 feet
lower down, the right wall is climbed via a big flake. A muddy path
leads right then back left to a platform above. Misses out the fun.
6 110 feet. Go up a groove on the right, then an 80-foot walk on
stones.

7 200 feet. Climb a narrow sloping chimney on the right of a rock rib, or surmount two mossy chockstones on its left. After 60 feet of scrambling go over a big jammed stone to another stone.
8 15 feet. Climb an awkward undercut chimney on the right of the stone, or the right wall starting slightly lower, then step into the top of the chimney. Or, the chimney left of the stone is even harder.
9 50 feet. The Great Cave Pitch, the crux and rightly so. Go up the left wall of the cave with difficulty, then traverse left to the outer of two chockstones. A tremendous ending to a stimulating outing.

Variation Finishes.
For non-climbers and non-Gallios.

Left Wall Exit 70 feet
8a 70 feet. Part way up pitch 8 there is a strenuous slanting chimney with blocks; climb this to the top.

Right Wall Exit 70 feet
8b 70 feet. Climb the broken chimney opposite the previous one then broken ground to finish. The least satisfactory finish.

The next three routes commence from the Great Gully, in the vicinity of 'The Chimney', pitch 5. The obvious approaches are to ascend or descend Great Gully.

Great Gully Pinnacle Direct 100 feet Very Severe   (1960)
Start 50 feet below 'The Chimney'. In the steep left wall of the gully is a corner crack leading to an obvious block pinnacle.
1 80 feet. Ascend the corner crack, easy but greasy. Rickety block belay on a saddle.
2 20 feet. Climb the right-hand edge of the pinnacle and descend the same way.

Invisible Chimney 130 feet Difficult   (1938)
A series of good short chimneys gives sustained interest. Start up the right wall flake pitch 5b of Great Gully and follow the muddy path right, but instead of traversing back left continue past a clump of ferns to a short chimney.
1 45 feet. Go up the chimney bed, past a jammed boulder, to a mossy cave. A deep twisting chimney leads behind another block in the bowels of the mountain and emerges at a pile of boulders.
2 60 feet. Go through a small hole on the right, then straight up a wet chimney to where it steepens. Back-up past tiers of blocks to a deep recess.
3 25 feet. Ascend a steep enclosed chimney, then move out from

beneath a roof to two jammed stones and a grassy ledge on the right.
Scramble to the ridge.

★**Great Gully Wall**   220 feet   E2 (1 pt. aid)   (1967)
A strenuous and continuously interesting route. Above 'The Chimney'
pitch of the gully is a large, shallow scoop, capped by an overhang,
in the left wall. Spike belay and well-appointed platform at the top of
'The Chimney'. There is a wet mossy cave immediately on the left.
1 60 feet. 5a. Traverse out left for a few feet, then go up to an
uncomfortable belay ledge below and to the left of the overhang.
2 100 feet. 5b. Traverse right, then cross the scoop to a point above
a perched block on the right. Using a thin peg in a horizontal crack,
move up to a muddy pocket, and continue traversing to a blunt arête.
Climb a wall above, trending right, to belay on the second of two
pulpit ledges.
3 60 feet. 5a. Follow an obvious line to gain an overhanging crack.
Layback up it, and continue up a corner to the top. Scramble off.

To the right of Great Gully, the crag becomes very broken and
unsatisfactory. One route has been recorded.

Shean Treuse   520 feet   Very Severe   (1941)
The climbing is quite good and varied, but its position detracts from
the interest and there is a break at mid-height. High up and to the
right of Great Gully is a substantial buttress of steep rock with slabs to
its right. Above the slabs is a massive block overhang, the most
distinctive feature hereabouts. Scramble up Great Gully for 150 feet,
then traverse right along a heather terrace to the right-hand side of
the steep buttress. The massive overhang is directly above. Belay at
the foot of a wet vegetated groove.
1 125 feet. 4b. Step left and go up a little rib to a heather ledge.
Traverse diagonally left round an awkward bulge, then go up to a
ledge. Step up right to yet another ledge, then climb a steep wall. A
bold pull leads into a short groove left of a block, then get on to the
block. Vegetation leads right to the foot of a 10-foot groove.
2 100 feet. 3b. Ascend the groove, then walk diagonally left across
a broad heather terrace, The Dancing Floor, to belay at the foot of
the big slab.
3 125 feet. 4a. Go diagonally left across the slab, to the foot of a
stepped crack in the left wall. Most of the vegetation can be avoided.
4 80 feet. 3b. Climb the stepped crack to a chock thread, then trend
right up a grass rake until a break on the left can be climbed to ash
trees.
5 90 feet. 4c. Climb a crack on the right, move on to the right wall
just below a small grass-floored cave, then awkwardly climb up into

the cave. Continue up a crack to a short groove which is avoided on the right. Only scrambling remains.

Approximately 100 yards right of Great Gully is Moss Gully which serves only to define the northern boundary of the crag.

The Obelisk or Craig Yr Ysfa Pinnacle

Some 300 yards north of Great Gully, amongst the broken rocks beyond the main crag, is a short wide gully where The Obelisk is situated. There are several alternatives leading to the summit none of which exceeds 40 feet in length.

First Ascents

1879 April 19	**Central Gully** (Ysgolion Duon) Probably an A C party *Originally called Bending Gully.*
1887	**South Gully** (Tryfan) R Williams *'The climber ascends jammed blocks and crawls into a small cave, but when he attempts to assume an erect posture, the roof and the floor conspire to overthrow him, the former juts over his head the latter slopes under his feet, and the further he steps back on the one in the effort to avoid the other, the nearer he comes to quitting both and returning to the foot of the pitch'. J M A Thomson 1910.*
1888	**North Gully** (Tryfan) T Williams, R Williams *'Between high walls are set five pitches... suitable for any number of climbers, provided close order is kept between the obstacles'. J M A Thomson 1910.*
1891 Sept 18	**Nor' Nor' Gully** (Tryfan) W E Corlett, M K Smith
1894 Oct	**Pinnacle Rib Route** (Tryfan) J M A Thomson, H Hughes *With its variations, the first route to move out of the gullies and on to the airier buttresses.*
1894 Nov 25	**Central Gully** (Glyder Fawr) J M A Thomson, H Hughes, H Edwards *'An auspicious opening to exploration in the Glyder area by an outstanding pioneer of Welsh climbs. The second was stuffed into the cave under the chockstones and the rope passed through a hole to protect the first hard moves. "The passage is severe, and the climber, if not unusually prehensile, should be preternaturally patient. 'The slabs above were covered with a "thin layer of quivering turf" but this was stripped off by the Great Frost of 1895'. In November 1980 Z P Leppert found a tunnel behind the impasse.*
1894 Nov	**West Gully** (Glyder Fach) H Edwards, J M A Thomson, H Hughes
1894	**Arête Climb** (Tryfan) J M A Thomson, H Hughes
1894	**Y Gully** (Tryfan) Notch Arête was probably done as a continuation to Y Gully.

1894 Nov   **Right Gully** (Braich Ty Du) J M A Thomson, H
                Hughes, H Edwards.
                *Haskett Smith was under the misapprehension that
                this gully was on a cliff called Craig yr Ysfa, then
                continued to describe them as 'These rugged and in
                parts, highly romantic rocks have attracted but
                few... quitting the road just beyond the eighth
                milestone from Bangor, reached, in twenty minutes,
                the mouth of a gully, broad except where it narrows
                into a gorge about half way up'.*

1895 or earlier **Eastern Gully** (Ysgolion Duon) probably Haskett
                Smith.
                *Right-hand branch was climbed by J M A Thomson
                and R Hughes in 1900.*

1895 or earlier **Eastern Ridge** (Ysgolion Duon) probably climbed
                by W P Haskett Smith

1895 May   **East Gully** (Glyder Fach) J M A Thomson, H
                Hughes
                *A hard pitch even for the gully epoch. 'The boulder
                can then be grasped by both hands, and the legs
                automatically swing free. There ensue some
                moments of suspense over the pitch, and a tough
                struggle before the climber lands, breathless, in the
                bed of the gully above the obstacle'. J M A Thomson
                1910. This was one of the routes originally
                classified as an Exceptionally Severe Course.*

1895 May   **East Gully** (Glyder Fawr) J M A Thomson, H
                Hughes, A E Elias, W P Elias
                *'If wet, the knob should be dried prior to the ascent,
                for it is the principle point of attachment, while the
                weight is drawn with a strenuous effort over a
                corner to the top of the obstacle'. Whilst Archer
                Thomson was renowned for his quietude, his
                descriptions concerning climbing were informative
                and showed his passion for the sport.*

1895 July   **Narrow Gully** (Glyder Fawr) J M A Thomson
                Thomson approached by climbing Idwal Staircase.

1895 July   **The Introductory Gully** (Idwal) J M A Thomson
                *To the right of the slab and West Wall and left of
                Idwal Buttress.*

1895 July   **Twisting Gully** (Glyder Fawr) H Hughes, H
                Edwards, J R Smith
                *'Here some have found it convenient to divest
                themselves of their coats in preparation for the
                struggle'.*

1895 July	**West Gully** (Glyder Fawr) J M A Thomson, H Hughes
1895 Oct	**Clogwyn Du Gully** (Cneifion) J M A Thomson, H Hughes
	By the Left and Right-Hand Branches. C H S R Palmer climbed a variation finish on 26th March 1926.
1895	**Grey Rib** (Glyder Fawr) J M A Thomson
	Credited to Thomson although he does not mention an ascent in his guidebook; this would certainly have been a bold lead for the times.
c. 1895	**Three Pitch Gully, Square Slabs, Square Furrow** (Glyder Fawr)
	Probably products of the explorations of Archer Thomson and his group.
1897 Aug 23	**Ordinary Route** (Idwal) T K Rose, C C B Moss
	'It soon took upon itself the mantle of prosperity and its repute flourished. The grass which covered its first 150 feet has long since been replaced by the marks of men'. 'A good route for beginners with a natural ineptitude for steep places'. J M Edwards 1936.
1898 May 7	**Devil's Kitchen Route** (Clogwyn y Geifr) W R Reade, W P McCulloch
	The Direct Finish was done by J W Jones and party on 16th August 1904. The Devil's Kitchen or Twll Du (The Black Pit) was first climbed by J M A Thomson and H Hughes on 3rd March 1895, when the waterfall was completely frozen. They used a hatchet surreptitiously removed from the worthy Mrs Jones's coal cellar at Ogwen Cottage. 'This implement proved of the utmost utility until the head took leave of the haft, and, glissading the snow slopes vanished out of sight. The head was recovered, and the hatchet, ingeniously repaired with string, continued to render us valuable service'. This amazing ascent was the first example of hard ice climbing in the area. The lower section up to the cave was climbed by J H Cliffe as early as June 1843.
1898 Whitsun	**Angular Chimney** (Clogwyn y Tarw) O G Jones, R Williams, J M A Thomson, W J Williams, H V Reade, G Collins, J W Puttrell
	'The Angular Chimney, which imposed a heavy task of gardening upon the first explorers, still offers scope for philanthropy... The lift over the edge

demands the most strenuous efforts. The second man should be close, and keep a watchful eye on the leader'. Certainly one of the strongest teams (for its day) ever to make a first ascent in Britain. The upper storey was climbed by R C Frost and F G Stangle on 4th August 1934.

1898	**Groove Route** (Glyder Fach) J M A Thomson	
1898	**Intermittent Gully** (Glyder Fach) T K Rose, C C B Moss	
1899 Easter	**Devil's Staircase** (Clogwyn y Geifr) O G Jones, G D Abraham	

They circumvented the first pitch by traversing in across the ledges from the foot of the Kitchen. 'The top pitch proved to be a veritable chimney, for a black hole leads upwards, apparently into the heart of the mountain; and we christened the place the Devil's Drainpipe... the leader crawled up into its dark recesses, and the sounds of progress gradually faded into the distance, until I heard a call from the open air some fifty feet above my head. At the same moment there was an ominous rumble in the Drainpipe! It took a second to realise that a rock was descending its dark interior, and there seemed every probability that it would sweep me off the small ledge on which I stood. It was a helpless feeling, but the suspense was soon over for the rock whizzed out of the dark hole, and before the real danger could be appreciated, it had scratched some skin off my left ear, and gone crashing down the cliff to the bottom of the gully'. Thus Jones and Abraham captured the best gully in the Ogwen area. It was climbed from its foot by W R Reade, O Eckenstein and G Bartrum in 1906. C F Kirkus did the left-hand direct exit in 1933.

1899 Easter	**Hanging Garden Gully** (Clogwyn y Geifr) O G Jones, G D Abraham, A P Abraham

The direct exit up the back of the gully was climbed by C F Kirkus in 1933.

1899 Easter	**Ordinary Route** (Milestone) O G Jones, G D Abraham, A P Abraham
1899 Easter	**North Buttress** (Tryfan) O G Jones, G D Abraham, J W Puttrell

'It is now recognised that the buttresses of Tryfan, with their wonderful firm, rough rocks, afford

climbing quite equal to the best of the gullies'. J M A Thomson had realised this earlier!

1899 Easter **Terrace Wall Variant** (Tryfan) O G Jones, G D Abraham, J W Puttrell
'The climb is exposed and should not be attacked with temerity'. J M A Thomson 1910

c. 1900 **East Gully and Rift, The Arête, North Chasm** (Craig Cwrwgl) J M A Thomson, R Williams, W J Williams
Thomson's guide is not specific about who did what, but it seems probable that all these climbs were done during the same period.

1900 April **Great Gully** (Craig yr Ysfa) J M A Thomson, R I Simey, W G Clay
Archer Thomson described the Great Cave Pitch thus: 'By utilising a small foothold on the right wall, the climber effects a lodgement on it, and then reaches its sharp upper edge by a struggle, in which he becomes near to defying all the laws of anatomy. A novel expedient is to lay the palm of the right hand on the block, using the arm as a pivot, perform a pirouette to the south; the climber thus lands in a sitting posture, with one leg thrust up to the roof to maintain equilibrium... any Gallio, however, will complacently demand a shoulder...'
Left Wall Exit 1901, J M A Thomson, R Hughes, R Williams
Door Jamb Direct April 1909, O Thorneycroft, G Pinsent, F W Hubback

1900 June **Bending Gully** (Craig yr Ysfa) J M A Thomson, H Hughes

1901 April **Arch Gully** (Craig yr Ysfa) J M A Thomson, R Williams, R F Backwell
'A bold pitch rises in front some forty five feet in height, and the clean straight walls on either side are impressive. The climbing is done on a protruding rock that occupies the centre, and the balance must be nicely adjusted, otherwise a feeling of being pushed out over the drop will cause discomfort'.

1901 August **Western Gully** (Ysgolion Duon) P H Cooke, T Brushfield, H Owen
Repeated by the Abraham brothers in 1905 and thought to be new. 'A magnificent, single-storeyed cave pitch is now entered and some sensational

> work is enjoyed in surmounting the steep 25 foot slab'. G D Abraham 1909
> '... better than the Great Gully on Craig yr Ysfa and much more serious an expedition as none of the pitches can be avoided'.

1902 Sept **Gashed Crag** (Tryfan) H B Buckle, G Barlow
The Left Way was found by F M Coventry and H Hartley on 12th July 1927.

1904 Nov **Vanishing Gully** (Craig yr Ysfa) G D Abraham, A P Abraham, C W Nettleton

1905 May **Amphitheatre Buttress** (Craig yr Ysfa) G D Abraham, A P Abraham, D Leighton, J W Puttrell
A classic and a tribute to a very distinguished party.

1905 May **Avalanche Gully** (Craig yr Ysfa) J W Puttrell, D Leighton
'In fine, this gully is dangerous, and its ascent should be deprecated in a book on climbing'. J M A Thomson 1910

1905 May **Hawk's Nest Buttress** (Glyder Fach) G D Abraham, A P Abraham, A Thompson
'... the rock was magnificent. The first stretch of about twenty feet proved to be rather a study in finger-tip holds... The difficulty of the place was aggravated by the annoying antics of the hawks. A well aimed piece of Glyder from our sheet-anchor rather allayed their aggressiveness'.

1905 May **Monolith Crack** (Clogwyn y Tarw) G D Abraham, A P Abraham
An outstanding lead as the chimney was climbed near to the front. 'I got too much inside the narrow crack, and found further progress impossible. In fact, it was a difficult matter to even extricate myself from the vice-like grip... As there was now little danger of falling out of such a quandary, we neglected the question of anchorage, and my brother mounted into the foot of the crack. It was an easy matter to climb over him and thus effect a splendid lodgement high up in the crack without undue fatigue... the upper portion demanded every iota of surplus energy and strength'.
M de Selincourt climbed his evasive variant in 1922 or 1923.'More speleology than rock climbing'. A J J Moulam

1905 Sept **Notch Buttress** (Tryfan) G Barlow, Miss E M Barlow

1905	**Cneifion Arête** G Barlow, Miss E M Barlow
1905-8	**Gullies A,B,C,D** and **The Nameless Rib** (Craig yr Ysfa) Abraham parties
	The parties may have been distinguished but the climbing certainly was not.
1907 April	**Oblique Gully** (Glyder Fach) K M Ward, H B Gibson
1907 April	**Slab Route** (Glyder Fach) K M Ward, H B Gibson
	The Spiral Variant was discovered about June 1917 by I A Richards and Mrs D E Pilley
1907 April	**Direct Route** (Glyder Fach) K M Ward, H B Gibson
	'... spoken of mysteriously for fifteen years as one of the most difficult climbs in the country'. J M Edwards and A R 'Sandy' Edge were to find The Winter Finish on 21st December 1930. J M Edwards climbed The Right Hand Crack of the Final Flake on 8th September 1931, '... can be horribly strenuous, indeed quite unbelievable for balance climbers'. The Left Hand Crack was climbed by P R Harding and J Wills on 21st August 1934. The more elegant Hodgkin's Variation was not solved until 10th January 1937, by R A Hodgkin and A D M Cox; even though the top crack had been reached from the right and led by J D Holland on 23rd July 1934. Brown's Corner was climbed by J Brown in August 1959.
1907 Whitsun	**Pillar Chimney** (Clogwyn Du) G Barlow, H B Buckle
1907 Sept	**Castle Rocks, V Buttress** (Tryfan) G Barlow, H B Buckle
	Wrinkled Slabs were climbed on an unknown date by A G Woodhead, T Wildbore.
1907 Sept	**East Arête** (Glyder Fawr) G Barlow, H B Buckle, A H Doughty
1909 Jan	**East Face of the Gribin** G H Mallory, R L Irving, D Murray, H E G Tyndale
	Dirty and dangerous.
1909 April	**Birch Tree Chimney** and **The Slab Climb** (Craig yr Ysfa) G W Young, G H L Mallory
	Another distinguished party.
1909 April	**Flake Crack** (Clogwyn y Tarw) O Thorneycroft
	At the time, various trees made the lower part easier.

1909 Whitsun	**Central Arête** (Glyder Fawr) G Barlow, H B Buckle
	The now more usual direct start was first led by Mrs E H Daniells in 1911.
1909 Aug	**Chimney Climb** (Bochlwyd Buttress) F C Aldous, A C Adams, O Thorneycroft
	The first route on a new cliff.
1910 Jan	**Old Route** (Gallt yr Ogof) K J P Orton, Mrs Orton
1910 Jan	**Rowan Route** (Milestone) H O Jones, K J P Orton, Mrs Orton
1910 Easter	**West Arête** (Glyder Fawr) J M A Thomson, H O Jones, F Dodd, L Noon
1910 Aug	**Direct Route, Superdirect** (Milestone) G Barlow, H Priestley-Smith
	The finish on the Central Block was added by J M Edwards on 3rd September 1941.
1910 Easter	**Chasm Route** (Glyder Fach) J M A Thomson, H O Jones, L Noon
	A most suitable route with which to close the gully era. Of the alternative finishes: Corkscrew Crack was done by D H Haworth and K Collins on 3rd June 1947; and Chasm Crack by P R J Harding and J Wills on 21st August 1946.
	At the Vertical Vice, Edwards was of the opinion that 'a stout man will need to climb outside and will need emphatically immoral support from the rope'.
1910	**Low Climb** (Craig yr Ysfa) G H L Mallory
1911	**Eastern Arête, Central Route** and **North Arête** (Craig Lloer) R B Henderson, Mrs E H Daniells
1911 April	**Grooved Arête** (Tryfan) E W Steeple, A G Woodhead, G Barlow, H E Bowron, A H Doughty
	'A breezy ascent for some 75 feet on splendidly sound rock led to an overhang, where divergence from the strict arête was found necessary... A cautious pull up a thin edge of rock then brought the leader to a heather shelf (the Haven)... the whole party assembled here. I was stopped a few feet higher by a bulge of rock in the groove... we finally decided that the pitch was unjustifiable. Moreover, the large slab on the left gives a much finer route'.
	The Superdirect and the Direct Route from the Haven were solved by C F Kirkus on 10th March 1929.
1911 Whitsun	**West End Buttress** (Ysgolion Duon) E W Steeple, G Barlow
1911 July	**Pulpit Route** (Milestone) G Barlow, Miss E M Barlow

1911 Aug 16	**Six Pitch Gully, Slanting Chimney** (Cwm Cywion) F H Parker with his brother.
1911 Aug	**Index Climb** (Tryfan) J Laycock, T I Cowlishaw
1912 Easter	**Cheek** (Tryfan) H E L Porter
1912 April	**Route 1** (Glyder Fach) G Barlow, R B Henderson, Mrs E H Daniells
1912 May	**South Rib** (Tryfan) J Laycock, M Wood, R Hodgkinson
1912 May	**Square Chimney** (Glyder Fach) J Laycock, S W Herford
1912 May	**Slab Climb** (Clogwyn y Tarw) J Laycock, S W Herford *More noted for their Lakeland explorations.*
1912 May	**Zig-Zag Climb** (Clogwyn y Tarw) S W Herford, J Laycock, W G Milligan, R Hodgkinson *The Direct Start was done by S H Jones and M A James on 7 September 1984.*
1912 May	**Herford's Crack** (Clogwyn y Tarw) S W Herford, J Laycock *The best single pitch they did on that visit. It provides a great deal of entertainment even today.*
1912 Aug	**Girdle Traverse of Glyder Fawr** E W Steeple, G Barlow, A H Doughty
1912 Aug	**Alpha, Beta** (Glyder Fach) S W Hereford, J Laycock
1913 May	**Green Gully** (Tryfan) G Barlow, A H Doughty *A late discovery for a gully climb.*
1913 Aug	**Chimney Route** (Milestone) E W Steeple, G Barlow
1914 Aug	**Route II** (Glyder Fach) E W Steeple, G Barlow, A H Doughty
1914 Sept	**Overlapping Rib Route** (Tryfan) E W Steeple, G Barlow, A H Doughty *'Behind this a yellow slab rises at a high angle. Its smoothness renders the lowest four yards hard to scale, but the second man is well-placed, and excellent holds soon come within reach'.* *The slab once made it into a 'Rogues Gallery' in a climbing magazine!*
1915 April	**Twisting Gully Buttress** (Glyder Fawr) Mrs E H Daniells, R B Henderson
1915 Aug 14	**Hope** (Idwal) Mrs E H Daniells, I A Richards, T J Roxburgh, R B Henderson *First named Minerva 'to mark the fact that it came from feminine skill and prudence', but then changed*

in 'hope' of continuing the route up Holly Tree Wall. Edwards surmised of the 'Twin Cracks' that "much energy has been expended here."

1916 April   **The Sylvan Traverse** (Milestone) E W Steeple, G Barlow
Variants by I A Richards and Captain Grenfell.

1916 April   **Charity** (Idwal) D R Pye, I A Richards, T Picton
There is a possibility that O G Jones and G D Abraham climbed this line in an ascent of the Slabs in Easter 1899.

1916 April   **Faith** (Idwal) D R Pye, I A Richards, T Picton
They started via Hope. C H S R Palmer climbed what is now the more usual start in March 1927.

1916 May   **The Tower Chimney** (Filiast) J Laycock, T H Cowlishaw

1916 Sept   **Cantilever Route, Holly Route, Postern Gate and Holly Crack, Canopy Route** (Milestone) E W Steeple, G Barlow

1917 April   **Primitive Route** and **Askant Chimney** (Llech Ddu) E W Steeple, G Barlow
These two climbs were originally linked as one route. It was the first of a series of routes on this crag by this indefatigable pair. Each of their routes demands a certain respect even to this day, and almost 30 years elapsed before further routes were made on Llech Ddu.
In 1950 Primitive Route was described as of only moderate difficulty but of excessive danger. It lies entirely up a steep wall of quivering vegetation.

1917 June   **Corridor Gully, The Pillar Traverse** and **Y-Chimney** (Llech Ddu) E W Steeple, G Barlow
The latter climb must have ranked high among Welsh routes of that time, for technical difficulty and seriousness. The Direct Finish was led by A J J Moulam in 1961.

1918 May 22   **Original Route** (Holly Tree Wall) I A Richards, C F Holland, Miss D E Pilley
The route was conceived as a finish to Hope. They started up what is now Piton Route, and then managed to get across to the Holly Tree. The tree was thick and tough then, which made the attempts on the chimney behind fairly safe. Despite this they failed, but Holland (in nails) succeeded on the wall to the left. Afterwards, they descended, gardening as they went, and produced the present pitch. The

alternative start was done by F E Hicks and W E Woosnam in 1929. Although C F Holland climbed in nails on this ascent he was one of the first to advance the use of rubber-soled shoes in rock-climbing.

The holly tree finally went in the '60s, under the weight of T Smythe, who was then working at Plas y Brenin. He was presented with the trunk at the bar that night!

1918 May	**Oblique Buttress** (Glyder Fach) C F Holland, I A Richards
1918 June	**Cave Route** and **The Corridor** (Llech Ddu) E W Steeple, G Barlow

Originally these were two separate routes, and it seems likely that The Corridor was climbed at an earlier date.

1919 April	**Far East Chimney** (Llech Ddu) E W Steeple, G Barlow, A H Doughty
1919 Aug	**Tennis Shoe** (Idwal) N E Odell

A route of distinction by a man who was to become famous for his Himalayan exploits. 'It maintained its rubber reputation for about 10 years.''A better climb than the other slab ones'. A J J Moulam 1958

1921 May	**The Tower** (Filiast) H E L Porter, D Benson, C E Benson
1921 May	**The Waved Slab** (Filiast) H E L Porter

This turned out to be a very apt route name. In fact the whole of the slabs are the uplifted and tilted remains of ripples formed in a shallow seabed about five hundred million years ago.

1921 May	**Central Slab Route** (Llech Ddu) E W Steeple, G Barlow
1922 Jan 9	**Home Climb** (Clogwyn y Tarw) I A Richards, Miss DE Pilley
1922 July 5	**Javelin Gully** (Idwal) A F Coventry, F M Coventry

The gully was finished directly by JL Longland in 1936.

1922 Aug	**Progressive Cracks** (Tryfan) S G Hughes, S R Ashton, E R Campbell
c.1922	**Lazarus** (Idwal)

It is not known who was responsible for this, though Richards and Pilley climbed the final difficulties during their ascent of Other Kingdom.

1923 May 21	**Slab Recess Route, Gully and Slab, Senior's Climb** (Clogwyn y Tarw) E W Steeple, G Barlow

1923 Oct 5   **Pont Pen y Benglog Buttress** (Braich Ty Du) B R Goodfellow, E A G Caroe

1924 Oct 8   **Central Route** (Filiast) F Graham

1925 April 11   **Javelin Buttress** (Idwal) F Graham, C E Jerram
A fine lead as the thread was not used as a stance.

1925 Nov 1   **Subwall Climb** (Idwal) S A Marples, W K Marples

1925 or 1926   **Needle's Eye Climb** (Glyder Fach) C H S R Palmer
Climbed in mistake for Hawk's Nest Buttress.

1926 Dec 11   **Groove Above** (Idwal) T S Knowles, H Poole

1926   **Gargoyle Traverse** (Bochlwyd) B L Bathhurst, K W McMillan

1927 March 27   **Arête and Slab** (Bochlwyd) C H S R Palmer, D G MacDonald

1927 May 14   **Long Chimney** (Tryfan) Pitch 1 only: I M Waller. Pitch 2: C W Marshall, Robertson Lamb, M G Bradley and Mrs Armstrong on the same day. Pitch 3 was done on 27 October 1929 by C F Kirkus and A B Hargreaves. The Right-Hand Branch was climbed in April 1936 by C W F Noyce and D M Murray-Rust.
They found that the new face was only small, and that a gramophone set on the terrace sufficed for the whole area'.

1927 June 7   **Belle Vue Bastion** (Tryfan) I M Waller, C H S R Palmer
'I M Waller did the already well-known bastion on a rope and then led it.'

1927 Sept 17   **Wall Climb** (Milestone) W R Reade, R P Bloor, C W Marshall.
Direct Finish J M Edwards 1932.

1927 Dec 8   **Devil's Cellar** (Clogwyn y Geifr) C H S R Palmer, C W Furlonge
J M Edwards and T E Davies made the Coal Chute Exit on 14 May 1933.

1927 Dec 10   **Routes 1 and 2** (Braich Ty Du) C H S R Palmer, G W Furlonge
The same party was also responsible for Another Route and The Gully hereabouts.

1928 July 11   **Kirkus's Route** (Craig Lloer) C F Kirkus
A fine solo. Harder, though not as exposed as Pinnacle Wall.
'The crack was about 40 feet high and overhung at the top. It looked very difficult. I tied the rope round my waist, with the other end hanging free, and

started up. The crack was just about wide enough to fit a boot, and I progressed chiefly by jamming my hands and my feet. In places there were small chockstones jammed in the crack and these were a great help, though I had first to test them to make sure they were firm.

After an exhausting struggle I arrived at the overhang. I felt tired, because when you are climbing a pitch that is really vertical you get no rest at all. And now I had the overhang to tackle, where my whole weight would come on my hands. There was a convenient little stone here, jammed firmly in the crack, and I threaded the whole length of my rope down behind it, hanging on meanwhile with my left hand only. Then I tied myself on to the chockstone and was able to rest my arms, hanging more or less bodily on the rope.

Before I started off again I untied the rope from the chockstone but still left it hanging down behind, hoping that it might jam and hold me if I did happen to fall off the next section. Then I started up the overhang. It was very strenuous, and I struggled frantically. Then, just at a crucial moment, my rucksack jammed in the crack. With a despairing effort I worked it off my shoulder and abandoned it, precious camera and all. Another blind struggle and I was up, surprised and relieved to find the rucksack still hanging over the other shoulder.'

To reach the base of the crack Kirkus had to make an'awkward manoeuvre'; which is, in fact, a mantelshelf move. Kirkus later described training for these moves. '… on an old-fashioned mantelpiece. It is easy to raise yourself on to your hands, but surprisingly awkward to obtain a footing; a very delicate balance is needed. It is a good plan first to crowd the mantelpiece with all the ornaments that you most detest – those china dogs presented by Uncle Joe can take a front place. A slight slip on your part – most unfortunate accident – and they are no more'.

1929 Easter Day	**Geography** (Idwal) F R G Chew, M Gordon, R C Wakefield
	'It is now a rather disappointed idol.'
1929 April 11	**Piton Route** (Idwal) F E Hicks, W E Woosnam Jones

*Pitch 1 had been climbed by Richards and Pilley as
a start to a rather circuitous ascent called Other
Kingdom during Whitsuntide 1922. A piton
fortuitously found at the foot of the wall was put to
good use safeguarding a meagre stance. Hicks was
to take a direct line up past Richards's piton. The
piton became part of folklore and Kirkus felt
compelled to comment: 'This venerable relic had too
many historical associations to be regarded with
any great distaste by even the most rabid purist: but
alas! when getting frail and weak with advancing
years it was uprooted by some ruthless vandal
having no respect for the antiquities of a bygone
age. Whereupon a dauntless enthusiast decided
that another piton must be inserted... the whole
procedure was carried out with almost medieval
pomp and splendour... the new arrival didn't long
survive'.*

1929 June 23   **The Arête** (Idwal) F E Hicks, C B M Warren, A L Spence

1929 June 25   **Lot's Groove** (Glyder Fach) C F Kirkus, F E Hicks
*'... was considerably steeper and more lacking in
holds than anything which it was customary to climb
at that time.' An early indication of Kirkus's ability.
'....a preliminary inspection on the rope is probably
advisable.' J M Edwards
'...this climb was alleged to be the most difficult in
the district. We merely goggled at the sheer corner
and turned away'. J Brown, on his second visit to
Wales, as a youth in 1948; but later 'couldn't
understand what all the fuss was about'.*

1929 June 26   **Central Route** (Tryfan) C F Kirkus
*'Kirkus was young and had the faculty of early
daring and confidence. No one was able to follow'.*

1929 June 28   **Ash Tree Wall** (Idwal) F E Hicks, J A Smalley
*This was the first breach in the East Wall. The
Stepped Corner start was tackled by D F Biggane
and P S Boston on 13 June 1940.*

1929 Aug 30   **Heather Wall** (Idwal) F E Hicks, A B Hargreaves, E A Stewardson
*'An apparently weak spot was attacked
lightheartedly in boots; after about an hour's hectic
work, in which the Helyg poker played its part
nobly, and during which the leader changed into
rubbers, a heaven sent belay was reached... after*

George White on *Mur y Niwl* (VS), Craig yr Ysfa. Photo: Paul Middleton

Don Roscoe on *The Grimmett* (VS), Craig yr Ysfa. Photo: John Cleare

*several abortive attempts on the holdless corner
above, an inspired lead across a rickety traverse
and up an impossible-looking bulge gave us Heather
Wall'. M P Ward led the 'holdless corner' finish in
1939.*

1929 Sept 14   **Cinderella** (Idwal) W Jackson, Lady Angharad
Jackson
*It was their first visit to the area. The Original Route
was crowded so they did this instead.*

1929 Sept 25   **Faith West Finish** (Idwal) F E Hicks, W E
Woosnam Jones

1929 Sept 26   **Wall Climb** (Bochlwyd) F E Hicks, C V A Cooper,
W E Woosnam Jones

1929 Sept 26   **Rowan Tree Slabs** (Idwal) F E Hicks, C V A
Cooper, W E Woosnam Jones
*Named after a tall rowan that grew below the slab,
but this has long since departed. A remarkably bold
lead though they did sneak up.
The modern way of doing this was first led by J
O'Neill in 1963 and the finish added by M A
Boysen and D Little in 1969.*

1929 Sept 26   **The Girdle Traverse of Holly Tree Wall**
(Idwal) F E Hicks, C V A Cooper, W E Woosnam
Jones
The completion of a fine series of routes by Hicks.

1929 Sept 28   **Central Rib** (Idwal) C F Kirkus, A B Hargreaves
*The original intention was to avoid any
nail-scratched rock.*

1929 Nov 9   **Rake End Chimney** (Idwal) C F Kirkus, F E Hicks,
A B Hargreaves
*For a time this was thought to be the hardest route
on the East Wall. 'The corner was wet. Hicks failed
on the overhang and the party was about to give up
and try a severe looking traverse onto the Ash Tree
Wall. Kirkus, however, was not to be beaten and
took off his boots and the overhang 'went' after a
struggle... This must have been one of the boldest
leads ever undertaken as the rocks were greasy and
the possibility of exit doubtful'.*

1929 Dec 15   **Grooved Wall** (Idwal) C F Kirkus, A B Hargreaves
*They must have approached from Ash Tree Wall as
the first pitch was credited to D F H Biggane and
party 13 May 1942.*

1930 Easter   **Javelin Blade** (Idwal) J L Longland, C Williams
An outstanding lead that stood as the most difficult

piece of Welsh climbing for many years, though few were aware of it. Moreover, Edwards gave no hint in his 1936 description 'The last part of the corner and the pull out are harder than the ordinary route.' 'Quite frankly, I'd lost my way. I'd come to the famous thread belay at the end of the first pitch of the normal route, and I didn't know that the route ought to go right. I was a pole vaulter, which I think gives you pretty strong fingers, and I remember the pull-out onto the actual blade of the javelin was very strenuous; though not dangerous – I had a belay about 40 feet below me'.

1930 Aug 14   **Saint's Wall** (Idwal) S A Marples, W H Marples

1930 Dec 20   **Route 5** (Idwal) J M Edwards, K W Gearey
'Here again much gardening has been done, indeed this route was discovered sod by sod'. Edwards finished by The Eaves on 7 August 1931.

1931 May 16   **Heather Weakness** (Idwal) J M Edwards, S B Darbishire, A R Edge
Climbed as a weak variation of Heather Wall.

1931 June 7   **Amphitheatre Rib** (Craig yr Ysfa) C F Kirkus, G G Macphee, A M Robinson
'Thousands of climbers had passed it without really noticing it'. C Kirkus

1931 June 20   **Lot's Wife** (Glyder Fach) C F Kirkus, A M Robinson

1931 June 21   **Pinnacle Wall** (Craig yr Ysfa) C F Kirkus
An exposed solo. C T Jones and D Walker added the left-hand finish in 1971.
'I used to sit, pretending to work with the drawer slightly open, so that I could see the photo inside. Then I would plan a route.' C Kirkus

1931 July 9   **Youth Crack** (Nant yr Ogof) J M Edwards, C H S R Palmer

1931 July 10   **Square Chimney Buttress** (Glyder Fach) C H R S Palmer, S B Darbishire

1931 July 12   **Sub-Cneifion Rib** (Cneifion) J M Edwards

1931 July 13   **Llyn** (Clogwyn y Tarw) C H S R Palmer, J M Edwards
Several others subsequently claimed ascents of this good little route.

1931 July 13   **East Wall Girdle** (Idwal) J M Edwards, C H S R Palmer
First climbed in boots. 'Owing to the unregenerate conditions of Rake End Chimney at the time, a lead

was taken straight from Heather Wall to Ash Tree Wall'.

1931 Aug 1   **Chasm Rib, Chasm Chimney** (Glyder Fach) J M Edwards, G H D Edwards, A Kerr

1931 Sept 7   **Balcony Cracks** (Idwal) J M Edwards, A M D'Aeth
'On the Idwal Slabs things are getting a trifle congested; there are so many people and so many scratches that it is very difficult to find fresh ground whereon to eat one's sandwiches, or leave people one may not want. Balcony Cracks is quite an arresting little piece...'

1931 Oct 11   **Crevassed Rib** (Tryfan) G M King, F E Wallbank, C E A Andrews
Though not much of this was new, forming part of the old Intermittent Arête.

1931 Dec 19   **Anvil Cracks** (Creigiau Gleision) J M Edwards, A M D'Aeth
A tribute to Edwards's ability to select the best from a very undistinguished crag.

1932 Feb 6   **West Groove** (Glyder Fawr) B McKenna, Miss E Lowe

1932 July 2   **Lost Boot Climb** (Glyder Fawr) A S Bullough, Cooper, J Marchington
A chance meeting between Ken Vickers and Arthur Bullough, while they were skiing in Cervinia in January 1988 led to an amazing story which has now been confirmed. Bullough made the first lead of Grey Slab predating the ascent by Edwards by 54 days – and the truth took 56 years to emerge. 'At first I wore my boots, but when it got harder I was forced to take them off and hang them round my neck. It was quite a long lead and near the top my boot laces broke and the boots fell to the foot of the cliff'. To avoid confusion the traditional name of Grey Slab has been retained.

1932 July 20   **The Crack** (Cwm Cywion) C F Kirkus, A M D'Aeth
D'Aeth did not complete the climb, as the rope jammed.

1932 July 21   **The Gully** (Cwm Cywion) C F Kirkus, A M D'Aeth
E W Steeple and G Barlow had climbed the gully section in 1915.

1932 July 23   **Little Woodhead** (Cwm Cywion) C F Kirkus, A M D'Aeth
The party used The Crack to start; an independent

approach was added by A J Lowe and O O Coupe on 26 June 1943.

1932 Aug 17   **Procrastination Cracks** (Glyder Fawr) J M Edwards, A M D'Aeth
A fine lead by Edwards. '...very spasmodic and youthful, but you may wait indefinitely between bits of it'. It is hardly surprising that, with virtually no protection, the climbing gave him food for thought.

1932 Aug 25   **Grey Slab** (Glyder Fawr) J M Edwards, F Reade
The second ascent of Lost Boot Climb! '...longer and more staid, and on the long second pitch there is less incitement to linger... It was on this that a small boy showed notable courage in trusting himself entirely to the pull of a rope for 100 feet'.

1932 Aug 28   **Devil's Buttress** (Clogwyn y Geifr) J M Edwards
'Done alone in rubbers on a dry day. This was the first of the buttress to yield. It had been seen previously on a rope in boots'.

1932 Dec 11   **High Pasture** (Glyder Fawr) J M Edwards, M M Williamson
'...a nice walk on soft yielding grass'.

1932   **The Crack** (Craig yr Ysfa) C F Kirkus, A B Hargreaves
This climb quickly earned a just reputation for difficulty.

c. 1932   **Grey Girdle** (Glyder Fawr) Probably dates from the period of Edwards's explorations.

1933 March 26   **Devil's Pasture** (Clogwyn y Geifr) J M Edwards, K Wormald

1933 April 13   **Jonah's Buttress** (Gallt yr Ogof) J M Edwards, G A Pixton

1933 April 15   **Devil's Dump** (Clogwyn y Geifr) J M Edwards, R M Bere
'...the steep bit is an interesting study in mosaics. But they did not finish if off very well. Alternatively it may be regraded as an excavation in the Dump, and you get holds on the bits sticking out: it is decidedly decomposing. Herein lies its charm'.

1933 May 14   **Cellar Buttress** (Clogwyn y Geifr) J M Edwards, T E Davies

1933 May 21   **Devil's Dive** (Clogwyn y Geifr) J M Edwards, C H French
It must have taken some daring to launch up the centre of this steep cliff.

1933 May 21   **North Slabs** (Clogwyn y Geifr) J M Edwards, C H French

1933 June 28   **Botany Bay Climb** (Clogwyn y Geifr) J M Edwards, W W Stallybrass, G G Macphee, R W Stallybrass
Edwards had previously attempted this alone and was forced to wait for rescue. 'Anon, there came a rope from above and the doughty explorer continued jerkily upwards... to the sound of heavy breathing in triplicate'.

1933 July 2   **South Nose** (Clogwyn y Geifr) J M Edwards, G H Pixton, F Mee

1933 July 22   **Staircase Traverse** (Clogwyn y Geifr) J M Edwards, A M D'Aeth

1933 July 23   **Hothouse Crack** (Clogwyn y Geifr) J M Edwards, C H S R Palmer
The direct approach was done by PRJ Harding and party in 1947.

1933 July 24   **Devil's Pipes** (Clogwyn y Geifr) J M Edwards, C H S R Palmer
The 'Pipes' were seen on a rope before being led. Palmer climbed the lower tower later that year.

1933 July 24   **Little Corner** (Clogwyn y Geifr) J M Edwards, C H S R Palmer

1933 Aug   **Deasel** (Braich Ty Du) R Elfyn Hughes and party

1933 Aug 31   **Grass Route** (Glyder Fawr) J M Edwards, R W Beard
It seems to have been a rather eventful ascent: Beard was stuffed into a little cave below the third pitch '... but he seemed to be deriving discomfort from falling materials, and his agitation appears to have been considerably increased by the sudden loosening of several large blocks in the roof of the cave itself... It is perhaps not generally realised that there are in the climbing world one or two seconds who display more courage and sagacity in the face of emergencies (e.g. the aforesaid cave) than has ever been shown by even the most reckless of leaders'.

1933 Sept 1   **Bee's Buttress** (Gallt yr Ogof) J M Edwards, W W Stallybrass
'... a good, if rather cumbersome, sort of climb. It starts with excellent, strong heather for some distance'. A better start was found in later years.

1933 Sept 2   **Piece by Piece Climb** (Clogwyn y Geifr) J M Edwards, T E Davies, R W Beard

1933 Sept 3   **Dump Crack** (Clogwyn y Geifr) J M Edwards, C H French
'… a tall spike rises above the fernery on the left. It is firm… Straight up into a good cave which obviously has not been wiped for years'.

1933 Sept   **Goat's Walk** (Clogwyn y Geifr) J M Edwards

1933 Oct 22   **South Gully** (Clogwyn y Geifr) C F Kirkus, M Linnel
They escaped to Botany Bay Climb, as the continuation looked improbable.
c. 1933
Central Groove (Clogwyn y Geifr) Probably climbed by Edwards.

1934 March 11   **Easy Pinnacle Route** (Gallt yr Ogof) J M Edwards, J N Mahler

1934 March 11   **Old Man Buttress** (Gallt yr Ogof) J M Edwards, J N Mahler

1934 March 31   **Rope Wall, Little Gully Wall** (Milestone) J M Edwards, A R Edge

1934 July 15   **Right Wall Route** (Clogwyn y Geifr) G H Kirkus, J F Ashton, G O'Flaherty
Seen on a rope first. 'The fame of the early attempts, the discouragement of its rock, and its numerous escapades and fatalities are still stirring in the Devil's Kitchen. It is essentially a climb of association'. J M Edwards

1934 Aug 29   **Hoyland's Route** (Ysgolion Duon) J D Hoyland, J R Jenkins, G Showell
Most of the pitches had been climbed at an earlier date as alternatives to Central Gully.

1934 Oct 21   **Frost's Climb** (Castell y Gwynt) R C Frost, V Unicombe, P G Barnett

1934 Nov   **Reed Rake** (Craig yr Ysfa) J R Jenkins and party
It seems likely that it was climbed earlier and not recorded.

1935 April 22   **Soapgut** (Milestone) J M Edwards, C W F Noyce
By The Squint Start. The direct, now normal, way was forced by the same strong pair on 4 September 1936.

1935 June 16   **Flat Chimney** (Drws Cwm Clyd) J M Edwards, C H S R Palmer

1935 June 25   **Steep Wall** (Gallt yr Ogof) C H S R Palmer
and the H and J variations 'in the old combination'.

1935 July 21	**Two Pitch Route, Five Pitch Route** (Bochlwyd) C F Kirkus, R C Frost
1935 July 21	**Marble Slab** (Bochlwyd) C F Kirkus, C Brennand

Kirkus recommended 'If you have a slate roof – say of an outhouse – not too far from the ground, you can learn the theory of slab-climbing. You can find that you can walk on it, with care, in climbing boots. The slates won't suffer much if you are careful, and anyhow it is all in a good cause.

Now imagine you are reaching up for a high handhold and lean inwards until you are almost against the slates. Your feet will slip, and you will probably slide down to the gutter. This should convince you that you must stand straight upright on slabs and not lean in at all. The lesson will be made even more convincing if you miss the gutter and break your neck in the yard below'.

1935 Aug 5	**Jacob's Ladder** (Ysgolion Duon) F H Jacob, E P Williams, R G Williams, I F Parry
1936 May 12	**Plain Crack, Whinberry Route, Barbed Corner** (Drws Nodded) J M Edwards, E W Lowe
1936 May 31	**Gamma** (Glyder Fach) C F Kirkus, G G Macphee
1936 June 21	**The Gully** (Craig y Cwmglas Bach) J R Jenkins, M S Taylor, A A Woodall
1936 July 1	**Munich Climb** (Tryfan) (2 pts) H Teufel, H Sedlmayr, J R Jenkins

F Scheuhuber, F Reiss and F Brandt made up the second assault team. Two pegs had been placed for aid and their removal became a point of national pride. These were swiftly dispatched in a free ascent by J M Edwards and J B Joyce in September 1936. Although Edwards did lasso a spike above to protect the moves across, the spike was loose! His method had '.... the advantage that the leader can climb with a rope above him all the way. I do not know why leaders do not make their rope precede them more frequently in this way. Saves a lot of trouble'.

The messy corner to the foot of Teufel's Crack was done by R V M Barry and Jenkins on 26 July 1936. South Gully Wall is made up of the independent variations to Munich Climb, the second pitch of which was discovered by I Clough on 15 July 1959.

1936 Aug 11	**Little Buttress** (Glyder Fach) C F Kirkus, G G Macphee

1936 Aug 24   **Bubbly Wall** (Tryfan) C W F Noyce, J M Edwards
1936 Aug 27   **North Side Route** (Tryfan) C W F Noyce, J M Edwards
1936 Aug 30   **Girdle Traverse of Terrace Wall** (Tryfan) C W F Noyce, J M Edwards
1936 Sept 1   **Yew Buttress** (Tryfan) C W F Noyce, J M Edwards
              'A short, severe and good little route, harder than one would expect, more difficult than Cheek, with which it is not comparable'. A J J Moulam 1956
1936 Sept 2   **Scars Climb** (Tryfan) C W F Noyce, J M Edwards
              A most improbable looking route. The Spider Wall variation was done by A R Dolphin and D C Birch on 9 August 1946.
1936 Sept 4   **Hangman Gut** (Milestone) C W F Noyce, J M Edwards
              They swung on a rope to start.
1936 Sept 6   **Arch Gully** (Glyder Fach) Pitches 1 to 4: C F Kirkus, P M Mahon. Pitches 5 and 6: C F Kirkus, R C Frost, G Dwyer, 13 Sept 1936.
1936 Sept 20 **Errant Route** (Glyder Fach) C F Kirkus, W W Stallybrass, R W Stallybrass
1936 Sept 26 **Stack Wall** (Gallt yr Ogof) J M Edwards, A M Keith
1936 Oct 11   **Hawk Slab** (Glyder Fach) C F Kirkus, G G Macphee
1936 Oct 18   **Main Gully Ridge** (Glyder Fach) CF Kirkus, R C Frost
1936 Oct 24   **Chalkren Stairs** (Gallt yr Ogof) J M Edwards, A T Leggate
              Pitch 3a was done by W Cox and D T Roscoe (1 pt. aid) on 1 May 1968.
1936 Oct 25   **Tower Rib** (Cwm Cneifion) C F Kirkus, A E Wood
1936 Nov 15   **Slab Intermediate Route** (Clogwyn y Tarw) G G Macphee, G C Williams
1936 Dec 20   **Pinnacle Edge** (Cwm Cneifion) C F Kirkus
1936   **Skyline Buttress** (Bristly Ridge) M S Taylor, J R Jenkins
              The crack on the third pitch was climbed direct by P Dahlr and A Edmonds in 1966.
1937 Jan 11   **Roughcast Flutings** (Ysgolion Duon) R A Hodgkin, A D M Cox, C Crichton Miller
1937 Mar 19   **Roughcast Wall** (Ysgolion Duon) R A Hodgkin, R L Beaumont
1937 May 10   **Great West Slab** (Glyder Fawr) P O Work
              This appears to have been a solo ascent on friable rock.

1937 July 31   **Devil's Appendix** (Clogwyn y Geifr) F H Jacob, R
G Williams
*The additional pitch across the line of the waterfall
was climbed during the drought in June 1970 by A
C Cain and D Lewis.*

1937 July 31   **Corrugated Cracks** (Craig Cwrwgl) A W Evans,
P Smith

1937 Aug 2   **The Terminal Arête** (Ysgolion Duon) F H Jacob, S
M Jacob, I B Williams, R G Williams
*On the same area of cliff as Jacob's Ladder starting
from Central Gully.*

1937 Aug 9   **Bivouac Buttress** (Craig Lloer) C H S R Palmer

1937 Aug 11   **Gnat's Gnose** (Gallt yr Ogof) C H S R Palmer, J A
B Gray

1937 Aug 13   **First Trinity Groove** (Craig Lloer) C H S R
Palmer, J A Ingham

1937 Aug 13   **Chimney Buttress** (Craig Lloer) J A Ingham, C H
S R Palmer

1937 Aug 20   **Second Trinity Groove** (Craig Lloer) C H S R
Palmer, J H Buzzard

1937 Aug 23   **Fence Climb** (Gallt yr Ogof) J H Buzzard, C H S R
Palmer
*Not a very inspiring series of routes by Palmer and
friends!*

1937 Sept 2   **Table Climb** (Gallt yr Ogof) J A B Gray, B Pownall

1937 Sept 2   **Slab Route** (Gallt yr Ogof) W N Coombes, J A B
Gray

1937 Sept   **Amphitheatre Slab, Black Chimney** and
Trident Route (Creigiau Gleision) J H Buzzard

1937 Sept   **Bird's Wing Buttress** (Creigiau Gleision) J H
Buzzard, H B Derbyshire, J F Mackeson
*The alternative start was climbed by L R Holliwell
and R A Lewis, in error, 1971.*

1937 Oct 6   **Autumn Buttress** (Creigiau Gleision) J H
Buzzard, H J A Thicknesse, H C H Crofton

1937 Nov 2   **Arch Wall** (Craig yr Ysfa) H E Kretschmer, A D M
Cox, J R Jenkins

1938 Mar 19   **Beaumont's Chimney** (Craig yr Ysfa) R L
Beaumont, P B Inchbald, A D Hardie, I F Rose, R H
Cardwell, J D Allen
*The initial chimney and the upper part of Original
Route were climbed by this party.*

1938 Mar 20   **Original Route** (Craig yr Ysfa) R L Beaumont, B A
Harwood, F H Allen

1938 April   **The Staircase** (Craig yr Ysfa) R L Beaumont

1938 July	**Gomorrah** and **Spiral Route** (Craig yr Ysfa) A D M Cox *Two fine solos.*
1938 July 24	**The Grimmett** (Craig yr Ysfa) A D M Cox, R L Beaumont
1938 Aug	**Nether Climb** (Craig yr Ysfa) J Martin, N J M Barry climbed pitches 1 to 3. H E Kretschmer, F J Dodd did pitches 4 to 7 *This climb was extended by pitch 4 on 12 August 1946 by H A Carsten and A.C.L.*
1938 Sept 8	**Linear Climb** (Tryfan) R A Hull, P Marsden *Much of this had been done before; because in 1911 F C Aldous, B Horsley, T Wildbore, F Mason and A C Adams climbed Ordinary Route starting by Cheek, and continuing up the Variant. To this F E Hicks and R M Bere added a direct start on 19 December 1936.*
1938 Nov 6	**Brace and Bit** (Castell y Geifr) J H Emlyn Jones, A Bellinger *This may have been climbed by Archer Thomson, however.*
1938 Dec 15	**Truant Rib** (Craig yr Ysfa) C W F Noyce, D M Craib, D C Thom
1939 May 14	**Original Route** (Gallt yr Ogof) J H Buzzard
1939 Nov 4	**The Rocking Stone Climb** (Gallt yr Ogof) J S T Gibson, J H Buzzard
1939 Dec 16	**Sub-Cneifion Chimney** (Cwm Cneifion) D F H B , J F W
1940 May 21	**Right Chimney** (Carreg Mianog) E Moss, J F Mathews, H A Standing
1940 July 22	**Hawk's Nest Arête** (Glyder Fach) P W W Nock, H Harrison *They accepted the real challenge of the Buttress.*
1940 Nov 4	**Capstone Climb** (Gallt yr Ogof) J H Buzzard
1941 Oct 4	**Shean Treuse** (Craig yr Ysfa) H E Kretschmer, F A Pullinger
1942 May 9	**Garden Path** (Drws Nodded) C W F Noyce *'Still needs much spade work.' D H Haworth continued in the crack, to surmount the overhang on 25 March 1949.*
1942 May	**Cinderella's Twin** (Idwal) C W F Noyce
1942 July 12	**Manx Wall** (Clogwyn Du) A J Lowe, W K J Pearson, J G Pearson, P Russell *The initial investigation of an impressive wall.*
1943 May 27	**Groove Route** (Castell y Geifr) H C J Hunt

1943 May 29	**Chastity** (Clogwyn Du) A J Lowe, P Russell
1943 June 26	**Fallacy** (Cwm Cywion) C P Brown, A R Jones, H C Hancock
1943 July 3	**Gawain** (Craig yr Ogof) H E Kretschmer, J H Emlyn Jones, R D S Carpendale, W H Ward
	The Direct line was climbed by D E Alcock and C E Davies (using 2 aid slings) on 7 June 1969. Free climbed by Z Leppert in 1989.
1943 July 4	**Travesty** (Clogwyn Du) A J Lowe, P Russell (AL), R Goodger
	The alternative finish was climbed at a later date. Climbed free by S Cardy, A Orton in May 1984.
1944 June 24	**Angle Groove** (Craig yr Ysfa) M P Ward, F H Keenlyside, A R H Worssam
1944 June 28	**Cockroach Crack** (Craig yr Ysfa) W H Ward, G G Freeman
1944 June 28	**Coffin Scoop** and **Cradle Chimney** (Craig yr Ysfa) J E Q Barford, J V S Glass
1944 June 28	**Figure of Eight** (Craig yr Ysfa) C A Fenner, R M P Hartog
1944 Aug 8	**Zip Wall** (Carreg Mianog) E Moss, H A Standing, J F Mathews
1944 Aug 10	**The Crawl Climb** (Carreg Mianog) E Moss, H A Standing, J F Mathews
1944 Aug 12	**Angle Gully** (Carreg Mianog) E Moss, H A Standing
1944 Aug 12	**Crack and Corner** (Carreg Mianog) H A Standing, E Moss
1944 Aug 26	**Clean Rib** (Craig yr Ysfa) J M Bechervaise
1944 Aug 26	**Skyline Chimney** (Craig yr Ysfa) C H S R Palmer, J M Bechervaise
	This included a scruffy start, now best forgotten. The start described was first climbed by P R J Harding and N L Horsfield on 27 March 1948.
1944 Aug 30	**The Overhangs**, **Crack and Wall** (Gallt yr Ogof) J M Bechervaise, C H S R Palmer
	The variation to the Overhangs was added much later, 18 September 1977, by Palmer.'Climbed alone, and as an elderly gent of my advanced age (72), I found some of the moves very difficult and the exposure considerable. But it amused me and might amuse a few others of my vintage'.
1944 Aug 30	**Airy Corner** (Gallt yr Ogof) C H S R Palmer, J M Bechervaise

1944 Sept 6 **Giant's Steps Buttress, Two Tower Buttress** (Bristly Ridge) C H S R Palmer, J M Bechervaise
The Chateau was climbed on 10 September 1944 by C H S R Palmer, J M Bechervaise, J P Walker and J B Williamson.

1944 Sept 6 **Great Tower Buttress** (Bristly Ridge) C H S R Palmer
Although A D M Cox and J R Jenkins climbed here on 13 June 1937.

1944 Christmas **Covent Garden** (Craig y Cwmglas Bach) E C Pyatt, K C King, C S Johnstone, R Howard

1945 May 21 **Cracked Arête** (Carreg Mianog) A D Ferguson, R A Williams

1945 Aug 3 **Central By-Pass** (Tryfan) E Byne, J B Alexander

1945 Sept 9 **Advocate's Wall** (Clogwyn y Geifr) C Preston, R G Morsley, D McKellar

1945 Sept 28 **Stoats' Groove** (Tryfan) D A Hanson, W Lathbury, H Mykura, J Butler

1945 Oct 7 **Suicide Wall Route 1** (Idwal) C Preston, R G Morsley, J Haines
This was a problem that had defeated both Edwards and Kirkus. Preston was extremely fit, hardened by army training. He had previously made an inspection of the route by abseil and climbed to the ledge, but unfortunately his seconds were unable to follow his example and he was forced to accept a top rope to finish. Preston returned with a strengthened team to make the successful ascent, finding it totally within his ability.
'The idea was to give Preston enough slack for him just to hit the ground if he fell off, so as not to pull the other two off their precarious perch'. A Rouse made a solo ascent in May 1970.

1945 **Christmas Staircase** (Pen Llithrig y Wrach) P R J Harding, A J J Moulam
An early contribution from two distinguished climbing careers.

1946 April 22 **Central Route** (Llech Ddu) G Dwyer, R G Morsley
This was the long awaited and much tried break through on the steep central section of the crag. In the late '30s, P O Work and I Ap G Hughes climbed three hard pitches before being forced to retreat.

1946 Aug 9 **Beeline** (Tryfan) A R Dolphin, D C Birch

1947 May 26   **Mare's Nest Climb** (Ysgolion Duon) J H Emlyn Jones, B Crowther

1947 June 1   **Pegasus** (Ysgolion Duon) J H Emlyn Jones, D J Watson
The Chimera Variation was added by A J J Moulam and A R Chapman 3 Sept. 1949.

1947 June 23   **Late Night Final** (Clogwyn y Tarw) D H Haworth, M J Ball, K E Berrill
The Away Variations were added by a University of North Wales party.

1947 Oct 9   **South Climb** (Cwm Cneifion) J K Rhoden, K T Jenkins

1947   **The Rampart** (Idwal) A J J Moulam
The hard pitch was first led by Hicks in 1929 during his Girdle Traverse.

1947 Dec 29   **Mordred** (Craig yr Ogof) H A Carsten, R E Meyer, N M Blackett

1948 Mar 16   **Biceps Wall** (Carreg Mianog) D H Haworth, G A Horridge

1948 March 24   **Suicide Groove** (Idwal) J B Lawton, D H Haworth
An obvious line, not as fierce as Suicide Wall, so it seems surprising it had to wait longer for an ascent. A Rouse and P Minks both made solo ascents in May 1970.
Direct Finish: N Shepherd, B Wayman, June 1977, a useful pitch on this upper section of Suicide Wall.

1948 April 10   **Lot's Child** (Glyder Fach) P R J Harding, C Bramfitt

1948 May 16   **Pilgrim's Progress** (Clogwyn y Geifr) P Shipley-Taylor, R G Morsley, P Russell, G Brittain

1948 July 27   **Cobweb Wall** (Craig yr Ysfa) M G Hughes, L L Turner

1948 Sept 1   **Hangman's Wall** (Milestone) J R Bradley, K U Ingold
K U Ingold, E L Hardy added the wall finish later, on 10 September 1948.

1948 Sept 18   **Northern Rib** (Tryfan) P Russell, G A Jeffrey, A L Sparshott

1948 Sept 26   **Analyst's Flue** (Drws Nodded) A G N Flew, H O Parker
A curious name for the route and leader!

1948 Sept 26   **Anniversary Route** (Creigiau'r Dena) E Byne, P Russell, C Bates
Originally done in nine pitches.

1948 Dec 16   **Pinnacle Route** (Clogwyn y Tarw) D H Haworth, A Parker

1949 May 1	**Omega, Back Door** (Glyder Fach) Bangor University MC party
1949	**Pieces of Eight** (Craig yr Ysfa) A J J Moulam, A R Chapman
1949 June 25	**Launcelot** (Craig yr Ogof) A J J Moulam, P R J Harding *Pitch 3 was added by A J J Moulam and H G Robertson on 27 August 1949.*
1949 July 2	**Dandelion Wall** (Gallt yr Ogof) N P Campbell, J M Edwards
1949 July	**Route 1** (Gallt yr Ogof) J M Edwards, L W Bennet, J O Hibling
1949 July 11	**Route II** (Gallt yr Ogof) J M Edwards, R W Beard
1949 Aug 19	**Crab Slab** (Castell y Gwynt) G C Norman, I C Bennett
1949 Aug 21	**Druid Route** (Glyder Fach) G C Norman, I C Bennett
1949 Aug 30	**Low Wall** (Craig y Cwmglas Bach) A J J Moulam, A R Chapman
1949 Sept 2	**Juno** (Ysgolion Duon) A J J Moulam, A R Chapman
1949 Sept 12	**Jupiter** (Ysgolion Duon) A J J Moulam, Miss P J Fearon, K U Ingold
1949 Sept 15	**Sigma** and **Troglodyte** (Craig yr Ysfa) A J J Moulam, T P Snell, G A Horridge (Sigma only) *The lower section of Troglodyte collapsed, and the route now described was climbed by L R Holliwell and A N Other in 1971.*
1949 Sept 18	**Enigma** (Craig yr Ysfa) A J J Moulam, T P Snell
1949 Sept 19	**Wide Chimney** (Cwm Cywion) A J J Moulam, T P Snell
1949 Sept 21	**Garden Cracks** (Castell y Dulyn) J Renshaw, J A Lewis
1949 Sept 21	**Sheep Pen Buttress** (Creigiau Gleision) A J J Moulam, B L Blake
1949 Sept 23	**The Banister** (Craig yr Ysfa) A J J Moulam, B L Blake
1949 Sept 25	**Anniversary Approach** (Creigiau'r Dena) E Byne, C Bates, P Russell
1949 Oct 1	**The Enigma Variation (to Nor' Nor' Buttress)** T D Bourdillon, K Norcross *Subsequently K Norcross and A G N Flew added Opus One.*
1950 Mar 12	**Avalanche Buttress** (Craig yr Ysfa) A J J Moulam, J B Nicholson *This party climbed pitches 1 and 2, but the*

remainder of the route was made much earlier,
probably by G W Young and G H L Mallory as a
continuation to Birch Tree Chimney.

1950 Mar 12   **Mitre** (Carreg Mianog) A J J Moulam, J B Nicholson
But it was not led clean until later.

1950 Mar 25   **The Lectern Grooves** (Braich Ty Du) A J J
Moulam and party
*Moulam's first venture into this confused area of
buttresses which he later was to describe 'Now
something has gone wrong. Some of the gullies
seem to have taken up their beds and walked,
together with the buttresses between them'.*

1950 Mar 26   **Jason** (Ysgolion Duon) A J J Moulam, K U Ingold

1950 Mar 27   **Third Trinity Groove** (Craig Lloer) K U Ingold, A
J J Moulam (AL)

1950 Mar 31   **Pinnacle Ridge Route** (Braich Ty Du) K U Ingold,
Miss P J Fearon, M J Ball

1950 Apr 5   **Jane (If she doesn't mind)** (Carreg Mianog) M
J Ball, Miss P J Fearon, T D Bourdillon

1950 Easter   **Introvert** and **Widdershins** (Braich Ty Du) A J J
Moulam, I G McNaught-Davis
*R Elfyn-Hughes climbed in the area of Widdershins,
but it is unlikely that he followed the line exactly.*

1950 May 3   **Pillar Face, The** (Clogwyn Du) P Nock, Mary
Hingley

1950 May 5   **Sentry Box Crack** (Craig yr Ysfa) A J J Moulam,
R E Meyer

1950 May   **Sidewalk** (Glyder Fach) Bangor University MC
Party

1951 June 18 **Custodian's Creep** (Braich Ty Du) A J J Moulam, J
D B Lindsay, J A Harrison

1951 Oct 7   **F-Sharp** (Braich Ty Du) A J J Moulam, Mrs D King

1952 Apr 23   **Easter Ridge** (Creigiau'r Dena) E Byne, R Arthur,
C Ashbury, R Goldsmith

1952 Apr 26   **Mur y Niwl** (Craig yr Ysfa) A J J Moulam, J B
Churchill
*A milestone in Carneddau climbing, the route
quickly became a Welsh classic. The Direct
variation was climbed by R Tresidder and C N
Stewart on July 22, 1967.*

1952 Sept 12 **Great Flake Crack** (Creigiau'r Dena) D Penlington

1952 Sept 21 **Left Ridge** (Creigiau'r Dena) E Byne, M Cully

1953 Apr 7   **Columbyne** (Tryfan) E Byne and party

1953 Whit   **Wit** (Llech Ddu) C J S Bonington, G G Francis
Sunday

1953 June 7   **Flake Cross** (Creigiau'r Dena) A J J Moulam, J M Barr

1953 Aug 2   **Humour** (Llech Ddu) A Kopczinski, G G Francis
The Laughing Finish, which avoids the principal difficulties was added by E A Wrangham, A Alvarez and D C Bull on July 10 1955. An alternative finish was also climbed by C Knowles, H Lagoe 1983.

1953 Aug 3   **Central Ridge** (Craig Lloer) I Clayton, B Cooke

1953 Aug 6   **Pierrot** (Tryfan) E Byne, C Ashbury, B Jones, B Wood, M Allbutt, J Turner, M Thomas, I Weighell
Pitch 4 was added by A J J Moulam and G W S Pigott.

1953 Aug 14   **Wall Direct** (Creigiau'r Dena) M Bridgewater, A Letts

1954 Apr 17   **Moonrise** (Craig Lloer) A J J Moulam, C M Dixon
It is doubtful if this party followed the route described precisely.

1954 June 12   **Puffin** (Pen Llithrig y Wrach) A J J Moulam, H L Richardson, Mrs E Upton

1954 July 25   **Yeoman Service** (Gallt yr Ogof) G W S Pigott, A J J Moulam, W R Cra'ster

1954 Oct 9   **Mea Route** (Tryfan) A J J Moulam, R M Viney, C W Brasher, E A Wrangham

1955 Mar 19   **Netts** (Gallt yr Ogof) A J J Moulam, Miss P D Chapman

1955 Apr 8   **Lower Dolmen Rib** (Glyder Fach) J W B Barnes, D Clutterbuck

1955 July 2   **Limax** (Craig yr Ysfa) M J Harris, J Neill

1955 Aug 2   **Hard Frost** (Castell y Gwynt) P M Hutchinson, P R Williams

1955 Sept 15   **Decameron Rib** (Braich Ty Du) S M Lane, F A Boydell
Boccaccio's Start by A J J Moulam and R F Jones on July 7 1956. The Direct Start by S M Lane, P J Crabb and D Price on April 27 1958.

1955 Nov 26   **Dover Road** (A2) (Craig yr Ysfa) T D Bourdillon, M P Ward
'Largely artificial climbing with a pleasing variety of technique'. This route was dropped from the last guidebook.

1956 June 23   **Girdle Traverse of East Buttress** (Glyder Fach) A J J Moulam, G J Sutton
Though Pitches 4-8 were climbed at least as early as 27 June 1942.

| 1956 July 7 | **Aaron** (Braich Ty Du) A J J Moulam, R F Jones |

The original finishes of this climb and Joyce have been interchanged for the sake of grade consistency.

1956 July 21	**Née Langley** (Clogwyn y Tarw) R James, R L Roberts, W M Macleod
1956 Aug 9	**Cannon Ridge** (Tryfan) E Byne, Miss U Milner White, F Tomney, B Thorneycroft
1956 Sept 15	**Shadow Arête** (Bochlwyd) R L Roberts, R Greenwood

F E Hicks and R M Bere made a route here on 16 December 1929, and others also, including Harding and Moulam in 1945, followed various pitches in this broken area.

1956 Sept	**Bishop's Gut** (Milestone) J R Lees, J W B Barnes, A R Gordon-Cumming
1957 May 5	**Snowstorm** (Tryfan) (1 pt aid) D T Roscoe, H MacInnes
1957 June 1	**Digitalis Direct** (Braich Ty Du) A J J Moulam, Mrs P D Moulam
1957 June 1	**Extrovert** (Braich Ty Du) A J J Moulam, R F Jones
1957 June 26	**Waterfall Climb** (Clogwyn y Geifr) J M Edwards, A Jones

'Suitable only for extremely dehydrated parties in dry, scorching weather'. Menlove Edwards's last contribution, and so typical of him.

| 1957 Aug 21 | **Yob Route** (Clogwyn y Tarw) (3 pts aid) K R C Britton, G N Crawshaw |

Two pitons and a sling were used. The modern finish was done by M G T Plant and P E Wright on 25 July 1967.

1957 Aug	**Girdle Traverse of Clogwyn y Tarw** K R C Britton, R Beasley
1958 June 1	**Central Route** (Carreg Mianog) (some aid) C Goodey, L Evans
1958 Nov 14	**Rocking Chair** (Clogwyn y Tarw) R L Roberts, E Birch
1959	**Apprentice's Route** (Braich Ty Du) Ogwen Cottage party
1959	**Knee Cap** and **Funny Bone** (Carreg Mianog) R James, R L Roberts
1959	**Jan Premiere** (Craig Eigiau) G Martin, T Goodwin
1959	**Jan Vin Ordinaire** (Craig Eigiau) A B Knox, V Leese
1959 May 21	**Maria** (Gallt yr Ogof) J Brown, C T Jones

1959 June	**Playtime** (Clogwyn y Tarw) R James, C T Jones

The alternative finish was added by M Crook and D Farrant on 8 July 1979.

1959 July 15	**Agrippa** (Craig yr Ysfa) (many aid pitons) J Wharton, D Isles

Caused a great deal of controversy at the time.

1959 Aug 13	**Vae** (Milestone) R F G Wrottesley, K S Vickers
1959 Aug 16	**Grey Arête** (Glyder Fawr) R James, P Benson

The first part had been climbed previously, on 8 August 1949, by M P Ward and J M Edwards as a variation start to Procrastination Cracks.

1959 Oct 2	**Devil's Nordwand** (Clogwyn y Geifr) R James, J V Anthoine

The first pitch had been climbed earlier by J Wharton and D Isles. James approached from the right.

1960 Easter	**Junior Slab** (Clogwyn y Geifr) (1 pt aid) J F Austin, F Spence (AL)
1960 May 18	**Cuckoo Groove** (Braich Ty Du) (1 pt aid) J R Lees, T R Wilkinson
1960 May 25	**Ring Ouzel** and **Stone Chat** (Braich Ty Du) T R Wilkinson, J R Lees
1960 June 1	**Shelf Edge** (Braich Ty Du) T R Wilkinson, F H Hardman
1960 July 2	**Hhier** (Craig Lloer) J R Lees, P R Janney
1960 July 6	**Temptation** (Braich Ty Du) J R Lees, R H Newby
1960 July 10	**Mexico Cracks** (Craig Cwrwgl) C T Jones, M Tweed
1960 Sept	**Sweet Sorrow** (Clogwyn y Tarw) J V Anthoine, R James, R Phillips

The start was added later.

1960	**Great Gully Pinnacle Direct** (Craig yr Ysfa) F A Wedgwood, J Cross
1960 Nov 19	**Patience** (Braich Ty Du) I F Cartledge, J R Lees
1961 Mar 19	**Primrose** (Braich Ty Du) A J J Moulam, J Cole
1961 June 18	**Garden Wall** (Castell y Dulyn) M A Reeves, J B Boyle (AL)
1961 June 24	**Lining Crack** (Braich Ty Du) A J J Moulam, Mrs P D Moulam
1961 June 25	**Pyramid Gully** (Ysgolion Duon) A J J Moulam, R G Hargreaves (AL)

This was the first recorded ascent, but it is certain that it was climbed at a much earlier date. The Direct Start was added by A J J Moulam and A N Other on October 1 1961.

1961 Summer	**Sinner's Corner** (Idwal) R James and party
1961 Oct	**The Groove** (Llech Ddu) (aid) J V Anthoine, I F Campbell

The first epic ascent took five days of toil through tons of vegetation and loose rock, which necessitated the use of five points of aid on pitch 2, some aid on pitch 3 and two points of aid on pitch 4. Soloed by P Livesey in 1975.

'How Mo Anthoine and Ian Campbell must have enthused at the prospect of this superb route! Any new climb is a unique challenge, but few can have equalled this five day epic for suspense and excitement. Loose rock, copious vegetation and the inevitable wet constituted infinitely more serious hazards than the technical difficulties involved'. Les Holliwell

1962 June	**Bochlwyd Eliminate** R James, R Barber

J Moffat and T Roper were first to climb straight up, instead of traversing, in 1980.

1962	**Soap Crack and Rib** (Milestone) J Clements, A Bell
1962 Aug 19	**Ancient's Wall** (Craig yr Ysfa) (1 pt aid) C T Jones, H I Banner (AL)

G J Streetly and E A Wrangham had climbed pitch 1 in 1952.

1962 Oct	**Moss Wall** (Carreg Mianog) J Cross, F A Wedgwood

The jamming crack had been climbed by A J J Moulam in 1949.

1963 Mar	**Cirque Rib** (Craig yr Ysfa) (3 pts aid) J A Austin, R B Evans (VL)

The aid was a peg, a sling and a shoulder.

1963 Easter	**Temper** (Carreg Mianog) C Goodey

Free climbed by A Pollitt and A Boorman 15 Feb 1982.

1963 June	**God's Little Acre** (Clogwyn y Geifr) D Yates, D H Jones
1963 Aug 28	**The Wrack** (Bochlwyd) T F Allen, W Hurford

Has now become a good route.

1963 Sept 22	**Suicide Wall Route 2** (Idwal) P Crew, B Ingle

A notable contribution from a strong partnership.

1963 Oct 14	**Draw** (Clogwyn y Tarw) A J J Moulam

It is likely that it had been done before.

1963 Dec 7	**Pocket Wall** (Idwal) A J Austin, A J J Moulam (AL), C T Jones

1964 Feb 8	**Finale Groove** (Cwm Cywion) A J J Moulam
1964 Feb 9	**Gubben Gully, Petrous** (Cwm Cywion) A J J Moulam, G D Roberts
1964 May 22	**Druid's Doghouse** (Clogwyn y Geifr) (1 pt aid) H I Banner, K Rhodes
1964 Aug 11	**Band Stand** (Creigiau Gleision) A J J Moulam, G Barker
1964 Oct 4	**Griseofulvin** (Craig yr Ysfa) (1 pt aid) A A Bell, J H Clements (AL)
1965 Easter	**Heron Slab** (Craig yr Ysfa) A J J Moulam, G D Roberts
1965 Apr 25	**Black Maria** (Gallt yr Ogof) M A Boysen, A Williams, D Little

1965 Apr 25 — *At one point the support climbers were reduced to hauling themselves up from the cord of a piton hammer.*

1965 May 30	**Elliw** (Llech Ddu) A A Bell, J H Clements (AL)

A fine find.

1965 June 4	**Endor** (Llech Ddu) (4 pts aid) A A Bell, J H Clements (AL)

Free climbed by M Fowler and E Hart 6 Sept 1981. Bell found the final few feet of the route loose and very dangerous. 'Much later I had a similar disarming experience with this compacted Weetabix-textured rock'. Les Holliwell

1965 June 16	**Joyce** (Braich Ty Du) J L Belton, P Thornton
1965	**Plumbagin** (Craig yr Ysfa) J H Clements, D Potts (AL)
1965 Aug	**The Great Corner** (Llech Ddu) J H Clements, D Potts (AL)

The Great Corner was the last of John Clements's contributions to the area before his untimely death. 'Clements and Potts cleared a wall of grass 50 feet high revealing superb rock beneath'. Now it provides '...one of the best corner climbs in Britain'.

1965 Aug 18	**Devil's Bastion** (Clogwyn y Geifr) T Herley, D Blythe (AL)

A route that exploited to the full the atmosphere of climbing on the main buttresses.
J Perrin bypassed the aid peg in 1971; the same year D Yates and W Barker did the Black Magic start.

1965 Oct 16	**Rake End Wall** (Idwal) H I Banner, R G Wilson
1965 Oct 17	**Cluck's Nook** (Braich Ty Du) A J J Moulam, G D Roberts

1965	**Synapse** (Clogwyn y Tarw) R Evans, T Herley (AL) *A long-standing problem solved by a powerful combination.*
1966 Apr 30	**Commuters Crack** (Llech Ddu) (1 pt aid) M P Hatton, C T Jones, A J J Moulam (VL)
1966 May 13	**Tower Line** (Idwal) (3 pts aid) R James, K C Gordon *A line from Ash Tree Wall to finish up the block of Tennis Shoe. cf The Tower on 5 September 1981.*
1966 Whit Sat.	**Girdle Traverse of the Lower Amphitheatre Wall** (Craig yr Ysfa) (1 pt aid) R James, J Wilkinson *A great route. Continuing, and satisfying, the somewhat idiosyncratic craving of the British for girdles. This is one of the best in North Wales.*
1966 June 4	**Billingsgate** (Craig y Cwmglas Bach) A C Cain, W K Carr (AL)
1966 June 19	**Auspice, White Horse** (Craig Cwrwgl) A J J Moulam, C T Jones (AL)
1966 July 1	**Devil's Delight** (Clogwyn y Geifr) R Edwards, E G Penman (AL) *A surprisingly good find.*
1966 July 9	**Sospan Bach, The Yazar** (Craig Cwrwgl) C T Jones, A J J Moulam, J G C Muirhead *Two routes that showed the possibilities of Elidir Slabs. Though the former should be 'Sospan Fach' to be totally correct; so much for the Jones's!*
1966 July 17	**Raven's Groove** (Craig Cwrwgl) A J J Moulam, G D Roberts (AL)
1966 July 17	**Raj Path** (Craig Cwrwgl) C T Jones, G D Roberts, A J J Moulam
1966 July 19	**Boot Crack** (Milestone) A J J Moulam, G D Roberts *A very useful find for this very busy buttress.*
1966 Sept 3	**Easy Slab** (Clogwyn y Geifr) A J J Moulam
1966 Aug 30	**Trindod** (Llech Ddu) I F Campbell, D H Jones, A S Hunt (VL)
1966 Aug 30	**Venom** (Llech Ddu) (1 pt aid) L E Holliwell, L R Holliwell *The first contribution to the Carneddau by the Holliwells. 'It was not well-protected. Lawrie had reached a point where further progress seemed in doubt and after several pressing attempts to gain height he reluctantly came to the conclusion that a peg was indispensable. Exasperated by what he considered to be momentary weakness, he swore that he would come down if further aid were*

necessary, and he meant it. The huge overhang
loomed ahead and I had taken it for granted that
aid would definitely be required to surmount this,
but I kept discreetly quiet, not wishing to aggravate
a delicate situation. Using the piton to gain a rib
which led to the roof, he continued. Several large
blocks parted company with the cliff accompanied
by grunts and muttering and I began to wonder if he
would be next. After a brief rest, or perhaps 'pause'
would be a more apt description, giving
consideration to the situation, he bridged and pulled
over the roof apparently without undue difficulty and
continued to the top'.
'Originally there were three of them, but the third, a
non-climber, after being conducted up Vector and
Great Corner by his brothers, opted for the less
precarious pleasures of the East End of London'.
Mountain magazine 1969.
Apparently, the third brother, who could have been
the better climber of the three, was seduced by golf.

1966 Sept 3	**Iota** (Llech Ddu) L E Holliwell, L R Holliwell
1967 June 4	**Smithfield** (Craig y Cwmglas Bach) A C Cain, T I M Lewis, C Boulton
	Previously the route was given the phonetically crude name 'Couldn't I'.
1967 Mar 5	**Alouette** (Braich Ty Du) F E R Cannings, D G Pears (AL)
1967 Apr 15	**The Jester** (Llech Ddu) M A Boysen, C E M Yates (AL)
1967 June	**Day-tripper** (Craig y Cwmglas Bach) M P Hatton, J A Maguire, M B Hodgins
1967 June 17	**Scarface** (Llech Ddu) L E Holliwell, L R Holliwell

'Climbing Scarface, like the majority of new routes
on Llech Ddu, was not so much an operation as an
excavation'.
'One unwary spectator was almost buried by a
large sod and a party doing Central Route had
some anxious moments as the precise direction of
the missiles could not be predicted with accuracy
any more than could their size and frequency'.
Les Holliwell was later to describe this technique as
'vertical bulldozing' and that 'Lawrie often carried a
swan-neck hoe and occasionally a stiff brush'. The
hoe can clearly be seen on the previous

guidebook's rear cover photograph of Lawrie, down by his feet!

1967 June 11   **Great Gully Wall** (Craig yr Ysfa) (1 pt aid) D S Potts, M A Boysen (AL)

1967 June 17   **Armour** (Craig Cwrwgl) C T Jones, A J J Moulam (VL)

1967 July 22   **Elidir Rib** (Craig Cwrwgl) P Gillman, D Charity

1967 Aug 26   **Gargoyle** (Braich Ty Du) B St John-Phillips, J Spencer (AL)

1967 Sept 17   **The Laxative** (Craig Cwrwgl) R Cole, C Osborne, A Tyler

Another useful find for the area.

1967   **Grey Eliminate** (Glyder Fawr) R James, J Heskett

Others made up the party on a number of visits.

1967   **Janos** (Craig Cwrwgl) A J J Moulam, C T Jones (AL)

1968 June 9   **Zenith** (Llech Ddu) L E Holliwell, L R Holliwell

'Pioneering on Llech Ddu certainly has its attractions but the effort involved is usually far greater than that expended on new routes in other areas. No doubt the mantle of greenery which adds so much to the atmosphere of this cliff will one day be lifted as has been the case elsewhere. This is my favourite crag'. Les Holliwell

1968 June 16   **Roseda Wall** (Gallt yr Ogof) D T Roscoe, W Cox (AL)

They produced a very airy climb. Several old pegs indicated that the niche had been reached at an earlier date. 'In fact, we did the route on the same day that Brown and Cain came to do it – we were sitting on the first ledge as they toiled up the scree. Brown observed that the wall was the "the only decent bit of rock on the cliff!" and they went off to console themselves with Curate's Egg'. B Cox.

1968 June 16   **The Curate's Egg** (Gallt yr Ogof) J Brown, A C Cain

1968 June 22   **Blitzkrieg** (Llech Ddu) L E Holliwell, L R Holliwell

The second pitch was led with only one doubtful runner due to the loose rock and vegetation. 'The huge heap at the bottom of the crag brought the wrath of the Nature Conservancy on to the brothers and their later explorations were accordingly concentrated on less vegetated rock'. Mountain 1969.

1968 June 30   **Skid Row** (Llech Ddu) L E Holliwell, L R Holliwell

Surely one of the very last classic chimneys. 'We

thoroughly enjoyed wallowing about in this wet chasm'. Les Holliwell

1968 July 7   **Herostratus** (Llech Ddu) (3pts aid) L E Holliwell, L R Holliwell
The top pitch was led in the rain, and found hard. A repeat ascent a month later confirmed this impression.
Free climbed by M Fowler, J Kingston 27 July 1978.
Lawrie undertook to demonstrate one of the moves by laybacking upon a Cornish pastie jammed in to a doorframe. Apparently, at the time, the rock was of a similar consistency.
'I have an unfortunate tendency to confuse terminology when I am preoccupied maintaining uncertain contact with the rock. Contrary to common belief, my brother and I do not always get along well and our intimate discussions about tactics on a route are often heard on Cloggy even when we are climbing on Llech Ddu. In spite of this he manages to tolerate me, no mean feat, and get up daunting chunks of rock first'. Les Holliwell

1968 July 13   **Cupid's Inspiration** (Llech Ddu) (1 pt aid) L E Holliwell, L R Holliwell
C Ayres and I Stevens made a free ascent on 27 April 1987, probably climbed without the aid before.

1968 July 27   **Gytrack** (Llech Ddu) L E Holliwell, L R Holliwell
1968 July 31   **Mosquito Slab** (Gallt yr Ogof) J F Kerry, G Arnold (AL)

1969 June 7   **Gawain Direct** (Craig yr Ogof) D E Alcock, C E Davies (2 pts aid)
Free climbed and extended by Z P Leppert.

1969 June 15   **The Crack** (Clogwyn Du) (2 pts aid) M A Boysen, D E Alcock
A fierce pitch climbed in poor conditions.

1969 June 15   **Hades** (Clogwyn y Geifr) M A Boysen, D E Alcock (AL)

1969 June   **Flanders** (Ysgolion Duon) (1 pt aid) P Crew, I Lowe, D E Alcock, J Brown (VL)
'Explorations have also commenced on the Black Ladders but information is shrouded in secrecy'.

1969 July 15   **Sodom** (Gallt yr Ogof) D G Peers, J E Brittain (AL)
1969 July 17   **The Mulberry Bush** (Gallt yr Ogof) D G Peers, J E Brittain (AL)
A good sort of traverse covering much new ground.

1969 Aug	**Pinnaclissima** (Craig yr Ysfa) (2 pts aid) C T Jones, R F Jones
	George Band and party climbed the first pitch as a start to Pinnacle Wall.
1969 Aug	**Top Storey** (Craig Dafydd) (1 pt aid) C T Jones, R F Jones
1969 Sept 1	**The Great Arête** (Llech Ddu) (4 pts aid) B Campbell-Kelly, E Drummond (AL)
	A typically audacious contribution from a controversial climber. Several days were taken on the first ascent. Pete Livesey and Steve Foster climbed the route without any aid in June 1975.
	'The main pitch of this climb demanded some tortuous tactics; pegs were placed in order to place others, the original pegs taken out before each section was led. A series of hard free moves, between each point of aid or protection was left...'
	'Ever inventive, Ward-Drummond has graded it 5c+, an interesting new variation on the existing numerical system'.
	Soloed by D Shaw in 1991.
1969 Oct	**Gettysburg** (Craig yr Ysfa) (1 pt aid) C T Jones, A J J Moulam, R Conway
1969 Oct 11	**Hebenwi** (Clogwyn Du) D Alcock, M A Boysen (AL)
	In June 1970 D G Peers and M D Swaine climbed the face believing it to be still virgin and added the variation finish.
1969 Oct 11	**The Devil Rides Out** (Clogwyn y Geifr) (A3 and HVS) K G Hipkiss, R Lavill, Z P Leppert
	'... for even He recognised the broken ethics of his influence'.
	An attempt by P Littlejohn to free climb the route in 1982 ended below the roof; S Boydon found a variation round this, which became The Devil Dries Out.
1970 Apr 18	**Gorballs** (Tryfan) K Wilson, D Griffiths
1970 May 23	**Witterer** (Llech Ddu) C T Jones, L R Holliwell (VL)
1970 May 26	**Throsher** (Clogwyn y Tarw) R Evans, K G Powell
1970 May 28	**West End** (Llech Ddu) L R Holliwell, C T Jones (VL)
1970 June 6	**Carpet Baggers** (Craig yr Ysfa) (1 pt aid) C T Jones, A J J Moulam, R F Allen
1970 June 7	**Shrapnel** (Llech Ddu) J W Kingston, L R Holliwell (AL) R Ford
1970 June 13	**The Ribbon** (Llech Ddu) L R Holliwell, Miss E Morse

1970 June 14	**Inferno** (Clogwyn y Geifr) Z P Leppert, K G Hipkiss (AL)
1970 June 21	**Tranquility** (Clogwyn y Geifr) Z P Leppert, K G Hipkiss (AL)
1970 June 26	**Thrasher** (Clogwyn y Tarw) R Evans, P Morris
1970 July 18	**Slabs Eliminate** (Idwal) R Evans, J Pasquill
1970 Oct 10	**The Chicken Run** (Cwm Cywion) (1 pt aid) D G Peers, M Holloway

Pitch 1 was Coronation Groove, climbed by P J Crabb and party in 1958.
Climbed without the aid by P Williams in 1977. Although the crag was originally given as the 'Cliff in the Cwm of the Chickens', it is fairly certain that none of these birds would survive the foul weather associated with these uplands. The word Cywion means the young of any animal, such as goats or sheep.

1971 Apr	**The Rib** (Craig Lloer) L R Holliwell, Mrs J Rodgers
1971 Apr 14	**Pectoral Wall** (Carreg Mianog) J Whittle, D G Peers
1971 May 2	**Homicide Wall** (Idwal) (2 pts aid) D G Peers, J Whittle

This problem was cracked '... perhaps unethically but practically by roping down and putting a sling in place'. The route is now done without this refinement.
Free climbed by L McGinley and 'Strappo' Hughes, May 1977. An escape to the right was found by D Midlane and W Church on 5 July 1971.
'the seriousness is more apparent than real' K Wilson, Z P Leppert.

1971 May 15	**Pluto** (Clogwyn y Geifr) (1 pt aid) K G Hipkiss, A Houghton (AL)

The first route from a rich untapped seam of rock.

1971 June 1	**The Trident** (Clogwyn y Geifr) Z P Leppert, J M Blears
1971 June 5	**Devil's Fissure** (Clogwyn y Geifr) Z P Leppert, J M Blears
1971 June 11	**The Sorcerer** (Clogwyn y Geifr) D Yates, W Barker, D H Jones (VL)
1971 June	**Petticoat Lane** (Craig y Cwmglas Bach) L R Holliwell, Miss R A Lewis
1971 July 11	**The Broiler** (Cwm Cywion) R Conway, C T Jones
1971 July 10 and 18	**The Fourth Dimension** (Llech Ddu) (3 pts aid) L E Holliwell, B Whybrow

This was the last of Lawrie Holliwell's new routes on the crag to which he contributed so much.
Free climbed by D Lampard, C Waddy (AL) 1989.

1971 July 22   **Cannon Rib** (Ysgolion Duon) J Pasquill, R Evans (AL)

1971 Sept 11   **Capital Punishment** (Idwal) (1 pt aid) M A Boysen, D E Alcock
'We had looked at it for years... finally summoning up the courage to try, I climbed almost unprotected to just a few feet below a tantalising thread but dared not make the moves to reach it... Dave tried with similar lack of success until a precariously placed piton allowed him to snatch it'.
R James and B James had previously climbed the top pitch as an escape whilst attempting a traverse of the area.
M Berzins, R Berzins and C Hamper made the second, and free, ascent in July 1976.
'A couple of small manky wires and that's your lot; just psych up and go for it, man! The layback moves into the groove seem too wild; a quick look to see how far the ground is below. Too far to jump'. N Shepherd

1971 Sept 12   **Suspended Sentence** (Idwal) (1 pt aid) M A Boysen, D E Alcock
Climbed free by C Hamper, M Berzins and R Berzins in July 1976.

1971 Sept 12   **The Garotte** (Idwal) (3 pts aid) D E Alcock, M A Boysen (AL)

1971 Sept   **Satan** (Clogwyn y Geifr) (1 pt aid) D Yates, D E Alcock (AL)
They took advantage of the scorching conditions.

1972 May 14   **Sundowner** (Craig Cwrwgl) D Yates, W Barker (AL)

1972 July   **Gehenna** (Clogwyn y Geifr) M A Boysen, A C Cain (AL)

1972 Aug 26   **Redemption** (Clogwyn y Geifr) Z P Leppert, J M Blears

1972 Aug 27   **Devil's Pulpit** (Clogwyn y Geifr) Z P Leppert, J M Blears

1972 Aug 28   **Faustus** (Clogwyn y Geifr) Z P Leppert, J M Blears
The second attempt brought success. The first having been thwarted by a long fall and much loss of dignity.

1972 Aug   **Samson** (Gallt yr Ogof) J Perrin, D Cook

1972 Aug	**The Psychlist** (Llech Ddu) (2pts aid) L R Holliwell, J Kingston
	Pitches 1 and 2. First complete ascent: T Millward, N Ingham 1974-1976.
	'The Psychlist initially involved 14 points of aid, primarily used to remove loose rock. Systematically, the aid was whittled down to four points, then by another party to two'.
1973 Jan	**Nick the Neck** (Craig Cwrwgl) N J Estcourt, C T Jones
	'Much better than poncing back down those odious gullies'.
1973 June 9	**Evening Flight** (Drws Nodded) Z P Leppert, M Hankey
1973 June 16	**Last Exit** (Idwal) K J Wilson, R Ford
1973 June 16	**Penthouse** (Idwal) R Ford, K J Wilson
	There were many subsequent claims of this obvious line.
1973 June 16	**Grey Slab Variant** (Glyder Fawr) M Rock, B Franklin
1973 Aug 18	**Cannon Ball** (Ysgolion Duon) R Evans, H Johnston, T Jepson
1975 May	**Aura** (Craig yr Ysfa) R Carrington, A Rouse, B Hall
	Once reported to be harder and better than Scorpio on Clogwyn Du'r Arddu. A fantastic find on an atmospheric crag!
1975 Sept 7	**Western Passage** (Glyder Fawr) Z P Leppert, M Hankey, B Hankey
	A successful probe into a neglected part of the cliff.
1975 Aug	**Devil's Appendage** (Clogwyn y Geifr) H I Banner, C T Jones
	'Much of this was removed in ascent'.
	Although the first ascensionists named this route Pitchfork, it was later claimed by Z Leppert, who gave it its current, and better known, name.
1976 July 2	**Trouble with Lichen** (Clogwyn y Tarw) J C Peart, J Holt
	A peg was used to reach the crack on pitch 2, but this was disposed of when R Fawcett soloed the pitch in 1979.
1976 July	**Last Rites** (Idwal) P Thexton, A Latham
	Although the route was given E2 5b/5c in one magazine; the start, as described, was found to be very hard.

1976 July	**Marathon** (Llech Ddu) R Evans, B Wyvill
	'... Ray was fighting to maintain contact whilst weeding an impending rock garden'.
1976 Aug	**Anubis** (Llech Ddu) L R Holliwell, G R Everitt
1976 Aug	**Cerberus** (Llech Ddu) L R Holliwell, G Rowlands
1976 Aug 14	**Hanging Garden Groove** (Clogwyn y Geifr) Z P Leppert, M Davies
	Leppert climbed pitch 1 the following day.
1976 Aug 21	**Tartarus** (Clogwyn y Geifr) Z P Leppert, R Lavill
1976	**Good Egg** (Craig Lloer)
	There are many eggs on this knobbly cliff, they are siliceous nodules, part of an acidic ash flow tuff.
1976 Sept	**Sirius** (Llech Ddu) L R Holliwell, A Cotton
1976 Sept	**One Flew Over the Cuckoo's Nest** (Craig yr Ysfa) L R Holliwell, R Laville
1977 June	**Death Row** (Idwal) N Shepherd, B Wayman
1977 Aug	**Penal Servitude** (Idwal) B Wayman, T Jepson
	It was thought necessary to pre-place an awkward thread runner before attempting the ascent. The name was changed from Life Imprisonment at the request of K Wilson.
1977 Sept 13	**Rising Damp** (Bochlwyd) J H S Ashton, J Jackson
	Most of this had been done before.
1977 Sept 13	**Rampart Corner** (Idwal) H I Banner, R Wilson
1978 Aug	**Solitary Confinement** (Idwal) P Davidson, G Healey, T Jones
	N Shepherd and I Leslie did a climb called The Reprieve in 1979, which made a fitting second pitch.
1979 June 30	**Mur y Meirwon** (Idwal) R Fawcett, C Gibb
	The peg runner was found to be in place. Livesey was to grade it at E3 5c/6a!
1979 July 3	**Wavelength Touch** (Idwal) G Gibson, J Walker
1979 July 14	**Breach of Promise** (Nant yr Ogof) Z P Leppert, R Lavill
1979 Aug 4	**Desecration Crack** (Milestone) M A Boysen, J Yates
1979 Aug 4	**Crosscut** (Milestone) J Yates, M A Boysen
1979 Aug	**Demetreus** (Idwal) D Beetlestone, G Gibson
	The last word in elegance.
1979 Oct 21	**Hawkwind** (Filiast) P G Martin, G Milburn (AL)
1979 Oct 22	**The Derelict** (Clogwyn y Tarw) R Fawcett (solo)
1979	**Diadem** (Clogwyn y Tarw) M Crook, D Farrant
	'We believe this to be a little gem. If it does not get popular we'll eat our EBs'.

1979	**Insidious Slit** (Clogwyn y Tarw) J Redhead, K W Robertson *A daring frontal attack, and John Redhead's first new route in Wales.*
1979	**Jailbreak** (Idwal) N Shepherd, T Hulme
1979	**Zero** (Idwal) P Livesey, Ms J Lawrence *A stunning and committing lead, which was to be 'Livesey's swan-song in Wales'.*
1980 Apr 3	**The Wrinkled Retainer** (Milestone) J Redhead, C Shorter *A climb with a fraught history. The crack was first climbed by stepping out of a well-established oak tree that grew at the foot of the Central Block. However, in the spring of 1980 attempts were made to climb the lower part of the line by mercilessly cutting down the tree (an act of sheer vandalism). As it was Redhead that claimed the route, Boysen blamed him for this and in a letter wrote:* *'Dear Mr. Blockhead, I congratulate you on 'creating' the variation start to Desecration Crack – a fine little route which I did with John Yates last year... It was a splendid tree and quite large to be growing in so inhospitable a place... Perhaps chain saws will soon be as small and convenient to carry as a large Friend'. Crags 26* *It was later to transpire that Redhead had been an innocent party to the proceedings and in order to clear his name, the real culprits Dave Nottidge and Chris Shorter came forward and wrote:* *'We cut it down and, having done so, found we could not get up the climb. So we enlisted the services of John Redhead. When he saw what we had done he was genuinely shocked... John is an artist and a painter of natural life. His subsequent silence on the matter was purely to protect us... It was a foolish, thoughtless, and irresponsible action' Mountain 78* *Further controversy ensued when the route appeared under the name of The Slash in the subsequent guidebook. Fortunately, the oak tree seems to be making a slow recovery, long may it grow in peace.*
1980 Apr 5	**London Lady** (Idwal) G Gibson, S Keeling

1980 Apr 6	**Excalibur** (Craig yr Ysfa) M Crook (unsec) *Pitch 1 only. Pitch 2 by M Crook, R Pritchard on 26 April 1980.*
1980 May 11	**The Watchtower** (Glyder Fawr) Z P Leppert, M Kellas
1980 May 11	**The Last Pretender** (Glyder Fawr) M Crook, S Durkin
1980 May 17	**Night Moves** (Clogwyn y Geifr) P Littlejohn, S Lewis *A bold modern climber leaves his mark.*
1980 Aug 2	**Solid Air** (Craig yr Ysfa) P Trower, G Tinning *A fine addition to a stupendous wall.* *The New Route Book entry was altered to read 'Solidarity', apparently put up by Bishop Glemp and Lech Walesa.*
1980 Aug 24	**Gryngolet** (Glyder Fach) H I Banner, Mrs J Yates, M Yates
1980 Aug 25	**Amadeus** (Craig yr Ysfa) G Gibson, P Gibson *Has stopped many a strong team.*
c. 1980	**Scimitar Crack** (Idwal) M Creasey, A N Other *Was to be claimed later as Yardheads by M Jones and P Baxter in 1990.*
1981 Apr 6	**Turn the Centuries Turn** (Craig yr Ysfa) G Gibson, D Beetlestone
1981 May 11	**Georgie Lad the Bricklayer** (Braich Ty Du) P Thomas, N Shepherd *What route name were they attempting to mimic?*
1981	**Time Served** (Braich Ty Du) N Shepherd, G Miller *The leader, in his youth, had a particularly hard time on Apprentice's Route, but by now he'd been initiated. The route was claimed by another team at E2 5b!*
1981	**Lazy Sunday** (Braich Ty Du) D Jones, B Pinion
1981	**Cobalt Dream** (Drws Nodded) C Shorter, J Redhead *The name describes the colour of the sky the first free ascensionists could see as they climbed the crack. The prospective second ascent failed due to the fact that they were told that nothing above a Friend 3 was required; about three Friend 4s would be considered adequate!*
1981 Aug 11	**Hell-Bent** (Clogwyn y Geifr) Z P Leppert, M Kellas *The start of the crack on pitch 1 was used by R James and J V Anthoine on their ascent of Devil's Nordwand.*

1981 Aug 12   **Grey Wall** (Glyder Fawr) Z P Leppert, M Kellas
The name was previously used as an alternative name for Procrastination Cracks.

1981 Sept 5   **The Tower** (Idwal) N Shepherd, B Wayman
Although R James and K C Gordon did Tower Line here on 13 May 1966, they approached via Ash Tree Wall and climbed Pitches 2 and 3, but used some aid on the steep twin cracks.

1981   **Let Your Feet Hang** (Braich Ty Du) G Dady

1982   **Street of Crocodiles** (Clogwyn y Tarw) M Crook, R Darnell

1982 Feb 15   **Funny Bone Variant** (Carreg Mianog) A Pollitt, A Boorman

1982 Mar 27   **Living Fossil** (Craig Cwrwgl) M A Boysen, J Yates

1982 Mar 27   **Manana** (Craig Cwrwgl) J Yates, M A Boysen

1982 Mar 28   **Siesta Cracks** (Craig Cwrwgl) M A Boysen, J Yates (AL)

1982 Mar 28   **Coelacanth** (Craig Cwrwgl) J Yates, M A Boysen

1982 Apr 16   **En Passant** (Milestone) Z P Leppert, M Kellas

1982 May 9   **Hell's Gate** (Clogwyn y Geifr) P Littlejohn, S B Jones

1982 June 5   **Stratosphere** (Clogwyn Du) S Boydon, S Cardy

1982 June 11   **Don't Just Stand There** (Clogwyn y Tarw) S Boydon, S Cardy

1982   **Saint Laurent** (Braich Ty Du) D Jones

1983 June 12   **Crazy Horse** (Milestone) J Harwood, A Sharp (AL)
Pitch 2 first climbed by M Crook, D Towse.

1983 June 20   **Sea of Dreams** (Craig yr Ysfa) M Crook, A Newton (VL)
The leader almost fell off his stance with laughter as the second grunted into sight frantically hand-traversing the footholds.
Combined with the Lower Girdle makes an excellent outing.

1983 June 21   **The Haunted** (Craig yr Ysfa) G Gibson, A Popp
Pitch 1 was climbed by G Gibson, J Walker on 18 June 1983. 'I gave the peg a tweak to test it and out it came! I tried to put it back in laying away off a tiny hold and had to prod for ages before I found the hole again!' C Waddy.
A curious case of a round peg in a round hole! This has now been replaced by a tighter fitting peg.

1983 July 3   **Spiral Scratch** (Craig yr Ysfa) G Gibson, A Hudson, A Popp

1983 July 9   **El Nino** (Craig yr Ysfa) M A Boysen, R Carrington

Unknown climber on *Pinnacle Wall* (Severe), Craig yr Ysfa. Photo: Simon Cardy

George White crossing the 'quartz pavement' on *Pinnacle Wall* (Severe),
Craig yr Ysfa. Photo: Paul Middleton

1983 July 9	**Drought** (Craig yr Ysfa) M A Boysen, R Carrington
	Certainly needs to be hot and dry.
1983 July 14	**The Black Vegetable** (Milestone) M Brothers, D Whitfield
1983 July	**The Last Starfighter** (Clogwyn y Tarw) M Crook, S Durkin
1983 Sept	**Ghostrider** (Drws Nodded) Z P Leppert, J Yeardsley
1983 Sept	**Friction, White Lightning, Bracken Corner** (Filiast) R Fletcher, A Bowman
1983	**Central Chimney, The Temple, The Flange** (Tryfan) H I Banner, P W Vaughan

1983   **Central Chimney, The Temple, The Flange** (Tryfan) H I Banner, P W Vaughan
Although H Banner and W Wynn had climbed the first pitch of The Temple and the second pitch of Central Chimney in 1968. In doing so they removed a large grass caterpillar which '...was full of stones and enraged a party way down on Grooved Arête'. The routes supersede a climb called Zephyr Wall by P Johnstone and A Newton climbed on 17 May 1988.

1984 May	**Yr Wydd Grug** (Llech Ddu) M W Lacey, I Barnett
1984 May 12	**Optical Illusion** (Drws Nodded) (1 pt aid) S Boydon, S Cardy
1984 May 5	**Eminence Grise** (Glyder Fawr) M A Boysen, R Carrington
1984 May 14	**Appendicitis** (Clogwyn y Geifr) S Boydon, S Cardy
	The first summer ascent of the line taken by the ice route The Devil's Appendix.
1984 May 27	**Teenage Menopause** (Idwal) N Dixon (unsec)
	One of the more desperate leads in Britain at the time.
1984 Aug 18	**Redstart** (Carreg Mianog) J Harwood, A Sharp (AL)
1984 Aug 22	**Red Cloud** (Gallt yr Ogof) A Sharp, J Harwood (AL)
1984 Aug 22	**Warhorse** (Gallt yr Ogof) A Sharp, J Harwood (AL)
1984 Aug	**Gobagape** (Idwal) N Dixon, C Brear
1984 Aug	**One More Calorie** (Idwal) N Dixon (unsec)
1984 Aug	**Thinking of the Girl** (Idwal) N Dixon
1984 Aug	**Breadline** (Idwal) N Dixon, A Popp
1984 Aug	**Ryvita** (Idwal) B Barnett, A Popp
1984 Aug	**Summer Pudding** (Idwal) A Popp, N Dixon
1985 Apr 27	**The Hollow Men** (Glyder Fach) A Newton, M Crook (AL)
	Both the team were numb with cold, but astonished that such an obvious line was unclimbed.

1985 Sept 29	**Oblique Buttress Direct** (Glyder Fach) H Banner, J Tombs

1985 Sept 29   **The Tombstone Crack** (Glyder Fach) J Tombs, H Banner

1986 June 21   **Afterburner** (Gallt yr Ogof) J de Montjoye, H Sharp, F Crook

1986 June 28   **The Hangman's Return** (Idwal) I Carr, C Hall

1986 July 5   **Au Suivant** (Milestone) I Carr, C Hall
Tragically Carr disappeared in the Himalaya.

1986 Aug 23   **Waved Slab Goodbye** (Filiast) D Moore, G Neil

1986 Sept 20   **Seagull** (Filiast) D Moore, G Neil, S Fahy

1986 Oct 4   **Gina's Traverse** (Filiast) D Moore, G Neil

1987 May 10   **Hell's Teeth** (Clogwyn y Geifr) S Boydon, S Cardy, P Harrison

1987 May 10   **The Devil Dries Out** (Clogwyn y Geifr) S Boydon, S Cardy, P Harrison
A free climb based on the old route The Devil Rides Out.

1987 May 16   **Poultry in Motion** (Cwm Cywion) S Boydon, S Cardy
One of the wittiest of names in the guide, pity the translation changed.

1987 June   **The Tree of Man** (Milestone) G Smith, M Crook

1987 July 4   **Game, Set and Match** (Idwal) S Boydon, S Cardy

1987 Aug 4   **Peglegs** (Clogwyn y Tarw) G Smith, R Wood
The start of a blitz on this crag. Also known as The Gribin Fact in New Climbs 1987.

1987 Aug 5   **Bubbling** (Clogwyn y Tarw) G Smith, M Thomas

1987 Aug 5   **Centrally Heated Big Top** (Clogwyn y Tarw) S Howe, G Smith, M Thomas

1987   **Antideluvian, Primordial** (Craig Cwrwgl) M A Boysen, R Carrington (AL)

1988 May   **Cricklewood** (Craig Cwrwgl) I Stevens, C Parkin

1988 June 14   **Recess Monkey** (Clogwyn y Tarw) E Stone, G Smith
A droll route name. However, the first ascensionists initially graded it at E5 6a, apparently it was dark!

1988 June 18   **Broadsword** (Craig yr Ogof) Z P Leppert, M A Kellas
Tom managed to keep the place secret for a long time.

1988 June 18   **Rhwyn** (Bochlwyd) C Greatwich, A Woodward

1988 June 24   **Couteau** (Clogwyn y Tarw) E Stone, G Smith

1988 June 24   **Le Fin** (Clogwyn y Tarw) G Smith, E Stone

1988 June 27	**Pocket Knife** (Clogwyn y Tarw) E Stone, P Baxter, S Howe
1988 June 29	**Rocking Chair Ridge** (Clogwyn y Tarw) G Smith (unsec)
1988 July	**Travelling People** (Clogwyn y Tarw) C Parkin, D O'Dowd
1988 July	**Stonehenge** (Clogwyn y Tarw) C Parkin, L Hardy
1988 July	**Hippy Invasion** (Clogwyn y Tarw) L Hardy, C Parkin
1988 July	**Blue Smartie** (Clogwyn y Tarw) C Parkin, D O'Dowd
1988 Aug 20	**Pentangle** (Craig yr Ogof) Z P Leppert, M A Kellas
1988	**Kaya** (Glyder Fach) N Craine (unsec)
	Direct finish added by J Dawes (unsec)
1989 May 14	**Llywelyn Ein Llyw Olaf** (Craig yr Ogof) Z P Leppert, M A Kellas
	A route of riddles, beth yw llw pysgodyn.
1989 May	**Tooty Frooty, Angharad** (Idwal) C Stephenson et al
1989 June	**Hyndsight** (Glyder Fach) C Parkin, L Hardy
1989 June	**Get Close** (Glyder Fach) L Hardy, C Parkin
1989 June 3	**Zippo** (Carreg Mianog) C Greatwich, G Russell
1989 June 18	**Meibion Glyndwr** (Llech Ddu) S Cardy, M Snell
	Perhaps the police would like their addresses?
1989 June 18	**The Straight to the Heart Start** (Llech Ddu) M Snell, S Cardy
1989 July	**Whirlwind** (Craig yr Ysfa) Z P Leppert, T Cumberland
1989 July	**The Fourth Dimension** (Llech Ddu) Free climbed by C Waddy, D Lampard (AL)
	Now the most serious route on the crag. Later described by Lampard as 'an excellent outing – certainly not in the modern idiom – indifferent gear and belays make this a must'.
	A belay ledge gave way during the first free ascent
1989	**Cadwaladr** (Craig yr Ogof) Z P Leppert, W Barker
	An Arthurian knight.
1990 May 11	**Foreplay** (Clogwyn y Tarw) E Stone
1990 May 11	**Grab and Flash It** (Clogwyn y Tarw) E Stone (unsec)
	Ed was accompanied by an irate porta-belay who thought himself entitled to a mention merely for holding the ropes! How he can be credited when signing himself as 'Scotch Mist' is a mystery.
1990 May 28	**Shorter Oak** (Gallt yr Ogof) S Cardy, A Orton

1990 May 28   **The Littlest Rebel** (Gallt yr Ogof) S Cardy, A Orton
Pre-inspected on a top-rope.

1990 June 14   **Sorrowful** (Clogwyn y Tarw) E Stone, R Potter

1990 July 11   **Pinnaclissimo** (Mianog) G Gilmore (solo)
It will now seem customary to jump off the summit of the pinnacle in the style of the first leap!

1990 July 18   **Bonfire of the Vanities** (Clogwyn y Tarw) K W Robertson, L Hardy, C Parkin

1990 July 18   **Arkwright's Reward** (Clogwyn y Tarw) C Parkin, L Hardy, K W Robertson

1990 July 20   **Gwynhyfryd** (Craig yr Ogof) Z P Leppert, P Holden

1990 July 20   **Meillionnydd** (Craig yr Ogof) P Holden, Z P Leppert

1990 July   **Morgan La Faye** (Craig yr Ogof) P Jenkinson, I A Jones
The route was described by a writer for one climbing comic as being 'On Clogwyn y Tarw. In the Carneddau... on Craig Eryl Farchog'. They clearly knew the way round the Mountain Crags.

1990 Aug 7   **Llofruddwyr** (Idwal) A George, P George, I A Jones, C Dwyer
Dwyer was so pleased with his ascent that he performed a pirouette – whilst climbing!

1990 Aug   **Clustfeinydd** (Craig yr Ogof) I A Jones, P R Allen

1990 Aug 11   **F-stop Fitzgerald** (Craig Blaen y Nant) E Stone, C Tickell
A good free climb created from an obscure aid pitch. The aid had been provided by Frank Cannings.

1990 Aug 27   **EEC** (Craig y Cwmglas Bach) S Wilson, C Haworth, P Kershaw

1990 Sept 2   **Pat's Crack (Keep Pullin' Cen)** (Braich Ty Du) L Lovatt, P Evans

1990 Sept 15   **Dead Calm** (Craig y Cwmglas Bach) S Wilson, D Kelly

1990   **Snuff** (Craig y Cwmglas Bach) S Wilson, A Bowering
'It took all my powers of persuasion to coax him on after he had laid eyes on the first pitch. The rest made him mutter something about not 'phoning him in future...' Steve Wilson after the first ascent.

1991 Jan 2   **K.C. Route** (Braich Ty Du) M Podd

1991 May 27	**Mother of Mercy** (Craig yr Ysfa) D Lampard, N Bonnett, C Fleck
1991 June 15	**Ysgyrnygu** (Craig Llethr Gwyn) S Cardy
1991 July 2	**Gwdihw** (Craig Braich Ty Du) S Cardy, P Harrison
1991 July 2	**The Pals** (Milestone) P Baxter, M Jones, M Neil
1991 July 14	**Mad Jack McMad** (Gallt yr Ogof) P Harrison, S Cardy
1991 July 14	**Y Blaidd** (Craig Llethr Gwyn) S Cardy, P Harrison
1991 Aug 30	**Y Meirwon Byw** (Idwal) E Stone, M Turner
1991 Sept	**Y Grug** (Idwal) J Brown, D H Jones
1992 May 15	**Blue Sunshine** (Craig Braich Ty Du) I A Jones, M Rowlands
1992 May 15	**Tyromancy** (Craig Braich Ty Du) I A Jones, M Rowlands
	Tyromancy is the art of fortune telling by the study of cheese mould development!
1992 May 17	**Sweating Peat** (Craig Ddaear) S Cardy, D Basford
1992 May 17	**Salt of the Earth** (Craig Ddaear) S Cardy, M Niklas, D Basford
1992 May 17	**Mother Earth** (Craig Ddaear) M Niklas, S Cardy, D Basford
1992 May 27	**Slim Pick Long Flap** (Idwal) E Stone, M Oliver
1992 May	**Glyder Crack** (Glyder Fach) G Smith, D Kendal
1992 June 14	**Surrogate Soils** (Craig Ddaear) S Cardy, D Basford
1992 June 14	**Earth Summit** (Craig Ddaear) S Cardy, D Basford
1992 July 5	**Moving Moss** (Craig Ddaear) S Cardy, M Niklas
1992 July 5	**Wet Roots** (Craig Ddaear) S Cardy, M Niklas
1992 July 5	**Whole Earth** (Craig Ddaear) S Cardy
1992 July 9	**Faenaldo** (Craig yr Ysfa) D Green, D Lampard
1992 July 14	**Ring of Scorpio** (Craig Braich Ty Du) S Boydon, P Harrison (AL)
1992 July 15	**Sluice Juice** (Idwal) N Biven (unsec)
1992 July 16	**Thorfinn Skullsplitter** (Idwal) N Biven (unsec)

Index

Mountain Rescue

In the event of a serious accident where assistance is required, a message giving all the factual information about the person(s), location (crag, climb, pitch etc.) should be passed on to the North Wales Police by dialling 999.

The Police will contact the respective Rescue Team and as co-ordinators will obtain further assistance (e.g. helicopter) as directed by those effecting the rescue.

After an accident, please report in writing directly to the Hon. Secretary, Mountain Rescue Committee, 18 Tarnside Fold, Simmondley, Glossop, Derbyshire, SK13 9ND, giving particulars of: date of accident, extent of injuries, name, age, and address of the casualty, details of the M.R.C. Equipment used and the amount of morphine used (so that it can be replaced). Normally this will be done by the local Police and/or the Rescue Team involved, who will also require the names and addresses of the persons climbing with the injured party.

Avoid making rash or unconsidered statements to the press; refer any journalist to the mountaineer who has overall charge of the rescue.

Helicopter Notes
In the event of a helicopter evacuation ALL climbers ON and OFF the cliff should take heed. A helicopter flying close to the cliff will make verbal communication between climbers difficult, and small stones will be dislodged by the rotor downdraught. All loose equipment must be secured and climbers in precarious positions should try to make themselves safe. A smoke grenade may be dropped from the helicopter to give wind direction.

The persons with the injured party should try to identify their location. No attempt should be made to throw a rope to the helicopter, but assistance should be given to the helicopter crew if requested.

A helicopter will always be flown into the wind to effect a rescue and on landing there are three danger points; the main rotor, the tail rotor and the engine exhaust. The helicopter should not be approached until directions to do so are given by the air crew.